THE EVERYMAN BOOK
OF
THEATRICAL ANECDOTES

THE EVERYMAN BOOK
OF
THEATRICAL ANECDOTES

Edited by Donald Sinden

J M Dent & Sons Ltd
London Melbourne

First published 1987
© Introduction, notes and selection Tresin Ltd and Victorama Ltd 1987

This book is set in Linotron Bembo by
Input Typesetting Ltd., London SW19 8DR
Printed and bound in Great Britain by
Mackays of Chatham Ltd
J M Dent & Sons Ltd
Aldine House, 33 Welbeck Street, London W1M 8LX

British Library Cataloguing in Publication Data

Sinden, Donald
  The Everyman book of theatrical anecdotes.
  1. Theatre——Anecdotes, facetiae, satire, etc
  I. Title
  792'.09'03   PN2095

  ISBN 0–460–04692–6

CONTENTS

INTRODUCTION

'No play-no pay' was the theatrical rule until very recently. An actor's salary was based on giving eight performances a week (six evenings and two matinées) so public holidays, when theatres closed, were bad news, and if Christmas fell on a matinée day he stood to lose a quarter of his pay that week. Nor were rehearsals paid for. It was quite possible therefore to rehearse for three or four weeks, open to bad reviews in the press, close at the end of the first week, and be paid for only the number of given performances. The theatre has always been a precarious occupation, with heartbreak often just around the corner, but actors have always entered the profession fully aware of the problem. For them the show must go on, the curtain must rise, so on with the motley. It's no good crying, the best thing to do is laugh. That is why so many of the best observations and pieces of advice in this book are wrapped in humorous form.

Over the centuries covered in this book other countries have produced better musicians, better painters and better sculptors, but the one art in which the British have excelled the world has been the art of Drama. For 400 years Britain has produced better playwrights, actors, directors and designers than any other country. During this time the theatre has undergone many changes and the anecdotes I have chosen include many contemporary accounts of those changes.

Speculate as we may, we still don't know exactly what an Elizabethan theatre looked like and sadly there are very few sources containing relevant information. Nor do we know anything of performances but, judging from the sheer size of the parts that Shakespeare allotted to the boy actors, who at that time played the women's roles, they must have been very convincing. Not until many years later when Colley Cibber described the last of them (no. 18) do we get a taste of their quality.

The Restoration of Charles II to the throne in 1660 brought the first actresses to the stage and from the *Diary* of Samuel Pepys we get many passing references to the conditions under which they had to work, and also to the divided attention of the playgoer: 'A dull play that did give us no content; and, besides, little company there, which made it very unpleasing.' A year later he went 'to the King's Playhouse and there saw, I think, *The Maiden Queen*'! We also find in his *Diary* several references to the uncouth behaviour of the gallants who seemed to have a perfect right to invade the dressing rooms of the actresses (no. 22). Gradually, privileges such as these were whittled away until David Garrick, in 1763, finally succeeded in keeping the footlights and the proscenium arch between him and the spectators.

Garrick's success as an actor was phenomenal, and he numbered all his great contemporaries among his friends. We find him living beside the River Thames at Hampton in a house designed by Robert Adam, with furniture by Chippendale, a statue of Shakespeare by Roubiliac in the garden, and having his portrait painted by all the great artists of the period – Hogarth, Reynolds, Gainsborough and Zoffany.

From Garrick's time onwards actors became increasingly respectable. Indeed, in the next generation the magisterial bearing of the Kemble family was awe-inspiring. At a recent gathering Emlyn Williams remarked of another actor, 'If you hear a loud c-r-r-a-c-k it will be that fellow unbending': that could so easily have been said of John Philip Kemble. It is interesting in entry 90 to find Kemble being amusing.

The theatres in eighteenth-century England were small, intimate buildings, as we can see at Richmond in Yorkshire, Bristol and Bury St Edmunds, but the theatre in which Edmund Kean burst upon an astonished London in 1814 held 3000 people, so it is surprising that everyone talked of his eyes. What eyes they must have been to register in such an enormous auditorium! Coleridge's statement that 'to see Kean act was like reading Shakespeare by flashes of lightning' has usually been assumed to have been the most exciting thing ever said of an actor. (It was Baliol Holloway who first drew my attention to the context in which it was made: the complete passage is actually derogatory.) After Kean's first great success he exclaimed, 'Charlie shall go to Eton!' And to Eton Charlie went – the son of a Rogue and Vagabond.

The next titan to appear was William Charles Macready, educated at Rugby and possibly even more pompous than Kemble.

The eighteenth century had seen the flowering of the gentlemen's clubs from their coffee-house roots, but actors, because of their unsavoury trade, were not admitted as members until a group headed by the Duke of Sussex decided to found a club 'in which actors and men of education and refinement might meet on equal terms'. To name it after a living actor could have been invidious – a name from the past would be better – so in 1831 the Garrick Club was formed.

The abolition in 1843 of the Patent Theatres Act resulted in hundreds of theatres being built all over the country and almost every town created its resident stock company with whom the Olympians of the metropolis would condescend to appear in much the same way as the international stars of the opera do today. Little or no rehearsal was allowed – the star just stood centre stage and the others fitted in as best they could.

Back in London, in 1869, an experiment was tried which has now become an accepted institution of the theatre – the matinée performance. It is fascinating to find in Sir Squire Bancroft's memoirs (no. 170) that the event is recorded almost as a footnote.

Each theatre run by an actor-manager at this time had its regular players, but not under permanent contract. If there was no part for an actor in the current play, there was bound to be one in the next. The story is told of an old actor at the Theatre Royal in the Haymarket who, not being wanted for the next production, waited at home. Months later the next production was announced, but there was still no part for him. Then came the next production and still no part. Of course, he argued to himself, it was quite possible for three consecutive plays to be performed without requiring his expertise, but when more months later the next play was produced without him he became genuinely worried. Down he went to the theatre and joined the queue at the box office. On arriving at the window he asked, 'Can you tell me if Mr Walter Plinge is appearing at this theatre?'

'No, he is not.'

Plinge rejoined the queue and, using a different voice, asked, 'Is Mr Plinge appearing in the current attraction?'

'No, he is not.'

Again he rejoined the queue; again in a different voice he asked, 'Can you tell me if that fine actor Mr Plinge is in the present play?'

'No, he is not.'

Six more times he went round asking similar questions until, on receiving the same answer, he finally replied, 'Ah – you might tell the management that *people* are asking.'

Henry Irving had been the acknowledged head of his profession for some 25 years before the momentous day in 1895 when he was honoured with a knighthood. Actors were now officially respectable. In 1921 Genevieve Ward became the first actress to be made Dame of the British Empire. Many similar honours followed and in 1970 Laurence Olivier became the first actor to be created a Life Peer – Baron Olivier of Brighton. But they are of course the leaders of the profession. The rank-and-file still find themselves misunderstood and discriminated against. During the First World War Felix Aylmer was serving in a minesweeper off the coast of Scotland. One night he found himself on the bridge listening for hours to the captain relating his peacetime adventures with the local fishing fleet. Eventually the captain paused and asked Aylmer what he had been doing before the war. 'I was–er–an–actor, sir,' explained Felix apologetically. 'What was that?' 'I was an actor, sir.' There was a long pause, then the captain looked disapprovingly at him and spoke: 'Paintin' yer face to make people laff at ye!'

Quite recently an actor friend of mine who loathed even the idea of flying was faced with no alternative but to go by air to join a film unit on location in Italy. At the airport he noticed a small booth advertising that for 10p his dependents would receive something like £100,000 if he should lose his life on that particular flight. He hastily filled in the required form: name, address, occupation, next of kin.

'Oh, an actor,' said the lady behind the desk, 'just a moment.' She consulted a booklet. 'Yes, as I thought, *actors* 50p.' My friend remonstrated, to no avail of course, that the plane was no more likely to crash because an actor was on board.

It hardly comes as a surprise, in the face of so much disdain, if actors are inclined to close ranks against the 'civilians' of this world. But out of adversity comes humour, both as a shield against the precarious nature of our job and as a sword with which to confront our assailants. More than most others, theatre people have been outspoken, garrulous and gossipy, inspiring and thriving on anecdotes, and the cumulative effect of the stories printed here is to reveal an informal and entertaining history of the theatre, not only in Britain but also in America where for so many years the leading players were actually British-born. In the famous nineteenth-century Macready-Forrest rivalry (nos. 128–130) we can see the conflict between the weight of the British tradition and the emerging American style.

Towards the end of the nineteenth century, American dramatists at last developed their own distinctive voices and although actors and actresses from each country would continue to cross the Atlantic, the British and American theatres began to lead separate lives. I have tried to respect the part played by America in the development of the theatre by including many anecdotes by and about American performers and producers, from William Dunlap and Thomas Cooper to the actors of today.

Although it would have been easy to fill this book by concentrating on a few of the more illustrious names on both sides of the Atlantic, I imposed a ceiling on the number of anecdotes concerning them in order to include less well-known names and stories. Laurence Olivier and Orson Welles now jostle with Jimmy Allen and Master Arnott. The entries are presented in chronological order of the date of birth of the central figure in each passage and where this has proved impractical I have placed the author centre stage. If the author's name is not apparent within the text I have placed it at the end of each extract.

Assembling a collection of anecdotes that spans 400 years has been an awesome task. I have been assisted by a number of people (including Adam Kean, Alan Hewitt, Clive Dickinson and Jacqueline Bayes) and it was intriguing to find that the quotations sent in by those who were actually employed in the theatre were always pertinent to the craft of acting, while the others were inclined to bolster a preconceived notion of actors and the world in which they work. I have included both so that the reader may enjoy differentiating between the two attitudes. There are almost 400 extracts printed here – as many as space would permit – so I hope that if your own favourite anecdote is not to be found, there are enough unfamiliar ones to interest you. I have scrupulously kept to published material and the notes at the end of the book give the source of each entry.

Donald Sinden
1986

THEATRICAL ANECDOTES

CHRISTOPHER MARLOWE (1564–93)

1 *After Shakespeare, the best known Elizabethan playwright. His Dr Faustus (?1588) was once the occasion of some considerable alarm for 'certaine players at Exeter'.*

"Certaine Players at Exeter acting *upon* the stage the tragicall storie of Dr. Faustus the Conjurer; as a certain number of Devels kept everie one his circle there, and as Faustus was busie in his magicall invocations, on a sudden they wer all dasht, every one harkning other in the eare, for they were all perswaded there was one devell too many amongst them; and so after a little pause desired the people to pardon them, they could go no further with this matter: the people also understanding the thing as it was, every man hastened to be first out of dores. The players (as I heard it) contrarye to their custome spending the night in reading and in prayer got them out of the towne the next morning."

From Gentleman's Magazine

WILLIAM SHAKESPEARE (1564–1616)

2 *Most people think of Shakespeare as the greatest dramatist in history, but he was also a professional actor – one of The Lord Chamberlain's Men (later, in the reign of King James I, the King's Men).*

Concerning Shakespear's first appearance in the playhouse. When he came to London, he was without money and friends, and being a stranger he knew not to whom to apply, nor by what means to support himself. – At that time coaches not being in use, and as gentlemen were accustomed to ride to the playhouse, Shakespear, driven to the last necessity, went to the playhouse door, and pick'd up a little money by taking care of the gentlemens horses who came to the play; he became eminent even in that profession, and was taken notice of for his diligence and skill in it; he had soon more business than he himself could manage, and at last hired boys under him, who were known by the name of Shakespear's boys: Some of the players accidentally conversing with him, found him so acute, and master of so fine a conversation, that struck therewith, they recommended him to the house, in which he was first admitted in a very low station, but he did not long remain so, for he soon distinguished himself, if not as an extraordinary actor, at least as a fine writer. His name is printed, as the custom was in those times, amongst those of the other players, before some old plays, but without any particular account of what sort of parts he used to play: and Mr. Rowe says, "that tho' he very carefully enquired, he found the top of his performance was the ghost in his own Hamlet."

Theophilus Cibber

3 It is well known that Queen Elizabeth was a great admirer of the immortal Shakspeare, and used frequently (as was the custom with persons of great rank in those days) to appear upon the stage before the audience, or to sit delighted behind the scenes, when the plays of our bard were performed. One evening, when Shakspeare himself was personating the part of a King, the audience knew of her Majesty being in the house. She crossed the stage when he was performing, and, on receiving the accustomed greeting from the audience, moved politely to the poet, but he did not notice it! When behind the scenes, she caught his eye, and moved again, but still he would not throw off his character, to notice her: this made her Majesty think of some means by which she might know, whether he would depart, or not, from the dignity of his character, while on the stage. – Accordingly, as he was about to make his exit, she stepped before him, dropped her glove, and re-crossed the stage, which Shakspeare noticing, took up, with these words, immediately after finishing his speech, and so aptly were they delivered, that they seemed to belong to it:

> "And though now bent on this high embassy,
> Yet stoop we to take up our *Cousin's* glove!"

He then walked off the stage, and presented the glove to the Queen, who was greatly pleased with his behaviour, and complimented him upon the propriety of it.

Anon

4 *Richard Burbage, the most famous tragedian of his day, was the original interpreter of some of Shakespeare's greatest characters.*

Upon a tyme when Burbidge played Richard III, there was a citizen grone soe farr in liking with him, that before shee went from the play shee appointed him to come that night unto hir by the name of Richard the Third. Shakespeare overhearing their conclusion went before, was intertained and at his game ere Burbidge came. Then message being brought that Richard the Third was at the dore, Shakespeare caused returne to be made that William the Conqueror was before Richard the Third. Shakespeare's name William.

John Manningham

5 Shakespeare, in his frequent journeys between London and his native place Stratford-upon-Avon, used to lie at Davenant's, at the Crown, in Oxford. He was very well acquainted with Mrs. Davenant, and her son (afterwards Sir William) was supposed to be more nearly related to him than as a godson only.

One day, when Shakespeare was just arrived, and the boy sent for from school to him, a head of one of the colleges (who was pretty well acquainted with the affairs of the family) met the child running home, and asked him whither he was going in so much haste? The boy said, 'To my godfather, Shakespeare.' 'Fie, child,' says the old gentleman, 'why are you so superfluous? Have not you learned yet that you should not use the name of God in vain?'

Joseph Spence

6 *The Globe Theatre caught fire on 29 June, 1613, during a performance of Shakespeare's* Henry VIII. *A few days later the diplomat and poet Sir Henry Wotton wrote to his nephew Sir Edmund Bacon.*

Now I will entertain you at the present with what hath happened this Week at the Banks side.* The King's Players had a new Play, called *All is true*, representing some principal pieces of the Reign of Henry the 8th which was set forth with many extraordinary circumstances of Pomp and Majesty, even to the matting of the Stage; the Knights of the Order, with their Georges and Garter, the Guards with their embroidered Coats, and the like: sufficient in truth within a while to make Greatness very familiar, if not ridiculous. Now King Henry making a Masque at the Cardinal Wolsey's House, and certain Cannons being shot off at his entry, some of the Paper, or other stuff, wherewith one of them was stopped, did light on the Thatch, where being thought at first but an idle smoak, and their Eyes more attentive to the show, it kindled inwardly, and ran round like a train, consuming within less than an hour the whole House to the very ground.

This was the fatal period of that virtuous Fabrique wherein yet nothing did perish, but Wood and Straw and a few forsaken Cloaks; only one Man had his Breeches set on fire, that would perhaps have broyled him, if he had not by the benefit of a provident wit put it out with Bottle-Ale.

---

*Bankside, the southern side of the Thames, between Southwark and Blackfriars Bridge, was the principal brothel district of London, but renowned, too, for its theatres such as the Globe, the Rose, the Swan and the Fortune.

BEN JONSON (1572–1637)

7 *Jonson's plays are less often staged today than they might be, for his comedies, in particular, parade a wonderful portrait-gallery of Elizabethan types. Johnson himself had an unusual upbringing, if John Aubrey's description is to be believed.*

His mother, after his father's death, maried a Bricklayer; and 'tis generally said that he wrought sometime with his father-in-lawe (and particularly on the Garden-wall of Lincoln's Inne next to Chancery Lane) and that a Knight, a Bencher, walking thro', and hearing him repeate some Greeke verses out of Homer, discoursing with him and finding him to have a Witt extraordinary, gave him some Exhibition to maintaine him at Trinity College in Cambridge.

Then he went into the Lowe-countreys, and spent some time (not very long) in the armie, not to disgrace, as you may find in his *Epigrammes*.

Then he came over into England, and acted and wrote, but both ill, at the Green Curtaine, a kind of Nursery or obscure Play-house, somewhere in the Suburbes (I thinke towards Shoreditch or Clarkenwell).

Then he undertooke again to write a Playe, and did hitt it admirably well, viz. *Every Man . . . [in His Humour]*, which was his first good one . . .

He was (or rather had been) of a clear and faire skin; his habit was very plaine. I have heard Mr. Lacy, the Player, say that he was wont to weare a coate like a coachman's coate, with slitts under the arme-pitts. He would many times exceed in drinke (Canarie was his beloved liquor) then he would tumble home to bed, and, when he had thoroughly perspired, then to studie.

8 Eastward Ho, *by Jonson, Chapman and Marston, made fun of King James I's Scottish courtiers.*

He was dilated by Sir James Murray to the King, for writting something against the Scots, in a play Eastward Hoe, and voluntarily imprissonned himself with Chapman and Marston, who had written it amongst them. The report was, that they should then have had their ears cut and noses. After their delivery, he banqueted all his friends; there was Camden, Selden, and others; at the midst of the feast his old Mother dranke to him, and shew him a paper which she had (if the sentence had taken execution) to have mixed in the prisson among his drinke, which was full of lustie strong poison, and that she was no churle, she told, she minded first to have drunk of it herself.

William Drummond

ROGER BOYLE, FIRST EARL OF ORRERY (1621–79)

9 *Samuel Pepys records the first performance of Orrery's play,* The Black Prince, *on 19 October, 1667.*

Full of my desire of seeing my Lord Orrery's new play this afternoon at the King's House, 'The Blacke Prince,' the first time it is acted; where, though we came by two o'clock, yet there was no room in the pit, but were forced to go into one of the upper boxes, at 4s. apiece, which is the first time I ever sat in a box in my life. And in the same box came, by and by, behind me, my Lord Berkeley and his lady, but I did not turn my face to them to be known, so that I was excused from giving them my seat. And this pleasure I had, that from this place the scenes do appear very fine indeed, and much better than in the pit. The house infinite full, and the King and Duke of York there. By and by the play begun, and in it nothing particular but a very fine dance for variety of figures, but a little too long. . . . the whole house was mightily pleased all along till the reading of a letter, which was so long and so unnecessary that they frequently began to laugh, and to hiss twenty times, that had it not been for the King's being there, they had certainly hissed it off the stage. But I must confess that, as my Lord Berkeley said behind me, the having of that long letter was a thing so absurd, that he could not imagine how a man of his parts could possibly fall into it; or if he did, if he had but let any friend read it, the friend would have told him of it; and, I must confess, it is one of the most remarkable instances of a wise man's not being wise at all times. . . . After the play done, and nothing pleasing them from the time of the letter to the end of the play, people being put into a bad humour of disliking, I home by coach, and could not forbear laughing almost all the way, and all the evening to my going to bed, at the ridiculousness of the letter, and the more because my wife was angry with me and the world for laughing, because the King was there.

KING CHARLES II (1630–85)

10 *The King's remark possibly concerns Titus Oates, the perpetrator of the 'Popish Plot' of 1678 in which Catholics were rumoured to want to murder the King and replace him with the Duke of York.*

It is not improbable, but that from Sandford's so masterly personating Characters of Guilt, the inferior Actors might think his Success chiefly owing to the Defects of his Person; and from thence might take occasion, whenever they appear'd as Bravo's, or Murtherers, to make themselves as frightful and as inhuman Figures, as possible. In King Charles's time, this low Skill was carry'd to such an Extravagance, that the King himself, who was black-brow'd, and of a swarthy Complexion, pass'd a pleasant

Remark, upon his observing the grim Looks of the Murtherers in *Macbeth;* when, turning to his People, in the Box about him, *Pray, what is the Meaning*, said he, *that we never see a Rogue in a Play, but, Godsfish! they always clap him on a black Perriwig? when, it is well known, one of the greatest Rogues in* England *always wears a fair one?* Now, whether or no Dr. Oates, at that time, wore his own Hair, I cannot be positive; Or, if his Majesty pointed at some greater Man, then out of Power, I leave those to guess at him, who may yet, remember the changing Complexion of his Ministers.

Colley Cibber

JOHN DRYDEN (1631–1700)

11 *The first Poet Laureate, Dryden was an influential critic in such works as his* Essays on Dramatic Poesy, *as well as a major poet and playwright. His 'rival' in this passage, John Crowne, was the author of a number of successful comedies (see below, p. 00).*

Even Dryden was very suspicious of rivals. He would compliment Crowne when a play of his failed, but was cold to him if he met with success.

He sometimes used to own that Crowne had some genius, but then he always added that 'his father and Crowne's mother were very well acquainted.'

Joseph Spence

SAMUEL PEPYS (1633–1703)

12 *Pepys's* Diary *is full of precise and vivid details of the Restoration period, including numerous reports of his own inveterate theatre-going.*

To the Duke of York's playhouse, and there saw 'Mustapha': which, the more I see, the more I like; and is a most admirable poem, and bravely acted; only both Betterton and Harris could not contain from laughing in the midst of a most serious part, from the ridiculous mistake of one of the men upon the stage; which I did not like.

To the Duke of York's House, and there saw 'Heraclius,' which is a good play; but they did so spoil it with their laughing, and being all of them out, and with the noise they made within the theatre, that I was ashamed of it, and resolved not to come thither again a good while, believing that this negligence, which I never observed before, proceeds only from their want of company in the pit, that they have no care how they act.

13 1 January, 1668

Thence I after dinner to the Duke of York's playhouse, and there saw 'Sir Martin Mar-all,' which I have seen so often, and yet am mightily pleased with it, and think it mighty witty, and the fullest of proper matter for mirth that ever was writ; and I do clearly see that they do improve in their acting of it. Here a mighty company of citizens, 'prentices, and others; and it makes me observe that when I began first to be able to bestow a play on myself I do not remember that I saw so many by half of the ordinary 'prentices and mean people in the pit at 2s. 6d. apiece as now; I going for several years no higher than the 12d. and then the 18d. places,* though I strained hard to go in when I did: so much the vanity and prodigality of the age is to be observed in this particular.

14 11 May, 1668

Took coach and called Mercer,** and she and I to the Duke of York's playhouse, and there saw 'The Tempest,' and between two acts I went out to Mr. Harris,*** and got him to repeat to me the words of the Echo, while I writ them down, having tried in the play to have wrote them; but, having done it without looking upon my paper, I find I could not read the blacklead.**** But now I have got the words clear, and, in going in thither, had the pleasure to see their actors in their several dresses, especially the seamen and monster, which were very droll: so in to the play again. But there happened one thing which vexed me, which is, that the orange-woman did come in the pit and challenge me for twelve oranges which she delivered by my order at a late play, at night, in order to give to some ladies in a box, which was wholly untrue, but yet she swore it to be true. But, however, I did deny it, and did not pay her; but, for quiet, did buy 4s. worth of oranges of her at 6d. apiece.

THOMAS BETTERTON (?1635–1710)

15 *Thomas Betterton was one of the principal actors of the Restoration theatre, making a great success of Shakespearean roles such as Hamlet and Lear. His dramatic powers overcame the disadvantages of a low voice, small eyes and ungainly figure.*

Archbishop Tillotson was very well acquainted with Betterton, and

---

*The admission prices to the upper gallery and the middle gallery respectively.

**Mary Mercer, former companion to Pepys's wife Elizabeth.

***Henry Harris, an actor whom some people preferred to Thomas Betterton.

****The 'Echo' referred to here was to Ferdinand's song 'Go thy way' in Act III sc.3, composed by John Banister, in which Ariel echoed the half-sentences sung previously by Ferdinand. Pepys had attended a production the previous year and had found the song 'mighty pretty' on the first hearing.

continued that acquaintance even after he was in that high station. One day when Betterton came to see him at Lambeth, that prelate asked him how it came about that after he had made the most moving discourse that he could, was touched deeply with it himself, and spoke it as feelingly as he was able, yet he could never move people in the church near so much as the other did on the stage?

'That,' says Betterton, 'I think is easy to be accounted for: 'tis because you are only *telling* them a story, and I am *showing* them facts.'

Joseph Spence

16 Not only was Betterton's range of characters unlimited, but the number he "created" was never equalled by any subsequent actor of eminence – namely, about one hundred and thirty! In some single seasons he studied and represented no less than eight original parts – an amount of labour which would shake the nerves of the stoutest among us now.

His brief relaxation was spent on his little Berkshire farm, whence he once took a rustic to Bartholomew Fair for a holiday. The master of the puppet-show declined to take money for admission – "Mr. Betterton," he said, "is a brother actor!" Roger, the rustic, was slow to believe that the puppets were not alive; and so similar in vitality appeared to him, on the same night, at Drury Lane, the Jupiter and Alcmena in *Amphitryon*, played by Betterton and Mrs. Barry, that on being asked what he thought of them, Roger, taking them for puppets, answered, "They did wonderfully well for rags and sticks."

John Doran

JOSEPH HAINES (1638–1701)

17 *Haines was a leading comedian and one of the first English Harlequins. Charles Hart excelled in heroic parts.*

About this time (1673) there happened a small pique between Mr. Hart and Joe, upon the account of his late negotiation in France, and there spending the company's money to so little purpose, or, as I may properly say, to no purpose at all. There happened to be one night a play called "Cataline's Conspiracy," wherein there was wanting a great number of senators. Now Mr. Hart, being chief of the house, would oblige Joe to dress for one of these senators, although his salary, being fifty shillings a week, freed him from any such obligation. But Mr. Hart, as I said before, being sole governor of the playhouse, and at a small variance with Joe, commands it, and the other must obey. Joe being vexed at the slight Mr. Hart had put upon him, found out this method of being revenged upon him. He gets a scaramouch dress, a large full ruff, makes himself whiskers from ear to ear, puts on a long merry cap, a short pipe in his mouth, a little three-legged stool in his hand, and in this manner follows Mr. Hart on the stage, sets himself down behind him, and begins to smoke his pipe, laugh and point at him, which comical figure put all the house in an uproar, some laughing, some clapping, and some hallooing. Now Mr. Hart, as those who knew him can aver, was a man of that exactness and grandeur on the stage, that let what would happen, he'd never discompose himself or mind anything but what he then represented, and had a scene fallen behind him he would not at that time look back to see what was the matter; which Joe knowing, remained still smoking; the audience continued laughing; Mr. Hart acting and wondering at this unusual occasion of their mirth – sometimes thinking it some disturbance in the house; again, that it might be something amiss in his dress. At last, turning himself towards the scenes, he discovered Joe in the aforesaid posture; whereupon he immediately goes off the stage, swearing he would never set foot on it again unless Joe was immediately turned out of doors; which was no sooner spoke than put in practice.

R. Wewitzer

EDWARD KYNASTON (?1640–1706)

18 *Actresses first appeared on the English stage during the Restoration period. Kynaston was one of the last boy-players of female roles. He played Juliet to Betterton's Romeo on several occasions.*

Tho' as I have before observ'd, Women were not admitted to the Stage, 'till the return of King Charles yet it could not be so suddenly supply'd with them, but that there was still a Necessity, for some time, to put the handsomest young Men into Petticoats; which Kynaston was then said to have worn, with Success; particularly in the Part of Evadne, in the *Maid's Tragedy*, which I have heard him speak of; and which calls to my Mind a ridiculous Distress that arose from these sort of Shifts, which the Stage was then put to – The King coming a little before his usual time to a Tragedy, found the Actors not ready to begin, when his Majesty not chusing to have as much Patience as his good Subjects, sent to them, to know the Meaning of it; upon which the Master of the Company came to the Box, and rightly judging that the best Excuse for their Default would be the true one, fairly told his Majesty that the Queen was not shav'd yet: The King, whose good Humour lov'd to laugh at a Jest, as well as to make one, accepted the Excuse, which serv'd to divert him, till the male Queen cou'd be effeminated. In a word, Kynaston, at that time, was so beautiful a Youth, that the Ladies of Quality prided themselves in taking him with them in their Coaches, to Hyde-Park, in this Theatrical Habit, after the Play; which in those Days, they might have sufficient time to do, because Plays then were us'd to begin at four a-Clock; The Hour that People of the same Rank, are now going to Dinner – Of this Truth, I had the Curiosity to enquire, and had it confirm'd from his own Mouth, in his advanc'd Age: And indeed, to the last of him, his handsomeness was very little abated.

Colley Cibber

WILLIAM PEER (d.1713)

19 *Sir Richard Steele wrote this obituary of a minor actor whose entire reputation rested on the delivery of a handful of lines.*

Though men see every day people go to their long home, who are younger than themselves, they are not so apt to be alarmed at that, as at the decease of those who have lived longer in their fight. They miss their acquaintance, and are surprised at the loss of an habitual object. This gave me so much concern for the death of Mr. William Peer of the Theatre-royal, who was an actor at the Restoration, and took his theatrical degree with Betterton, Kynaston and Harris. Though his station was humble, he performed it well; and the common comparison with the stage and human life, which has been so often made, may well be brought out upon this occasion. It is no matter, say the moralists, whether you act the prince or the beggar, the business is to do your part well. Mr. William Peer distinguished himself particularly in two characters, which no man ever could touch but himself; one of them was the speaker of the prologue to the play, which is contrived in the tragedy of Hamlet, to awake the conscience of the guilty princes. Mr. William Peer spoke that preface to the play with such an air, as represented that he was an actor, and with such an inferior manner as only acting an actor, as made the others on the stage appear real great persons, and not representatives. This was a nicety in acting that none but the most subtle player could so much as conceive. I remember his speaking these words, in which there is no greater matter but in the right adjustment of the air of the speaker, with universal applause:

> 'For us and for our tragedy,
> Here stooping to your clemency,
> We beg your hearing patiently.'

Hamlet says very archly upon the pronouncing of it, 'Is this a prologue, or a posy of a ring;' However, the speaking of it got Mr. Peer more reputation than those who speak the length of a puritan's sermon every night will ever attain to.

Besides this, Mr. Peer got a great fame on another little occasion. He played the Apothecary in Caius Marius, as it is called by Otway; but Romeo and Juliet, as originally in Shakespear; it will be necessary to recite more out of the play than he spoke, to have a right conception of what Peer did in it. Marius, weary of life, recollects means to be rid of it after this manner:

'I do remember an apothecary
That dwelt about this rendezvous of death;
Meagre and very rueful were his looks,
Sharp misery had worn him to the bones.'

When this spectre of poverty appeared, Marius addressed him thus:

'I see thou art very poor,
Thou may'st do any thing, here's fifty drachmas,
Get me a draught of what will soonest free
A wretch from all his cares.'

When the apothecary objects that it is unlawful, Marius urges,

'Art thou so base and full of wretchedness
Yet fear'st to die? Famine is in thy cheeks,
Need and oppression stareth in thy eyes,
Contempt and beggary hang on thy back;
The world is not thy friend, nor the world's laws:
The world affords no law to make thee rich;
Then be not poor, but break it, and take this.'

Without all this quotation the reader could not have a just idea of the visage and manner which Peer assumed, when in the most lamentable tone imaginable he consents; and delivering the poison, like a man reduced to the drinking it himself, if he did not vend it, says to Marius,

'My poverty, but not my will, consents,
Take this and drink it off, the work is done.'

It was an odd excellence, and a very particular circumstance this of Peer's, that his whole action of life depended upon speaking five lines better than any man else in the world. But this eminence lying in so narrow a compass, the governors of the theatre observing his talents to lie in a certain knowledge of propriety, and his person admitting him to shine only in the two above parts, his sphere of action was enlarged by the addition of the post of property-man. This officer has always ready, in a place appointed for him behind the prompter, all such tools and implements as are necessary in the play, and it is his business never to want billet-doux, poison, false money, thunderbolts, daggers, scrolls of parchments, wine, pomatum, truncheons and wooden legs, ready at the call of the said prompter, according as his respective utensils were necessary for promoting what was to pass on the stage. The addition of this office, so important to the conduct of the whole affair of the stage, and the good economy observed by their present managers in punctual payments, made Mr. Peer's subsistence very comfortable. But it frequently happens, that men lose their virtue in prosperity, who were shining characters in the contrary condition. Good fortune indeed had no effect on the mind, but very much on the body of Mr. Peer. For in the seventieth year of his age he grew fat, which rendered his figure unfit for the utterance of the five lines above mentioned. He had now unfortunately lost the wan distress necessary for the countenance of the apothecary, and was too jolly to speak the prologue with the proper humility. It is thought this calamity went too near him. It did not a little contribute to the shortening his days; and as there is no state of real happiness in this life, Mr. Peer was undone by his success, and lost all by arriving at what is the end of all other men's pursuits, his ease.

JOHN CROWNE (?1640–?1703)

20 *The dashing of an author's hopes of royal preferment.*

It was at the very latter End of King Charles's Reign, that Mr. Crown being tyr'd with the Fatigue of Writing, and shock'd by the Uncertainty of Theatrical Success, and desirous to shelter himself from the Resentments of those numerous Enemies which he had made by his City Politicks, made his Application immediately to the King himself; and desir'd his Majesty to establish him in some Office, that might be a Security to him for Life. The King had the Goodness to assure him he should have an Office, but added that he would first see another Comedy. Mr. Crown endeavouring to excuse himself, by telling the King that he plotted slowly and awkwardly; the King replyed, that he would help him to a Plot, and so put into his Hands the Spanish Comedy called *Non pued Esser*. Mr. Crown was oblig'd immediately to go to work upon it; but, after he had writ three Acts of it, found to his Surprise, that the Spanish Play had some time before been translated, and acted, and damn'd, under the Title of *Tarugo's Wiles, or the Coffee-house*. Yet, supported by the King's Command, he went boldly on and finish'd it; and here see the Influence of a Royal Encouragement . . .

. . . The Play was now just ready to appear to the World; and as every one that had seen it rehears'd was highly pleas'd with it; every one who had heard of it was big with the Expectation of it; and Mr. Crown was delighted with the flattering Hope of being made happy for the rest of his Life, by the Performance of the King's Promise; when, upon the very last Day of the Rehearsal, he met Cave Underhill coming from the Play-House as he himself was going towards it: Upon which the Poet reprimanding the Player for neglecting so considerable a Part as he had in the Comedy, and neglecting it on a Day of so much Consequence, as the very last Day of Rehearsal: Oh Lord, Sir, sayd Underhill, we are all undone. Wherefore, says Mr. Crown, is the Play-House on Fire? The whole Nation, replys the Player, will quickly be so, for the King is dead. At the hearing which dismal Words, the Author was little better; for he who but the Moment before was ravish'd with the Thought of the Pleasure, which he was about to give to his King, and of the Favours which he was afterwards to receive from him, this Moment found, to his unspeakable Sorrow, that his Royal Patron was gone for ever, and with him all his Hopes. The King indeed reviv'd from his Apoplectick Fit, but three Days after dyed, and Mr. Crown by his Death was replung'd in the deepest Melancholy.

John Dennis

WILLIAM WYCHERLEY (1641–1716)

21 *Accomplished and witty, Wycherley personified the Restoration Gentleman: his plays – realistic and bawdy – enjoyed great vogue. 'One of King Charles's Mistresses' was the Duchess of Cleveland.*

Upon the writing his first Play, which was *St. James's Park*, he became acquainted with several of the most celebrated Wits both of the Court and Town. The writing of that Play was likewise the Occasion of his becoming acquainted with one of King Charles's Mistresses after a very particular manner. As Mr. Wycherley was going thro' Pall-mall towards St. James's in his Chariot, he met the foresaid Lady in hers, who, thrusting half her Body out of the Chariot, cry'd out aloud to him, *You*, Wycherley, *you are a Son of a Whore*, at the same time laughing aloud and heartily. Perhaps, Sir, if you never heard of this Passage before, you may be surpris'd at so strange a Greeting from one of the most beautiful and best bred Ladies in the World. Mr. Wycherley was certainly very much surpris'd at it, yet not so much but he soon apprehended it was spoke with Allusion to the latter End of a Song in the foremention'd Play.

> *When Parents are Slaves*
> *Their Brats cannot be any other,*
> *Great Wits and great Braves*
> *Have always a Punk to their Mother.*

As, during Mr. Wycherley's Surprise, the Chariots drove different ways, they were soon at a considerable Distance from each other, when Mr. Wycherley recovering from his Surprise, ordered his Coachman to drive back, and to overtake the Lady. As soon as he got over-against her, he said to her, *Madam, you have been pleased to bestow a Title on me which generally belongs to the Fortunate. Will your Ladyship be at the Play to Night?* *Well*, she reply'd, *what if I am there? Why then I will be there to wait on your*

Ladyship, tho' I disappoint a very fine Woman who has made me an Assignation. So, said she, *you are sure to disappoint a Woman who has favour'd you for one who has not. Yes,* he reply'd, *if she who has not favour'd me is the finer Woman of the two. But he who will be constant to your Ladyship, till he can find a finer Woman, is sure to die your Captive.* The Lady blush'd, and bade her Coachman drive away. As she was then in all her Bloom, and the most celebrated Beauty that was then in England, or perhaps that has been in England since, she was touch'd with the Gallantry of that Compliment. In short, she was that Night in the first Row of the King's Box in Drury Lane and Mr. Wycherley in the Pit under her, where he entertained her during the whole Play. And this, Sir, was the beginning of a Correspondence between these two Persons, which afterwards made a great Noise in the Town.

John Dennis

NELL GWYNN (1650–87)

22 *Samuel Pepys records a meeting with Nell Gwynn when she was an actress (she retired from the stage at the age of nineteen). As the next two anecdotes show, actresses on the Restoration stage did not expect privacy in their dressing rooms.*

. . . to the King's House: and there, going in, met with Knipp,* and she took us up into the tiring-rooms and to the women's shift, where Nell was dressing herself and was all unready, and is very pretty, prettier than I thought. And so walked all up and down the house above, and then below into the scene-room,** and there sat down, and she gave us fruit: and here I read the questions to Knipp, while she answered me, through all her part of 'Flora's Figaries,' which was acted today. But, Lord! to see how they were both painted would make a man mad, and did make me loathe them; and what base company of men comes among them, and how lewdly they talk! and how poor the men are in clothes, and yet what a show they make on the stage by candle-light, is very observable. But to see how Nell cursed, for having so few people in the pit, was pretty.

REBECCA (BECK) MARSHALL (fl. 1667)

23 The 'tiring rooms of the actresses were then open to the fine gentlemen who frequented the house. They stood by at the mysteries of dressing, and commented on what they beheld and did not behold, with such

---

*Mrs Knepp, an actress with whom Pepys was more than a little infatuated.
**Part of the stage in which scenery in the form of painted wings and back-cloths was kept.

breadth and coarseness of wit, that the more modest or least impudent ladies sent away their little handmaidens. The dressing over, the amateurs lounged into the house, talked loudly with the pretty orange girls, listened when it suited them, and at the termination of the piece crowded again into the 'tiring room of the most favourite and least scrupulous of the actresses. Among these gallants who thus oscillated between the pit and the dressing bowers of the ladies, was a Sir Hugh Middleton. On the second Saturday of February 1667, Sir Hugh was among the joyous damsels dressing for the play, behind the stage of old Drury. The knight was so unpleasantly critical on the nymphs before him, that one of them, sharp-tongued Beck Marshall, bade him keep among the ladies of the Duke's House, since he did not approve of those who served the King. Sir Hugh burst out with a threat, that he would kick, or what was worse, hire his footman to kick, her. The pretty but angry Rebecca nursed her wrath all Sunday; but on Monday she notified the ungallant outrage to the great champion of insulted dames, the King. Nothing immediately came of it; and on Tuesday, there was Sir Hugh glowering at her from the front of the house, and waylaying her, as she was leaving it with a friend. Sir Hugh whispers a ruffianly-looking fellow, who follows the actress, and presses upon her so closely, that she is moved by a double fear – that he is about to rob, and perhaps stab her. A little scream scares the bravo for a minute or so. He skulks away, but anon slinks back; and, armed with the first offensive missile he could pick up in a Drury Lane gutter, he therewith anoints the face and hair of the much-shocked actress, and then, like the valiant fellows of his trade, takes to his heels. The next day, sweet as Anadyomene rising from the sea, the actress appeared before the King, and charged Sir Hugh with being the abettor of this gross outrage. How the knight was punished, the record in the State Paper Office does not say; but about a fortnight later a royal decree was issued, which prohibited gentlemen from entering the 'tiring rooms of the ladies of the King's Theatre. For some nights the gallants sat ill at ease among the audience; but the journals of the period show that the nymphs must have been as little pleased with this arrangement as the fine gentlemen themselves, who soon found their way back to pay the homage of flattery to the most insatiable of goddesses.

John Doran

Mrs Susannah Mountfort (?1667–1703)

24 The most interesting performance of Ophelia that I have met with on record, was that of Mrs. Susannah Mountfort . . . Mrs. Mountfort, during her last years, became deranged, but, as her disorder was not outrageous, she was not placed under any rigorous confinement, but

was suffered to walk about her house. One day, in a lucid interval, she asked what play was to be performed that evening, and was told it was to be 'Hamlet.' Whilst she was on the stage she had acted Ophelia with great applause; the recollection struck her, and, with all that cunning which is so frequently allied to insanity, she found means to elude the care of her attendants, and got to the theatre, where, concealing herself till the scene where Ophelia was to make her appearance in her mad state, she pushed upon the stage before the person appointed to play the character, and exhibited a representation of it that astonished the performers as well as the audience. She exhausted her vital powers in this effort, was taken home, and died soon after.

Thomas Campbell

COLLEY CIBBER (1671–1757)

25 *Actor, dramatist, Poet Laureate and sometime manager of Drury Lane Theatre. His adaptation of Shakespeare's* Richard III *held the stage for well over a hundred years. This version contained the famous line, 'Off with his head – so much for Buckingham'.*

Cibber and Verbruggen were two dissipated young fellows, who determined, in opposition to the advice of friends, to become great actors. Much about the same time, they were constant attendants upon Downes, the prompter of Drury-lane, in expectation of employment. What the first part was, in which Verbruggen distinguished himself, cannot now be known. But Mr. Richard Cross, late prompter of Drury-lane theatre, gave me the following history of Colley Cibber's first establishment as a hired actor. He was known only, for some years, by the name of Master Colley. After waiting impatiently a long time for the prompter's notice, by good fortune he obtained the honour of carrying a message on the stage, in some play, to Betterton. Whatever was the cause, Master Colley was so terrified, that the scene was disconcerted by him. Betterton asked, in some anger, who the young fellow was that had committed the blunder. Downes replied, 'Master Colley.' – 'Master Colley! then forfeit him.' – 'Why, Sir,' said the prompter, 'he has no salary.' – 'No!' said the old man; 'why then put him down ten shillings a week, and forfeit him 5s.'

To this good-natured adjustment of reward and punishment, Cibber owed the first money he received in the treasurer's office.

Thomas Davies

26 Cibber persisted so obstinately in acting parts in tragedy, that at last the public grew out of patience, and fairly hissed him off the stage. The following anecdote was many years since authenticated to me. When

Thomson's Sophonisba* was read to the actors, Cibber laid his hand upon Scipio, a character, which, though it appears only in the last act, is of great dignity and importance. For two nights successively, Cibber was as much exploded as any bad actor could be. Williams, by desire of Wilks,** made himself master of the part; but he, marching slowly, in great military distinction, from the upper part of the stage, and wearing the same dress as Cibber, was mistaken for him, and met with repeated hisses, joined to the music of catcals; but, as soon as the audience were undeceived, they converted their groans and hisses to loud and long continued applause.

Thomas Davies

27 *Colley Cibber himself narrates this splendid piece of inter-theatre rivalry. Powell and Doggett are the actors George Powell and Thomas Doggett.*

As it has been always judg'd their natural Interest, where there are two Theatres, to do one another as much Mischief as they can; you may imagine it could not be long, before this hostile Policy shew'd itself, in Action. It happen'd, upon our having Information on a Saturday Morning, that the Tuesday after, *Hamlet* was intended to be acted at the other House, where it had not yet been seen; our merry menaging Actors (for they were now in a manner left to govern themselves) resolv'd, at any rate, to steal a March upon the Enemy, and take Possession of the same Play the Day before them: Accordingly, *Hamlet* was given out that Night, to be acted with us on Monday. The Notice of this sudden Enterprize, soon reach'd the other House, who, in my Opinion, too much regarded it; for they shorten'd their first Orders, and resolv'd that *Hamlet* should to *Hamlet* be oppos'd, on the same Day; whereas, had they given notice in their Bills, that the same Play would have been acted by them the Day after, the Town would have been in no doubt which House they should have reserv'd themselves for; ours must certainly have been empty, and theirs, with more Honour, have been crowded: Experience, many Years after, in like Cases, has convinc'd me that this would have been the more laudable Conduct. But be that as it may; when, in their Monday's Bills, it was seen that *Hamlet* was up against us, our Consternation was terrible, to find that so hopeful a Project was frustrated. In this Distress, Powell, who was our commanding Officer, and whose enterprising Head wanted nothing but Skill to carry him thro'

*James Thomson (1700–48), poet and playwright, wrote *Sophonisba* in 1729. One luckless line, 'O Sophonisba, Sophonisba O' was quickly met with the parody, 'O Jemmy Thomson, Jemmy Thomson O', which killed off what little life the piece possessed. See also p. 27.

**Robert Wilks, with Cibber and Barton Booth, managed Drury Lane Theatre from 1710 till his death in 1732.

the most desperate Attempts; for, like others of his Cast, he had murder'd many a Hero, only to get into his Cloaths. This Powell, I say, immediately call'd a Council of War; where the Question was, Whether he should fairly face the Enemy, or make a Retreat, to some other Play of more probable Safety? It was soon resolv'd that to act *Hamlet* against *Hamlet*, would be certainly throwing away the Play, and disgracing themselves to little or no Audience; to conclude, Powell, who was vain enough to envy Betterton, as his Rival, propos'd to change Plays with them, and that, as they had given out the *Old Batchelor*, and had chang'd it for *Hamlet*, against us; we should give up our *Hamlet*, and turn the *Old Batchelor* upon them. This Motion was agreed to, *Nemine contradicente;* but upon Enquiry, it was found, that there were not two Persons among them who had ever acted in that Play: But that Objection, it seems (though all the Parts were to be study'd in six Hours) was soon got over; Powell had an Equivalent, *in petto*, that would balance any Deficiency on that Score; which was, that he would play the *Old Batchelor* himself, and mimick Betterton, throughout the whole Part. This happy Thought was approv'd with Delight, and Applause. Accordingly, the Bills were chang'd, and at the bottom inserted,

> The Part of the *Old Batchelor*, to be perform'd in Imitation
> of the Original.

Printed Books of the Play were sent for in haste, and every Actor had one, to pick out of it the Part he had chosen: Thus, while they were each of them chewing the Morsel, they had most mind to, some one happening to cast his Eye over the *Dramatis Personae*, found that the main Matter was still forgot, that no body had yet been thought of for the Part of Alderman Fondlewife. Here we were all a ground agen! nor was it to be conceiv'd who could make the least tolerable Shift with it. This Character had been so admirably acted by Dogget, that though it is only seen in the Fourth Act, it may be no Dispraise to the Play, to say, it probably ow'd the greatest Part of its Success to his Performance. But, as the Case was now desperate, any Resource was better than none, Somebody must swallow the bitter Pill, or the Play must die. At last it was recollected, that I had been heard to say, in my wild way of talking, what a vast mind I had to play Nykin, by which Name the Character was more frequently call'd. Notwithstanding they were thus distress'd about the Disposal of this Part, most of 'em shook their Heads, at my being mention'd for it; yet Powell, who was resolv'd, at all Hazards, to fall upon Betterton, and having no concern for what might become of any one that serv'd his Ends or Purpose, order'd me to be sent for; and, as he naturally lov'd to set other People wrong, honestly said, before I came, *If the Fool has a mind to blow himself up, at once, let us ev'n give him a clear Stage for it.* Accordingly, the Part was put into my Hands, between Eleven and

Twelve that Morning, which I durst not refuse, because others were as much straitned in time, for Study, as myself. But I had this casual Advantage of most of them; that having so constantly observ'd Dogget's Performance, I wanted but little Trouble, to make me perfect in the Words; so that when it came to my turn to rehearse, while others read their Parts, from their Books, I had put mine in my Pocket, and went thro' the first Scene without it; and though I was more abash'd to rehearse so remarkable a Part before the Actors (which is natural to most young People) than to act before an Audience, yet some of the better-natur'd encourag'd me so far as to say they did not think I should make an ill Figure in it: To conclude, the Curiosity to see Betterton mimick'd drew us a pretty good Andience, and Powell (as far as Applause is a Proof of it) was allow'd to have burlesqu'd him very well. As I have question'd the certain Value of Applause, I hope I may venture, with less Vanity, to say how particular a Share I had of it, in the same Play.

MRS BOUTWELL (fl. 1677)

28 This story is told by Campbell, in his "Life of Mrs. Siddons," of Mrs. Boutwell. "She was," he says, "the original *Statira* of Lee's 'Alexander,' and acted the 'Rival Queens' successively with Mrs. Marshall and Mrs. Barry.* Once when playing with the latter of the ladies, she was in danger of dying on the stage in earnest. Before the curtain drew up the two Queens, *Statira* (Boutwell) and *Roxana* (Barry) had a real rivalship about a lace veil, which was at last awarded to the former by the property-man. This decision so enraged *Roxana* that she acted her part rather too naturally, and in stabbing *Statira* sent her dagger, though it was a blunted one, through Mrs. Boutwell's stays, about a quarter of an inch into the flesh."

From *Representative Actors*

MR KING (fl. 1680s)

29 *By prudent management of their salaries, theatre staff could sometimes become wealthier than their employers. Booth and Wilks were the actors Barton Booth and Robert Wilks.*

Box-keepers, whatever they may be now, by the managers' keeping an eye over their conduct, were formerly richer than their masters. A remarkable instance of it I heard many years since. Colley Cibber had, in a prologue, or some part of a play, given such offence to a certain great man in power, that the playhouse, by order of the Lord-chamberlain,

---

*Nathaniel Lee's *The Rival Queens; or the Death of Alexander the Great* (1677)

was shut up for some time; Cibber was arrested, and the damages laid at ten thousand pounds. Of this misfortune Booth and Wilks were talking very seriously, at the playhouse, in the presence of a Mr. King, the box-keeper; who asked if he could be of any service, by offering to bail Cibber. – 'Why, you blockhead,' says Wilks, 'it is for ten thousand pounds.' – 'I should be very sorry,' said the box-keeper, 'if I could not be answerable for twice that sum.' The managers stared at each other; and Booth said, with some emotion, to Wilks, 'What have you and I been doing, Bob, all this time?'

Thomas Davies

CHRISTOPHER RICH (d. 1714)

30 *How to drop a theatrical brick. Rich was the manager of Drury Lane Theatre; Mich was the comic actor Michael Stoppelaer.*

It was Mich's faculty to utter absurd speeches and disagreeable truths, without any design to give offence. I shall quote one anecdote, which will give the reader an idea of his character. Rich was talking to some of the actors, when Stoppelaer was present, concerning the disproportioned agreement he had made with Hallam, who acted Aumerle. Stoppelaer shook his head and said, *Upon my soul, Sir, he got on the blind side of you there.* Rich, apprehensive of hearing something more offensive, left the company: somebody present observed that Stoppelaer's speech was exceedingly improper, and really affronting, because every body knew that Mr. Rich had a great blemish in one of his eyes. – '*Upon my word*', said Mich, '*I never heard of it before, and I will go immediately and ask his pardon.*'

Thomas Davies

JOHN RICH (?1692–1761)

31 *The son of Christopher Rich, John was a theatrical manager himself, and probably the greatest Harlequin and pantomime performer of his day. Foote is Samuel Foote, the actor and dramatist.*

The education of Mr. Rich had been grossly neglected; for though his understanding was good, his language was vulgar and ungrammatical: he was a perfect male Slip-slop.* However, he had much entertainment in his conversation, and loved a private party where he could unbend himself. From an habitual inattention, he had contracted a strange and perverse custom of calling every body Mister; and this gave occasion to

*A character in Henry Fielding's novel *Joseph Andrews*

an unmannerly bon mot of Foote. After Mr. Rich had called him Mister several times, Foote grew warm, and asked him the reason of his not calling him by his name. "Don't be angry," said Mr. Rich; "for I sometimes forget my own name." – "That's extraordinary indeed," replied Foote; "I knew you could not write your own name, but I did not suppose you could forget it."

Thomas Davies

WILLIAM PINKETHMAN (d. 1725)

32 It must be confessed, that the actors, termed low comedians, are too guilty of adding to their author's text. Sometimes, indeed, it happens, that the wit, or happy imagination of the actor, is of service to the situation in which he is placed, and unexpectedly gives a relief or embellishment to that which would otherwise be neglected, or perhaps disapproved.

The contrary practice is, however, much more common . . . Will Pinkethman, of merry memory, was in such full possession of the galleries, that he would hold discourse with them for several minutes. To fine him for this fault was in vain; he could not abandon it, and the managers were too generous to curtail him of his income. At length, I was told, he and Wilks came to this whimsical agreement: Pinkey consented, that whenever he was guilty of corresponding with the gods, he should receive, on his back, three smart strokes of Bob Wilks's cane. – This fine, however, was, I believe, never exacted. I shall give the reader one specimen of his unseasonable drollery.

In the play of the Recruiting Officer*, Wilks was the Captain Plume, and Pinkethman one of the Recruits. The Captain, when he enlisted him, asked his name: instead of answering as he ought, Pinkey replied, 'Why! don't you know my name, Bob? I thought every fool had known that!' Wilks, in rage, whispered to him the name of the Recruit, Thomas Appletree. The other retorted aloud, 'Thomas Appletree! Thomas Devil! my name is Will Pinkethman:' and immediately addressing an inhabitant of the upper regions, he said, 'Hark you, friend: don't you know my name?' – 'Yes, Master Pinkey (said a respondent) we know it very well.' The play-house was now in an uproar; the audience, at first, enjoyed the petulant folly of Pinkethman and the distress of Wilks; but, in the progress of the joke, it grew tiresome, and Pinkey met with his deserts, a very severe reprimand in a hiss; and this mark of displeasure he changed into applause, by crying out, with a countenance as melancholy as he could make it, in a loud and nasal twang, *Odsfo! I fear I am wrong!*

Thomas Davies

*By George Farquhar (1678–1707)

JAMES QUIN (1693–1766)

33 *Quin was one of the last of the school of declamatory acting soon to be eclipsed by Garrick.*

Mrs. Hallam was unhappy in a large unwieldy person: notwithstanding this unfavourable circumstance, the public always wished to see her in characters which received no advantage from her figure. Monimia was a part which her good understanding would have taught her to resign; but neither the public nor the manager would permit it. You may guess at the unfitness of her figure for young and delicate ladies by Quin's sarcasm. He observed one morning, at rehearsal, a large tub, or barrel, in which the mad Englishman, in the Pilgrim, rolls about the stage; he asked the prompter what it was; but, before he could receive an answer, he cried out, *I see what it is: Mrs. Hallam's stays, in which she played Monimia last night.*

Thomas Davies

CHRISTIANA HORTON (?1696–?1756)

34 The queen was personated by Mrs. Horton; one of the most beautiful women that ever trod the stage. She was married, when very young, to a musician, who was insensible to her charms, and treated her, as it has been said, very brutally. The first notice that was taken of her was at Windsor, in the summer of 1713; where she acted Marcia, in *Cato*, in a company of miserable strollers, who were drawn there on account of Queen Anne's making it the place of her residence several months in the year. Cato and his senate met with little respect from the audience; and poor Juba was so truly an object of ridicule, that, when he cried out, in a transport of joy, on hearing Marcia's confession of her passion for him, "What do I hear?" my Lord Malpas, wilfully mistaking the actor, loudly said, from behind the scenes, *Upon my word, sir, I do not know: I think you had better be any where else:* and this joke, I believe, put an end to the play. However, Mrs. Horton was so superior in merit to the rest, and so attractive in her person, that she was soon after very powerfully recommended to the managers of Drury-lane Theatre, who engaged her at a moderate salary.

Thomas Davies

CHARLES MACKLIN (?1699–1797)

35 *Born in Ireland, Macklin acted in Dublin long before he came to England.*

It was said of him that at nineteen he could not read. It is however certain that he was servant, similar to what at Oxford is called a "scout," at

Trinity College, Dublin. The custom was for these servants to wait in the courts of the college in attendance on the calls of the students. To every shout of "Boy!" the scout, first in turn, replied, "What number?" and on its announcement went up to the room denoted, for his orders. After Macklin by his persevering industry had gained a name as author and actor, in one of his engagements at the Dublin Theatre some unruly young men caused a disturbance, when Macklin in very proper terms rebuked them for their indecent behaviour. The audience applauded; but one of the rioters, thinking to put him down by reference to his early low condition, with contemptuous bitterness shouted out "Boy!" Poor Macklin for a moment lost his presence of mind, but recollecting himself, modestly stepped forward, and with manly complacency responded, "What number?" It is unnecessary to add that the plaudits of the house fully avenged him on the brutality of his insulters.

William Charles Macready

36 *Macklin was a particularly good teacher of other actors. Thomas Davies said that he was 'the only player I ever heard of that made acting a science.'*

Miss Ambrose was a pupil of Macklin, who lived at that time in Dorset-street, far on as you go to Drumcondra: next to his was a nunnery, a small house, with a large garden, which was divided from Macklin's by a wall not very high.

Macklin had another pupil, Philip Glenville, a handsome, tall, fine young man, whom he was also preparing for the stage. In Macklin's garden, there were three long parallel walks, and his method of exercising their voices was thus. His two young pupils with back boards (such as they use in boarding schools) walked firmly, slow, and well, up and down the two side walks; Macklin himself paraded the centre walk: at the end of every twelve paces he made them stop; and turning gracefully, the young actor called out across the walk, "How do you do, Miss Ambrose?" – she answered, "Very well, I thank you, Mr. Glenville." They then took a few more paces, and the next question was, "Do you not think it a very fine day, Mr. Glenville?" "A very fine day, indeed, Miss Ambrose," was the answer. Their walk continued; and then, "How do you do, Mr. Glenville?" – "Pretty well, I thank you, Miss Ambrose." And this exercise continued for an hour or so (Macklin still keeping in the centre walk) in the full hearing of their religious next-door neighbours. Such was Macklin's method of training the management of the voice: if too high, too low, a wrong accent, or a faulty inflection, he immediately noticed it, and made them repeat the words twenty times till all was right. Soon after this, Glenville played Antonio to his Shylock in "The

Merchant of Venice;" and Miss Ambrose, Charlotte in his own "Love-à-la Mode."

John O'Keefe

37 Macklin was tenacious, and very properly so, of the performers throwing in words of their own. Lee Lewes one morning at Covent-Garden, at the rehearsal of "Love à-la-mode," in which he played Squire Groom, said something which he thought very smart. "Hoy, hoy!" said Macklin, "what's that?" – "Oh," replied Lee Lewes, "'tis only a little of my nonsense." – "Ay," replied Macklin, "but I think *my* nonsense is rather better than *yours;* so keep to that, if you please, Sir." Though so particular in drilling the performers at rehearsals, aware of the consequence of irritability, he kept his temper down. An instance of this happened in Dublin, one morning at rehearsal:-one of the performers got tired with over-particularity as he called it, and said, "Why, this is worse than the Prussian exercise!" Macklin, after a pause, looked at the refractory actor, and said, "Suppose we all go and sit down a little in the green-room?" He walked in, and they followed; he sat down, and they seated themselves; he then took out his watch, looked at it, and laid it on the table, "Now," said he, "we'll just sit here one hour." The performers, knowing his great money-drawing importance, acquiesced, and kept rather an awful silence. The hour being expired, he took up his watch, "Now," he said, "we are all in good humour, and we'll go upon the stage and begin our rehearsal."

John O'Keefe

38 *Macklin's play* The Man of the World *was an undisguised attack on the influence of the Scottish Lord Bute at the court of King George III. Its performance in England was officially delayed for seventeen years. It left Macklin with a lasting hatred of the Scots.*

After he had left the stage, which the utter loss of memory compelled him to do, my father paid him a visit in London, and his account of it gave curious evidence of an inveterate prejudice surviving the decay of physical and intellectual power. The old man, with lack-lustre eye, was sitting in his arm-chair unconscious of any one being present, till Mrs. Macklin addressed him. "My dear, here is Mr. Macready come to see you." "Who?" said Macklin. "Mr. Macready, my dear." "Ha! who is he?" "Mr. Macready, you know, who went to Dublin to act for your benefit." "Ha! my benefit? what was it? what did he act?" "I acted Egerton, sir," said my father, "in your own play." "Ha! my play? what was it?" " 'The Man of the World,' sir." "Ha, 'Man of the World!' Devilish good title! Who wrote it?" "You did, sir." "Did I? Well! What

was it about?" "Why, sir, there was a Scotchman" – "Ah d — n them!"
My father finding it useless to prolong this last interview with his old
preceptor, took his leave.

William Charles Macready

JAMES THOMSON (1700–48)

39 *Apart from being a poet and playwright, Thomson may also have been the author of
'Rule Britannia'. His play* Agamemnon *was written in 1738.*

Thomson, in reading his play of Agamemnon to the actors, in the green-
room*, pronounced every line with such a broad Scotch accent, that
they could not restrain themselves from a loud laugh. Upon this, the
author good-naturedly said to the manager, 'Do you, Sir, take my play,
and go on with it; for, though I can write a tragedy, I find I cannot read
one.'

Thomas Davies

40 Agamemnon, though well acted, was not written agreeably to the taste
of the critics, who very justly observed that he had not entirely preserved
ancient manners and characters; Clytemnestra did not resemble the
portrait drawn of her by Aeschylus, which is more consistent and
agreeable to history. The displeasure of the audience shown to certain
scenes produced a whimsical effect upon the author; he had promised to
meet some friends at a tavern as soon as the play was ended, but he was
obliged to defer his attending them to a very late hour. When he came,
they asked him the reason of his stay; he told them that the critics had
sweated him so terribly by their severe treatment of certain parts of his
tragedy, that the perspiration was so violent as to render his wig unfit to
wear; and that he had spent a great deal of time among the peruke-makers
in procuring a proper cover for his head.

Thomas Davies

MARY ANN PORTER (d. 1765)

41 She excelled greatly in the terrible and the tender – the great actor Booth
speaking in raptures of her *Belvidera* – and Dr. Johnson saying that in the
vehemence of tragic acting he had never seen her equal. For many years

---

*For performances the stage was always covered with a green cloth which simulated grass for
exterior scenes or a green carpet for interior. The stage is still known to actors as 'the green'
and the room where they await their entrances is 'the green-room'. Many of the anecdotes in
this book contain references to the green room.

she acted, though absolutely a cripple, having had her hip-joint dislocated by a fall from her chaise in an encounter with a highwayman, whom she terrified into supplication by the sight of a brace of pistols. Finding he had been driven to desperation by want, she gave him ten guineas, and afterwards raised sixty pounds by subscription for relief of his family. In acting *Elizabeth* in the "Rival Queens" she had to support herself on a crutched cane; and after signing Mary's death-warrant, she expressed her agitation by striking the stage with her cane so violently as to draw bursts of applause. At last she herself subsisted on charity; and Dr. Johnson, who paid her a visit of benevolence some years before her death, said she was then so wrinkled that a picture of old age in the abstract might have been taken from her countenance. –

From *Blackwood's Magazine*

JOHN THURMOND (1700–49)

42 Was an Actor of Repute in this Kingdom about Thirty Years past, and stood in many capital Parts, being then a Sharer in old Smock-Alley Theatre* with Mr. Thomas Elrington, & c.

To let you see how formerly even Tragedy Heroes were now-and-then put to their Shifts, I'll tell you a short Story that befel Mr. Thurmond.

It was a Custom, at that Time, for Persons of the First Rank and Distinction to give their Birth-Day Suits to the most favoured Actors. I think Mr. Thurmond was honour'd by General Ingoldsby with his. But his Finances being at the last Tide of Ebb, the rich Suit was put in Buckle (a Cant Word for Forty in the Hundred Interest): One Night, Notice was given that the General would be present with the Government at the Play, and all the Performers on the Stage were preparing to dress out in the Suits presented. The Spouse of Johnny (as he was commonly called) try'd all her Arts to persuade Mr. Holdfast the pawnbroker (as it fell out, his real Name) to let go the Cloaths for that Evening, to be returned when the Play was over: But all arguments were fruitless; nothing but the ready, or a Pledge of full equal Value. Well! what must be done? The whole Family in Confusion, and all at their Wits-End; Disgrace, with her glaring Eyes, and extended Mouth, ready to devour. Fatal Appearance! At laft Winny the Wife (that is, Winnifrede) put on a compos'd Countenance (but, alas! with a troubled Heart); stepp'd to a neighbouring Tavern, and bespoke a very hot Negus, to comfort Johnny in the great Part he was to perform that Night, begging to have the Silver Tankard with the Lid, because, as she said, *a Covering, and the Vehicle Silver, would retain Heat longer than any other Metal*. The request was

*The best-known theatre in Dublin, also known as the Orange Street Theatre.

comply'd with, the Negus carry'd to the Play-house piping hot – popp'd into a vile earthen Mug – the Tankard *L'argent* travelled Incog under her Apron (like the Persian Ladies veil'd), popp'd into the Pawnbroker's Hands, in exchange for the Suit – put on, and play'd its Part, with the rest of the Wardrobe; when its Duty was over, carried back to remain in its old Depository – the Tankard return'd the right Road; and, when the Tide flow'd with its Lunar Influence, the stranded Suit was wasted into safe Harbour again, after paying a little for dry Docking, which was all the Damage receive'd.

W.R. Chetwood

SAMUEL JOHNSON (1709–84)

43 *Johnson was only eight years older than his pupil, David Garrick. Both were born in Lichfield and travelled together, sharing a horse, on their first foray to London. Johnson's achievements as poet, critic, essayist and lexicographer are not in doubt. As a dramatist, however, he was not so successful: his tragedy,* Irene, *staged by Garrick, was short-lived. Although the two men often argued with and criticized one another, they remained friends for the rest of Garrick's life. On being told of his demise, Johnson remarked, 'I am disappointed in that death which has eclipsed the gaiety of nations and impoverished the public stock of harmless pleasure.'*

Johnson thought the opportunity fair to think of his tragedy of *Irene*, which was his whole stock on his first arrival in town, in the year 1737. That play was accordingly put into rehearsal in January 1749. As a precursor to prepare the way, and awaken the public attention, *The Vanity of Human Wishes*, a Poem in Imitation of the Tenth Satire of Juvenal, by the Author of *London*, was published in the same month. In the Gentleman's Magazine, for February, 1749, we find that the tragedy of *Irene* was acted at Drury-lane, on Monday, February the 6th, and from that time, without interruption, to Monday, February the 20th, being in all thirteen nights. Since that time it has not been exhibited on any stage. *Irene* may be added to some other plays in our language, which have lost their place in the theatre, but continue to please in the closet. During the representation of this piece, Johnson attended every night behind the scenes. Conceiving that his character, as an author, required some ornament for his person, he chose, upon that occasion, to decorate himself with a handsome waistcoat, and a gold-laced hat. The late Mr. Topham Beauclerc, who had had a great deal of that humour which pleases the more for seeming undesigned, used to give a pleasant description of this Green-room finery, as related by the author himself; 'But,' said Johnson, with great gravity, 'I soon laid aside my gold-laced hat, lest it should make me proud.' The amount of the three benefit nights for the tragedy of *Irene*, it is to be feared, was not very considerable, as the profit, that stimulating motive, never invited the author to another dramatic attempt. Some years afterwards, when the present writer was intimate with Garrick, and knew Johnson to be in distress, he asked the manager why he did not produce another tragedy for his Lichfield friend? Garrick's answer was remarkable: 'When Johnson writes tragedy, declamation roars, and passion sleeps: when Shakespeare wrote, he dipped his pen in his own heart.'

From *Johnsonian Miscellanies*

44 When Garrick was one day mentioning to me Dr. Johnson's illiberal treatment of him, on different occasions; 'I question,' said he, 'whether, in his calmest and most dispassionate moments, he would allow me the high theatrical merit which the public have been so generous as to attribute to me.' I told him that I would take an early opportunity to make the trial, and that I would not fail to inform him of the result of my experiment. As I had rather an active curiosity to put Johnson's disinterested generosity fairly to the test, on this apposite subject, I took an early opportunity of waiting on him, to hear his verdict on Garrick's pretensions to his great and universal fame. I found him in very good and social humour; and I began a conversation which naturally led to the mention of Garrick. I said something particular on his excellence as an actor; and I added, 'But pray, Dr. Johnson, do you really think that he deserves that illustrious theatrical character, and that prodigious fame, which he has acquired?' 'Oh, Sir,' said he, 'he deserves every thing that he has acquired, for having seized the very soul of Shakspeare; for having embodied it in himself; and for having expanded its glory over the world.' I was not slow in communicating to Garrick the answer of the Delphic oracle. The tear started in his eye – 'Oh! Stockdale,' said he, 'such a praise from such a man! – *this* atones for all that has passed.'

Percival Stockdale

45 *The Shakespearean commentator George Stevens is talking to Dr Johnson. Goldsmith's play was* She Stoops to Conquer.

'Though you brought a Tragedy, Sir, to Drury-Lane, and at one time were so intimate with Garrick, you never appeared to have much theatrical acquaintance.' – 'Sir, while I had, in common with other dramatic authors, the liberty of the scenes, without considering my admission behind them as a favour, I was frequently at the theatre. At that period all the wenches knew me, and dropped me a curtsey as they passed on to the stage. But since poor Goldsmith's last Comedy, I scarce recollect having seen the inside of a playhouse. To speak the truth, there

is small encouragement there for a man whose sight and hearing are
become so imperfect as mine. I may add that, Garrick and Henderson*
excepted, I never met with a performer who had studied his art, or could
give an intelligible reason for what he did.'

From *Johnsonian Miscellanies*

46 Mrs B. having recently desired Johnson to look over her new play of the
'Siege of Sinope' before it was acted, he always found means to evade it;
at last she pressed him so closely that he actually refused to do it and told
her that she herself, by carefully looking it over, would be able to see if
there was anything amiss as well as he could. 'But, sir,' said she, 'I have
no time. I have already so many irons in the fire.' 'Why then, madam,'
he said (quite out of patience), 'the best thing I can advise you to do is,
to put your tragedy along with your irons.'

From *Johnsonian Miscellanies*

WILLIAM HAVARD (1710–78)

47 Havard undertook the tragedy of "Charles I." at the desire of the manager
of the company of Lincoln's Inn Fields, to which he then belonged, in
1737. The manager had probably read of the salutary effects produced
on the genius of Euripides by seclusion in his cave, and he was determined
to give Havard the same advantage in a garret during the composition
of his task. He invited him to his house, took him up to one of its airiest
apartments, and there locked him up for so many hours every day, well
knowing his desultory habits; nor released him till the unfortunate bard
had repeated through the keyhole a certain number of new speeches in
the progressive tragedy.

Thomas Campbell

DAVID GARRICK (1717–79)

48 *For nearly thirty years, until his retirement in 1776, Garrick dominated the London stage,
giving superb portrayals both in tragic roles such as Hamlet and Richard III, and in comic
roles such as Abel Drugger in Ben Jonson's* The Alchemist. *He was small in stature,
but had great stage presence. In this first anecdote Garrick gets himself into hot water on
account of his powers of mimicry.*

---

*This is John Henderson (see also p. 53), often called 'the Bath Roscius' – after Quintus
Roscius, the most famous of Roman actors, whose name became used as a generic title for all
actors of genius in later times.

When Garrick first undertook to play Bayes in *The Rehearsal,** he had
some doubts of the propriety of taking-off his brother performers; and
therefore made a proposal to Giffard the manager of the theatre in
Goodman's Fields,** to permit him to begin with him, as a kind of an
apology for the rest. Giffard supposing that Garrick would only just
glance at him to countenance the mimicry of the others, consented: but
Garrick hit him off so truly, and made him so completely ridiculous, at
rehearsal, that Giffard, in a rage, sent him a challenge; which Garrick
accepting, they met the next morning, when the latter was wounded in
the sword arm.

The comedy of *The Rehearsal* had been during this time advertised for
the Saturday night ensuing; but the duel intervening (which none but
the parties and their seconds knew of at that time, and very few ever
since), the play was put off for a fortnight longer, *on account of the sudden
indisposition of a principal performer.* At the end of that time it came out,
with imitations of most of the principal actors, but Giffard was totally
omitted.

Thomas Davies

49 *Garrick removed spectators from the stage of Drury Lane in 1763 in order to put a stop to
such interruptions as went on in Dublin. Mrs Woffington is Margaret (Peg) Woffington,
a leading actress and for some years Garrick's mistress.*

Mr. Garrick indeed must have called to mind a very ridiculous circumstance that happened on the Dublin theatre when he acted the part of
King Lear. When the old King was recovering from his delirium, and
sleeping with his head on Cordelia's lap, a gentleman stepped at that
instant from behind the scenes, upon the stage, and threw his arms round
Mrs. Woffington, who acted that character; nor did I hear that the
audience resented, as they ought, so gross an affront offered to them,
and to common decency; so long had they been accustomed to riotous
and illiberal behaviour in the theatre.

Thomas Davies

50 Upon their return from Dublin, Mrs. Woffington lodged in the same
house with Macklin; and as Garrick often visited there, there was a
constant course of society between the parties; a fourth visitor, too,
sometimes made his appearance, but in *private* – who was a Noble Lord,
now living, and who was much enamoured with Miss Woffington's

---

*By George Villiers, the Duke of Buckingham (1671)

**Garrick made his professional début at Goodman's Fields Theatre in 1741. This playhouse,
not licensed under the Licensing Act of 1737, closed at the end of 1742.

many agreeable qualifications. It, however, unfortunately happened one night, that Garrick had occupied Miss Woffington's chamber when his Lordship took it in his head to visit his favourite Dulcinea. A loud knocking at the door announced his arrival; when Garrick, who had always a proper presentiment of danger about him, jumped out of bed, and gathering up his clothes as well as he could, hurried up to Macklin's apartments for security.

Macklin was just out of his first sleep when he was roused by his friend, who told him the particular cause of disturbing him, and requested the use of a bed for the remainder of the night. But what was Garrick's surprise, when, on reviewing the articles of his dress which he brought up with him, "in the alarm of fear," he found he had left his scratch wig below in Miss Woffington's bed-chamber! Macklin did all he could to comfort him – the other lay upon tenter-hooks of anxiety the whole night.

But to return to his Lordship: he had scarcely entered the apartment, when finding something entangle his feet in the dark, he called for a light, and the first object he saw was this unfortunate scratch! which taking up in his hand, he exclaimed with an oath, "Oh! Madam, have I found you out at last? So here has been a lover in the case!" and then fell to upbraiding her in all the language of rage, jealousy, and disappointment. The lady heard him with great composure for some time, and then, without offering the least excuse, "begged of him not to make himself so great a fool, but give her her wig back again." "What! Madam, do you glory in your infidelity? Do you own the wig then?" – "Yes to be sure I do," said she: "I'm sure it was my money paid for it, and I hope it will repay me with money and reputation too." This called for a farther explanation. At last she very coolly said, "Why, my Lord, if you will thus desert your character as a man, and be prying into all the little peculiarities of my domestic and professional business, know that I am soon to play a breeches part,* and that wig, which you so triumphantly hold in your hand, is the very individual wig I was practising in a little before I went to bed: and so, because my maid was careless enough to leave it in your Lordship's way – here I am to be plagued and scolded at such a rate, as if I was a common prostitute."

This speech had all the desired effect: his Lordship fell upon his knees, begged a thousand pardons, and the night was passed in harmony and good humour.

Thomas Davies

---

*A male role considered appropriate in the eighteenth century for an actress to play, e.g. Peg Woffington herself as Sir Henry Wildair in Farquhar's *The Constant Couple*.

51 *Garrick had a reputation in some quarters for guarding his money carefully. Others thought him downright mean.*

Mr. Garrick gave a dinner at his lodgings to Harry Fielding, Macklin, Havard, Mrs. Cibber, &c. &c.; and, vails to servants being then much the fashion, Macklin, and most of the company, gave Garrick's man (David, a Welshman) something at parting – some a shilling, some half a crown, &c. while Fielding, very formally, slipt a piece of paper in his hand, with something folded in the inside. When the company were all gone, David seeming to be in high glee, Garrick asked him how much he got. 'I can't tell you yet, Sir,' said Davy; 'here is half a crown from Mrs. Cibber, Got pless hur – here is a shilling from Mr. Macklin – Here is two from the Poet, Got pless his merry heart.' By this time Davy had unfolded the paper; when, to his great astonishment, he saw it contain no more than *one penny!* Garrick felt nettled at this, and next day spoke to Fielding about the impropriety of jesting with a servant. 'Jesting!' said Fielding, with a seeming surprise: 'so far from it, that I meant to do the fellow a real piece of service; for had I given him a shilling, or half a crown, I knew you would have taken it from him; but by giving him only a penny, he had a chance of calling it his own.' "

Thomas Davies

52 Mr. Peter Garrick [David's brother] once told Dr. Johnson the following anecdote: A grocer in the town of Lichfield, a neighbour of Peter Garrick's, having occasion to come up to London on business, the latter gave him a letter of recommendation to his brother David. The grocer came to town late in the evening, and seeing Garrick's name up in the bills for Abel Drugger, he went to the two shilling gallery, and there waited in anxious expectation of seeing, in the person of this townsman, the greatest actor of the age. On Garrick's appearance he was for some time in doubt whether it could be he or not: at last being convinced of it by the people about him, he felt so disgusted with the mean appearance and mercenary conduct of the performer (which, by a foolish combination, he attached to the *man*), that he went out of town without delivering the letter.

On his arrival at Lichfield, Peter Garrick asked him how he was received by his brother, and how he liked him? The man at first wished to parry the question, but at length owned that he never delivered the letter.

"Not deliver my letter!" says Peter; "how came that about?" – "Why, the fact is, my dear friend," said the other, "I saw enough of him on the stage to make that unnecessary. He may be rich, as I dare say any man who lives like him must be; but, by G-d" (and here, said the Doctor, the man vociferated an oath), "though he is your brother, Mr. Garrick, he is one of the shabbiest, meanest, most pitiful hounds I ever saw in the whole course of my life."

Thomas Davies

53 *In January 1763 a man named Fitzherbert and some of his friends led a revolt at Drury Lane against Garrick's abolition of the time-honoured concession of allowing entry at half-price at the end of the third act. They had rioted at the previous night's performance of* The Two Gentlemen of Verona *and were out to repeat their action the following night. Moody is the actor John Moody.*

The next night a new tragedy, called Elvira, written by Mr. Mallet, was acted at Drury Lane. The rioters, headed by their spokesman, enforced their former demand in the same violent and laconic manner. When Mr. Garrick appeared, they cried out with one voice, "Will you, or will you not, give admittance for half price, after the third act of a play, except during the first winter a pantomime is performed?" The manager, who had learnt the lesson of obedience by the losses which he had sustained the preceding evening, replied in the affirmative. But, however, peace was not to be restored till some of the players had made an *amende honorable*, for daring to espouse the cause of their master. Mr. Moody was called upon to apologize for the offence he had given, in stopping a madman's hand who was going to set fire to the playhouse. He, imagining that he should bring the audience into good humour by a laughable absurdity, in the tone and language of a low-bred Irishman, said, "He was very sorry that he had displeased them by saving their lives in putting out the fire." This speech was so ill taken, that it rather inflamed than cooled their rage; and they loudly and vehemently insisted that he should go down on his knees, and ask their pardon. Moody was so far from complying with this positive command, that he had the courage absolutely to refuse, saying, "I will not by G – ." When he came off the stage, Mr. Garrick was so pleased with his behaviour, that he received him with open arms, and assured him, that whilst he was master of a guinea, he should be paid his income; but that, if he had been so mean as to have submitted to the required abasement, he never would have forgiven him.

Thomas Davies

54 *Garrick played almost continually on the London stage, his only long rest being a trip to the Continent in 1763–5, when he fancied that his popularity was in danger of diminishing. His absence, however, seems to have made audiences' hearts grow fonder.*

Before his going abroad, Garrick's attraction had much decreased; Sir

William Weller Pepys said that the pit was often almost empty. But, on his return to England, people were mad about seeing him; and Sir George Beaumont and several others used frequently to get admission into the pit, before the doors were opened to the public, by means of bribing the attendants, who bade them "be sure, as soon as the crowd rushed in, to pretend to be in a great heat, and to wipe their faces, as if they had just been struggling for entrance."

Samuel Rogers

55 *In later life John Bannister became a famous comic actor. Here he receives some early-morning advice from Garrick.*

'I was a Student of Painting in the Royal Academy, when I was introduced to Mr. Garrick – under whose superior genius the British Stage then flourished beyond all former example.

One morning I was shewn into his dressing-room, when he was before the glass preparing to shave – a white night-cap covered his forehead – his chin and cheeks were enveloped in soap-suds – a razor-cloth was placed upon his left shoulder, and he turned and smoothed the shining blade with so much dexterity, that I longed for a beard, to imitate his incomparable method of handling the razor.

"Eh! well – what young man – so – eh! You are still for the stage? Well, now, what character do you, should you like to – eh?"

"I should like to attempt Hamlet, Sir."

"Eh! what Hamlet the Dane? Zounds! that's a bold – a – Have you studied the part?" "I have, Sir." "Well, don't mind my shaving. Speak your speech, the speech to the Ghost – I can hear you. Come, let's have a roll and a tumble." (A phrase of his often used to express a probationary specimen.)

After a few hums and haws, and a disposing of my hair, so that it might stand on end, "like quills upon the fretful porcupine," I supposed my father's ghost before me, "arm'd *cap à piè*," and off I started.

"Angels and ministers of grace defend us! (*He wiped the razor.*)
Be thou a spirit of health, or goblin damn'd! (*He strapped it.*)
Bring with thee airs from heav'n, or blasts from hell! (*He shaved on.*)
Thou com'st in such a questionable shape,
That I will speak to thee. I'll call thee Hamlet!
King, Father, Royal Dane! – O, answer me!
Let me not burst in ignorance." (*He lathered again.*)

I concluded with the usual

"Say, why is this? wherefore? what should we do?"

but still continued in my attitude, expecting the praise due to an exhibition, which I was booby enough to fancy was only to be equalled by himself. But, to my eternal mortification, he turned quick upon me, brandished the razor in his hand, and thrusting his half-shaved face close up to mine, he made such horrible mouths at me, that I thought he was seized with insanity, and I shewed more natural symptoms of being frightened at him than at my father's Ghost. "Angels and ministers! yaw! whaw! maw!" However, I soon perceived my vanity by his ridicule. He finished shaving, put on his wig, and, with a smile of good-nature, he took me by the hand. "Come," said he, "young gentleman, – eh, let us see now what we can do." He spoke the speech – *how* he spoke it, those who have heard him never can forget. "There," said he, "young gentleman; and when you try that speech again, give it more *passion*, and less *mouth*." '

James Boaden

56 *One of the innumerable letters and documents held by the Garrick Club in London is from Garrick to a lady who had tried to win his interest in the potentialities of a young man ambitious to go on the stage.*

To Her Grace the Duchess of Portland: 29th October, 1767

I shall always be happy to obey your Grace's commands, but our Company at present is so full and all the Parts dispos'd of, that I could not without great injustice to those Actors I have already engag'd, employ the person you recommend.

I have given Mr Collins the best advice in my Power, and appris'd him that I should be ready at the End of the season to examine his qualifications for the stage. If your Grace will permit me to speak my mind, I think he has the most unpromising Aspect for an Actor I ever saw. A small pair of unmeaning Eyes stuck on a round unthinking face are not the most desirable requisites for a Hero or a fine Gentleman. However I will give him a Tryal if he is unemployed at that time of the year so if he can be of the least service to me or himself I shall most certainly obey Your Grace's Commands.

SAMUEL FOOTE (1719–88)

57 *Samuel Foote was an actor who put his talent for caricature and mimicry to good use in the plays he wrote as well as in the performances he gave – off stage as well as on.*

They are remarkable in Dublin, when pleased, to continue applauding till the curtain falls, often not suffering the play to finish. This was a compliment frequently paid to Mr. Sheridan.*

Foote once said to that gentleman, very seriously, "My dear Sheridan, I wish you would relieve yourself of a great deal of labour and trouble!"

"In what manner!" says Sheridan, "do inform me, and I shall be obliged to you."

"Why," says Foote, "instead of Richard the Third, act King Henry in that tragedy."

"Good God, Mr. Foote! why should I relinquish Richard, where you are a witness I get such universal applause! – Give me your reason."

"O'!" says Foote, "the best reason in the world; for if you will perform Henry instead of Richard, the play will finish in the first act, and the players may all go home in good time to supper."

Tate Wilkinson

58 I made a visit with him [Garrick] by his own proposal to Foote at Parson's Green; I have heard it said he was reserved and uneasy in his company; I never saw him more at ease and in a happier flow of spirits than on that occasion.

Where a loud-tongued talker was in company, Edmund Burke declined all claims upon attention, and Samuel Johnson, whose ears were not quick, seldom lent them to his conversation, though he loved the man, and admired his talents: I have seen a dull damping matter-of-fact man quell the effervescence even of Foote's unrivalled humour.

But I remember full well, when Garrick and I made him the visit above-mentioned poor Foote had something worse than a dull man to struggle with, and matter of fact brought home to him in a way, that for a time entirely overthrew his spirits, and most completely frighted him from his propriety. We had taken him by surprise, and of course were with him some hours before dinner, to make sure of our own if we had missed of his. He seemed overjoyed to see us, engaged us to stay, walked with us in his garden, and read to us some scenes roughly sketched for his Maid of Bath. His dinner was quite good enough, and his wine superlative: Sir Robert Fletcher, who had served in the East Indies, dropt in before dinner and made the fourth of our party: When we had passed about two hours in perfect harmony and hilarity, Garrick called for his tea, and Sir Robert rose to depart: there was an unlucky screen in the room, that hid the door, and behind which Sir Robert hid himself for some purpose, whether natural or artificial I know not; but Foote, supposing him gone, instantly began to play off his ridicule at the expence of his departed guest. I must confess it was (in the cant phrase) *a way that*

---

*The Irish actor, father of Richard Brinsley Sheridan

he had, and just now a very unlucky way, for Sir Robert bolting from behind the screen, cried out – "I am not gone, Foote; spare me till I am out of hearing; and now with your leave I will stay till these gentlemen depart, and then you shall amuse me at their cost, as you have amused them at mine."

Richard Cumberland

JOHN MOODY (?1727–1813)

59 Among the traits of stupidity put to the account of actors, by which droll unrehearsed effects have been produced on the stage, there is none that is supposed to convey greater proof of stupidity than that which distinguished the actor who originally represented Lord Burghley in the "Critic."* The names of several players are mentioned, each as being the hero of this story; but the original Lord Burghley, or Burleigh was Irish Moody, far too acute an actor to be suspected for a fool. When Sheridan selected him for the part, the manager declared that Moody would be sure to commit some ridiculous error, and ruin the effect. The author protested that such a result was impossible; and according to the fashion of the times, a wager was laid, and Sheridan hurried to the performer of the part to give him such instructions as should render any mistake beyond possibility. Lord Burghley has nothing to say, merely to sit awhile; and then, as the stage directions informed him, and as Sheridan impressed it on his mind, "Lord Burghley comes forward, pauses near Dangle, shakes his head, and exit." The actor thoroughly understood the direction, he said, and could not err. At night he *came* forward, *did* pass near Dangle, shook his – Dangle's – head, and went solemnly off.

From Cornhill Magazine

HENRY MOSSOP (?1729–?74)

60 *An Irish actor who enjoyed initial success alongside Garrick at Drury Lane until jealousy of the latter proved his undoing. At the time of these anecdotes Mossop was in charge of the famous Smock Alley Theatre in Dublin.*

I was one night witness to an untoward circumstance at Smock-alley Theatre. Congreve's "Mourning Bride" was the tragedy; Mossop was Osmin, and a subordinate actor, Selim: Selim being stabbed by Osmin, should have remained dead on the stage, but seized with a fit of coughing, he unluckily put up his hand and loosened his stock, which set the audience in a burst of laughter. The scene over, the enraged manager and

---

*By Richard Brinsley Sheridan (1779).

actor railed at his underling for daring to appear alive when he was dead, who, in excuse, said he must have choked had he not done as he did: Mossop replied, "Sir, you should choke a thousand times, rather than spoil my scene."*

At a period when the payments were not very ready at the Smock-alley treasury, one night Mossop, in Lear, was supported in the arms of an actor who played Kent, and who whispered him, "If you don't give me your honour, Sir, that you'll pay me my arrears this night, before I go home, I'll let you drop about the boards." Mossop alarmed, said "Don't talk to me now." "I will," said Kent, "I will; I'll let you drop." Mossop was obliged to give the promise, and the actor thus got his money, though a few of the others went home without theirs.

John O'Keefe

OLIVER GOLDSMITH (1728–74)

61 *Both these anecdotes concern Goldsmith's most famous play,* She Stoops to Conquer.

It has been said that Goldsmith's comedy of *She Stoops to Conquer*, originated in the following adventure of the author. Some friend had given the young poet a guinea, when he left his mother's residence at Ballymahon, for a school in Edgworth's Town, where, it appears, he finished his education. He had diverted himself by viewing the gentlemen's seats on the road, until night-fall, when he found himself a mile or two out of the direct road, in the middle of the streets of Ardagh. Here he inquired for the best house in the place, meaning an inn; but a fencing-master, named Kelly, wilfully misunderstanding him, directed him to the large, old-fashioned residence of Sir Ralph Featherstone, as the landlord of the town. There he was shown into the parlour, and found the hospitable master of the house sitting by a good fire. His mistake was immediately perceived by Sir Ralph, who being a man of humour, and well acquainted with the poet's family, encouraged him in the deception. Goldsmith ordered a good supper, invited his host and the family to partake of it, treated them to a bottle or two of wine, and, on going to bed, ordered a hot cake for his breakfast; nor was it until his departure, when he called for his bill, that he discovered that, while he imagined he was at an inn, he had been hospitably entertained at a private family of the first respectability in the country.

J.H. Leigh Hunt

---

*Nearly 200 years later (see p. 229), Flora Robson had a not-dissimilar experience.

62 *Richard Cumberland recalls the first night of* She Stoops To Conquer *in 1773.*

We were not over-sanguine of success, but perfectly determined to struggle hard for our author: we accordingly assembled our strength at the Shakespeare Tavern in a considerable body for an early dinner, where Samuel Johnson took the chair at the head of a long table, and was the life and soul of the corps . . . Our illustrious president was in inimitable glee, and poor Goldsmith that day took all his raillery as patiently and complacently as my friend Boswell would have done any day, or every day of his life. In the mean time we did not forget our duty, and betook ourselves in good time to our separate and allotted posts, and waited the awful drawing up of the curtain. As our stations were pre-concerted, so were our signals for plaudits arranged and determined upon in a manner, that gave every one his cue where to look for them, and how to follow them up.

We had amongst us a very worthy and efficient member, long since lost to his friends and the world at large, Adam Drummond, of amiable memory, who was gifted by nature with the most sonorous, and at the same time the most contagious, laugh, that ever echoed from the human lungs. The neighing of the horse of the son of Hystaspes was a whisper to it; the whole thunder of the theatre could not drown it. This kind and ingenuous friend fairly fore-warned us that he knew no more when to give his fire than the cannon did, that was planted on a battery. He desired therefore to have a flapper at his elbow, and I had the honour to be deputed to that office. I planted him in an upper box, pretty nearly over the stage, in full view of the pit and galleries, and perfectly well situated to give the echo all its play through the hollows and recesses of the theatre. The success of our manoeuvres was complete. All eyes were upon Johnson, who sate in a front row of a side box, and when he laughed every body thought themselves warranted to roar. In the mean time my friend followed signals with a rattle so irresistibly comic, that, when he had repeated it several times, the attention of the spectators was so engrossed by his person and performances that the progress of the play seemed likely to become a secondary object, and I found it prudent to insinuate to him that he might halt his music without any prejudice to the author; but alas, it was now too late to rein him in; he had laughed upon my signal where he found no joke, and now unluckily he fancied that he found a joke in almost every thing that was said; so that nothing in nature could be more mal-a-propos than some of his bursts every now and then were. These were dangerous moments, for the pit began to take umbrage; but we carried our play through, and triumphed . . .

W.R. CHETWOOD (d.1776)

63 *Chetwood was the author of* A General History of the Stage *published in 1749.*

I remember, above twenty Years past, I was one of the Audience, at a new Play: Before me sat a Sea-Officer, with whom I had some Acquaintance; on each Hand of him a Couple of Sparks, both prepar'd with their offensive Instruments vulgarly term'd *Cat-calls,** which they were often tuning, before the Play began. The Officer did not take any Notice of them till the Curtain drew up; but when they continued their Sow-gelder's Music (as he unpolitely call'd it), he beg'd they would not prevent his hearing the Actors, tho' they might not care whether they heard, or no; but they took little Notice of his civil Request, which he repeated again and again, to no Purpose: But, at last, one of them condescended to tell him, *If he did not like it, he might let it alone. Why, really,* reply'd the Sailor, *I do not like it, and would have you let your Noise alone; I have paid my Money to see and hear the Play, and your ridiculous Noise not only hinders me, but a great many other People that are here, I believe, with the same Design: Now if you prevent us, you rob us of our Money, and our Time; therefore I intreat you, as you look like Gentlemen, to behave as such.* One of them seem'd mollified, and put his Whistle in his Pocket; but the other was incorrigible. The blunt Tar made him one Speech more. *Sir,* said he, *I advise you, once more, to follow the Example of this Gentleman, and put up your Pipe.* But the Piper sneer'd in his Face, and clap'd his troublesome Instrument to his Mouth, with Cheeks swell'd out like a Trumpeter, to give it a redoubled, and louder Noise; but, like the broken Crow of a Cock in a Fright, the Squeak was stopt in the Middle by a Blow from the Officer, which he gave him with so strong a Will, that his Child's Trumpet was struck thro' his Cheek, and his Companion led him out to a Surgeon; so that we had more Room, and less Noise; and not one that saw or heard the Affair, but what were well pleased with his Treatment; and, notwithstanding his great Blustering, he never thought it worth his while to call upon the Officer, tho' he knew where to find him.

GEORGE ANNE BELLAMY (1728–88)

64 *George Anne Bellamy (christened thus because of the clergyman's impaired hearing of the proposed name Georgiana) was more at home in society than on the stage. It should be remembered that, during this period, all plays were performed in contemporary dress.*

Early in the season, the tragedy of "All for Love, or the World well

---

*The 'cat-call', which today is a whistling noise, started life as the whistle itself.

Lost," was revived; in which Barry and Sheridan* stood unrivalled in the characters of Antony and Ventidius. The getting it up produced the following extraordinary incidents. The manager, in an excursion he had made during the summer to London, had purchased a superb suit of cloaths that had belonged to the Princess of Wales, and had been only worn by her on the birth-day. This was made into a dress for me to play the character of Cleopatra; and as the ground of it was silver tissue, my mother thought that by turning the body of it in, it would be a no unbecoming addition to my waist, which was remarkably small. My maid-servant was accordingly sent to the theatre to assist the dresser and mantua-maker in preparing it; and also in sewing on a number of diamonds; my Patroness [Mrs Butler] not only having furnished me with her own, but borrowed several others of her acquaintance for me. When the women had finished the work, they all went out of the room, and left the door of it indiscreetly open.

Mrs. Furnival, who owed me a grudge, on account of my eclipsing her, as the more favourable reception I met with from the public . . . accidentally passed by the door of my dressing-room in the way to her own, as it stood open. Seeing my rich dress thus lying exposed, and observing no person by to prevent her, she stepped in, and carried off the Queen of Egypt's paraphernalia, to adorn herself in the character of Octavia, the Roman matron, which she was to perform. By remarking from time to time my dress, which was very different from the generality of heroines, Mrs. Furnival had just acquired taste enough to despise the black velvet in which those ladies were usually habited. And without considering the impropriety of enrobing a Roman matron in the habiliments of the Egyptian queen; or perhaps not knowing that there was any impropriety in it, she determined, for once in her lifetime, to be as fine as myself, and that at my expence. She accordingly set to work to let out the cloaths, which, through my mother's economical advice, had been taken in.

When my servant returned to the room, and found the valuable dress, that had been committed to her charge, missing, her fright and agitation were beyond expression. She ran like a mad creature about the theatre, enquiring of every one whether they had seen any thing of it. At length she was informed that Mrs Furnival had got possession of it. When running to that lady's dressing-room, she was nearly petrified at beholding the work, which had cost her so much pains, undone. My damsel's veins, unfortunately for Mrs Furnival, were rich with the blood of the O'Bryens. And though she had not been blest with so polished an education as such a name was entitled to, she inherited at least the *Spirit*

*Spranger Barry, 1719–77, Irish actor, was thought by many to be the best romantic actor of the day. Sheridan is Thomas Sheridan. The play was taking place in Dublin.

of the Kings of Ulster. Thus qualified for carrying on an attack even of a more important nature, she at first demanded the dress with tolerable civility; but meeting with a peremptory refusal, the blood of her great fore-fathers boiled within her veins, and without any more ado, she fell tooth and nail upon poor Mrs. Furnival. So violent was the assault, that had not assistance arrived in time to rescue her from the fangs of the enraged Hibernian nymph, my theatrical rival would probably have never had an opportunity of appearing once in her life adorned with *real* jewels.

When I came to the theatre, I found my servant dissolved in tears at the sad disaster; for notwithstanding her heroic exertions, she had not been able to bring off the cause of the contest. But so far was I from partaking of her grief, that I could not help being highly diverted at the absurdity of the incident. Nothing concerning a theatre could at that time affect my temper. And I acknowledge I enjoyed a secret pleasure in the expectation of what the result would be. I sent indeed for the jewels; but the lady, rendered courageous by Nantz, and the presence of her paramour, Morgan, who was not yet dead, she condescended to send me word, that I should have them after the play.

In this situation I had no other resource than to reverse the dresses, and appear as plain in the character of the luxurious Queen of Egypt, as Antony's good wife, although the sister of Caesar, ought to have been. In the room of precious stones, with which my head should have been decorated, I substituted pearls; and of all my finery I retained only my diadem, that indispensible mark of royalty.

Every transaction that takes place in the theatre, and every circumstance relative to it, are as well known in Dublin as they would be in a country town. The report of the richness and elegance of my dress had been universally the subject of conversation, for some time before the night of performance; when, to the surprize of the audience, I appeared in white sattin. My kind patroness, who sat in the stage-box, seemed not to be able to account for such an unexpected circumstance. And not seeing me adorned with the jewels she had lent me, she naturally supposed I had reserved my regalia till the scene in which I was to meet my Antony.

When I had first entered the green-room, the manager, who expected to see me splendidly dressed, as it was natural to suppose the inchanting Cleopatra would have been upon such an occasion, expressed with some warmth his surprize at a disappointment, which he could only impute to caprice. Without being in the least discomposed by his warmth, I coolly told him, "that I had taken the advice Ventidius had sent me by Alexis, and had parted with both my cloaths and jewels to Antony's wife." Mr. Sheridan could not conceive my meaning; but as it was now too late to make any alteration, he said no more upon the subject. He was not however long at a loss for an explanation; for going to introduce

Octavia to the Emperor, he discovered the jay in all her borrowed plumes. An apparition could not have more astonished him. He was so confounded, that it was some time before he could go on with his part. At the same instant Mrs. Butler exclaimed aloud, "Good Heaven, the woman has got on my diamonds!" The gentlemen in the pit concluded that Mrs. Butler had been robbed of them by Mrs. Furnival; and the general consternation, occasioned by so extraordinary a scene, is not to be described. But the house observing Mr. Sheridan to smile, they supposed there was some mystery in the affair, which induced them to wait with patience till the conclusion of the act. As soon as it was finished, they bestowed their applause upon Antony and his faithful veteran; but as if they had all been animated by the same mind, they cried out, "No more Furnival! No more Furnival!" The fine dressed lady, disappointed of the acclamations she expected to receive on account of the grandeur of her habiliments, and thus hooted for the impropriety of her conduct, very prudently called fits to her aid, which incapacitated her from appearing again.

65 Mrs. Bellamy played Alicia in "Jane Shore"* in presence of the King of Denmark (who was then on a visit to George III), who, wearied with very fast living, was in a sound sleep during one of her finest scenes. The angry lady had to exclaim, "Oh, thou false lord!" and she drew near to the slumbering monarch, and shouted it close to his ears with such astounding effect that he started up, rubbed his eyes, became conscious of what was going on, and how it had come about, and remarked that he would not have such a woman for his wife though she had no end of kingdoms for a dowry. –

From *Cornhill Magazine*

CHARLES HOLLAND (1733–69)

66 The Stage was at 5s. – Pit and Boxes all joined together at 5s. There was only one entrance on each side the stage, which was always particularly crowded. First, they sported their own figures to gratify self consequence, and impede and interfere with the performers, who had to come on and go off the stage. Affronting the audience was another darling delight – particularly, offending the galleries, and thereby incurring the displeasure of the gods, who shewed their resentment by dispersing golden showers of oranges and half-eaten pippins, to the infinite terror of the ladies of fashion seated in the pit on such public nights, where they were so closely

*Tragedy by Nicholas Rowe (1674–1718).

wedged as to preclude all possibility of securing a retreat, or obtaining relief till the *finale*.

The stage spectators were not content with piling on raised seats, till their heads reached the theatrical cloudings; which seats were closed in with dirty worn out scenery, to inclose the painted round from the first wing, the main entrance being up steps from the middle of the back scene, but when that amphitheatre was filled, there would be a group of ill-dressed lads and persons sitting on the stage in front, three or four rows deep, otherwise those who sat behind could not have seen, and a riot would have ensued: So in fact a performer on a popular night could not step his foot with safety, less he either should thereby hurt or offend, or be thrown down amongst scores of idle tipsey apprentices.

The first time Holland acted Hamlet it was for his own benefit, when the stage was in the situation here described. On seeing the Ghost he was much frightened, and felt the sensation and terror usual on that thrilling occasion, and his hat flew *à-la-mode* off his head. An inoffensive woman in a red cloak, (a friend of Holland's) hearing Hamlet complain the air bit shrewdly, and was very cold, with infinite composure crossed the stage, took up the hat, and with the greatest care placed it fast on Hamlet's head, who on the occasion was as much alarmed in *reality* as he had just then been feigning. But the audience burst out into such incessant peals of laughter, that the Ghost moved off without any ceremony, and Hamlet, scorning to be outdone in courtesy, immediately followed with roars of applause. The poor woman stood astonished, which increased the roar, &c. It was some time before the laughter subsided; and they could not resist a repetition (that merry tragedy night) on the re-appearance of the Ghost and Hamlet.

Tate Wilkinson

JAMES WILLIAM DODD (1734–96)

67 *Dodd won wide acclaim for his portrayal of characters such as Sir Andrew Aguecheek in* Twelfth Night *and Sir Benjamin Backbite in* The School for Scandal

There was a gossiping anecdote told of Dodd, for the truth of which I will not be answerable. He sojourned in lodgings near the theatre with a *chère amie* belonging to the company. This perhaps he might have found to be a snug arrangement in the summer months, if the tranquillity of the *téte-à-téte* had not been daily disturbed by discussing frivolous points, upon which the fond pair very furiously differed; insomuch that the gentleman was wont to enforce his arguments more by missiles than by metaphors; in short, he threw chairs, tables, and chimney-piece crockery all about the room. In the heat of one of these domestic fracas, which happened at an early dinner upon a shoulder of mutton, while Dodd clattered, and the *chère amie* screamed, the landlord rushed upon the scene of action in hopes, if he could not prevent a further breach of the peace, to hinder their breaking more of his property. "How dare you, mister," ejaculated Dodd, who was brandishing the shoulder of mutton in his hand, "obtrude into our apartments while we are *rehearsing?*" – "Rehearsing!" cried the enraged landlord, while the broken bits of sham china were crunching under his feet, "I could have sworn you were fighting." – "No, sir," said Dodd; "we were rehearsing the supper scene in 'Catherine and Petruchio, or the *Taming of a Shrew.*' " – "Why, it does look," observed his landlord, giving a glance round the room, "as if you had been trying to tame a shrew, sure enough." "Don't you know, fellow," asked Dodd, sternly, "that we are advertised to act the parts this very night?" – "Not I, truly," returned the host – "Then go downstairs, sir," cried the comedian, "and read the bill of the play; and read it every morning, sir, to prevent your repeating this impertinence." History records not whether the landlord read the playhouse bill; but it sets forth that he did not forget *his own.* –

From *Representative Actors*

THOMAS WESTON (1737–76)

68 *Comedy rather than tragedy was Weston's forte: his performance as Abel Drugger was as good as his Richard III was bad.*

You should have seen Weston. It was impossible, from looking at him, for any one to say that he was acting. You would suppose they had gone out and found the actual character they wanted, and brought him upon the stage without his knowing it. Even when they interrupted him with peals of laughter and applause, he looked about him as if he was not at all conscious of having anything to do with it, and then went on as before. In Scrub, Dr. Last, and other parts of that kind, he was perfection itself. Garrick would never attempt Abel Drugger after him. There was something peculiar in his face; for I knew an old schoolfellow of his who told me he used to produce the same effect when a boy, and when the master asked what was the matter, his companion would make answer, 'Weston looked at me, sir!'

James Northcote

69 In *The Rival Candidates,** * this year he spoke the epilogue in the company of a big dog, nearly as high as his waist, which he led by the ring in its collar. It is a most engaging beast and stares up into its droll companion's

*By Sir Henry Bate Dudley, 1775.

face, while he is speaking, with an almost human expression; the latter strokes him with so much condescension that it is obvious to all that they are kindred spirits. On the second occasion on which I saw the play Weston, for the first time, wearied of speaking this epilogue and refused to appear; the audience took this in very bad part, and 'Epilogue! Epilogue!' resounded from all the throats which had done their best to wake Richard the Third from the dead; but still Weston did not appear. Several persons left the boxes, but I had made up my mind to await the outcome of the matter. Suddenly there came a shower, first of pears, then oranges, and next quart bottles, on to the stage, one of them, containing, I should think, three quarts, striking one of the glass chandeliers; and it looked like turning into a riot, when Weston came on the stage with Dragon (that is the dog's name) as calmly as though he were always called for like this. There was a little hissing here and there, but this soon died down. Now there is a passage in the epilogue, in which, I believe, he is speaking of the critics, where he addresses the dog thus: 'But why do you put your tail between your legs, Dragon, they will not hurt you?' On the spur of the moment, without detriment either to rhyme or couplet, Weston altered the passage into: 'And why do you put your tail between your legs, you tom-fool? They won't throw any bottles at your head.' The situation was saved at a very critical juncture by this excessively witty alteration, so aptly expressed in rhyme. There was no end to the clapping and shouting. But Weston did not move a muscle, his face being as expressionless as a brick, not the least trace of pleasure or complacency, no more than on the face of his four-footed friend.

Georg Christoph Lichtenberg

WILLIAM BENSLEY (1738–1817)

70 *'He had the fine poetical enthusiasm', declared Charles Lamb, 'the rarest faculty among players.' It was put to the test in the following incident.*

He had to play Henry VI in "Richard the Third." After the monarch's death in the early part of the play, he had to appear for a moment or two as his own ghost, in the fifth act. The spirits were at that time exhibited *en buste* by a trap. Now our Henry was invited out to supper, and being anxious to get there early, and knowing that little more than his shoulders would be seen by the public, he retained his black velvet vest and bugles, but discarding the lower part of his stage costume, he drew on a jaunty pair of new, tight, nankeen pantaloons, to be as far dressed for his supper company as he could. When he stood on the trap, he cautioned the men who turned the crank not to raise him as high as usual, and of course they promised to obey. But a wicked low comedian was at hand, whose love of mischief prevailed over his judgment, and he suddenly applied himself with such goodwill to the winch, that he ran King Henry up right to a level with the stage; and moreover, gave his majesty such a jerk that he was forced to step from the trap on to the boards to save himself from falling. The sight of the old Lancastrian monarch in a costume of two such different periods – mediæval above, all nankeen and novelty below – was destructive of all decorum both before the stage and upon it. The audience emphatically "split their sides," and as for the tyrant in the tent, he sat bolt upright, and burst into such an insane roar that the real Richard could not have looked more frantically hysterical had the deceased Henry actually so visited him in the spirit.

John Doran

TATE WILKINSON (1739–1803)

71 *Wilkinson was a celebrated actor and theatre manager, who has left us his high-spirited Memoirs of theatre life in the late eighteenth century.*

One morning a letter was brought in at Southampton Street, introducing a young man who wished to go on the stage. Garrick received him kindly, listened to his declamation, which was poor enough, and comforted the aspirant by telling him that his shyness was a very good sign of success. This young fellow had hung about the green-room in Covent Garden, and for all this shyness was a pert, forward, impudent *gamin*, whose precocious talents of mimicry had been overpraised by friends. He offered to "take off" some of the well-known actors, to show the manager his gifts. "Nay, now," said Garrick, in his peculiar mixture of hesitation and repetition, which made his "talk" a favourite subject of imitation. "Nay, now, sir, you must take care of this; for I used to call myself the first at this business." But the young fellow knew the manager's weak place. He began, leading off with Foote. The likeness amused the manager immensely, and the performance was repeated. "Hey, now! now – what – all," went on Mr. Garrick. "How – really this – this – is – why, well, well, well, do call on me on Monday, and you may depend on my doing all I can for you." This broken style of speech was Mr. Garrick's characteristic when addressing his inferiors, and was, in fact, his *managerial* manner, and may have been found very useful in helping him to any positive declaration. It was not a bad auxilliary for one who was asked for so much, and had to refuse so much.

On the Monday the youth came again, and was welcomed warmly. He was told that inquiries had been made about his widowed mother, and that he was to be put on the books at thirty shillings a week – a fortune indeed. The youth's name was Tate Wilkinson, who has left behind a very curious history of himself and other players, which is a mass of truth, blunders, and falsehoods – a mass, too, of meanness, vanity, and egotism.

Percy Fitzgerald

72 *Wilkinson himself relates the next two anecdotes.*

. . . Alexander the Great was the play, got up with great attention: I was the Alexander . . . All went off with great eclat till the latter part of the fourth act, soon after the death of Clytus. – Some olive leaves, &c. intended for decorations, being twisted and interwoven with little bits of wax, caught fire from the lights, and the flame continuing to blaze, the burnt particles occasioned a strong stench – an universal cry of "Fire! fire!" prevailed, on which every person was alarmed, but not one so horridly aghast as the dead Clytus, who had expired by the rage of Alexander: he rose with the agility of a tumbler that would not have disgraced the Royal Circus; his uprise and exit were so quick that he threw the immortal Alexander on his back. The late noble Earl of Effingham, who was remarkably corpulent, evinced equal alacrity with dead nimble-footed Clytus, and gave evident proofs of superior agility; for instead of making his way to the box-door, he with one spring of the utmost ease, swiftness, and dexterity, vaulted over the side-box, and lighted on his feet on a row in the middle of the pit, standing erect; the seat gave proof to the credit of the carpenter; for it did not yield, but firmly supported its ponderous and noble weight.

In a few minutes the trifling cause that occasioned this universal panic subsided, and was soon extinguished; the audience called to order, the ladies instead of fainting, being surrounded by martial heroes, smiled; Lord Effingham returned to his box, but not by the way he went into the pit: No sooner was his Lordship settled in *statu quo* than all the gentlemen of the army (for he was universally beloved) gave a general salutation, which his Lordship returned, and after a hearty laugh on all sides the play was ordered to go on, and old grey-headed Clytus made his second appearance after death, and prostrated himself once more a victim at the feet of Alexander. It appeared so truly ridiculous, that the convulsive fits of laughter which involuntarily ensued, may easier be conceived than described; it was truly whimsical, and mutually entertaining.

73 The next day I accidentally stepped into a milliner's shop, where a little elderly lady sat knitting in the corner, and without once looking at me on my entrance (or if she had she would *not* have known me) said, "Well, I am sure, Nanny, you never shall persuade me to go to the play again to see that hunch-backed Barber: Give me the Mourning Bride, and Mr. Frodsham, and then there is some sense in it: But for that man, that Wilkinson, as you call him, from London, pray let him go back and stay there, for he is the ugliest man I ever saw in my life; and so thought Jenny. I am sure if he was worth his weight in gold he should never marry a daughter of mine." – Miss Priestley who knew me, looked confounded, and said, "My dear aunt, you would alter the severe opinion you are delivering to Nanny if you were to see Mr. Wilkinson in some of his principal characters; therefore, dear aunt Doughty, go some other night, and that gentleman will make a convert of you." – "No, that he never will," replied the old lady hastily, "for I shall never bear the sight of him again." I turned round to her, and said, "Dear madam, do not be so very hard hearted – try the theatre once more when *I play*, and I will exert my best abilities to make you amends and deserve your better sentiments." – The old lady stared, down dropped the spectacles, the knitted garters followed, (which had busily employed her attention while speaking) and without a single word she took to her heels (which were nimble) and ran away out of the back door into New Street: I laughed immoderately: but with Miss Priestley the odd circumstance had not such a whimsical effect: She appeared much hurt, and genteelly apologized for Mrs. Doughty as not being a competent judge of plays, though a worthy woman, which indeed was her true character.

JOHN PALMER (?1742–98)

74 Upon the subject of this representation of Lord Russell,* Palmer's brother once told me a ludicrous anecdote, to which I incline to give some credit. It seemed that Palmer had done with Lord Russell, as he did with many other characters, that is, totally neglected to study the words of the part; and in this dilemma he bethought himself of an expedient, which answered astonishingly, and, indeed, by the audience was never suspected. As much of Lord Russell was unlearned on the night of its performance, he thought it was better to speak from some character that he did know, than one that he did not; whenever, therefore, he felt himself at a loss, he dexterously introduced some passages from the Earl of Essex, which he contrived to fit into the cues received by Lord Russel; and thus, really giving some parts, and masking others, he gained another day to perfect himself in the character. It will be remembered that to his audience this play was completely new; while the dialogue was in progress, and not seemingly irrelevant, there were no means of detection.

James Boaden

*The title role in a play by the poet and biographer William Hayley (see also p. 73).

JOHN O'KEEFE (1747–1833)

75 *Although this passage refers to an 'opera', The Young Quaker, O'Keefe's operas (of which he wrote more than 20) were really plays with breaks for songs. George Colman (the Elder) was a theatrical manager; John Edwin (the Elder) played the part of Clod.*

On showing it to Mr. Colman and mentioning my musical purpose, "Opera," he said, "it is a good five-act comedy; if you will let me have it, I will bring it out this summer." I gave it to him. This was "The Young Quaker." It was acted, July, 1783. I did not go to see it the first night, but sent my servant to bring me back the result. I stayed at home, passing the time anxiously enough. As soon as the curtain dropped, Mr. Colman packed off John to me at Acton with the joyful news of its complete success. I ventured to town a few nights after to please myself, as I thought I had some right to share in the amusement I had given to the public, and was indeed gratified by Edwin's Clod, John Palmer's Reuben Sadboy, Parsons's Chronicle, Wewitzer's Shadrach Boaz, and Miss Frodsham's Dinah Primrose. This was her first appearance in London, and most graceful, modest, and interesting she was in my beautiful Quakeress.

The first night there was throughout the play only a single hiss, and that only from one person: this was at Edwin in Clod, stopping at a table to drink a glass of wine. Edwin said to me the next day, "Never introduce drinking into a piece that comes out in the summer theatre; for in the gallery they are so confoundedly squeezed, and hot, and parched, that last night a great thirsty fellow envied seeing me alone in a large room with a bumper of cooling wine at my grasp."

MR AND MRS MATTOCKS (d.1804 and 1746–1826 respectively)

76 *He was a theatrical manager; she was more famous as an actress, formerly Isabella Hallam.*

Mattocks was manager of the Portsmouth Theatre at this time – his company consisted of Mrs. Mattocks, Mrs. Kennedy, Whitfield, Booth, Wheeler, Perry, Dutton, Townshend, &c., the latter I remember a student at Dublin College. Mrs. Mattocks, agreeable to what was due to her professonal talents (which were of the first order), imagined that her name being up, must fill the house each time she played. – One night, on which the opera of the "Maid of the Mill" was to be acted, she walked from her dressing-room and looked through the curtain, and on seeing a half-empty house, returned, sat down, and sent for Mattocks; – he came, she told him to dismiss the house for that she certainly would not play: – he, with his usual politeness, and calm good-humour, seemed to acquiesce, and to approve of her spirited determination, at the same time expressing himself rather angry at the want of taste in the public, thus exceeding her in his remarks upon such neglect.

This matrimonial colloquy took up about twenty minutes. – "Make yourself easy, my dear," he said, "for I'll go this instant, and dismiss the house." – He left her, and walking leisurely towards the front of the stage, gave the Prompter the private order to ring the band into the orchestra, and begin the Overture. He was obeyed; he then ordered the curtain to ring up, – and up it went. Mrs. Mattocks, by this time, having heard musicals which she did not expect, ventured to quit her dressing-room, and go towards the stage, where, to her astonishment and vexation, she heard the full chorus of,

> "Free from sorrow, free from strife,
> Oh! how blest the miller's life!" – &c.

Angry with Mattocks, she reproached him for the deception he had put upon her, when he with mildness said, "Come with me down to the wing, and throw your eye round the house, then try what you can say on this occasion." – She complied, looked out, and saw the theatre, boxes, pit, and gallery, all full; – before the conclusion of the first scene, it was an overflow. The fact was, it happened to be a very fine evening – the King had been on the water, and on the ramparts, and all the people out on their walks and rambles, boating and sailing, every one eager to have even a distant sight of his Majesty. – Mrs. Mattocks was, perhaps, right, but the manager, who well knew the danger of what is called "dismissing a house," was aware of this; and, in reality, it is wiser for actors, if there is only as much in the theatre as will pay for the lights, never to dismiss an audience; it throws a damp upon the public spirit and feelings, and many persons, after such a circumstance, will keep from a theatre, always doubting whether the night they fix on to go to the play, there will be any play at all.

Mrs. Mattocks recovered her good-humour, and performed the charming Patty with all her usual delightful and delighting powers.

John O'Keefe

JOHN HENDERSON (1747–85)

77 *Henderson – the 'Bath Roscius' (see p. 31) – enjoyed brief but widely acclaimed success in major dramatic roles during his short life. Professor Dugald Stewart, who recounts Henderson's feat, was an eminent Scottish philosopher.*

Professor Dugald Stewart, who knew Henderson, told me that his power of memory was the most astonishing he had ever met with. In the philosopher's presence he took up a newspaper, and, after reading it once, repeated such a portion of it as to Mr. Stewart seemed utterly marvellous. When he expressed his surprise, Henderson modestly replied, "If you had been obliged, like me, to depend, during many years, for your daily bread, on getting words by heart, you would not be so much astonished at habit having produced this facility."

Thomas Campbell

RICHARD BRINSLEY SHERIDAN (1751–1816)

78 The Rivals, The School for Scandal *and* The Critic *are the three plays for which Sheridan is most highly regarded. He was also owner of Drury Lane Theatre, in succession to Garrick, besides being in the House of Commons from 1780 to 1812. This famous anecdote has been recounted ever since the fire of 1809 destroyed Drury Lane and bankrupted Sheridan.*

Such was the state of this luckless property, – and it would have been difficult to imagine any change for the worse that could befall it – when, early in the present year, an event occurred, that seemed to fill up at once the measure of its ruin. On the night of the 24th of February, while the House of Commons was occupied with Mr. Ponsonby's motion on the Conduct of the War in Spain, and Mr. Sheridan was in attendance, with the intention, no doubt, of speaking, the House was suddenly illuminated by a blaze of light; and, the Debate being interrupted, it was ascertained that the Theatre of Drury Lane was on fire. A motion was made to adjourn; but Mr. Sheridan said, with much calmness, that, "whatever might be the extent of the private calamity, he hoped it would not interfere with the public business of the country." He then left the House; and, proceeding to Drury Lane, witnessed, with a fortitude which strongly interested all who observed him, the entire destruction of his property.

(It is said that, as he sat at the Piazza Coffee-house, during the fire, taking some refreshment, a friend of his having remarked on the philosophic calmness with which he bore his misfortune, Sheridan answered, "A man may surely be allowed to take a glass of wine *by his own fire-side*.")

Thomas Moore

FANNY BURNEY (1752–1840)

79 *Fanny Burney was successful as a novelist but quite the opposite as a dramatist. Her play* Edwyn and Elgiva – *in spite of John Philip Kemble and Mrs Siddons being in the cast – lasted just one night.*

On the 21st of March, 1795, a tragedy, called "Edwyn and Elgiva," written by Miss Burney, afterwards Madam D'Arblay, was produced at Drury Lane. "We are sorry," says the *London Chronicle*, the following day, "that we cannot congratulate the fair authoress on the success of her first dramatic essay: for even the benedictions of the three bishops, whom she chose for her heroes, were not able to procure the salvation of it; – a circumstance which will probably induce her hereafter to employ something more than spiritual aid in support of a temporal cause."

Miss Burney was peculiarly unfortunate in bringing bishops into her tragedy. At that time there was a liquor much in popular use, called Bishop: it was a sort of negus or punch, I believe, though the origin of its name I must leave more learned antiquaries to determine. But, be that as it may, when jolly fellows met at a tavern, the first order to the waiter was, *to bring in the Bishop*. Unacquainted with the language of taverns, Miss Burney made her King exclaim, in an early scene, *"Bring in the Bishop!"* and the summons filled the audience with as much hilarity as if they had drank of the exhilirating liquor. They continued in the best possible humour throughout the piece.

Thomas Campbell

SARAH SIDDONS (1755–1831)

80 *The leading tragedienne of the late eighteenth century, and sister of John, Charles and Stephen Kemble, Sarah Siddons was an actress of considerable force and expressiveness. All these anecdotes, except the last, come from Thomas Campbell's biography.*

"My door was soon beset by various persons quite unknown to me, whose curiosity was on the alert to see the new actress, some of whom actually forced their way into my drawing-room, in spite of remonstrance or opposition. This was as inconvenient as it was offensive; for, as I usually acted three times a week, and had, besides, to attend the rehersals, I had but little time to spend unnecessarily. One morning, though I had previously given orders not to be interrupted, my servant entered the room in a great hurry, saying, 'Ma'am, I am very sorry to tell you there are some ladies below, who say they must see you, and it is impossible for me to prevent it. I have told them over and over again that you are particularly engaged, but all in vain; and now, ma'am, you may actually hear them on the stairs.' I felt extremely indignant at such unparalleled impertinence; and, before the servant had done speaking to me, a tall, elegant, invalid-looking person presented herself, (whom, I am afraid, I did not receive very graciously;) and, after her, four more, in slow succession. A very awkward silence took place; when presently the first lady began to accost me, with a most inveterate Scotch twang, and in a dialect which was scarcely intelligible to me in those days. She was a person of very high rank: her curiosity, however, had been too powerful for her good breeding. 'You must think it strange,' said she, 'to see a person entirely unknown to you intrude in this manner upon your

privacy; but, you must know, I am in a very delicate state of health, and
my physician won't let me go to the theatre to see you, so I am to look
at you here.' She accordingly sat down to look, and I to be looked at,
for a few painful moments, when she arose and apologised; but I was in
no humour to overlook such insolence, and so let her depart in silence."

81 How much more pleasantly people tell their history in social converse
than in formal writing. I remember Mrs. Siddons describing to me the
same scene of her probation on the Edinburgh boards with no small
humour. The grave attention of my Scottish countrymen, and their
canny reservation of praise till they were sure she deserved it, she said,
had well-nigh worn out her patience. She had been used to speak to
animated clay; but she now felt as if she had been speaking to stones.
Successive flashes of her elocution, that had always been sure to electrify
the South, fell in vain on those Northern flints. At last, as I well
remember, she told me she coiled up her powers to the most emphatic
possible utterance of one passage, having previously vowed in her heart,
that if this could not touch the Scotch, she would never again cross the
Tweed. When it was finished, she paused, and looked to the audience.
The deep silence was broken only by a single voice exclaiming, "*That's
no bad!*" This ludicrous parsimony of praise convulsed the Edinburgh
audience with laughter. But the laugh was followed by such thunders of
applause, that, amidst her stunned and nervous agitation, she was not
without fears of the galleries coming down.

82 I was at Edinburgh one year when she was electrifying the Northern
metropolis with many characters, and with none more than this. One of
her fellow-performers, Mr. Russell, told me an instance of her power in
the part. A poor fellow who played the Surveyor, in "Henry VIII," was
met by Mr. Russell coming off the stage, having just received the Queen
Katherine's (Siddons's) rebuke, "*You were the Duke's surveyor, and lost
your office on the complaint o' the tenants.*" The mimetic unjust steward was
perspiring with agitation. "What is the matter with you?" said Mr.
Russell. "The matter!" quoth the other, "that woman plays as if the
thing were in earnest. She looked on me so through and through with
her black eyes, that I would not for the world meet her on the stage
again."

83 Mrs. Siddons and her friend proceeded to Ireland by the way of Holyhead.
At first her spirits were extremely depressed, but they recovered, at last,
by the change of air and scenery. She, very naturally, stopped at Stratford,

to visit the house of Shakespeare. Here, in spite of her melancholy, she was forced to smile at the cool impudence of a woman who shewed them the mansion of the mighty poet, and endeavoured to palm upon their credulity a little monster of a boy, with a double tongue, by the name of William Shakespeare, as a great grandson's grandson of his immortal namesake. The shew-woman was marvellously loquacious, and Mrs. Siddons remarked that nature had endowed *her* also with a double allowance of tongue.

84 She took her professional farewell of the stage on the 29th of June, 1812. The play was "Macbeth." At an early hour a vast crowd assembled around the theatre of Covent Garden, and, when the doors were opened, the struggle for places became a service of danger. After the sleep-walking scene, in the tragedy, the applause of the spectators became ungovernable: they stood on the benches, and demanded that the performance of the piece should not go further than the last scene in which she appeared. As this wish seemed to be felt by the great majority, the actor Chapman came forward, and signified that it should be complied with.

85 From intense devotion to her profession she derived a peculiarity of manner, of which I have the fullest belief she was not in the least conscious, unless reminded of it; – I mean the habit of attaching dramatic tones and emphasis to common-place colloquial subjects. She went, for instance, one day, into a shop at Bath, and, after bargaining for some calico, and hearing the mercer pour forth an hundred commendations of the cloth, she put the question to him, *"But will it wash?"* in a manner so electrifying as to make the poor shopman start back from his counter. I once told her this anecdote about herself, and she laughed at it heartily, saying, "Witness truth, I never meant to be tragical."

86 One night, when Mrs. Siddons had occasion to drain "the poisoned cup," a ruffian bawled out, to the overthrow of all order in the rest of the house, "That's right, Molly; soop it up, ma lass." Once during her engagement, the evening being hot, Mrs. Siddons was tempted by a torturing thirst to avail herself of the only relief to be obtained at the moment. Her dresser, therefore, despatched a boy in great haste to "fetch a pint of beer for Mrs. Siddons." Meanwhile the play proceeded, and on the boy's return with the frothed pitcher, he looked about for the person who had sent him on his errand, and not seeing her, inquired, "Where is Mrs. Siddons?" The scene-shifter whom he questioned, pointing his finger to the stage, where she was performing the sleeping-scene of *Lady Macbeth*, replied, "There she is." To the horror of the performers, the boy promptly walked on to the stage close up to Mrs. Siddons, and with a total unconsciousness of any impropriety, presented the porter! Her distress may be imagined; she waved the boy away in her grand manner several times without effect. At last the people behind the scenes, by dint of beckoning, stamping, &c., succeeded in getting him off with the beer, while the audience were in an uproar of laughter, which the dignity of the actress was unable to quell for several minutes.

From *Representative Actors*

GEORGE FREDERICK COOKE (c. 1756–1812)

87 *One of Covent Garden's leading actors, Cooke was persuaded to become one of the first English actors to tour America, where his early performances won him widespread acclaim. Soon, however, his 'old complaint' began to get the upper hand and the bottle, which had dogged much of his career in England, speeded his end.*

He rambled about the suburbs of the city in his solitary manner, for some hours, and then directed his steps to the Tontine Coffee-house, the place at which he lodged upon his landing. Here he dined, and repeated his maddening draughts, till late at night, or in the morning, he again sunk to rest; if sinking to partial oblivion, overwhelmed by intemperance, deserves that quiet appellation.

On the next day Cooke, still under the influence of his long continued intemperance, left the Tontine Coffee-house, with the avowed purpose of removing his baggage from the hospitable asylum he had enjoyed at the house of the Manager.

This day, the 19th Dec., had been appointed for his benefit. "Cato" was the play. The bills announced the last night of Mr. Cooke's engagement previous to his proceeding to Boston; the tragedy of "Cato" and the farce of "Love-à-la-Mode," for Mr. Cooke's benefit. The rehearsals of "Cato" had been called, but the tragedy of "Cato" was rehearsed without the presence of the hero. Cooke looked into the theatre on his way from the Coffee-house to the Manager's, and asked the prompter if "all was well." His appearance indicated too strongly that all was not well with him. He came into the green-room, and hearing the call-boy call, as usual, the performers to come to the stage, by the names of the characters they were to represent – Juba – Syphax – Cato – he beckoned the boy to him.

"My good lad, don't you know it's a benefit – we'll rehearse the play to-night."

He then proceeded with the intent of removing his trunks to the Coffee-house. Fortunately for him, a friend prevented him from carrying this design into execution, and upon being assured that no notice would be taken of his conduct, he gladly relinquished his plan, and dismissed the images of resentful enmity which he had conjured up to stimulate him to the act.

In the mean time he had never read a line of Cato, and he was now incapable of reading to any purpose. The house filled. An audience so numerous, or more genteel, had never graced the walls of the New-York theatre. The money received was eighteen hundred and seventy-eight dollars.

Soon, very soon, it was perceived that the Roman patriot, the godlike Cato – was not to be seen in Mr. Cooke. The mind of the actor was utterly bewildered; he hesitated, repeated speeches from other plays, or endeavoured to substitute incoherencies of his own – but the audience which had assembled to admire, turned away with disgust.

After the play, I walked into the Green-room. He was dressed for Sir Archy M'Sarcasm [one of his greatest roles]. As soon as he saw me, he came up to meet me, and exclaimed, "Ah, its all over now, we are reconciled – but I was very wild in the play – quite bewildered – do you know that I could not remember one line, after having recited the other – I caught myself once or twice giving Shakspeare for Addison;" and then with his chuckle and his eyes turned away, "Heaven forgive me! – If you have ever heard any thing of *me* you must have heard that I always have a frolic on my benefit day – If a man cannot take a liberty with his *friends*, who the devil can he take a liberty with?"

By the time the curtain drew up for the farce, he was so far recovered, that the words, being perfectly familiar, came trippingly from the tongue, and he being encouraged by finding himself in possession of his powers again, exerted them to the utmost, and played Sir Archy as well as ever he had done, and I need not say that *that* was as well as 'tis possible to conceive.

William Dunlap

88 *Later in Cooke's American tour William Dunlap (his biographer) recounts his attendance at a dinner party where he was 'full of wine, life and whim, the very spirit of the party surrounding him'.*

Among the guests was a young and distinguished actor, who, enlivened by surrounding circumstances, descanted rather fully upon his own talents. Cooke led him on, praised him, made him praise himself, until having worked him up to the point he wished, he asked him who had been his model?

"Mr. — , Sir; I have studied him in Hamlet, Sir, and in Benedict – but his Romeo – did you see my Romeo – there was – himself: when he says, turning to Juliet, which brings his back to the audience,

"There is more peril in thine eye – "

then whirling round and making a lunge at the audience,

" – than twenty
"Of *their* swords – ."

– there, Sir, is a fine instance of suiting the action – ha, Sir?"

"I see you have studied your profession attentively, and taken lessons from great actors; you have every thing from nature that can be wished; you have person, manner, voice – every requisite to make a great actor; and you have acquired great knowledge of the profession, very great indeed, Sir, and now I would advise one thing."

"What is that, Sir."

"Forget all you have learned as quick as possible."

JOHN PHILIP KEMBLE (1757–1823)

89 *Besides being an actor of distinction, John Philip Kemble was also known for his efforts, as manager, to defend the increased price of admission to Covent Garden Theatre after it had burned down in 1808. Rebuilt almost instantly, it re-opened in September 1809, provoking the Old Price Riots, an extraordinary battle of wits between the audience and the manager, which Kemble, in the end, lost gracefully.*

On the 13th of April 1779, Murphy's tragedy of *Zenobia* was performed,* and a Mrs. Mason was the heroine of the evening. The stage-box was unfortunately occupied by a lady of some distinction, whose ill-nature vented itself in the form of criticism; and Mrs. Mason became the object of her derision, which she expressed by loud and ill-bred laughter, to the annoyance of the poor victim, and of every body but the persons in her immediate suite.

Mr. Kemble too, because he perhaps could not shout like Cummins, or because he had a dark complexion; because he had the reputation of learning or because the lady cared not about a reason when she wanted to amuse herself, he also became a mark for this silly woman's annoyance.

I do not suppose that she was aware of Dr. Johnson's opinion of *Zenobia*, that it had too much Tig. and Teri. in it (the names of two of the characters being Tigranes and Teribazus); but Mr. Kemble performed the part of the latter, who is the lover of the piece, and shared with Mrs. Mason the contempt and derision of Miss S. and her party. In the interesting scenes of the last act, she found full gratification for her spleen, as both her objects were together upon the stage, and she redoubled her

---

*Arthur Murphy's tragedies, farces and comedies are hardly ever seen today.

efforts to cover them with disgrace. The actress had made little impression on any body, but Kemble was shocked at the brutal treatment she received. As to the insults designed for himself during the evening, he had retorted them by looks of infinite disdain. His sensibility was noticed in the box by loud and repeated peals of laughter from the lady and her echoes. At this, Kemble suddenly stopped, and being called upon by the audience to proceed, with great gravity and a pointed bow to the stage-box, he said "he was ready to proceed with the play as soon as THAT lady had finished her conversation, which he perceived the going on with the tragedy only interrupted."

The audience received this rudeness of the stage-box as an insolent attempt to control their amusements, and with shouts, which could not be laughed down, ordered the lady and her party out of the theatre.**

James Boaden

90 A translation of the popular French piece, 'Richard Coeur de Lion', was produced at Drury Lane Theatre on the twentieth of October [1786], with the original music by Grétry. Miss Romanzini (afterwards Mrs. Bland) sang the pretty chanson, 'The Merry Dance', with great naiveté and effect. The character of Richard was acted by Mr. John Kemble, who, though he had not a singing voice, got through the two-part song, on which the plot hinges, better than expected. At one of the rehearsals of the piece Kemble, who had got the tune of it tolerably well, being very deficient in keeping the time, Mr. Shaw, the leader of the band, impatiently exclaimed, "Mr. Kemble, that won't do at all! – you *murder* time abominably!" – "Well, Mr. Shaw," replied Kemble, "it is better to *murder* it, than to be continually *beating* it as you are."

W. T. Parke

91 Covent Garden Theatre was burned on September 19th, 1808, and was now in rapid progress of rebuilding. Its re-opening led to the most extraordinary theatrical riots that this country ever witnessed. Immediately after the destruction of the theatre Kemble solicited a subscription to rebuild it, which was speedily filled up, and the Duke of Northumberland contributing ten thousand pounds. The first stone of the new building was laid by the Prince of Wales on the last day of the year 1808, and it was completed with such rapidity that on the 18th of September 1809, it was opened with *Macbeth*, Kemble himself appearing in the character

---

*This reminds me of a similar story in which a child was screaming in the gallery with such gusto that Kemble was finally forced to tell the audience, 'If the play be not stopped the child cannot possibly continue.'

of Macbeth. In the new arrangement a row of private boxes formed the third tier under the gallery. The furniture of each box and of the adjoining room was to be according to the taste of the several occupants. To make these extraordinary accommodations for the great the comforts of the rest of the audience were considerably diminished. To crown all, the theatre opened with an increase of the prices, the pit being raised from 3s. 6d. to 4s., and the boxes from 6s. to 7s. The manager said that this was necessary to cover the great expense of rebuilding the theatre; but the public declared that the old prices were sufficient, and that the new ones were a mere exaction to enable Kemble to pay enormous salaries to foreigners like Madame Catalani (who had been engaged at 150*l.* a week to perform two nights only). On the first night of representation, which was Monday, the curtain drew up to a crowded theatre, and the audience seemed to be lost in admiration at the beauty of the decorations until Kemble made his appearance on the stage. A faint attempt at applause got up by his own friends was in an instant drowned by an overpowering noise of groans, hisses, yells, which drove him from the stage. Mrs. Siddons then came forward, but met with no better reception. Kemble had declared he would not give in to the popular clamour, but the next night and the nights following it was continued with greater fury. On Wednesday night the manager came forward to address the audience, and attempted to make a justification of his conduct, which was not accepted. On Friday he presented himself again, and proposed that the decision of the dispute should be put to a committee composed of the Governor of the Bank of England, the Attorney-General, and others. On Saturday night this was agreed to, and the theatre was shut up until the decision was obtained, the obnoxious Catalani having in the meantime agreed to cancel her engagement. On the Wednesday following the theatre was re-opened, but the report of the committee being of a very unsatisfactory kind, the uproar became greater than ever. The manager is said to have hired a great number of boxers, and on the Friday night following, the various fights in the pit gave it the appearance of a boxing-school. During this period everything distinguished by the epithet O. P. (old prices) became fashionable. There was an O. P. Dance. Finding it utterly impossible to appease the rioters in any other way, Kemble gave it to them. A public dinner was held, at which no less than five hundred people attended, and Kemble came in person to make an apology for his conduct. After dinner there was a crowded theatre, and amid considerable uproar a humble apology was accepted from the manager. After their demands had been complied with a large placard was unfurled, containing the words, "We are satisfied." Thus ended this extraordinary contest.

from *Wright's Caricature History*

STEPHEN KEMBLE (1758–1822)

92 *The younger, less successful and much fatter brother of John Philip Kemble and Sarah Siddons.*

Stephen Kemble, who died in Durham, conducted the Sunderland circuit for years, and was also manager of the Glasgow Theatre. His Falstaff was an attraction; for this gross character he could act without stuffing. There were others, too, he appeared in, such as Othello and Hamlet. An engraving is still in existence of Stephen Kemble in the *Prince of Denmark*, in an old-fashioned black coat, breeches, vest, shoes, buckles, and a large flowing auburn wig. I am not in possession of his costume for Othello, but should imagine from this that he dressed the noble Moor such as Garrick was in the habit of doing – coat, breeches, and a white judge's wig. He selected white as it matched his complexion. What ideas they had of costume in those days! In 1815, in Scotland, I have seen Macbeth dressed in an officer's red coat, sash, blue pants, Hessian boots, and a cocked hat. Stephan Kemble personated Othello one night in the Glasgow Theatre, and a circumstance occurred in the last scene which turned the tragedy into a comedy. When the bed of Desdemona was arranged, the property man, being a new hand, and in eager anxiety to have everything right and proper, fit for a *chambre accouché*, placed something under the bed which is always dispensed with. The curtain drew up and Kemble entered, speaking the soliloquy, "My soul, it is the cause, it is the cause!" A tittering took place, and then a laugh. Stephen Kemble stopped, looked around, and perceiving the cause of the hilarity, rushed off the stage, seized the unlucky property man by the neck as he would Iago, and roared out, "Villain! villain!" The terrified wretch cried, "Oh, sir, pardon me! I assure you I couldn't get the loan of a white one anywhere."

from *Representative Actors*

JOSEPH MUNDEN (1758–1832)

93 *Munden was a comedian who appeared at Covent Garden for over twenty years before transferring to Drury Lane. He was excellent, said James Northcote, 'but an artificial actor' – and probably not very popular.*

Munden had an unpleasant way of discouraging, if not extinguishing, the flame of ambition in the youthful dramatic author's breast. During a green-room reading of a comedy he would sit making hideous faces, and when the three or five acts were concluded, plaintively remark, "My precious eyes, sir, but where's the comedy?"

Munden had a foolish way of boasting of his ignorance. "I never read any book but a play," said this son of a poulterer; "no play but one in which I myself acted, and no portion of that play but my own scenes."

When this was told to Charles Lamb, he said, "I knew Munden well, and I *believe* him."

from *Representative Actors*

WILLIAM DUNLAP (1766–1839)

94 *Manager of New York's Park Theatre and biographer of the actor George Frederick Cooke (see p. 58). He also wrote plays and was the author of the* History of the American Theatre*, which alone assures him a place among the founding figures of America's theatrical tradition.*

On the last day of October a new drama from Dunlap's pen, "The Mysterious Monk," was performed with Hodgkinson in the leading part. Its reception was not enthusiastic. Quiet now seems to have prevailed in the greenroom, but the theatre was not to be the abode of tranquillity. One night in November, two sea captains became drunk (it was then permissible to bring liquor into the house), and began calling for "Yankee Doodle" during the overture. Not receiving the desired solace for their patriotic ears, they hurled missiles at the orchestra and defied the indignant audience. A riot ensued, which resulted in the ejection of the offenders; but returning later with a number of sailors, they assailed the doors of the play-house until the city watch took them into custody. This fracas resulted in the prohibition of intoxicants until the end of the first piece.

Oral Sumner Coad

95 *When Dunlap took over the post of manager at the Park Theatre in 1798 he found it difficult to alter the athletic nature of its productions.*

Soon after assuming the reins of government Dunlap had discovered that the audiences were not sufficiently cultivated to dispense with diversions of a physical kind, and, much as he deplored the custom, he was compelled frequently to introduce acrobatics and other spectacles. For instance, in 1798 an evening was concluded by a leap through the throat of a fiery dragon. In 1799 a pantomime on the career of *Don Juan* ended with that hero's precipitation into the inferno amid a tremendous shower of fire. Late in 1802 a marvelous person was advertised to stand on his head and revolve from sixty to a hundred times a minute, an act aptly styled "The Antipodean Whirligig." A few months later one Signor Manfredi charmed the audience by performing on the tight-rope as a prelude to "Romeo and Juliet."

Oral Sumner Coad

96 *The destruction by fire of the theatre at Richmond, Virginia in 1811 was one of the greatest tragedies in the history of early American theatre. Placide was the actor Alexandre Placide, who, until fleeing the French Revolution, had been rope dancer to Louis XVI.*

A new play and pantomime had been advertised for the benefit of Mr. Placide. The house was fuller than on any night of the season. The play was over, and the first act of the pantomime had passed. The second and last had begun. All was yet gaiety, all so far had been pleasure, curiosity was yet alive, and further gratification anticipated – the orchestra sent forth its sounds of harmony and joy – when the audience perceived some confusion on the stage, and presently a shower of sparks falling from above. Some were startled, others thought it was a part of the scenic exhibition. A performer on the stage received a portion of the burning materials from on high, and it was perceived that others were tearing down the scenery. Some one cried out from the stage that there was no danger. Immediately afterwards, Hopkins Robinson ran forward and cried out, "The house is on fire!" pointing to the ceiling, where the flames were spreading like wild-fire. In a moment, all was appalling horror and distress. Robinson handed several persons from the boxes to the stage, as a ready way for their escape. The cry of "Fire! fire!" ran through the house, mingled with the wailings of females and children. The general rush was to gain the lobbies. It appears from the following description of the house and the scene that ensued, that this was the cause of the great loss of life.

The general entrance to the pit and boxes was through a door not more than large enough to admit three persons abreast. This outer entrance was within a trifling distance of the pit door, and gave an easy escape to those in that part of the house. But to attain the boxes from the street it was necessary to descend into a long passage, and ascend again by an angular staircase. The gallery had a distinct entrance, and its occupants escaped. The suffering and death fell on the occupants of the boxes, who, panic-struck, did not see that the pit was immediately left vacant, but pressed on to gain the crowded and tortuous way by which they had entered. The pit door, as we have said, was so near the general entrance, that those who occupied that portion of the house gained the street with ease. A gentleman who escaped from the pit among the last, saw it empty, and, when in the street, looked back upon the general entrance to the pit and boxes, and the door had not yet been reached by those from the lobbies. A gentleman and lady were saved by being thrown accidentally into the pit, and most of those who perished would have escaped if they had leaped from the boxes and sought that avenue to the street. But all darted to the lobbies. The stairways were blocked up. All was enveloped in hot scorching smoke and flame. The lights were extinguished by the black and smothering vapour, and the shrieks of despair were appalling. Happy for a moment were those who gained a window and inhaled the air of heaven. Those who had reached the street cried to the sufferers at the windows to leap down, and stretched out their arms to save them. Some were seen struggling to gain the apertures to inhale the fresh air. Men, women, and children precipitated themselves from the first and second stories. Some escaped unhurt – others were killed or mangled by the fall. Some with their clothes on fire, shrieking, leaped from the windows to gain a short reprieve and die in agonies.

"Who can picture," says a correspondent of The Mirror, "the distress of those who, unable to gain the windows, or afraid to leap from them, were pent up in the long narrow passages?" The cries of those who reached the upper windows are described as being heart-sickening. Many who found their way to the street were so scorched or burnt as to die in consequence, and some were crushed to death under foot after reaching the outer door.

William Dunlap

ROBERT ELLISTON (1774–1831)

97 *Robert Elliston, a reasonable actor, was also a successful theatre manager, running numerous theatres throughout England, including Drury Lane from 1819 to 1827.*

Elliston had become proprietor of the Olympic Pavilion, as it was then called, in Wych Street, built originally by old Astley for equestrian performances. At his suggestion I wrote a speaking harlequinade, with songs for the *Columbine*, the subject being "Little Red Riding Hood." On the first night of its representation (December 21, 1818) every trick failed, not a scene could be induced to close or to open properly, and the curtain fell at length amidst a storm of disapprobation.

I was with Mr. Elliston and his family in a private box. He sent round an order to the prompter that not one of the carpenters, scene-shifters, or property-men was to leave the theatre till he had spoken to them. As soon as the house was cleared, the curtain was raised, and all the culprits assembled on the stage in front of one of the scenes in the piece representing the interior of a cottage, having a door in one half and a latticed window in the other. Elliston led me forward, and standing in the centre, with his back to the foot-lights, harangued them in the most grandiloquent language – expatiated on the enormity of their offence, their ingratitude to the man whose bread they were eating, the disgrace they had brought upon the theatre, the cruel injury they had inflicted on the young and promising author by his side; then, pointing in the most tragical attitude to his wife and daughters, who remained in the box, bade them look upon the family they had ruined, and burying his face in his handkerchief to stifle his sobs, passed slowly through the door in the scene, leaving his auditors silent, abashed, and somewhat affected, yet rather relieved by being let off with a lecture. The next minute the casement in the other flat was thrown violently open, and thrusting in his head, his face scarlet with fury, he roared out "I discharge you all!"

I feel my utter incapacity to convey an idea of this ludicrous scene, and I question whether any one unacquainted with the man, his voice, action, and wonderful facial expression, could thoroughly realize the glorious absurdity of it from verbal description.

George Raymond

98 Under the various phases of Elliston's character, we must here exhibit an instance of forbearance and good nature. Amongst the persons employed at the Olympic was a scene-painter, who had the misfortune of not being highly popular with his fellow-labourers in the establishment – in fact, a most disagreeable fellow. One of the carpenters projected a trick to mortify him, and this was placing a vessel nearly full of red paint on the upper edge of his working-room door, as it stood ajar, which, on any one entering, would consequently be capsized, like "Prone-descending rain," right over his person. The vessel being all ready, the next purpose was to induce the said artist to make his way to the room in question.

But by some mismanagement, at the moment, Elliston himself came by, and having business to transact in the scenic department, with his usual dignity of action, threw open the charged door, when the vermilion shower fell with a precision over his head and shoulders, which almost threatened suffocation. Consternation filled the minds of the skulking conspirators – and well it might. As soon as Elliston could recover his breath, in terrific accents he commanded that the whole establishment should be summoned before him; this was instantly obeyed. Red and fiery, he yet sat down with imperturbed dignity, when, shaking his gory locks, or rather the cardinal's hat, with which he had just been invested, he demanded instant explanation of the event, and the surrender of the offender.

The real culprit now stood forward, and at once confessed himself both the adviser and perpetrator of the plot, but thoroughly explaining for whom the revenge was intended.

"Ay!" said Elliston – "for Mr. — , say you?"

"Upon my honour!" was the reply.

"Then I forgive you!" rejoined the manager, and off he marched to incarnadine the Olympic pump with the evidence of his dishonour.

George Raymond

99 Elliston was another early manager of my father's. He was a man whose pomposity and majesty in private life were absolutely amazing; but he was a great actor for all that and an intelligent manager. For example, King George IV was a most theatrical man in all he did, and when his coronation took place he dressed all his courtiers and everybody about him in peculiarly dramatic costumes – dresses of Queen Elizabeth's time. It was all slashed trunks and side cloaks, etc. Of course, the dukes, earls and barons were particularly disgusted at the way they had to exhibit themselves, and as soon as the coronation ceremonies were over these things were thrown aside and sold, and Elliston bought an enormous number of them. He was then the lessee of the Surrey Theatre, where he got up a great pageant and presented "The Coronation of George IV." He had a platform made in the middle of the pit, and in one scene he strutted down among the audience in the royal robes; at which, with some good-natured chaff, there was a tremendous round of applause. For the moment Elliston became so excited that he imagined he was really the King himself, and spreading out his arms he said, amid silence: "Bless you, my people!"

Lester Wallack

100 Poor Elliston at last was so overcome with the gout that he could not act at all. He was then lessee of Drury Lane and my father was his stage-manager, appearing in Elliston's old parts, Captain Absolute, Charles Surface and the like. At that time there was no zoölogical garden in London, but there was a place called Exeter Change, in which were kept a lot of monkeys and parrots, a few wild animals, some lions (particularly the lion Wallace, who fought the six bull-dogs), and, if not the first, very nearly the first elephant that was ever exhibited alive in England. They did not know as much about taking care of animals then as they do now, and this elephant went mad, and became so dangerous that it was feared he would break out of his cage and do bodily damage to his keepers and the public, and it was determined he should be killed. A dozen men were sent from the barracks of the Foot Guards, who fired five or six volleys into the poor beast before they finished him.

At that time "The Belle's Stratagem" was being played with my father as Doricourt, one of Elliston's great parts. Elliston was in the habit of going to the theatre every night, particularly if one of his own celebrated characters was performed, and being wheeled down to the prompter's place in an invalid's chair, he would sit and watch all that was going on. In the mad scene in "The Belle's Stratagem" Doricourt, who is feigning insanity, has a little extravagant "business," and, at a certain exit, he utters some wildly absurd nonsense such as, "Bring me a pigeon pie of snakes." On the night in question, when the town talked of nothing but the great brute who had been killed by the soldiers the day before, my father on his exit after the mad scene shouted: "Bring me a pickled elephant!" to the delight of the easily pleased house, but to the disgust of the sensitive Elliston, who, shaking his gouty fist at him, cried: "Damn it, you lucky rascal; they never killed an elephant for *me* when *I* played Doricourt!"

Lester Wallack

JOHN LISTON (?1776–1846)

101 *One of London's principal comic actors for a period of thirty years.*

Walking one day through Leicester Square with Mr. Miller, the theatrical bookseller of Bow Street, Liston happened to mention casually that he was going to have tripe for dinner, a dish of which he was particularly fond. Miller, who hated it, said, "Tripe! Beastly stuff! How can you eat it?" That was enough for Liston. He stopped suddenly in the crowded thoroughfare in front of Leicester House, and holding Miller by the arm, exclaimed in a loud voice, "What, sir! So you mean to assert that you don't like tripe?" "Hush!" muttered Miller, "don't talk so loud: people are staring at us." "I ask you sir," continued Liston, in still louder tones, "do you not like tripe?" "For heaven's sake, hold your tongue!" cried Miller; "you'll have a crowd round us." And naturally people began to stop and wonder what was the matter. This was exactly what Liston wanted, and again he shouted, "Do you mean to say you don't like tripe?" Miller, making a desperate effort, broke from him, and hurried in consternation through Cranbourne Alley, followed by Liston, bawling after him, "There he goes! – that's the man who doesn't like tripe!" to the immense amusement of the numerous passengers, many of whom recognised the popular comedian, till the horrified bookseller took to his heels and ran, as if for his life, up Long Acre into Bow Street, pursued to his very doorstep by a pack of young ragamuffins, who took up the cry, "There he goes! – the man that don't like tripe!"

J. R. Planché

CHARLES MATHEWS (1776–1835)

102 *An amazing memory and a tremendous talent for mimicry and impersonation were Charles Mathews's principal theatrical characteristics. He presented his one-man shows, 'At Homes', throughout England and America.*

The infinite variety of his transformations will be best shown by a brief description of the characters he personated. On the rising of the curtain he entered as *Multiple*, a strolling actor in great agitation at being refused an engagement by *Velinspeck*, a country manager, who, it appears, had expressed doubts of his talents, and particularly of his versatility. In a short soliloquy he announced his determination to convince this insulting manager of the grossness of his error, and departed to make the requisite preparations. We are next introduced to *Mr. Velinspeck*, who gives a ludicrous detail of the disasters which had befallen the various members of his company, and the straits to which he is in consequence reduced. His complaints are interrupted by a knocking at the door, and Mathews enters disguised as *Matthew Stuffy*, an applicant for a situation as prompter, for which he says he is peculiarly qualified by that affection of the eyes commonly called squinting, which enables him to keep one eye on the performers, and the other on the book at the same time. This *Stuffy* is one of the richest bits of humour we ever witnessed; his endless eulogies upon the state of things "in the late immortal Mr. Garrick's time" are highly ludicrous. The prompter now departs, but is immediately succeeded by a *French tragedian*, who proposed to *Velinspeck* an entertainment of recitation and singing. This character is intended for a portrait of Talma,* and the resemblance must be instantly felt and acknowledged by all who are acquainted with the peculiarities of that Roscius of the French stage. It is always received with clamorous applause by those who have seen Talma, for its fidelity. The command of countenance which Mathews here displays is wonderful; never was anything more completely French than the face he assumes, and never was any character dressed more to the life. Next enters *Robin Scrawkey*, a runaway apprentice, smit with the desire of "cleaving the general ear with horrid speech." After a ludicrous colloquy between him and the manager, he expresses his apprehension of being pursued by his master, and takes refuge in a room on the first floor, which is open to the audience. He here quickly changes his dress, slips down the back stairs, and in the lapse of two minutes enters again as *Andrew M'Sillergrip*, a Scotch pawnbroker in search of his runaway apprentice, the aforesaid *Robin Scrawkey*, whom he pursues upstairs, and is heard to assail with blows and violent abuse. He again alters his dress, and re-appears immediately as *Mrs. M'Sillergrip*, who expresses great fears of an attack upon her honour by the manager, and joins the imaginary party upstairs. The skill of Mathews in carrying on a conversation between three persons is here exercised with most astonishing effect. Finally, he enters as a fat *Coachman* out of patience at waiting for three worthies, whom he has engaged to convey to Dover; and presently, to the utmost astonishment and confusion of the manager, convinces him that the whole of the characters

---

*François-Joseph Talma (1763–1826), the leading French actor of the period.

who have appeared before him have been personated by the identical comedian whose talents he had just before estimated so lightly.

from *Representative Actors*

THOMAS A. COOPER (1776–1849)

03 *One of the first English-born actors to become an American citizen. He was an outstanding exponent of the new style of acting evolved by the Kembles and became the leading tragedian of the American stage. Barrett was another English-born actor, eighteen years Cooper's junior.*

In the company of the old Chestnut Street Theatre at this epoch was a young actor, Mr. George Barrett, called generally "Gentleman George." He was a juvenile actor of great local repute in Philadelphia, and moved among all the young swells of that day. He was to play Laertes in "Hamlet" with Cooper, who arrived from Baltimore too late for rehearsal; so George went to his dressing-room in order to ascertain the arrangement of the fencing match in the last scene. Mr. Cooper was morose, and said, "Go to the prompter, sir, and find out!" When the fencing began Barrett would not let Cooper disarm him, and the audience could see this fact and became excited. Finally Barrett, with sword down, stood quietly to be run through by Cooper. When the curtain fell Cooper started up in a towering passion, and exclaimed to Barrett, "What did you mean by your conduct, sir?" Drawing himself up to his full height, six feet two inches, Barrett replied, "Go to the prompter, sir, and find out!"

Mrs John Drew

RICHARD JONES (1778–1851)

04 *The elegance and finery of William Lewis, actor-manager of Covent Garden Theatre from 1773 to 1809, led to him being nicknamed 'Gentleman' Lewis. He groomed younger light comedians, like Jones, in the same genteel mould.*

In 1809 Richard Jones made his *début* at Covent Garden, in Macklin's comedy of *Love à la Mode*, as Squire Groom. Lewis attended behind the scenes to witness his *protégé's* first attempt. When the cue was given for his entrance, Jones became transfixed with fear, and instead of giving the "view halloo," was struck dumb. Lewis perceiving the dilemma of the new actor, roared, "Yoicks! yoicks!" The audience hearing those well-known sounds exclaimed, "A second Lewis!" Slapping Jones on the back, Lewis told him to go in and win. Jones, lacking courage, dashed on the stage amid the most deafening plaudits; and as he paced about in his jockey-dress – thus showing off his slim, tall, and well-formed person

– minutes absolutely elapsed before he could utter a word for the applause. His success was most complete, and Jones remained in London as the true successor of Lewis as long as the legitimate drama had a home.

from *Representative Actors*

JOSEPH GRIMALDI (1778–1837)

105 *Grimaldi was responsible for developing the character of the clown in the harlequinade in a way that influenced pantomime throughout the nineteenth century. His health broke down at the peak of his fame and he was a cripple at the age of 45. Richard Findlater's biography of Grimaldi contains these two descriptions.*

In October he appeared in Brighton for the first time, with Bologna as Harlequin in a pantomime, and it was also at this period, according to the *Memoirs*, that he made his first expedition to Manchester and Liverpool, an expedition that was nearly his last. It began with an accident on the road, when Grimaldi's coach overturned and 'five stout men' fell on top of him – a Dickensian touch, this! That was not serious, but at Manchester he suffered a severe shock, of a kind which was not uncommon in his profession. The casualty rate among pantomimists was high: when Harlequins jumped through windows, sometimes there were no stage-hands ready to receive them (like Tom Ellar): when Pantaloons performed in comic duels, their eyes were thrust out by swords (like James Parsloe); when Clowns shot up through stage-traps, the ropes were likely to break. This is what happened to Grimaldi at Manchester. Just as he reached the level of the stage, he fell back into the cellar below, stunned and shaken; although he was in acute pain he continued to play the scene as if nothing was amiss, and by the end of the evening – with the help, no doubt, of the embrocation – he had quite recovered. He had been his own doctor, but he was not anxious to test the cure again, and when he travelled with the company to Liverpool for a one-night stand he implored the master-carpenter to ensure that there was no recurrence of such an accident at that theatre. Nevertheless, it happened all over again. Just as Grimaldi's head showed above the stage, to be greeted with applause by the people of Liverpool, the ropes snapped, and after holding on for a few seconds to the edge of the trap he fell right down into the machinery below. Again, he was in agony; again, he insisted on continuing his performance, but with considerable difficulty. After the pantomime was over, he could scarcely walk to the stage door, and it took him some time to recover from the effects of his injuries.

106 A month after the pantomimes opened, the mad old King of England [George III] died at last, on 29th January 1820. (The three weeks of compulsory closure had a disastrous effect upon the theatres' exchequers.) The Regency was over – and so, too, was the golden age of pantomime, and the ascendancy of Covent Garden.

It is a curious fact that it was only now that Grimaldi's name was distinguished upon the Covent Garden bills by bigger type from his colleagues of the harlequinade. Perhaps it was the controversy over Sancho Panza which prompted the change; perhaps the management was anxious to make the most of its assets in a bad year; but, whatever the reason, the new Easter piece gave the Clown, for the first time, the honour of star billing – thirteen years after *Mother Goose*. It was unusual to stage a new pantomime at Easter, but *Harlequin and Don Quixote* had been unsuccessful and the theatre hoped to make up for its failure with *Harlequin and Cinderella: or The Little Glass*. During the harlequinade, Clown lost his arm in some violent horse-play, but a few minutes later an arm sprang up from a stage-trap and hopped about as if in derision. He chased this tantalizing member all over the stage in a frenzy, and when he at last caught it he threw the arm furiously on the ground and began to stamp on it. As he did so, however, he let out a scream of agony – he had forgotten that it was his *own* arm. Is it too fanciful to see in this buffoonery a symbol of Grimaldi's own ill-treatment of his body, which now racked him continually with intimations of the day of reckoning? Moreover, he was beginning to lose his grip over the audience – or so it seemed, for he was roundly hissed for his strip-tease in the Baroness's bedroom when she 'exhibited the mysteries of her dress rather too plainly': taste was changing, and the Clown was failing to catch up with the new prudery seeping in from the provinces. It was a sign of the times that Covent Garden closed down early after 'one of the most disastrous campaigns it has ever experienced'.

THOMAS HARRIS (d. 1820)

107 *Like all managers, Harris had to cope with aspiring authors – in this instance with William Hayley.*

In 1784 a Reverend Doctor brought with him from Ireland, his native country, five tragedies and five comedies, all to be acted at Drury-Lane and Covent-Garden: he plagued me much to bring him to Mr. Harris at Knightsbridge; but, before I could do so, the doctor himself found means to slip through Hyde Park turnpike. The circumstances of their interview I had from Mr. Harris himself, who thus humorously hit upon an effectual method to get rid of him and his ten plays.

One of his tragedies was called "Lord Russell," and one of his comedies "Draw the long bow." Mr. Harris received him at his house with his usual politeness, and sat with great patience and much pain listening to the Doctor reading one of his plays to him; when he had got to the fourth act, Mr. Harris remarked that it was very fine indeed – excellent; "But, Sir, don't you think it time for your hero to make his appearance?" – "Hero, Sir! what hero?" – "Your principal character, Lord Russell. You are in the fourth act, and Lord Russell has not been on yet." – 'Lord Russell, Sir!" exclaimed the Doctor; "why, Sir, I have been reading to you my comedy of 'Draw the long bow." – "Indeed! I beg you a thousand pardons for my dulness; but I thought it was your tragedy of 'Lord Russell' you had been reading to me." The angry author started from his chair, thrust his manuscript into his pocket, and ran down stairs out of the house. When I again met the Doctor, he gave a most terrible account of the deplorable state of the English stage, when a London manager did not know a tragedy from a comedy. I laughed at his chagrin so whimsically detailed to me, and he was all astonishment and anger at my ill-timed mirth. This Reverend gentleman (his dramatic mania excepted) was a man of piety and learning; and I believe Mr. Harris's witty expedient effectually cured him of profane play-writing, and changed a mad scholar into an edifying divine.

John O'Keefe

WILLIAM OXBERRY (1784–1824)

108 *When my own son Marc was beginning his career in repertory, I felicitously wrote to him, 'If your leading man falls ill, don't send for the doctor – learn his lines!' Oxberry seems to have had similar ideas two centuries ago.*

Advice to the Players

As the purpose of acting is to obtain profit, notice and applause, the following Rules are laid down, by following which the 'summum bonum' notoriety may easily be obtained.

1: There is no necessity to subject yourself to the slavery of studying your part:– *what's* the use of the prompter? Besides, it's ten to one, that in a modern play, you substitute something from your own mother wit much better than the author wrote. If you are entirely at a loss and out, you will get noticed both by the audience and the critic, which would otherwise, perhaps, have never been the case. As to the feelings of the poet, did he shew any for you, when he put you in the part? And, as he is paid for his play by your master, why mayn't you do what you like with it?

2: Another excellent mode of acquiring *notice*, is never to be ready to go on the stage, and to have apologies made for you as often as possible.

3: Never attend to another actor in the same scene with you. You may be much better employed in arranging your dress, or in winking and nodding at your friends in the boxes. You must always keep your eye on your *benefit*.

4: If you have any witticism, or good saying to deliver *aside*, bawl it out as loud as you can. How are they to laugh and applaud at the back of the one shilling gallery, if they don't hear what you say? If you have no lungs, give up the profession.

5: Never part with your hat: *what are you to do with your fingers?*

6: If in a tragedy, your friend, the hero, is dying at the farther end of the stage, let him die and be damned. You come forward and look about you. *Every man attend to his own business.*

7: In singing, never mind the music – observe what time you please. It would be a pretty degradation indeed, if you were obliged to run after a fiddler – no, let him keep your time, and play your tune.

8: If you can force another actor to laugh, by making ugly faces at him – you'll get the character of being – *so droll!* The play may suffer by this – but *you* must look to your *reputation*.

9: Never speak a good word of the manager. I can't well explain why, but mind, I caution you not to do it!

10: Go to rehearsal very rarely. You are not a schoolboy, nor are you to think yourself a parrot, that nothing but repetition will beat the words into your head.

11: After you have *said your say*, drop your character directly. *You are only paid to play your own part, and not to assist another to play his.* Never aid to set him off – it may make the scene better, but it will surely lead to comparisons to your disadvantage. *Complain, if he serves you so.*

12: In making love always whine. These are the tones that go to the heart.

13: In the middle of a speech, if there's the least applause, stop, turn around, come forward and bow. It's respectful. In general, the plaudits will arise from the sentiment, and not at all from your acting – bow nevertheless.

WILLIAM HENRY WEST BETTY (1791–1874)

109 *Master Betty – 'the young Roscius' – was a child prodigy who enjoyed a brief period of phenomenal success on the London stage, from 1804 to 1806, before disappearing into obscurity for the rest of his life.*

The whole country was armed, drilled, and well accoutred, and Rugby furnished its two companies of well-equipped, well-marshalled volunteers. The elder boys had their blue coats cuffed and collared with scarlet, and exercised after school-hours with heavy wooden broad-swords. Nothing was talked of but Bonaparte and invasion. Suddenly a wonderful boy, a miracle of beauty, grace, and genius, who had acted in Belfast and Edinburgh, became the theme of all discourse. My father had brought him to England, and his first engagement was at Birmingham, where crowded houses applauded his surprising powers to the very echo. In London, at both Drury Lane and Covent Garden Theatres, throughout the whole country, "the young Roscius" became a rage, and in the *furore* of public admiration the invasion ceased to be spoken of. He acted two nights at Leicester, and on a half-holiday, my cousin Birch having sent a note to excuse me and his eldest son from the afternoon's callings-over at my father's request, Tom Birch and myself were smuggled into a chaise, and reached Leicester in time for the play – 'Richard III.' The house was crowded. John Kemble and H. Harris, son of the Patentee of Covent Garden, sat in the stage box immediately behind us. I remember John Kemble's handkerchief strongly scented of lavender, and his observation, in a very compassionate tone, "Poor boy! he is very hoarse." I could form little judgment of the performance, which excited universal enthusiasm, and in the tempest of which we were of course borne along. In subsequent engagements with my father we became playfellows, and off the stage W. H. West Betty was a boy with boys, as full of spirits, fun, and mischief as any of his companions, though caressed, fondled, and idolised by peeresses, and actually besieged for a mere glimpse of him by crowds at his hotel door. An instance of the "madness that ruled the hour" was given at Dunchurch, where he stopped to dine and sleep, being prevented from acting at Coventry in Passion Week by Cornwallis, Bishop of Lichfield and Coventry. One of the leading families in the country, who were on their way to Coventry to see him were stopped by the news at Dunchurch. The lady begged and entreated the landlord to get her a sight of "the young Roscius." She would "give anything." The landlord unwilling to disoblige his patrons, suggested that there was but one way in which her wish could be gratified: "Mr. and Mrs. Betty and their son were just going to dinner, and if she chose to carry in one of the dishes she could see him, but there was no other way." The lady, very grateful in her acknowledgements, took the dish, and made one of the waiters at table. I mention this as one among the numerous anecdotes of his popularity. The Prince of Wales made him handsome presents, and in short he engrossed all tongues.

William Charles Macready

LOUISA BRUNTON (?1785–1860)

110 My objection to the dramatic profession on the score of its uselessness, in this letter, reminds me of what my mother used to tell me of Miss Brunton, who afterwards became Lady Craven; a very eccentric as well

as attractive and charming woman, who contrived, too, to be a very charming actress, in spite of a prosaical dislike to her business, which used to take the peculiar and rather alarming turn of suddenly, in the midst of a scene, saying aside to her fellow-actors, "What nonsense all this is! Suppose we don't go on with it." This singular expostulation my mother said she always expected to see followed up by the sudden exit of her lively companion, in the middle of her part. Miss Brunton, however, had self-command enough to go on acting till she became Countess of Craven, and left off the *nonsense* of the stage for the *earnestness* of high life.

Fanny Kemble

EDMUND KEAN (1787–1833)

111 *Anne Carey, Kean's mother, deserted him as a child and he was brought up by her friend, the actress Charlotte Tidswell. As a young man he spent several penurious years tramping the provinces, but in January 1814 he appeared at Drury Lane as Shylock to tumultuous applause. Full of energy and enthusiasm in all his roles, Kean became the most admired actor of his day. Drunkenness and extravagance, however, made his last years unhappy ones.*

It was on my return home for one of my Christmas holidays that in passing through Birmingham I found the manager of the theatre there (which my father had relinquished on entering on his Manchester speculation) had sent tickets for a box. Conceiving it proper that the civility should be acknowledged by the appearance of some of our family, I went with one of my sisters and a friend. 'Richer, the Funambulist!' was the large-lettered attraction of the playbills. The play was 'The Busy-body,' very badly acted, and the after-piece a serious pantomime on the ballad of 'Alonzo and Imogene.' Richer represented the Baron "all covered with jewels and gold," and a female porpoise, rejoicing in the name of Watson, being the manager's wife, ungainly and tawdry, was the caricature of the "fair Imogene." As if in studied contrast to this enormous "hill of flesh," a little mean-looking man, in shabby green satin dress (I remember him well), appeared as the hero, "Alonzo the Brave." It was so ridiculous that the only impression I carried away was that the hero and heroine were the worst in the piece. How little did I know, or could guess, that under that shabby green satin dress was hidden one of the most extraordinary theatrical geniuses that have ever illustrated the dramatic poetry of England! When, some years afterwards, public enthusiasm was excited to the highest pitch by the appearance at Drury Lane of an actor of the name of Kean, my astonishment may easily be conceived on discovering that the little insignificant Alonzo the Brave was the grandly impassioned personator of Othello, Richard, and Shylock!

William Charles Macready

112 *Kean returned to Shylock for this performance on 1 April, 1816. This review appeared in* The Examiner *six days later.*

Mr. Kean's friends felt some unnecessary anxiety with respect to his reception in the part of Shylock, on Monday night at Drury-Lane, being his first appearance after his recovery from his accident, which we are glad to find has not been a very serious one. On his coming on the stage there was a loud burst of applause and welcome; but as this was mixed with some hisses, Mr. Kean came forward, and spoke nearly as follows:

> "Ladies and Gentlemen, for the first time in my life I have been the unfortunate cause of disappointing the public amusement.
>
> "That it is the only time, on these boards, I can appeal to your own recollection; and when you take into calculation the 265 times that I have had the honour to appear before you, according to the testimony of the managers' books, you will, perhaps, be able to make some allowance.
>
> "To your favour I owe all the reputation I enjoy.
>
> "I rely on your candour, that prejudice shall not rob me of what your kindness has conferred upon me."

This address was received with cordial cheers, and the play went forward without interruption. As soon as the curtain drew up, some persons had absurdly called out "Kean, Kean," though Shylock does not appear in the first scenes. This was construed into a call for "God save the King:" and the Duke of Gloucester's being in one of the stage-boxes seemed to account for this sudden effusion of loyalty.

William Hazlitt

113 Buckstone* and Sydney Cooper, the one as "general utility," and the other as scenic artist, made their first essay in dramatic life at Hastings. The season proceeded with varying success until Wombwell's Menagerie entered the town and presented a rival attraction, and then receipt fell off and fortunes ran low. Cooper, always a prudent lad, had accumulated savings to the amount of £5, which, in the form of a note, he kept for safety inside the case of a large, old-fashioned, silver watch which he wore. When fortune was at its lowest, the scenic artist woke one morning

*see also p. 88.

to find both watch and note had disappeared. The company was assembled, and the serious nature of the financial position considered, and it was determined to put on a celebrated melodrama then playing at the Surry Theatre, in the hope of retrieving fortune. In this Buckstone was cast for an important part, to perfect himself in which he used to wander away to the neighbouring downs for privacy and quiet. Here, on one accasion, he met a gentleman, actually on the same errand bent, who, noticing the lad's earnest attention to his book, and perhaps divining the cause, asked him the subject of his reading. The boy handed the book to the stranger, and told him that he was a member of the company then performing at Hastings. The gentleman said that he had a great taste for dramatic works, particularly Shakespeare's tragedies. "Ah!" said the rustic actor, "William Shakespeare is not a gentleman of my acquaintance yet, but I hope in time to be on speaking terms with him." "Very good," said the stranger, and then proceeded to inquire as to the business done at the theatre, eliciting the tale of misfortune with which the reader has already been made familiar. The gentleman next suggested that he should like to look over the theatre, and the young actor offered himself as guide. The gentleman's person was decorated by a blue coat with brass buttons, light pants, and Hessian boots with corresponding tassels. After visiting the theatre, the unknown was about to depart, when a post-chaise drove hastily up to the door. Out jumped R. W. Elliston, the then manager of Drury Lane Theatre, and taking the stranger by the hand, said: "My dear Kean, you must return with me to town to-morrow; since your absence the business has been ruinous. I must announce you for Richard the III for Monday." "Oh, no," said Edmund, "I came hither with your consent to study my part in the new tragedy." "Never mind the new part; we can put that off," said Elliston. "Well," said the great tragedian, "I will make a compact with you. If you will remain here and perform with me for the benefit of our unfortunate brethren to-morrow night, I will return with you on the following morning." The terms were joyfully accepted. The morrow came. The bill included *The Merchant of Venice* – Shylock by the Roscius of the world – and the farce, *The Liar*, with Elliston in the character of Wildrake. The house was crammed to suffocation, and the performance resulted in money enough being taken to pay all back salaries, not forgetting the lost watch and its contents, and to furnish the company with sufficient means to take them on with comfort to Dover.

Alfred Miles

114 And now the public began to grow discontented with the notoriously libertine life which Kean led. He had never, I believe, yet disappointed a London audience, but on one occasion. The circumstances of this one he

often related to me. He had gone to dine somewhere about ten miles from town with some old friends of early days, players, of course, fully intending to be at the theatre in time for the evening's performance. But temptation and the bottle were too strong for him. He out-stayed his time, got drunk, and lost all recollection of Shakespeare, Shylock, Drury Lane, and the duties they entailed on him. His friends, frightened at the indiscretion they had caused, dispatched Kean's servant, with his empty chariot, and a well-framed story that the horses had been frightened, near the village where Kean had dined, at a flock of geese by the road-side; that the carriage was upset, and the unfortunate tragedian's shoulder dislocated. This story was repeated from the stage by the manager; and the rising indignation of the audience (who had suffered the entertainments to be commenced by the farce) was instantly calmed down into commiseration and regret.

The following morning Kean was shocked and bewildered at discovering the truth of his situation. But how must his embarrassment have been increased on learning that several gentlemen had already arrived from town to make inquries for him? He jumped out of bed; and, to his infinite affright, he saw, amongst the carriages, those of Sir Francis Burdett, Mr. Whitbread, and others of his leading friends, whose regard for him brought them to see into his situation in person.

Luckily for him, his old associates the actors had, with great presence of mind, carried on the deception of the preceding night. The village apothecary lent himself to it and with a grave countenance confirmed the report; and Kean himself was obliged to become a party, *nolens volens*, in the hoax. His chamber was accordingly darkened, his face whitened, his arm bandaged. A few of the most distinguished inquirers were admitted to his bed-side. No one discovered the cheat; and, to crown it completely, he appeared, in an incredibly short time, on the boards of old Drury again, the public being carefully informed that his respect and gratitude towards them urged him to risk the exertion, notwithstanding his imperfect convalescence, and to go through the arduous parts of Richard, Macbeth, and Othello, on three successive nights, with his arm in a sling!

Thomas Grattan

115 Towards the close of his second visit to America, Kean made a tour through the northern part of the State, and visited Canada; he fell in with the Indians, with whom he became delighted, and was chosen a chief of a tribe. Some time after, not aware of his return to the city, I received, at a late hour of the evening, a call to wait upon an Indian chief, by the name of Alantenaida, as the highly finished card left at my house had it. I repaired to the hotel, and was conducted up stairs to the folding-doors

of the hall, when the servant left me. I entered, aided by the feeble light of the room; but at the remote end I soon perceived something like a forest of evergreens, lighted up by many rays from floor-lamps, and surrounding a stage or throne; and seated in great state was the chief. I advanced, and a more terrific warrior I never surveyed. Red Jacket or Black Hawk was an unadorned, simple personage in comparison. Full dressed, with skins tagged loosely about his person, a broad collar of bear-skin over his shoulders, his leggings, with many stripes, garnished with porcupine quills; his moccasons decorated with beads; his head decked with the war-eagle's plumes, behind which flowed massive black locks of dishevelled horse-hair; golden-colored rings pendant from the nose and ears; streaks of yellow paint over the face, massive red daubings about the eyes, with various hues in streaks across the forehead, not very artistically drawn. A broad belt surrounded his waist, with tomahawk; his arms, with shining bracelets, stretched out with bow and arrow, as if ready for a mark. He descended his throne and rapidly approached me. His eye was meteoric and fearful, like the furnace of the cyclops. He vociferously exclaimed, Alantenaida! the vowels strong enough. I was relieved; he betrayed something of his raucous voice in imprecation. It was Kean. An explanation took place. He wished to know the merits of the representation. The Hurons had honored him by admission into their tribe, and he could not now determine whether to seek his final earthly abode with them for real happiness, or return to London, and add renown to his name by performing the Son of the Forest. I never heard that he ever afterwards attempted, in his own country, the character. He was wrought up to the highest pitch of enthusiasm at the Indian honor he had received, and declared that even Old Drury had never conferred so proud a distinction on him as he had received from the Hurons. My visit was of some time. After pacing the room, with Indian step, for an hour or more, and contemplating himself before a large mirror, he was prevailed upon to change his dress and retire to rest. A day or two after, he sailed for Europe, with his Indian paraphernalia.[1]

[1]The professional receipts of Kean during his engagement in New York, were, I believe, at least equal to those for a like number of nights which he received at the acme of his renown in London. His average income for some twelve or fifteen years was not less than ten thousand pounds per annum. He rescued Old Drury from bankruptcy, yet he is said to have been often in need, and died almost penniless. There was no one special extravagance chargeable to him; but he was reckless in money matters, and figures entered not into his calculations. He had a helping hand for all applications, and he never forgot his early friends.

John W. Francis

116 Craven's Head Tavern, Drury-lane, William Oxberry, a Drury Lane comedian, was the host. Edmund Kean loved a social glass, and never forgot old companions of his former wanderings. Star now of the dramatic hemisphere, he still indulged in his former habits. Oxberry held a musical club at his tavern weekly, at which Edmund Kean presided. A club-night happened to fall upon a 'Richard the Third' night at Drury. 'What's to be done?' thought Oxberry; 'the chair will be vacant.' Visitors were wont to crowd the Craven's Head to look at the town's wonder, Kean – a thing to remember and talk about – especially for those who were privileged to hear him sing. 'The Jolly Dogs' (our clubbites' name) became as difficult to enter as the 'Carlton' or 'United Service' of our day.

OXBERRY: 'Ned, you'll never be able to take the chair to-night in time.'

'Won't I, Billy? For a dinner and a bottle of port, I am there.'

The wager was accepted by Billy, Kean acted Gloster very quickly, and in his fight, a great feature, whispered to Wallack (who played Richmond):

'Kill me quickly to-night, I'm due at the "Jolly Dogs." '

The curtain down, wrapped in a greatcoat, rapidly he ran down the Lane, jumping into the chair a few minutes before the club opened, amidst thunders of applause. There sat the last 'Plantagenet' in the habit as he lived (Kean had not taken off his Richard's dress), won his wager, and filled Billy's till that evening to repletion.

Edmund Stirling

117 The version [of Richard III] I played was of course, Shakespeare's, not Cibber's.* It is amazing how long the bombastic fustian of Cibber held the stage, and how hard his version was to dislodge from it. Edmund Kean, who made his great success in Cibber's version, revolted at last and tried to force Shakespeare, pure and unadulterated, upon the public; but they would have none of it, and he had to return to Cibber. The oft-quoted line "Off with his head! so much for Buckingham!" which according to tradition never failed to bring down the house was Cibber's.[1] I think Irving was the first to win over the public for Shakespeare's unspoiled, original version?

[1]The applause which followed this absurd line was naturally very precious to the actor who was playing 'Richard.' Harry Loveday, whose father had played with Kean, told me a good story. One night a small part player [Yarnold] from sheer nervousness, rushed on to the stage and shouted "My Lord, the Duke of Buckingham is taken and we've cut off

*see p. 18.

his head." Kean, absolutely nonplussed, could only murmur: "Oh! . . . then there's nothing more to be said."*

John Martin-Harvey

118 Leman Rede is the authority for a story which might be taken as an epitome not only of Kean in relaxation, but of a great many of his kind. Though it belongs to a period later in his life it applies equally to any part of it. Phillips, Kean's secretary, is supposed to be waiting while his employer makes merry in another room in the tavern.

Time, two in the morning
Phillips. Waiter, what was Mr. Kean doing when you left the room?
Waiter. Playing the piano, sir, and singing.
Phillips. Oh, come, he's all right, then.

Quarter-past two
Phillips. What's Mr. Kean doing now?
Waiter. Making a speech sir, about Shakespeare.
Phillips. He's getting drunk; you'd better order the carriage.

Half-past two
Phillips. What's he at now?
Waiter. He's talking Latin, sir.
Phillips. Then he *is* drunk. I must get him away.

H. N. Hillebrand

JOHN VANDENHOFF (1790–1861)

119 Old Vandenhoff played his farewell engagement in Edinburgh, at the Queen's Theatre, in 1858. In the *Merchant of Venice*, Irving** played Bassanio to his Shylock. In Act I., scene 3, where Shylock and Bassanio enter, an odd thing occurred. I give it in Irving's words as he told me of it:

"Vandenhoff began: 'Three thousand' – there was then a sort of odd click of something falling and the speech dried up. I looked up at him and saw his mouth moving, but there was no sound. At that moment my eye caught the glitter of something golden on the stage. I stooped to pick it up, and as I did so saw that it was a whole set of false teeth. This I handed to Shylock, keeping my body between him and the audience so that no one might see the transaction. He turned away for an instant,

---

* . . . or as I first heard the story, 'Then bury him! So much for Buckingham' – a spontaneous and better line in perfect iambics.

**Sir Henry Irving, see below p. 117.

putting both hands up to his face. As he turned back to the audience his words came out quite strong and clearly: 'Three thousand ducats – well!' "

Bram Stoker

WILLIAM CHARLES MACREADY (1793–1873)

120 *One of the finest of all tragedians, Macready was the chief rival of Kean in the early nineteenth century. He was noted for the lengthy pauses he developed for dramatic effect. Such an effect is still used by actors and is called 'A Macready Pause'. Although he had no great love for his profession, he did a great deal for it, insisting on adequate rehearsals for instance, and also restoring the texts of Shakespeare's plays, by then often corrupted. A somewhat earnest actor and manager, Macready nevertheless could see humour in the theatre, as his* Journals *and* Reminiscences *show.*

My experience of country theatres never presented me with any scenes resembling the barn of Hogarth's Strolling Players, but it was not altogether without its whimsical expedients and ludicrous mishaps. On the first representation of the grand Ballet of Action of Macbeth I was most busily and anxiously engaged in looking after the working of the machinery, which was very complicated, and urging on the performers. In the scene after Duncan's murder there was scarcely three minutes' time for Macbeth and Lady Macbeth to wash the blood from their hands. Macbeth, poor Conway, on rushing from the stage in an agony of despair, exclaimed, "Oh! my dear sir, my dresser is not here! What shall I do?" (the old man with water, soap, and towel was at the opposite side). There was not an instant for reflection. "Here," I cried, "come here:" dragging him up to the gentlemen's first dressing-room, where he plunged his hands into a jug of water. "There is no towel, my dear sir!" in continued agony he cried. I snatched up the first semblance of cloth that lay to hand, with which he dried his half-washed hands, and dashed back to the stage again. With the water and cloth in my hands I met at the foot of the stairs Lady Macbeth in equal perplexity, who hastily availing herself of the ready aid, rushed back to her place on the stage. The jug &c., I hastily deposited in my own room, and returned to watch the closing of the scene. The curtain fell that night with much applause on our barbarous violation of Shakespeare, and I went to my lodgings through a deep snow, insensible to the cold from the satisfaction I felt in the success of the evening. The next morning the acting manager met me with a very grave countenance, foretelling "the nature of a tragic volume," and opened his tale of woe with, – "Sir, I am very sorry to tell you, there are thieves in the theatre!" "Good heavens!" I answered, "is it possible? Let every inquiry be made, that they may be punished, or at least turned out of the place. What has been stolen?" "Why, sir, Mr

Simkin's breeches! When he went to dress himself at the end of the evening, his breeches were gone, and he was obliged to walk home to his lodgings through the snow without any." I desired the strictest search and inquiry to be made, and no pains spared to detect the offender. After a little time, however, a thought crossed me, and I asked the manager what kind of small clothes they were. When he told me they were brown kerseymere, it flashed across me that I had seized them for Conway's towel, and had thrown them under the table in my own room. The injury was repaired, but the story of Simkin's small clothes was for some time repeated as against my impetuosity.

121 *Macready's support for James Sheridan Knowles led to the latter's* Virginius *being staged at Covent Garden in 1820. Both of them triumphed, Macready confirming his reputation. Then the play toured the English provinces.*

One of the most ludicrous attempts to follow out the stage directions of the author at the least possible expense that I ever had the ill-luck to witness was at Kendal. The *corps dramatique* arrived in the town too late for the rehearsal of 'Virginius,' and I had to undergo during the two first acts a succession of annoyances in the scenic deficiencies and in the inaccuracies of the players. My unhappy temper was severely tried under the repeated mortifications I experienced, but in the third act of the play, where Siccius Dentatus should be discovered on a bier with a company of soldiers mourning over it, I saw the old man, who represented the Roman Achilles, lying on the ground, and two men standing near. This was too absurd! the body having to be borne off in sight of the audience. I positively refused to go on. "Oh, pray, Sir," urged the manager, "go on: the men have rehearsed the scene, and you will find it all right." In vain I represented that the men "could not carry off the old man." "Oh, yes, indeed, Sir," reiterated the manager, "they perfectly understand it." There was nothing for it but submission. After some delay the scene was drawn up, and disclosed the three as described. On I went and uttered my lamentation over the prostrate veteran, but when I gave the order "Take up the body, bear it to the camp" – to my agony and horror the two men, stooping down, put each an arm under the shoulder of the dead Dentatus, raised him upon his feet, he preserving a corpse-like rigidity, his eyes closed, and his head thrown back, and arm-in-arm the trio marched off at the opposite side of the stage amid roars of laughter from the convulsed spectators.

122 *William Robertson was manager of the Lincoln circuit.*

Louth, November 29. Walked with Mr Robertson to the theatre, which answers also the double purpose of a Sessions House; it is not the worst I have seen. Dressed in magistrates' room – 'quite convenient'. When ready to go on the stage, Mr Robertson appeared with a face full of dismay; he began to apologise, and I guessed the remainder. 'Bad house?' 'Bad? Sir, there's no one!' 'What? nobody at all?' 'Not a soul, sir – except the Warden's party in the boxes.' 'What the d—l! not one person in the pit or gallery?' 'Oh yes, there are one or two.' 'Are there five?' 'Oh, yes, five.' 'Then go on; we have no right to give ourselves airs, if the public do not choose to come and see us; go on at once!' Mr Robertson was astonished at what he thought my philosophy, being accustomed, as he said, to be 'blown up' by his *Stars*, when the houses were bad. I never acted Virginius better in all my life – good taste and earnestness.

123 *Bath was obviously not Macready's favourite place.*

January 17. In going through the box-office heard a woman inquiring for something entertaining for children. Brownell mentioned that Mr Macready and Dowton would play on Monday. 'Oh, no' she replied, 'they are very good actors, but I want something entertaining for children; when will *Aladdin* be done?' So much for Bath taste!

124 To Bath, March 6 . . . [*In the stage-coach*] Captain Bourchier [*a passenger*], as I soon learned his name to be, talked much; among other subjects mentioned young Kean's success at Bath, told me that he knew him, and that his dresses cost him £300 per annum, that he was very pleasant, and related many amusing stories about the theatre. One of Macready, who is a good actor, but he can never play without applause. He went on one night to play and no notice was taken of him, on which he said to the manager, 'I cannot get on, if they do not applaud me'. Upon which the manager went round and told the audience that Mr Macready could not act if they did not applaud him. When Macready reappeared, the applause was so incessant as to disconcert him, and he observed, 'Why, now I cannot act, there is so much applause'. I told him I rather discredited the story, 'In short,' I observed, 'perhaps I ought to apologise to you for allowing you to tell it without first giving you my name – my name is Macready.' He was very much confused, and I as courteous in apologising as I could be.

Bath, March 8 . . . [*Virginius*] The Icilius (a Mr Savile) was either half-stupidly drunk, or, as is very probable, a born ass. Virginia would have made an excellent representation of Appius' cook, as far as appearance went, added to which she seemed to think that she was playing Virginius, not Virginia, and fortified herself for some extraordinary efforts by a stimulant which was too easily detected on a near approach to her. The whole business was most slovenly – and last year this play was actually a *pattern* of correctness. Therefore last year there was a loss on the theatre, and now there is a considerable profit. So much for the judgement and taste of a Bath public. Pshaw! It is all quackery. . . .

..Exeter, March 18 . . . Between the third and fourth acts [of *Virginius*] the manager came into my room to apologise for a delay of some minutes, while Mr Hughes stripped the togas and decemviral insignia from Appius Claudius, a Mr H. Bartlett, and invested himself with them to finish the character, Mr Bartlett having been so excessively drunk as to tumble from the *sella curulis* in the Forum. Oh Rome! If the man had been acting Cato, it might have been taken for a point of character.

125 When playing Macbeth one night at Manchester his servant, who should have been in the wings with a bowl of cochineal which Macready used to smear on his hands to represent blood, failed to put in an appearance. Macready's exit was only a very momentary and rapid one, and finding that the blood he relied on for the next scene was not there, he rushed up to an inoffensive commercial traveller, who had been allowed as a great treat by his friend, the local stage-manager, to come and watch the mighty star from the side, and without any warning struck him a violent blow on the nose, smothered his hands in the blood that flowed freely, and ran on to the stage again to finish the Act.

When the curtain fell he apologised to the commercial for his apparent rudeness, as he put it, in the most courtly and chivalrous manner, at the same time presenting the object of his attentions with a five-pound note.

Seymour Hicks

126 I have frequently been asked, both by interviewing people and by my friends, what my method of study is, almost every actor having a method; and apropos of this there comes in an anecdote about Macready. He always objected to a redundancy of gesture, and once said to my father: "My dear Wallack, you are naturally graceful; I am not. I know that in gesture I do not excel, and facial expression is what I principally depend upon. In fact I absolutely make Mrs Macready tie my hands behind my back, and I practice before a large glass and watch the face." My father replied: "Well, Macready, I suppose that is all very good, but did you ever try it with your legs tied?"

Lester Wallack

JOHN BALDWIN BUCKSTONE (1802–79)

127 *Actor and dramatist, as well as being manager of the Theatre Royal, Haymarket (where his ghost still walks) from 1853 until 1876. (See also p. 78.)*

Mr Buckstone was rather happy-go-lucky in his attitude towards new plays. There were not nearly so many theatres in the West End of London as there are to-day, the competition was less and with his command of the chief authors, Mr Buckstone could afford to be rather lax in his treatment of casual manuscripts.

One day, an author who had submitted a five-act play to him arrived at the theatre and demanded the return of the manuscript which he had previously written for and it had not been found.

He was shown in to Mr Buckstone. "I'm sorry that your play cannot be found," he said genially, "but go up into my room. You will find a lot of three-act plays and a lot of two-act plays. Take one of each and make up for your lost five-acts."

Madge Kendal

EDWIN FORREST (1806–72)

128 *The foremost American tragedian for almost thirty years, and the first American actor to challenge the masters of the English stage. In spite of a tendency to rant in his early years he won a popular and devoted following at home and rivalled Macready for the plaudits of London's audiences when he appeared at Drury Lane in 1836–7. A second visit, however in 1845–6 led to an open feud, sparked by Macready's jealousy and Forrest's undoubtedly competitive attitude. In order to appreciate the extraordinary sequence of events surrounding this feud, we have first to read a passage from Macready's Diaries which describes the occasion when Forrest hissed him on stage in Edinbuurgh. The piece of business that so offended Forrest was Macready's introduction of a pas de mouchoir (a dance with a handkerchief) during the play scene in Hamlet.*

Edinburgh, March 2nd.–Acted Hamlet really with particular care, energy, and discrimination; the audience gave less applause to the first soliloquy than I am in the habit of receiving, but I was bent on acting the part, and I felt, if I can feel at all, that I had strongly excited them, and that their sympathies were cordially, indeed, enthusiastically, with me. On reviewing the performance I can conscientiously pronounce it one of the very best I have given of Hamlet. At the waving of the handkerchief before the play, and "I must be idle," a man on the right side of the stage – upper boxes or gallery, but said to be upper boxes – hissed! The audience took it up, and I waved the more, and bowed derisively and contemptuously to the individual. The audience carried it, though he was very staunch to his purpose. It discomposed me, and, alas, might have ruined many; but I bore it down. I thought of speaking to the audience, if called on, and spoke to Murray about it, but he very discreetly dissuaded me. Was called for, and very warmly greeted. Ryder came and spoke to me, and told me that the hisser was observed, and said to be a Mr. W —, who was in company with Mr. Forrest! The man writes in the *Journal,* a paper, depreciating me and eulogizing Mr.F., sent to me this place.

March 3rd.–Fifty-three years have I lived, to-day. Both Mr. Murray and Mr. Ryder are possessed with the belief that Mr. Forrest was the man who hissed last night. I begin to think he was the man.

129 *Macready won considerable sympathy from this episode and public feeling ran against Forrest. When Forrest again visited England in 1845 he was received with marked hostility, which he attributed to Macready's manoeuvrings. It is hardly surprising therefore that Macready's visit to America in 1848 should have aroused similar national passions against him. In the circumstances it was simply asking for trouble.*

On the 20th of November, 1848, Mr. Macready appeared at the Arch Street Theatre, Philadelphia. It was then, and for the first time, that an unsuccessful attempt was made to drive him from the stage. Upon his being called before the curtain he addressed the audience as follows:

> "He had understood, at New York and Boston, that he was to be met by an organized opposition, but he had abiding confidence in the justice of the American people." (Here the noise and confusion completely drowned his voice, and three cheers were attempted for Forrest, and three hearty ones were given for Macready.) He resumed by saying, "It was the custom in his country never to condemn a man unheard." (Cheers and calls, a voice crying out, "Did you allow Forrest to be heard in England?") He said, "I never entertained hostile feelings towards any actor in this country, and have never evinced a feeling of opposition to him. The actor alluded to had done that towards him, what he was sure no English actor would do – he had openly hissed him." (Great noise and confusion, hisses and hurrahs.) "That up to the time of this act he had never entertained towards that actor a feeling of unkindness, nor had he ever shown any since." (Collision in boxes and great uproar throughout the house.) He said, "That he fully appreciated the character and feelings of the audience, and, as to his engagement, if it was their will, he was willing to give it up at once; (no, no, cheers and hisses;) but that he should retain in his memory the liveliest recollection of the warm and generous sentiments of regard shown him, and should speak of the American people, whom he had known and studied for the past twenty years, with the same kind feelings that he ever had done."

This, the third speech delivered by Mr. Macready, before Mr. Forrest had uttered a syllable, called forth from the latter gentleman this scathing card. The editor of the *Pennsylvanian,* of Nov. 22nd, 18488, introduced it thus: "We received the following card last evening. It is a reply to the speech of Mr. Macready, at the Arch Street Theatre, on Monday evening:"

A CARD FROM EDWIN FORREST.

Macready, in his speech, last night, to the audience assembled at the Arch Street Theatre, made allusion, I understand, to 'an American actor' who had the temerity, on one occasion, 'openly to hiss him.' This is true, and, by the way, the only truth which I have been enabled to gather from the whole scope of his address. But why say 'an American actor?' Why not openly charge me with the act? for I did it, and publicly avowed it in the *Times* newspaper of London, and at the same time asserted my right to do so.

"On the occasion alluded to, Mr. Macready introduced a fancy dance into his performance of Hamlet, which I designated as a *pas de mouchoir,* and which I hissed, for I thought it a desecration of the scene, and the audience thought so too, for in a few nights afterwards, when Mr. Macready repeated the part of Hamlet with the same tomfoolery, the intelligent audience of Edinburg greeted it with a universal hiss.

"Mr. Macready is stated to have said last night, that up to the time of this act on my part, he had 'never entertained towards me a feeling of unkindness.' I unhesitatingly pronounce this to be a wilful and unblushing falsehood. I most solemnly aver and do believe that Mr. Macready, instigated by his narrow, envious mind, and his selfish fears, did *secretly*—not *openly*—suborn several writers for the English press to write me down. Among them was one Forster, a 'toady' of the *eminent tragedian*—one who is ever ready to do his dirty work; and this Forster, at the bidding of his patron, attacked me in print even before I appeared on the London boards, and continued his abuse of me at every opportunity afterwards.

"I assert also, and solemnly believe that Mr. Macready connived when his friends went to the theatre in London to hiss me, and did hiss me with the purpose of driving me from the stage—and all this happened many months before the affair at Edinburg, to which Mr. Macready refers, and in relation to which he jesuitically remarks that 'until that act he never entertained towards me a feeling of unkindness.' Pah! Mr. Macready has no feeling of kindness for any actor who is likely, by his talent, to stand in his way. His whole course as manager and actor proves this—there is nothing in him but self— self—self—and his own countrymen, the English actors, know this well. Mr Macready has a very lively imagination, and often draws upon it for his facts. He said in a speech at New York, that there, also, there was an 'organized opposition' to him, which is likewise false. There was no opposition manifested towards him there—for I was in the city at the time, and was careful to watch every movement with regard to such a matter. Many of my friends called upon me when Mr. Macready was announced to perform, and proposed to drive him from the stage for his conduct towards me in London. My advice was, do nothing— let the superannuated driveller alone—to oppose him would be but to make him of some importance. My friends agreed with me it was, at least, the most dignified course to pursue, and it was immediately adopted. With regard to an 'organized opposition to him' in Boston, this is, I believe, equally false; but perhaps in charity to the poor old man, I should impute these 'chimeras dire' rather to the disturbed state of his guilty conscience, than to any desire upon his part wilfully to misrepresent.

The only mistake we think Mr. Forrest made in this letter, was the expression calling Mr. Macready a "superannuated driveller." Mr. Macready was born in the year 1793, consequently at the time this article was written, 1848, he was but fifty-five years of age. A man cannot be called or considered superannuated at that age.

To this letter, Mr. Macready replied in a card "to the public," dated Jones' Hotel, Nov. 22nd, 1848:

> "In a card, published in the *Public Ledger* and other morning papers of this day, Mr. Forrest having avowed himself the author of the statement, which Mr. Macready has solemnly pledged his honor to be without the least foundation, Mr. Macready cannot be wanting in self-respect so far as to bandy words upon the subject; but, as the circulation of such statements is manifestly calculated to prejudice Mr. Macready in the opinion of the American public, and affect both his professional interests and his estimation to suspend their judgment upon the questions, until the decision of a legal tribunal, before which he will prove his veracity, hitherto unquestioned, shall place the truth beyond doubt."

James Rees

130 *The quarrel reached fever-pitch within a few months, and when Macready visited New York, to play Macbeth at the Astor Place Opera House, actual tragedy occurred; in the affray outside 22 people were killed and 36 injured. A pamphlet published shortly afterwards offered this account of the 'Terrific and Fatal Riot'.*

On the night of the tenth of May, 1849, the Empire City, the great metropolis of the Union, was the scene of one of those horrors of civilization, which for a time make the great heart of humanity stop in its beatings. In the darkness of night, thousands of citizens were gathered in a central square of the most aristocratic quarter of New York – gathered around one of its most conspicuous and magnificent edifices, the Astor Place Opera House . . .

Around this edifice, we say, a vast crowd was gathered. On the stage the English actor Macready was trying to play the part of MACBETH, in which he was interrupted by hisses and hootings, and encouraged by the cheers of a large audience, who had crowded the house to sustain him. On the outside a mob was gathering, trying to force an entrance into the house, and throwing volleys of stones at the barricaded windows. In the house the police were arresting those who made the disturbance – outside they were driven back by volleys of paving stones.

In the midst of this scene of clamor and outrage, was heard the clatter of a troop of horses approaching the scene. "The military – the military are coming!" . . . Further on was heard the quick tramp of companies of infantry, and there was seen the gleam of bayonets. A cry of rage burst from the mob. The appearance of an armed force seemed to inspire them with a sudden fury. They ceased storming the Opera House and turned their volleys against the horsemen. Amid piercing yells and execrations, men were knocked from their horses, the untrained animals were frightened, and the force was speedily routed, and could not afterwards be rallied to perform any efficient service.

Now came the turn of the infantry. They marched down the sidewalk in a solid column; but had no sooner taken up a position for the protection of the house than they were assailed with volleys of missiles. Soldiers were knocked down and carried off wounded. Officers were disabled. An attempt to charge with the bayonet was frustrated by the dense crowd seizing the muskets . . . At last the awful word was given to fire – there was a gleam of sulphurous light, a sharp quick rattle, and here and there in the crowd a man sank . . . with a deep groan or a death rattle. Then came a more furious attack, and a wild yell of vengeance! Then the rattle of another death-dealing volley . . . The ground was covered with killed and wounded – the pavements stained with blood. A panic seized the multitude, which broke and scattered in every direction. In the darkness of the night, yells of rage, screams of agony, and dying groans were mingled together. Groups of men took up the wounded and the dead, and conveyed them to the neighbouring apothecary shops, station-houses, and the hospital.

The horrors of the night can never be described. We looked over the scene that misty midnight. The military . . . were grimly guarding the Opera House. Its interior was a rendezvous and a hospital for the wounded military and police. Here and there around the building . . . were crowds of men talking in deep tones of indignation. There were little processions moving off with the dead or mutilated bodies of their friends and relations. A husband, uttering frenzied curses, followed his mortally wounded wife to the hospital. An aged mother found her only son . . . in the agonies of death. Many a wife sat watching at home, in terror and alarm for her absent husband . . .

131   *Following these riots Forrest became something of a theatrical outcast, although he was highly popular with the masses who felt he was standing up for American theatre against the weight of the English tradition. He certainly didn't suffer fools gladly, and could be quite intimidating, as the next few anecdotes, from James Rees's* Life of Edwin Forrest, *reveal.*

On one occasion, Mr Edwin Forrest, then a young man, gave a

tremendous display of really powerful acting. He was supposed to represent a Roman warrior, and to be attacked by six minions of a detested tyrant. At the rehearsals, Mr Forrest found a great deal of fault with the supers who condescended to play the minions. They were too tame. They didn't lay hold of him. They wouldn't go in as if it were a real fight. Mr Forrest stormed and threatened; the supers sulked and consulted. At length the captain of the supers inquired in his local slang, "Yer wan this to be a bully fight, eh?" "I do," replied Mr Forrest. "All right," rejoined the captain; and then the rehearsal quietly proceeded. In the evening the little theatre was crowded, and Mr Forrest was enthusiastically received. When the fighting scene occurred, the great tragedian took the centre of the stage, and the six minions entered rapidly and deployed in skirmishing order. At the cue "Seize him!" one minion assumed a pugilistic attitude, and struck a blow straight from the shoulder upon the prominent nose of the Roman hero, another raised him about six inches from the stage by a well-directed kick, and the others made ready to rush in for a decisive tussle. For a moment Mr Forrest stood astounded, his broad chest heaving with rage, his great eyes flashing fire, his sturdy legs planted like columns upon the stage. Then came the few minutes of powerful acting, at the end of which one super was seen sticking head foremost in the bass drum in the orchestra, four were having their wounds dressed in the green-room, and one finding himself in the flies, rushed out upon the roof of the theatre, and shouted "Fire!" at the top of his voice; while Mr Forrest, called before the curtain, bowed his thanks pantingly to the applauding audience, who looked upon the whole affair as part of the piece and "had never seen Forrest act so splendidly."

Mr Forrest was once playing in Richmond, Va., when one of the minor actors annoyed him terribly by persisting in reading his few lines in *Richelieu* incorrectly. Forrest showed him several times how to do it, but to no purpose, and then commenced abusing him. "Look here, Mr Forrest," finally said the poor fellow, in sheer despair, "if I could read it in that way I wouldn't be getting six dollars a week here." Forrest said only: "You are right; I ought not to expect much for that sum," and left him alone, but on the conclusion of the engagement sent him a check for forty dollars, with a recommendation to act up to the worth of that.

To use a slang word, he was extremely apt to "bully" all in the theatre, from the manager down. But he once met his match. It was when he was playing at the old Broadway Theatre, near Pearl Street. His pieces were followed by an exhibition of lions by their tamer, a certain Herr Driesbach. Forrest was one day saying that he had never been afraid in all his life – could not imagine the emotion. Driesbach made no remark at the time, but in the evening, when the curtain had fallen, invited Forrest home with him. Forrest assented, and the two, entering a house, walked a long distance, through many devious passages, all dark, until finally Driesbach, opening a door, said: "This way, Mr Forrest." Forrest entered, and immediately heard the door slammed and locked behind him. He had not time to express any surprise at this, for at the same moment he felt something soft rubbing against his leg, and, putting out his hand, touched what felt like a cat's back. A rasping growl saluted the motion, and he saw two fiery, glaring eyeballs looking up at him. "Are you afraid, Mr Forrest?" asked Driesbach, invisible in the darkness. "Not a bit." Driesbach said something; the growl deepened and became hoarser, the back began to arch and the eyes to shine more fiercely. Forrest held out for two or three minutes; but the symptoms became so terrifying that he owned up in so many words that he was afraid. "Now let me out, you infernal scroundrel," he said to the lion-tamer; "and I'll break every bone in your body." He was imprudent there, for Driesbach kept him, not daring to move a finger, with the lion rubbing against his leg all the time, until Forrest promised not only immunity, but a champagne supper into the bargain.

Forrest was once playing an engagement at Pittsburg. Already dressed for the character of Richelieu, he was in the act of going on the stage in the first scene, when he discovered that the sleeve of the dress he wore was either too short or drawn up; he called to his dresser, and told him to pull the sleeve down, so as the lace frill would show. The man commended pulling the robe instead of the under-sleeve, when Forrest, in a loud voice exclaimed: – "Hell and fury! what are you about? The under-sleeve, d — n you." Being near the first entrance, he was heard in front, and a round of applause followed – the audience imagining it part of the play. "What are they applauding?" exclaimed Forrest. The prompter promptly replied: – "Your first speech, sir, off the stage."

132 *Forrest did, however, have a charitable side to his character, as reflected, finally, in Louisa Lane Drew's affectionate recollection of an appearance she made with him in New York's Park Theatre.*

On one occasion, at the old Park Theatre, we were playing, as an afterpiece, "Therese, the Orphan of Geneva." He, as Carwin, rushes with a drawn dagger into the pavilion where he believes that Therese is sleeping. Immediately the place is struck by lightning; he then staggers out of the pavilion, exclaiming, "'Tis done; Therese is now no more." Then Therese enters and rushes into the pavilion to rescue her benefactress. On this occasion I, as Therese, rushed from the house before

Carwin had time to come out, and we met, face to face, in the apartment of the murdered countess, who had hardly finished screaming for her life. I was horror-stricken at my error. "Oh! horrors, Mr Forrest, what shall I do?" He smiled the beautiful smile which illuminated his face, and said: "Never mind. I'll go out by the back door!"

WILLIAM EWART GLADSTONE (1809–98)

133 *The Prime Minister often came to see Henry Irving's productions, usually ensconcing himself on the same cushioned seat by the corner of the stage. This particular visit, to a double bill starring Sir Henry, is described by Bram Stoker, Irving's personal manager and assistant at the Lyceum, his biographer, and also the author of* Dracula.

The Corsican Brothers was, so far as my knowledge goes, the first play – under Irving's management – which Mr Gladstone came to see. The occasion was January 3, 1881 – the first night when *The Cup* was played. He sat with his family in the box which we called in the familiar slang of the theatre "The Governor's Box" – the manager of a theatre is always the Governor to his colleagues of all kinds and grades. This box was the stage box on the stall level, next to the proscenium. It was shut off by a special door which opened with the pass key and thus, as it was approachable from the stage through the iron door and from the auditorum by the box door, it was easy of access and quite private. After *The Cup* Mr Gladstone wished to come on the stage and tell Irving and Ellen Terry how delighted he was with the performance. Irving fixed as the most convenient time the scene of the masked ball, as during it he had perhaps the only "wait" of the evening – a double part does not leave much margin to an actor. Mr Gladstone was exceedingly interested in everything and went all round the vast scene. Seeing during the progress of the scene that people in costumes were going in and out of queer little alcoves at the back of the scene he asked Irving what these were. He explained that they were the private boxes of the imitation theatre; and added that if the Premier would care to sit in one he could see the movement of the scene at close hand, and if he was careful to keep behind the little silk curtain he could not be seen. The statesman took his seat and seemed for a while to enjoy the life and movement going on in front of him. He could hear now and again the applause of the audience, and by peeping out through the chink behind the curtain, see them. At last in the excitement of the scene he forgot his situation and, hearing a more than usually vigorous burst of applause, leaned out to get a better view of the audience. The instant he did so he was recognised – there was no mistaking that eagle face – and then came a quick and sudden roar that seemed to shake the building. We could hear the "Bravo Gladstone!" coming through the detonation of hand-claps.*

WALTER LACY (1809–98)

134 *A good character actor who became Professor of Elocution at the Royal Academy of Music.*

My chief work in London was at the Princess's, where, in Mr Maddox's time, I often played twenty-four parts a week, such as the Gamin in "The Angel of the Attic," Charles Paragon in "The Little Devil," Alfred Highflyer, and Bounce in the "Ojibbeway Indians." On one occasion a laughable incident occurred. A party of Ojibbeways in the pit-box became suddenly so excited at witnessing my scalping Oxberry, as the "ring-tailed roarer of the backwoods," that uttering a war-whoop, they prepared to make a rush for the stage, but seeing me take the low comedian's wig off only, they all burst into peal after peal of laughter. With Charles Kean, I started a team of three – i.e. Rouble (original) in the "Prima Donna," Chateau Renaud in the "Corsican Brothers," and Alfred Highflyer in a "Roland for an Oliver," and ran them three months. These were brilliantly contrasted characters, affording splendid opportunity for an artist to establish himself. Of such an opportunity the severity of my early training, and the various experience of my career, enabled me to take full advantage. The author was to have ridden the middle horse, but owing to a difference with the management, my name was put in the cast at three days' notice. Fortunately I remembered being in a theatre in Paris in Louis Philippe's time (where I observed Dion Boucicault in a side box), when a man entered the parterre with hair and beard black as night, the hair cut close to the skull. I at once said to myself, "If ever I play a Frenchman, *that* shall be the head." It was odd that author, actor, and model should come together! I ordered the wig; wrote to Angelo, who, with prompt kindness came up from Brighton to his chambers in Curzon Street, where, after we had discussed a brief luncheon, we took off our coats, and in two hours I was able to master the combat with rapiers. After the first act of the "Prima Donna," Charles Kean came to my dressing-room to congratulate me on my "make-up" and acting in Rouble; and at the conclusion of the "Corsican Brothers" I was cheered by the whole house. The manager and manageress were delighted, and Mr Bayle Bernard came on the stage with the late Douglas Jerrold to compliment me on the "originality and finish of my acting." Next morning, Charles Mathews and Madame Vestris called me to their

---

*Winston Churchill was another Prime Minister who often visited the theatre. He sometimes bought three seats, one for himself, one for his daughter Mary, and one for his hat and coat.

carriage in the middle of Regent Street, and heartily congratulated me, Charles Mathews saying, "If that isn't a Frenchman, I don't know what is." My make-up hit the house, and was the keynote of the new rendering of the part.

CHARLES KEAN (1811–68)

135 *The son of Edmund Kean, he was meticulous about production standards.*

He was easily upset, when acting, by even a trifling noise. Years ago, in a seaport town he visited, a habit prevailed among the occupants of the gallery of cracking nuts throughout the performance. This played havoc with Kean when he acted there. On the following morning he called those who travelled with him together, and after loudly bewailing his sufferings and anathematising the gallery boys, gave instructions to his followers to go into the town and buy up every nut within its walls, either in the shops or on the quays. This was done. The result for the two following evenings was perfect success, crowned by the chuckles of the tragedian.

But oh, the third night! The fruiterers, perplexed by the sudden and unaccountable demand for nuts, had sent to Covent Garden and other sources for a plentiful supply to meet its hoped-for continuance; the demand fell off, there was a glut in the local market, the nuts so deluged the town that they were sold more abundantly and cheaper than ever. Crack! – crack! – crack! was the running fire throughout the succeeding performances, and the rest of Kean's engagement was fulfilled in torment.

The carpenters of country theatres always dreaded Charles Kean's advent among them, for, in his earlier days on the stage, when he rehearsed, he would steadily go through his own scenes just as at night. During this time silence was strictly ordered to be observed all over the theatre; a creaking boot, a cough, a sneeze, the knocking of a hammer, would distress the tragedian beyond measure. It was on pain of dismissal that any carpenter or other servant caused the smallest interruption during Mr Kean's scenes. This naturally caused much ill-humour amongst the men, and when it became known by the carpenters that "Kean was coming," there would be various expressions of discontent. At the commencement of one particular engagement these men formed a conspiracy amongst themselves. The opening play was *Hamlet*, and they conceived a plot by which the Royal Dane might be induced to "cut short" his long soliloquies. One particular man was to place himself at the back of the gallery, being quite hidden from sight, and just as Kean began his great soliloquy was to call out in a muffled voice to an imaginary fellow-workman. This was the result:

KEAN (in slow, measured tones): To be or *not* to be (long pause) – that is the question.

VOICE (far off in front of house, calling): Jo Attwood!

KEAN (stopping and looking in the direction, then commencing again): To be – or *not* – to – be – that is the question.

VOICE: Jo Attwood!

KEAN (bewildered and annoyed): Will somebody find Mr Attwood? (A pause.) To be or *not* to be – that is the question.

VOICE: Jo Attwood!

KEAN: Until Mr Attwood is found I cannot go on! "Mr Attwood" could *not* be found, and the voice did not cease interrupting Kean, who, at last, gave up his attempt to rehearse and went home; upon which the carpenters rejoiced in a sort of triumphant war-dance.

Sir Squire and Lady Bancroft

MR AND MRS ROBERT WYNDHAM
(his dates were 1814–94, hers are not known)

136 Mrs Robert Wyndham, the wife of the manager of the Theatre Royal, Edinburgh, was a remarkable woman. Her resourcefulness in getting out of a difficulty was most felicitous, as a story told me by Mr Harry Kemble, who was a member of their company at the time, will prove.

On a certain Friday evening she and her husband found themselves without sufficient money in the bank to meet the salaries at noon next day, when all the members of the company attended "treasury", as it used to be called. Having considered the accounts, Mrs Wyndham said to her husband: "You must go to — and get him to lend you a hundred pounds."

Mr Wyndham expostulated. In vain. His wife had the final word, as wives should; and as he had been well trained in husbandry, he went.

Mrs Wyndham put on her cloak and hat, went to the theatre and put the office clock forward half an hour. The moment it struck twelve, she left the treasury, that fatal treasury with nothing in it, and, locking the door after her, said to the first comer, "Late again! How terrible all this is; here have I been waiting until my patience is exhausted and I am not going to open the door again. I shall make a new rule. Anyone who is not here by twelve o'clock must wait until the evening for his salary. If I do this two or three times, perhaps the ladies and gentlemen will learn the meaning of the word 'punctuality.' "

Everybody was distressed at the inconvenience he or she had caused and then all apologised humbly to her for being late.

Mrs Wyndham hurried home and found that her husband had

borrowed the money. The various sums due to the actors were put out into small envelopes with their names written on them.

In the evening she handed each actor the appropriate envelope and with a most delightful smile said, "I have taught you your lesson to-day, and, perhaps, I may have to teach it to you again."

She was a genius, God bless her. She was a wife indeed.

Madge Kendal

ANNA CORA MOWATT (1819–70)

137 *Anna Cora ('Lily') Mowatt was an American actress and dramatist of considerable accomplishment. On one occasion in Cincinatti, in her early career, she found certain problems in* Romeo and Juliet.

The play also required properties: ladders, and daggers, and vials of sleeping-potion or poison. These presented complications. Lily developed a distinct complex about the dagger with which she kills herself in the final act. She invariably forgot it. Usually she could furtively extract Romeo's from his belt and make use of that, but this was hazardous. Her stabbing was always carried out with a certain realistic emphasis. Once, having forgotten her own weapon, she reached down for Romeo's, and holding it high above her head was about to plunge it against her bosom when the voice of the dead scion of the Montagues suddenly shattered the silence:

"Look out – it's very sharp!"

On another occasion Anna Cora almost came to grief with the sleeping-potion. At the last moment it was discovered by the property-man that he had forgotten the right kind of vial. Friar Laurence was just about to make his entrance to give Juliet the vial, and the distraught property-man seized the nearest small bottle he could find and gave it to the actor playing the Friar. The bottle was duly turned over to Juliet on the stage, with some whispered injunction of which Anna Cora caught only the words ". . . so take care". She thought no more about the matter until she had swallowed the potion. Then she noted a brilliant red stain on her fingers when they came away from her mouth. Viewed from the audience it must have been very picturesque. Lily's own reactions were less pleasant, when at the close of the scene the prompter rushed on, crying:

"Good gracious, you have been drinking from my bottle of ink!" She smiled bravely and uttered the words of the dying wit under similar circumstances:

"Let me swallow a sheet of blotting-paper . . ."

Eric Wollencott Barnes

JOHN JOHNSTONE (LESTER) WALLACK (1820–88)

138 *The Wallack family, of English origin, were instrumental in the development of the theatre in New York. James Wallack bought the New York Lyceum in 1852, renaming it Wallack's. During the 1860s his nephew John Johnstone, who took the stage name of Lester, maintained the tradition of staging mainly English plays there, particularly T.W. Robertson's comedies, despite the demand for plays of American origin and significance. Before reaching America, however, Lester Wallack had spent some time in Dublin, experiencing the 'outspoken criticism, shrewdness and humour' of the Dublin gallery (what Gordon Craig later called, less politely, 'the roughest public known to the northern world').*

I remember one particular occasion when a man named Morrison, who led the chorus, a gigantic fellow and very ugly, afforded no little amusement to the audience and his fellow-singers. We had at that period what are called "Ticket Nights." After the benefits of the regular performers the underlings of the theatre, the leader of the chorus, the ushers in front and the ticket takers, would have a benefit in common, when it was the custom to give them half the receipts; the manager doing it because he knew perfectly well that the house would be jammed full to the ceiling, as the beneficiaries sold their tickets among their friends and in great quantities. The curious part was the fact that the ushers and ticket takers, who, of course, never played anything themselves, made up for it by pestering the management for some particular play which they preferred. The people on the stage, chorus singers, etc., naturally wanted to do something, to get a chance they never had in any other part of the season. This man Morrison, who, by the way, was known as "Nigger Morrison," because of his dusky complexion, had a baritone voice and insisted upon singing a ballad between the acts on this particular "Ticket Night." Now the occupants of the gallery were original in their methods and ingenious in the application of them. They would wait until there was a gap in the play, as there always is, and then say their say. The expected chance came when Morrison went on and began: "Oh, I was young and lovely once" – pausing a moment to draw his breath. "And a bloody long toime ago it must have been, Morrison, me boy!" was the response from the gods. There was no more song for Morrison!

139 *Wallack recounts two slips of the tongue at moments of high drama, the first in a production of Lord Lytton's* Money, *the second during a run of* The School for Scandal.

Some of the experiences in my profession are very amusing. There are many instances of misapplication of a word or of a too quick inclination to carry a joke or a telling line to the audience. There was an old actor named Harry Hunt. He was a bass singer and was the husband of the present Mrs John Drew. Hunt was playing with us at the Broadway Theatre when I first came here. The play was "Money." George Vandenhoff played Evelyn and I Sir Frederick Blount. In the celebrated gambling scene there is a character called the Old Member, who has nothing to do but to call continually for the snuff-box. When Sir Edward Bulwer wrote that play I often thought how curious it was that in a first-class club there should be only one snuff-box. The characters, as they got excited, kept taking the snuff-box off the table. The Old Member is reading the paper all the time. Presently he looks for the snuff-box, and it is gone. He calls out to the waiter: "Waiter, the snuff-box!" and the servant goes to Blount, or whoever has taken it, and puts it back on the table. Hunt never was perfect in the words of anything he played; but on this occasion he had before him, inside the newspaper, all the cues and his own part; so he had nothing to do but read it, and he was determined to be right for once. When the scene is culminating, in the midst of all the confusion and the roar that is caused by certain necessities of the play, the last thing that is heard is this Old Member shouting: "Waiter, the snuff-box!" There was a momentary pause, when Hunt hallooed out: "Waiter, the buff-snox!" Of course, the scene closed with more laughter than ever before.

Another very curious thing of that sort occurred to me when I was playing Charles Surface at Wallack's Theatre. An actor named H. B. Phillips was Crabtree, and in the scene in which Crabtree and Sir Benjamin Backbite come on with the mass of scandal and stuff and a lot of information with regard to what has previously occurred in the four acts, they proceed to say, "Have you heard the news?" and so on. They are describing this thing, and, of course, telling all sorts of stories that are not a bit true; and Sir Benjamin Backbite, who is the first to enter, has to say, "Then Charles and Sir Peter began to fight with swords," and Crabtree rushes on, "Pistols, nephew; pistols, nephew," all of which is, of course, false. Sir Benjamin says: "Oh, no, no, no, no; then Sir Peter was wounded. I know it was swords, because he was wounded with a thrust in the *seconde*." "No, no, no, no," the other says; "a bullet in the thorax, a bullet in the thorax," and he was so anxious that he said, "No, no, no, no, a thullet in the borax!" Very curious to say, the audience hardly noticed this then, and would not have noticed it at all but for John Brougham, who never spared anybody (he was playing Sir Oliver Surface), and who said directly: "What the devil is his borax?"

140 *Wallack recalls how singularly prejudiced the old managers were against anything like an innovation.*

It was thought an extraordinary thing when Garrick first put on a pair

of Elizabethan trunks for *Richard III*. He played Macbeth in a squarecut
scarlet coat, the costume of an English general, and a regulation wig with
a pigtail of his own period, while Mrs Pritchard, who played Lady
Macbeth wore an enormous hoop. Garrick desired very much to wear
a Scotch tartan and kilt, and a plaid, with bare legs, the traditional
Highland costume. But this was in the days of the Pretender, when no
one was allowed to show a plaid in the streets of London. After Garrick
had brought in a great deal of wise reform in the way of dress there was
a lull again, and no one dared to do anything new. Many generations
later my father was cast for the part of Tressel, in Cibber's version of
"Richard III." Tressel is the youthful messenger who conveys to King
Henry VI the news of the murder of his son after the battle of Tewkesbury.
My father, a young, ambitious actor, came on with the feather hanging
from his cap, all wet, his hair dishevelled, one boot torn nearly off, one
spur broken, the other gone entirely, his gauntlet stained with blood,
and his sword snapped in twain; at which old Wewitzer, who was the
manager, and had been a manager before my father was born, was
perfectly shocked. It was too late to do anything then, but the next
morning Wewitzer sent for him to come to his office, and addressed him
thus: "Young man, how do you ever hope to get on in your profession
by deliberately breaking all precedent? What will become of the profession
if mere boys are allowed to take these liberties? Why, sir, you should
have entered in a suit of decent black, with silk stockings on and with a
white handkerchief in your hand." "What! after defeat and flight from
battle?" interrupted my father. "That has nothing at all to do with it,"
was the reply; "the proprieties! Sir, the proprieties!"*

DION BOUCICAULT (1820–90)

141 *He found success early with* London Assurance, *a five-act comedy produced in 1841 at
Covent Garden, using the very first 'box' set.** In the first passage here, Lester Wallack
recalls the opening night. Further plays, like* The Corsican Brothers *and* Louis XI,
*followed during the next decade. In 1853 Boucicault eloped with Charles Kean's ward to
New York where they acted together and he, appreciating the demand for 'the actual, the
contemporaneous, the photographic', wrote a string of successful melodramas.* The
Shaughraun, *mentioned in the second passage, dates from 1874 and helped to establish
Boucicault as the principal Anglo-Irish dramatist of his time.*

Talking of "London Assurance," I remember standing behind the scenes
at the Haymarket one night during the run of Bulwer's [Lord Lytton]

---

*'The audience was satisfied', Wallack adds, 'even if the management was not'.

**With scenery on three sides of the stage in place of the former 'wings', an innovation that
should be attributed to the manager of Covent Garden, Madame Vestris. It was this innovation
that led Tom Robertson to write the first drawing-room comedies.

"Money," then at the very zenith of its first and great success, when some one came hurrying in and announced, "An enormous hit at Covent Garden; the third act is over and it is tremendous. If the other two acts go in the same way it is an immense go." This was "London Assurance." I saw it the second night. It was really the first time that the perfection of the modern boxed-in scenery was displayed to the public. It was most beautifully done; I can see the whole thing now, the scenes and everything. It was, as I have said, something quite novel; and was of course a great success. When the curtain went down on the first act, the first night, there was a dead silence. It is a very ineffective ending and the scene was simply an anteroom in which there was no chance for very great display; but when the curtain rose on the second act, the outside of "Oak Hall," there was an enormous amount of applause; and that act went with the most perfect "snap." The audience was in good humour from the moment of the entrance of that most perfect actress, Mrs Nisbett, as Lady Gay, for whom Boucicault wrote that part. He describes her as the seventh daughter of an earl, the baby of the family, married to a man considerably older than herself. Mrs Nisbett's tall, lovely figure, her baby face, her silvery laugh, carried the whole house; while the contrast with Keely, who was the original Dolly was delicious. He was a country squire of about forty years of age, dressed to perfection in his top-boots, etc. The fault of all later Dollys is that they are made to look and act too young. The first cast of "London Assurance" was a wonderful one throughout, even to the actor who played Cool, Mr Brindal; and to the afterwards celebrated Alfred Wigan, who played Solomon Isaacs, and had about four words to say. That *ensemble* was one of the most perfect I ever saw. It had for that time a very great run, and it built up the declining fortunes of Covent Garden.

142 Now, I will say something by way of anecdote to show how utterly unnecessary it is for you to bother your minds so much about your dress. I was producing *The Shaughraun* in New York. I generally had enough to employ my time. I get the actors and actresses to study their characters, and generally leave myself to the last. But the last morning before the play was produced I saw my dresser hobbling about, but afraid to come to the stage. At last he said, "Have you thought of your costume?" I said I had not done any such thing. It was about three o'clock in the afternoon, and I had to play about seven o'clock in the evening. I went upstairs, and said, "Have you got a red coat?" "Yes, we have got a uniform red hunting coat." "Oh, that is of no use!" "We have got one that was used in *She Stoops to Conquer*." That was brought, but it had broad lapels, and looked to belong to about one hundred and fifty years ago. "Oh!" said the man, "there is an old coat that was worn by Mr Beckett as Goldfinch."

When he came to that it reached all down to my feet, and was too long in the sleeves. So I cut them off with a big pair of shears, and by the shears and the scissors I got some sort of a fit. Then I got an old hunting cap, a pair of breeches, and sent for some old boots that cost about 2s 6d, and did not fit me, and that is how I came on the stage. The editor of one of the newspapers said, "Where on earth did you get that extraordinary costume from?"

Dion Boucicault

RACHEL (ÉLISA FÉLIX) (1821–48)

143 *Rachel, the French actress, was one of the greatest tragediennes of all time. She made her London debut in 1841, went to America in 1855, encountered critical audiences, and returned to France suffering from consumption.*

Rachel, though fancy-free, to be sure, evidently was still subject to the ties of blood. When her adored sister [Rebecca] died, friends came to her house to inform her of the tragedy. On hearing the terrible news, she fell in a dead faint and could not be revived for quite some minutes. When she regained consciousness and found herself lying on a chaise, she realized what had transpired and became extremely agitated. Her genuine grief was replaced by her professional need to examine it. Her companions began to console her but she sat up and shouted, "What did I do? How did I fall? Did I distort my face in any way? Tell me!"

She had truly loved her sister and she had truly fainted, but she was an actress. That special eye. That insatiable curiosity. It is both terrible and marvelous.

Helen Hayes

BARRY SULLIVAN (1821–91)

144 *Tragedian who made tours of America and Australia and was for a while lessee of the Holborn Theatre. George Bernard Shaw preferred him to Henry Irving.*

Barry was giving this impersonation one night at Portsmouth to an audience largely composed of the breeziest British sailors, who had been "revelling" before arriving. After listening to the tragedy of *Hamlet* with commendably little interruption, suddenly, when Barry started "To be or not to be" one of the Jack tars in the gallery stopped him, and shouted, "Hi, Barry, give us a hornpipe!"

Barry scowled, as only he could scowl, at the irreverent interrupter, and started to continue his soliloquy, when several other Jack tars took up the cry, and said, "Yes . . . give us a hornpipe, Barry! . . . " Then added a deep-voiced mariner, "Mind as it's the sailor's one!"

This demand being repeated rather peremptorily Barry felt it his duty to step down to the footlights and to reprove these dance demanders! Having done so, he returned to the throne chair and resumed the great soliloquy on Life and Death, when a Herculean tar from a corner of the gallery shouted, "'Ere, Barry! . . . are you going to give me and my friends that hornpipe or am I to come down and make yer?"

Barry, by this time inwardly convulsed with laughter at this extraordinary joke, retorted: "Gentlemen, as you insist upon my performing a Sailor's Hornpipe in the midst of this sublime tragedy, I will e'en do so."

And Barry did it! And he did it well, for, like most of the tragedians of his time, he had gone through the theatrical mill so much and had played Black-Eyed Susan's William* so often, that to dance a hornpipe at a moment's notice was the most natural thing in the world.

Having thus performed this famous dance to the tune of "Jack Robinson," Barry Sullivan resumed his tragic and touching impersonation of Hamlet without further interruption!

H. Chance Newton

145 *Sullivan was involved in the opening of the Shakespeare Festival at Stratford-upon-Avon in 1879.*

When Charles Edward Flower, of the brewing family, proposed the erection of a permanent Memorial in Stratford, he was called presumptuous and foolish by the day's professional critics, their horizon bounded on one side by Leicester Square, on the other by Clare Market. For them a rumble of wheels in the Strand spelt life; the ripple of the Avon nothing but bucolic boredom. Flower, like his father a man of character, sent the work forward, personally subscribing much of the cost of the 'striped sugar-stick' theatre, with its plum-cake turrets and gables, its walls of staring brick, that rose in Stratford for the Birthday of 1879. It cost twenty thousand pounds: a motley block, half-timbered, and from a distance flimsy, as if it were a cardboard cut-out against the sky. Within, its stage was cramped; but it managed to be a friendly place, excellent for speaking and listening, and able to seat 800 persons on the ground floor and in dress circle and gallery. This Memorial began its life on a drenching night in 1879, with Barry Sullivan as the Benedick of *Much Ado About Nothing.* Helen Faucit, in her farewell to the stage, was Beatrice. Sullivan, relentless heavy-weight actor and sympathetic man, could be domineering in the theatre. At Stratford, though he gave a hundred guineas to the fund and refused to take a fee, he became

---

*William is the sailor hero of Douglas Jerrold's *Black-Ey'd Susan*, probably the most famous nautical melodrama of the nineteenth century.

something of a bore. Charles Flower fitted up the theatre green-room as a dressing-room for Helen Faucit, who was there for only one night. Sullivan, observing this, would not appear unless his dressing-room was similarly arranged. 'You, my dear', said Charles Flower gravely to his wife, 'must send across silver candlesticks, vases of flowers, and a lace pincushion for Mr Sullivan.'

J.C. Trewin

J. B. HOWE (1828–1908)

146 *This string of disasters is told by Howe in his autobiography* A Cosmopolitan Actor.

When the 'bus arrived at the Eyre Arms, I saw several of the company waiting to receive me. It was now twenty-five minutes past eight.

"What's the meaning of this? Not dressed? My G – !"

Judge of my horror when I alighted being saluted with — "Oh, my boy, my dear fellow! We were just giving you up altogether. Wherever have you been?"

"Where? don't ask me now," I gasped; "but why are you not dressed?"

"What was the use of dressing without Hamlet?"

"What are they doing, then?" I asked, and Crauford answered:

"Why, there's a Mr — (I forget the name now) on the stage reciting the soliloquy upon death."

He had already got through several others.

"There is! Well, of all the infernal impudence!"

This was said while we were running along towards the Abbey, out of breath, indignant, furious, raving. I arrived at the top of the balcony at the entrance door facing the stage, when I saw and heard the gentleman named uttering the last three or four lines of the soliloquy.

I shouted at the top of my voice –

"Go off, sir; go off! How dare you?"

And there ensued, as might be expected, a perfect babel of tongues in an instant. Suffice that I mounted to the stage and claimed the attention of the audience for a few minutes while I briefly stated the dilemma I had been placed in by the untimely arrival of the wardrobe, and politely claimed their indulgence while the artists were fitly costumed, and then we would go through the entire tragedy from beginning to end.

This announcement was received with *éclat*, and I descended to the "realms of darkness" beneath the stage to dress with the rest, when – Well, can you imagine? – no, of course you can't – my torture on being told that Mr Frank Huntly, who had promised so faithfully to get permission from his manager at the Bower to do the Ghost, had given it up at the last moment. What was I to do?

"I'll do the Ghost," said Crauford, "and here is a young gentleman, who knows almost every line of the piece, who can go on for Laertes."

This was "his nibbs" who had been spouting during my absence, and for whom I did not feel at that moment the most cherished friendship. However, what was I to do? I consented. The piano and cornet had been going it ever since the announcement. The audience were getting more impatient every instant. Crauford took off his Laertes dress and began to put on the "complete steel" (made of grey glazed lining) of the Ghost, the helmet was at least a little more real (papier maché); and while we were thus engaged he loquaciously informed me that he didn't know a line.

Here was another crusher!

Never mind. I was equal to the occasion. I knew every line of at least the "Platform Scene," so I told him simply to go on at the proper cues, and I would speak for him as well as myself. After a long delay – it was now nine o'clock – the little bell went, and by my direction the bed curtains were drawn from the centre to the sides, and all the artists clung to each other as far out of sight as the gap between the tables and the wall would allow.

When the play commenced in earnest everything went swimmingly. When your humble servant made his appearance – well, my "natural modesty forbids, &c."; however, it was, candidly speaking, all right.

Mind, I am supposing that you here know the first, second, and third scenes are over; we are now into the "Platform Scene". The dialogue went all right, and I believe not one of the spectators ever dreamt but that it was Crauford himself speaking the Ghost's lines, as I artfully turned my head to the back each time I had to do the ventriloquial for him, and as persistently faced the audience whilst uttering the heart-rendering speeches of the melancholy Dane.

When I had to speak the last lines of the Ghost, "Adieu! Adieu! remember me," I put in an aside to every word thus – "Adieu! (step back) Adieu! (farther) remember (go on) me." Crauford took step after step as instructed, until, not thinking of the treacherous gap at the side of the wall, he fell backwards off the edge of the table stage, and as a drowning man will clutch at a straw so did the poor Ghost clutch at the bed curtains, and down came the whole of the proscenium, exposing to view all the company, who at once tried to rush off the tables through the door at the back in the wall leading to the private house of the proprietor.

I have heard laughter in my time, and have often been the means of creating it in the various rôles I have assumed; but no shout ever greeted my ears equalled for length or strength the continued roar of that night. And the incident appeared so ludicrous to me that, notwithstanding the former annoyance I had been subjected to, I literally had to hold my sides with laughter, while poor Will Crauford lay in the gap, with his helmet off, part of his body down the gap and his heels in the air, the chintz curtains tightly clutched in his hands forming a sort of tent over him. Whether he was enjoying the fun underneath I could not say.

After the roaring was over, I put in an amendment to the text thus –
"Remember thee? Yea, thou poor ghost; I shall never forget thee!"
Nor have I, as the above lines, I hope, fully prove.

JOSEPH JEFFERSON (1829–1905)

147 *Jefferson imbibed his theatrical expertise during tours around America. He became an overnight success in* Our American Cousin *in 1858. Boucicault then hired him for the 1859 New York season at the Winter Garden Theatre, where he created the role of Salem Scudder in Boucicault's* The Octoroon – *keeping himself fit during rehearsals by sparring in his dressing room with an ex-professional boxer.*

Among the well-remembered characters of my dramatic life was an actor named Salisbury. The only influence that he exerted upon the stage during his career was, I regret to say, anything but a good one. "Guying" was formerly a slang term, but it has of late years become a technical one for trifling with a part upon the stage. The art of guying was Mr Salisbury's forte, and it was the only thing that he did well. Life was one huge joke to him: he treated nothing seriously. He was the delight of actors and the bane of managers. It is related of him that he once sent a telegram to Mr Rice of the Chicago Theatre applying for an engagement. The manager sent back this answer: "I would not engage you if you would come for nothing"; to which Salisbury replied: "Terms accepted. Will be with you to-morrow."

This man's memory was so wonderful that it was almost impossible to ask him a question without getting a Shakespearean quotation in reply. If he was imperfect in his part, which was generally the case with him, he would interpolate speeches from other characters, talking the most absurd nonsense, and turning a serious scene into ridicule. Sometimes the audience, detecting this impertinence, would hiss. This rebuke was the only thing that would check him, for any slight put upon himself was keenly felt; but the next night the chastisement would be forgotten, and he would repeat his indiscretion. It was said of him that he was generous to a fault; and I think he must have been, for he never paid his washerwoman. One morning the poor old laundress was dunning him for her hard earnings. He was standing at the stage door, surrounded by a circle of admirers, and turning furiously upon the old woman, he paraphrased *Macbeth's* speech to the ghost of *Banquo* in the following words: "Avaunt, and quit my sight! Thy tubs are marrowless; there is no starch in my fine shirts that thou didst glare withal! Approach thou like the Russian manager, the Hyrcan critic, or the 'Old Rye whisky-us'; or, be alive again, and make it salary day. If, trembling then, I do inhibit thee, confess me but a babe of a Salisbury." The laundress fled in despair, only too glad to escape unpaid from the supposed lunatic.

148 *After the death of his first wife in 1861 Jefferson visited Australia where, for four years, he was a great success in* The Octoroon *and in the play for which he is best known,* Rip Van Winkle.

My engagement at the Princess [in Melbourne] extended to one hundred and sixty-four consecutive nights. At its conclusion my agent and I dissolved our temporary partnership, he assuming the management of the new Haymarket Theatre, and I going into the small mining and provincial towns to reap the benefit of the reputation I had acquired in the two larger cities. Ballarat, Bendigo, and Adelaide had all good stock companies, and were visited in their turn, generally with pleasant and profitable results.

During this provincial tour I was acting in one of the mining towns called Castlemaine, and after tea as I was strolling leisurely towards the theater my ears were suddenly saluted by the violent ringing of a bell, and a sonorous bass voice roaring out my name in full. I looked in the direction of this unaccountable noise and saw a little fat man, in a high white hat and a seedy suit of black, standing on a barrel in front of the theater and surrounded by a crowd of boys. Gesticulating violently with his left hand, he swung in the right an enormous bell. Now suddenly stopping, he seemed to swell and got red in the face as he delivered himself of the following: "Oh, yes! Oh, yes! Oh, yes! Step up, ladies and gentlemen; now or never is your only chance to see the greatest living wonder of the age, Joseph Jefferson, the great hactor from Amerikee. His power of producing tears and smiles at vun and the same time is so great that he caused the Emperor of Roushia to weep on his weddin' night, and made her gracious Majesty the Queen bu'st out laughin' at the funeral of Prince Albert. He is the bosom friend of the President of Amerikee and the hidol of 'is Royal 'Ighness the Prince of Wales."

I always had a horror of orators. They are seldom sincere, and never hesitate to say the wrong thing instead of the right one if they can say it best. To most of them epigram is more sacred than truth, and we are often so fascinated with the manner that we forget somewhat the matter. It must have been the comical earnestness and bombastic attitude of this extraordinary creature that had interested the crowd; certainly they did not believe what he was saying, for they were roaring with laughter at every word, while his face was as serious as the fifth act of a tragedy. At this juncture I rushed into the theater and demanded that the manager should make the bellman stop. "Why, we always have it done here, and thought you'd like it," replied the manager.

"Like it!" said I. "If he is not stopped at once I shall not act." So the little fat man was ordered to cease his harangue and come down from his barrel: but no, he said he wouldn't budge; he wasn't half through, and it would injure his business and ruin his reputation to be cut off "in the heye of the public," and he would "be blowed" if he stirred till he finished. The manager now appealed to me to let him go on. "Now, mark me," said I. "If he rings that bell again, or opens his mouth, I don't act." This settled it. The little fat man now stood with his arms folded, glaring defiance at the manager and his myrmidons, but they seized him and a tremendous struggle ensued. The tall white hat was completely mashed over his eyes, and in stamping violently with his rage the head of the barrel burst in, letting him through till only a fat head just appeared above the top. They tipped the barrel over and rolled him off inside, to the great amusement of the bystanders, who had been roaring with laughter all the time.

149 *Jefferson stopped in London in 1865 on his way home to America to put on* Rip Van Winkle *at the Adelphi. The intensity of 'the most important dramatic moment of my life' was clear for all to see.*

On Sunday evening, being alone in my lodgings, I got out for my own admiration my new wig and beard – the pride of my heart – which I was to use in the last act. I could not resist trying them on for the twentieth time, I think; so I got in front of the glass and adjusted them to my perfect satisfaction. I soon became enthused, and began acting and posing in front of the mirror. In about twenty minutes there came a knock at the door.

"Who's there?" said I.

"It's me, if you please," said the gentle but agitated voice of the chambermaid. "May I come in?"

"Certainly not," I replied; for I had no desire to be seen in my present make-up.

"Is there anything wrong in the room, sir?" said she.

"Nothing at all. Go away," I replied.

"Well, sir," she continued, "there's a policeman at the door, and he says as 'ow there's a crazy old man in your room, a-flingin' of his 'arnds and a-goin' on hawful, and there's a crowd of people across the street a-blockin' up the way."

I turned towards the window, and to my horror I found that I had forgotten to put down the curtain, and, as it seemed to me, the entire population of London was taking in my first-night. I had been unconsciously acting with the lights full up, to an astonished audience who had not paid for their admission. As I tore off my wig and beard a shout went up. Quickly pulling down the curtain, I threw myself in a chair, overcome with mortification at the occurrence. In a few minutes the comical side of the picture presented itself, and I must have laughed for half an hour. I had been suffering from an attack of nervous dyspepsia, consequent upon the excitement of the past week, and I firmly believe that this continuous fit of laughter cured me.

150 *Tom Robertson, the English playwright, dined frequently with Jefferson while he was in London. One night, after Jefferson's performance had ended, they slipped round to see the last two acts of* Macbeth *at Drury Lane.*

We arrived at the theater just at the opening of the fourth act, and ensconced ourselves snugly in a private box. It seemed that matters had gone wrong during the whole play, and when mishaps do occur in the earlier scenes of a drama, particularly a Shakesperean one, they are apt to continue to the end. We were seated well back in the private box and could enjoy the tragedy without being observed, which as it happened was quite fortunate. The solemn cave scene opened with the three witches at their ghastly work about the caldron. Mr Phelps, as Macbeth, came upon the stage with the martial stride and dignity that characterized this excellent actor, and the weird sisters summoned their phantom confederates to appear. At last one of the apparitions slowly rose to the surface only to disappear suddenly without giving Macbeth warning or receiving any himself; there was a slight crash, but nobody was hurt. Next came the passing by of the six ghostly kings, the first one of whom lost his crown, and in stopping to recover it was run down by the other five monarchs, who came so rapidly upon the heels of their leader that the several dynasties were all in a heap, creating a spiritual revolution that fairly convulsed the audience.

In the last scene, just as Mr Phelps had given orders to have his banners hung on the outer wall, that frail edifice gave way before it was besieged, and tumbled the king of Scotland into the middle of the stage, where, with uplifted claymore and in a sitting posture, he presented a sight of harmless indignation that would have revenged Macduff for the murder of his entire family.

I have no idea what ever became of the tyrant after this, for Tom and I were compelled to flee from the theater and seek some dark alley in Drury Lane, where we pounded each other in the exuberance of our mirth.

LAURA KEENE (c. 1830–73)

151 *English-born actress who was the first woman in America to become a manager. Her career was characterized by a delicacy of charm and taste, although her greatest claim to fame lies in a very different quarter.*

Though she made no lasting impression on the American theatre and though her popularity and success declined long before she quit the stage, her name is associated with the careers of many great stars of the American theatre, her acting was a worthy example of feminine charm and emotionalism, and her name is forever linked with American history because she was the star of the play being presented in Ford's Theatre the night Abraham Lincoln was assassinated, and she was the one who recognized John Wilkes Booth as he made his escape and who, it is said, held the dying President's head in her lap until he was carried from the theatre.

Garff B. Wilson

EDWIN BOOTH (1833–93)

152 *During Booth's record-breaking run as Hamlet at the Winter Garden Theater, his brother, John Wilkes Booth (who, a year later, was to assassinate Abraham Lincoln) confided, 'Between ourselves, he is Hamlet – melancholy and all.' Edwin was dogged by this disposition throughout his life, through domestic grief (his first wife died early, the second went mad), the shame of his brother's national crime and financial catastrophes. Nevertheless for thirty years he reigned as the leading tragic actor of the American stage.*

In 1845 the Booths were living on North Front Street, but a year later moved to a home on Exeter Street, where a spacious arbor in the back yard served as a theatre in which many ambitious youths who grew to be prominent actors played their first parts. There they performed, before select juvenile audiences, classic and romantic dramas with the female rôles left out. Edwin organized the company and was its manager. Booth's [his father] disapproval soon forced them to move to a cellar in Triplet Alley.

The cellar was under a hotel kept by John Lutz (afterward associated with Laura Keene), who knew nothing of the rental arrangements they had made with his Negro janitor by promising him all the pennies he collected at the door. The admission fee was three cents for reserved seats, one cent for standing room, and there was no free list. Edwin was the star, George L. Stout was prompter and leading man, and Sleepy Clarke, as he was called, was stage manager. Other company members included Theodore Hamilton, Summerfield Barry, Samuel Knapp Chester, and Henry Stuart, who was to be known professionally as Stuart Robson.

Stage properties and funds to promote the venture were obtained by borrowing surreptitiously from their elders. Robson's mother had an old iron stove which was not in use, and the others pointed out to him that he might add something to the treasury by turning it into cash. The fact that his mother never spared the rod on a certain part of his anatomy made him hesitate, but the sale was finally accomplished and the money used to buy an abandoned set piece from a resort at Fell's Point. By some such means, they financed also the purchase of an old nag at the horse market and hired an organ-grinder to fill in as orchestra.

Edwin, whose great desire was to be a clown in a circus, was advertised to perform a daring equestrian act on the opening night, but when they got the old nag into the ring and Edwin was lifted onto his back the horse refused to budge. Efforts to force him into action had no effect, until a rasping tune from the hand organ sent him gallivanting around the circle. One boy's father owned a livery stable, and unknowingly, furnished feed for the animal, who grew so fat that they had to remove a partition to get him out. An account of these Triplet Alley days was given by George L. Stout in his *Recollections:*

> It was in this cellar that Edwin Booth made his first appearance as *Richard III*, and a tragedy indeed it turned out to be. He was anxious to get armour and finally solved the puzzle by getting pieces of oilcloth and covering them with large spangles cut from the gaberdine worn by his father as *Shylock*. He cut up the garment and transferred the spangles without detection, and had made beautiful armour. Unfortunately, just about this time the old man had a sudden call to play *Shylock*, and in looking over his wardrobe discovered the loss. He went at once to Wilkes and began thrashing him without more ado, promising to keep up until told who did the mischief. On this hint, Wilkes spoke, and confessed that Edwin was responsible, moreover, that he was at the moment wearing the stolen ornaments. The old man lost no time in hastening to the cellar, but was held up at the door by the janitor, who refused to let him pass without the tribute of three cents. Whereupon Booth pitched into the negro and fought his way to the cellar, his anger now at boiling point. Edwin was just saying, "A horse! A horse! My kingdom for a horse!" before an entranced audience, when he heard the well known voice. With a lightning appreciation of his father's form blocking the door, he made a wild dash for the window. He got half way through when the armor stuck, and the old man began to "lay on" with a vigor that produced realistic shrieks from *Richard* who was on the other side of the window being tugged vigorously by a policeman, who thought he was climbing out of the window with burglarious spoils! Between his father and the policeman, poor Edwin was literally torn with contending emotions.

The plays were so well patronized by the boys and girls of the neighbourhood that they were kept up for several weeks, and the Negro often took in more than a dollar at each performance. But rivalry among members of the company divided them and led to much trouble. Robson and Hamilton organized another group, claimed all the stage properties they had scraped together, and stole the set. Edwin and his associates fought them and got it back. They foiled further attempts with clubs and sticks, and moved it, when not in use, to a secret hiding place.

Stanley Kimmel

153 As a means of gaining truth and conviction in his performances, Booth tried to "think himself" into his roles. He attempted, imaginatively, to *become* the characters so he could better understand how they felt. On nights when he could not sleep, he let the moods of his roles "flood through his mind." Before a performance, he tried to avoid distractions which might break his mood. One night in the "Tubal scene" of *The Merchant of Venice*, the actress playing Jessica watched the scene from the wings where Booth could see her. When the scene was over, Booth asked her never to do it again, explaining: "I go into that scene with a clear picture of Jessica. My own flesh and blood has betrayed me . . . I am deserted . . . I am hopeless – alone. I charge my voice with Shylock's agony, and then look up and see you – my daughter – standing before me, come back to me. My picture breaks up! I lose my scene!"

Garff B. Wilson

HENRY JAMES BYRON (1834–84)

154 *Under Byron's régime, theatres in Liverpool and in London, such as the Strand Theatre and the Prince of Wales's Theatre, were famous for satire and burlesque (which on the nineteenth-century English stage took the form of a spirited parody of some play that was currently popular).*

It was during Byron's lesseeship of the Theatre Royal, Liverpool, that he made an astounding *mot* to his box-office keeper. Barry Sullivan, the tragedian, who was one of the greatest provincial stars of his time, was due to open at Byron's house in his famous impersonation of Richard III.* He gave a great performance in this part, I believe, and held the house spellbound when he cried: "Off with his head; so much for Buckingham."

Business had not been too good during the season, and, as Sullivan was an enormous attraction, Byron put on an extra fee for reserving seats. It was with delight, therefore, that he saw a lengthy queue waiting at the box office to book for the coming engagement. As he stood happily

---

*Colley Cibber's version, not Shakespeare's; see above p. 18.

watching the number of people who wanted stalls increasing every moment, he heard an altercation begin, which soon developed from a wrangle into a row. Becoming anxious to know what was the matter, he elbowed his way up to the box-office and inquired of the clerk what all the trouble was about. "It's no good, Mr. Byron," the man said; "they won't stand for it." "Stand for what?" said Byron. "Why," shouted an infuriated playgoer, "stand paying an extra shilling for booking seats for 'Richard III.' " "Oh, well," said Byron, "if that's all it is, it shall be remedied"; and wearily turning to his manager he said: "Off with the 'bob'; so much for booking 'em!"

It was a wonderful quip and undoubtedly deserved full marks.

Sir Squire and Lady Bancroft

155 When his play *Dearer than Life* was produced at another theatre, in which both Irving and Toole had parts, all had gone well until the end of the second act, after which there was a long delay. The audience grew more and more impatient, the band played waltz after waltz, still the curtain was not taken up. Byron was walking uneasily up and down the corridor at the back of the dress circle, chafing over the mishap, and tugging, as he always did when agitated, at one side of his moustache, when a friendly critic asked, "What, in the name of goodness, are they doing?" "I don't know," moaned Byron. At that moment the sound of a saw, hard at work behind the scenes, was heard above the uproar – saw-saw-saw! "I think they must be cutting out the last act," he said.

Seymour Hicks

SIR CHARLES WYNDHAM (1837–1919)

156 During the run of *David Garrick*, the play which opened the new Wyndham's Theatre in 1899, and in which the actor-manager portrayed the title part of the great English actor of the eighteenth century, Wyndham used to spend his afternoon sitting in the Garrick Club next to the bust of Garrick there. One day another member went up to the gallant-looking old actor. "You get more and more like Garrick every day," he assured him. "And less and less like him every night."

Cedric Hardwicke

AUGUSTIN DALY (1838–99)

157 *For the last forty years of the nineteenth century this critic, manager, director and playwright was the leading figure of the American stage. Daly had an innate sense of theatre, not*

always matched by dramatic finesse, but one that ensured widespread success at home, in London and in Europe.

Within a year or two the lease of the New York Theatre passed to one William Worrell, formerly a circus acrobat or clown, who had saved money, and with the aid of a good wife had reared three daughters – Sophia, Irene, and Jennie – for the stage. Mr. Daly, having the scheme of a new sensational play in his head, offered to hire the theatre for a summer season. Even at the present day a New York manager would yield at least half the gross receipts for such an enterprise (in which he took no risk); but the shrewd old circus man, seeing the enthusiasm of young Daly, offered him a quarter of the gross and it was accepted.

The play Daly had in mind was to be called "Under the Gaslight," and was destined to become immediately famous and to hold the stage from that time to the present, to be imitated even by Boucicault, the master of stage sensation, and to be played in every country under various disguises. As we walked home one night, discussing the need of a culminating incident, my brother said: "I have got the sensation we want – a man fastened to a railroad track and rescued just as the train reaches the spot!"

The class of plays presenting some feature of physical peril and rescue were familiar, and usually called in disparagement the "sensational drama" – as if every great play were not in one sense a sensational drama. The murder of Cæsar and the harangue of Antony to the mob are colossal sensations, as is the Ghost in "Hamlet" and the play within the play, and, above all, the scene of the attempted mutilation of little Arthur in "King John." The screen scene in "The School for Scandal" is one of the greatest of sensations. Without some episode to hold the spectator in breathless suspense no drama can be successful. Whether the effect be produced with or without the aid of scenic adjuncts and of action is not important. With regard to this new play, the effect was wrought by moral agencies which were potent without the climax of the visible railroad train.

On the first night the audience was breathless. In spite of many drawbacks – the insufficiency of the stage, the nervousness of the stage hands, and all the accidents of a first performance – the play gained its decisive victory. The intensely wrought feelings of the spectators found vent in almost hysterical laughter when the "railroad train" parted in the middle and disclosed the flying legs of the human motor who was propelling the first half of the express. Had the effect of the scene depended not upon the suspense and emotion created by the whole situation, but upon the machinery, the piece had been irretrievably lost; but the real sensation was beyond chance of accident. It became the town talk. The houses were thronged. An old theatre-goer who stood up in the rear of the crowded seats turned to those about him after a long-drawn breath and said, "It is the climax of sensation!"

Joseph Francis Daly

158 *Daly was also a pioneer in other aspects of theatre life.*

In the course of this eventful year [1885], Daly did the American playwrights and the American playgoers signal service. He broke up an establishment in Chicago for the sale of pirated copies of popular plays, and his act led to the formation of a protective society of managers, publishers, and authors; and he invented and put in operation a scheme to defeat speculation. He had been a consistent foe of that form of monopoly, even obtaining judicial recognition of the manager's right to exclude from his theatre purchasers from sidewalk operators. But those traders had so many ways of eluding detection in buying seats at the box-office to sell at a hundred per cent profit on the streets, that Augustin devised the following plan. The purchaser of seats for a particular night received simply a slip of paper with a number on it, exchangeable at night for the actual ticket purchased. As speculators could not sell slips, containing merely a numeral, and no indication of the number or location of seats, they retired from the field.

Joseph Francis Daly

SIR HENRY IRVING (1838–1905)

159 *The son of a Somerset tradesman, Henry Irving made his name in London in 1871 when he played Matthias in* The Bells. *In 1874 he played Hamlet for 200 nights, his interpretation creating much controversy. Shylock was another role in which he excelled. Indeed he was the greatest classical actor of the period. In 1878 he became manager of the Lyceum, making it into the first theatre in the country, with Ellen Terry as his leading lady. He toured North America several times, and in 1895 was the first actor to receive a knighthood.*

In *The Bells*, the hurricane of applause at Irving's entrance was no interruption. It was no boisterous greeting by an excitable race, for a blustering actor – it was something which can only be described as part and parcel of the whole, as right as rain. It was a torrent while it lasted. Power responded to power. This applause was no false note, whereas silence would have been utterly false; for though Irving endured and did not accept the applause, he deliberately called it out of the spectators. It was necessary *to them* – not to him; it was something they had to experience, or to be rid of, or rather released from, before they could exactly take in what he was going to give them.

So then the applause came down like thunder as Irving appeared in the doorway with the ordinary cry: "It is I." Now no one has ever been known to hear these words distinctly – they resolved themselves into a single exclamation. The door flung open – the figure is in the room, God knows how – with arms extended, face alight, and this single ejaculation: "'t's I."

In those days – as in the noble days of the Greek drama – as in those of the Nō drama of Japan – an important entrance was to be preceded by suspense, and then to come as a surprise, or like a chapter-heading of some grand old romance: it thrilled, and was intended to thrill. . . .

I can only speak of Irving's entrances, but I believe that with Edmund Kean an entrance was also something to experience . . .

To prepare for this entrance in *The Bells*, the entire first fifteen minutes of the play conspired.

The talk all hovered around the thought of the man who was coming, and about other things somehow connected with him.

The storm raging outside the house; the sudden blowing open of a window in the next room, which smashed a whole trayful of crockery and glass as it swung open – the looking at the clock which told of the overdue traveller – the slow, quiet talk which mumbled on – and, above all, the queer "hurry music," as it is called, which was astonishingly dramatic: all these things led up to the first point to be made, and made with decision: "Here is the man!" And now watch what he will do – better still, how he will do it – best of all, watch his face and figure, and follow what it is these are hinting at.

Irving once on, the shout of applause going up he lowers his arms, he lowers his head, he relaxes his force all over, seems to turn it off to an almost dead calm, while the applause rolls on and up. Twice, maybe three times, he, as it were, shifts one foot (his right I think it was), and by this slight and meaningless gesture a limit is being reckoned to the applause which goes on and on – no other motion, except that the foot in shifting sends a slight vibration also without significance, through the whole person before us – and then as the applause dies away, at the first sign of it dying, the actor clips it off by a sudden gesture of awakening from his long and patiently-endured ordeal – flings cap and whip to right and left, and begins to shed his coat, his muffler, as his wife and daughter run to help him off with them.

Edward Gordon Craig

160 . . . which reminds me of Henry Irving's first entrance in *The Bells*. The printed version states that:

(Mathias is seen passing the window. The door opens. Lights up.
Chord.)
MATHIAS: It is I.

Of course you needed to be an actor-manager to arrange for all the lights
to be turned up and the full orchestra to strike a chord on your entrance.
Gordon Craig, in his biography of Irving, remarks upon his idiosyncratic
pronunciation and says that his first line sounded like 'Tsi' ('t's I). Years
later Baliol Holloway, who had seen the great man in *The Bells*, explained
that he only did that out of necessity because, as he had been seen through
the window, the entire audience expected the arrival of their hero and
were prepared to greet him with a storm of applause. He had no time to
say the full 'It is I'. So the opening of the door, the lights up, the chord,
'Tsi' were simultaneous, a fraction of a second before the applause.

Donald Sinden

161 Here is a little story of a strange thing that happened to Henry Irving
when he was just reaching his two hundredth performance of *Hamlet;*
and when large posters were to be seen announcing that coming "record"
all over London.

It chanced that Irving was standing in the Lyceum vestibule one
afternoon, talking with his manager of this impending bi-centenary
performance, when he noticed the famous actor Charles Dillon passing
by. "Why, there's dear old Dillon!" he exclaimed, and dashed out to
greet that then still vigorous veteran.

"Ah, Mr. Dillon!" said Irving. "This is indeed a pleasure! It is years
since we met. I hope you are well?"

"Sir!" thundered Dillon, "you have the advantage of me! Who *are*
you, sir?"

"I am Henry Irving," gently responded the Lyceum star. "Surely you
recall me, Mr. Dillon! Why, I had the pleasure of supporting you in the
provinces on the occasion of several of your starring engagements – "

"*No*, sir!" growled Dillon. "I do *not* recall you! Nothing occurs to me
concerning you – or your name!"

Irving went on attempting to arouse some slight recollection of himself
in Dillon.

"I might perhaps remind you," quoth Irving, "that more than once I
had the great privilege of playing Cassio – yes, even Cassio – to your
grandly pathetic Othello" (and Dillon's Othello was *that*), "and I
remember with great gratitude your kind words of encouragement so
welcome to so young an actor as I was. I remember, and with pride,
dear Mr. Dillon, that you said to me: 'I regard you as showing a good
deal of promise, Irving, my boy!' "

And then Dillon, in front of the very theatre placarded with posters of "Henry Irving as Hamlet," retorted meditatively: "Irving? H'm, ye – es. Irving! I seem to remember the name. . . . *And what are you doing NOW, Irving?"*

H. Chance Newton

162   Henry Irving's Shylock dress was designed by Sir John Gilbert. It was never replaced, and only once cleaned by Henry's dresser and valet, Walter Collinson. Walter, I think, replaced "Doody," Henry's first dresser at the Lyceum, during the run of "The Merchant of Venice." Walter was a wig-maker by trade – assistant to Clarkson the elder. It was Doody who, on being asked his opinion of a production, said that it was fine – "not a join* to be seen anywhere!" It was Walter who was asked by Henry to say which he thought his master's best part. Walter could not be "drawn" for a long time. At last he said Macbeth.

This pleased Henry immensely, for, as I hope to show later on, he fancied himself in Macbeth more than in any other part.

"It is generally conceded to be Hamlet," said Henry.

"Oh, no, Sir," said Walter, "*Macbeth*. You sweat twice as much in that."

Ellen Terry

163   One more funny matter there was in the doing of the play [*The Corsican Brothers* staged by Irving in 1880]. The supper-party at Baron Montgiron's house was supposed to be a very "toney" affair, the male guests being the *crème de la crème* of Parisian society, the ladies being of the *demi-monde;* all of both classes being persons to whom a "square" meal was no rarity. As, however, the majority of the guests were "extras" or "supers" it was hard to curb their zeal in matters of alimentation. When the servants used to throw open the doors of the supper-room and announce "*Monsieur est servi!*" they would make one wild rush and surround the table like hyenas. For their delectation bread and sponge-cake – media which lend themselves to sculptural efforts – and *gâteaux* of alluring aspect were provided. The champagne flowed in profusion – indeed in such profusion and of so realistic an appearance that all over the house the opera-glasses used to be levelled and speculations as to the brand and *cuvée* arose. Indeed a rumour went round the press that the

---

*In films, to deceive the eye of the camera, the front part of wigs and hairpieces are mounted on very fine net which is then glued to the *forehead*. It was not until 1945 that the make-up artist Stanley Hall brought his expertise to bear on wigs worn in the theatre. Before that time all such wigs had a canvas fore-piece which covered half the forehead and this the actors had to cover with greasepaint to make it look like skin. The line or 'join' where it met the face was remarkably difficult to disguise.

nightly wine bill was of colossal dimensions. In reality the champagne provided was lemonade put up specially in champagne bottles and foiled with exactness. It certainly *looked* like champagne and foamed out as the corks popped. The orgy grew nightly in violence till at the end of a couple of weeks the noblesse of France manifested a hunger and thirst libellous to the Faubourg St. Germain. Irving pondered over the matter, and one day gave orders that special food should be provided, wrought partly of plaster-o'-Paris and partly of *papier-mâché*. He told the Property Master to keep the matter secret. There was hardly any need for the admonition. In a theatre a joke is a very sacred thing, and there is no one from highest to lowest that will not go out of his way to further it. That night when the emaciated noblesse of France dashed at their quarry, one and all received a sudden check. There were many unintentional ejaculations of surprise and disappointment from the guests, and much suppressed laughter from the stage hands who were by this time all in the secret and watching from the wings.

After that night there was a notable improvement in the table manners of the guests. One and all they took their food leisurely and examined it critcally. And so the succulent sponge-cake in due time reappeared; there was no need for a second lesson against greed.

Bram Stoker

164 *The play in which 'Lily' appeared was* Don Quixote, *produced by Irving in 1895.*

Another interesting engagement was that of the famous mare 'Lily' for the equine *rôle* of 'Rosinante.' I suppose few leading ladies had played a wider range of parts than Lily. I had the honour of bestriding her in her assumption of "White Surrey" in *Richard III*. She certainly filled Sir Henry's formula of being "clean and sober" – if she was not "word-perfect", she was always perfect in her cues. Neither the discharge of villainous salt-petre nor the clash of steel against steel in those furious battles waged by the supers "off" could ever disturb her slightly contemptuous calm. Even the application of the long fifteenth-century spur left her cold. She certainly fitted the ideal of Tattersall's auctioneer and was "quiet to ride and drive." Those qualifications and bearing recommended her to Irving when casting the part of "Rosinante," for our chief was certainly no horseman. At rehearsal, he walked round her quarters at a respectful distance; "HNH" – (this spelling does not convey the peculiar nasal comment which, with our chief, was tantamount to another man's "Humph," but I do not know any combination of letters which will). "Hnh . . . quiet?" he enquired. "Oh, yes sir," Hales, her trainer, assured him. "Ah!" said the Chief, "good horse," stroking Lily's nose and flanks. "Never knew her to shy or give any trouble," continued

Hales, "never knew her mind anyone mounting her – except one gentleman – and him she wouldn't have at any price!" "Ah," said Irving, "who was that, eh?" "Gentleman you may have heard of, sir – Mr. Beerbohm Tree." "Ah," said Henry Irving, putting an added touch of affection and approbation into his caress of Lily's muzzle, "Nice beast! Critic, too, eh?"

John Martin-Harvey

165   I recall, too, a delightful incident about which Edith Craig told me. Irving, Miss Terry and she were once driving from Rye to Winchelsea, and Irving was carrying a large paper bag of shrimps which they had bought. The water in which they had been recently boiled began to percolate through the brown paper parcel and overflow on to Irving's lap. When Edie Craig drew his attention to this he murmured sympathetically: "Ah, poor things, they're *nervous!*"

John Martin-Harvey

166   They say Edmund Kean told his wife, after his performance of Richard III, that during the last act he could not feel the stage beneath him. During my conversation with Henry Irving I am not sure I felt the chair under me. He could never resist taking a gentle rise out of anyone, if he felt he'd like to, and on this night he, in wishing most kindly to advise me as to my future, led me on by praise to heights of dizziness, and then dashed me into the boneyard with a short sentence. He was telling me how he had enjoyed the afternoon performance, in his sudden and staccato way, and ended, after being eulogistic to a degree, with: "I liked your acting, my boy." I had played a rough-character part of a cruel, badly-brought-up youth, who ill-treated animals, and who ultimately killed his own father. "Yes," he said, "I liked your work. It was strong, it was natural, it was good – um, yes, good, powerful. You held the audience in the big scenes; you held them, my boy, in your hand, by your rugged strength." "Did I, sir?" I ventured; "I am proud you think so." "Yes," he said, "I do, I do; *but light comedy is your game; I shouldn't annoy them with the other stuff, if I were you!*" I felt as if I could have sunk through the floor, but he patted me on the shoulder and said, with his wonderful smile: "Never mind about that; you'll be all right if you stick to it." . . .

Many years afterwards Irving saw me in a French farce, and when the curtain fell said: "Well, you're at the comedy game, I see, eh? Do you know you remind me of Charles Mathews; very like him, very." "I'm so glad," I replied. "Yes," he said, "you wear the same sort of collars."

Seymour Hicks.

167 When on our Western tour in 1899–1900 we visited Kansas City for three nights, playing in the Opera House afterwards destroyed by fire. At that time limelight for purposes of stage effect had been largely superseded by electric light, which was beginning to be properly harnessed for the purpose. It was much easier to work with and cheaper, as every theatre had its own plant. Irving, however, preferred the limelight or calcium light, which gives softer and more varied effects, and as it was not possible to get the necessary gas-tanks in many places we took with us a whole railway waggon-load of them. These would be brought to the theatre with the other paraphernalia of our work. As we had so much stuff that it was not always possible to find room for it, we had to leave some of the less perishable goods on the sidewalk. This was easy in Kansas City, as the theatre occupied a block and its sidewalks were wide and not much used except on the main street. Accordingly the bulk of our gas-tanks were piled up outside. The scarlet colour of the oxygen tanks evidently arrested the attention of a local reporter and gave him ideas. On the morning after the first performance his paper came out with a sensational article to the effect that at last the treasured secret was out: Henry Irving was in reality a dying man, and was only kept alive by using great quantities of oxygen, of which a waggon-load of tanks had to be carried for the purpose. The reporter went on to explain how, in order to investigate the matter properly, he had managed to get into the theatre as a stage hand and had seen the tanks scattered about the stage. Further, he went on to tell how difficult it was to get near Irving's dressing-room as rude servants ordered away any one seen standing close to the door. But he was not to be baffled. He had seen at the end of the act Irving hurry into his room to be reinvigorated. He added, with an inconceivable *naïveté*, that precautions were taken to prevent the escape of the life-giving oxygen – *for even the keyhole was stopped up.*

Bram Stoker

MASTER ARNOTT (fl, 1870)

168 One of these men, Arnott, the Property Master and a fine workman, had had an odd experience during the Bristol week. Something had gone wrong with the travelling "property" horse used in the vision scene of *The Bells,* and he had come up to town to bring the real one from the storage. In touring it was usual to bring a "profile" representation of the gallant steed. "Profile" has in theatrical parlance a special meaning other than its dictionary meaning of an "outline." It is thin wood covered on both sides with rough canvas carefully glued down. It is very strong and can be cut in safety to any shape. The profile horse was of course an outline, but the art of the scene-painter had rounded it out to seemingly natural dimensions. Now the "real" horse, though a lifeless "property", had in fact been originally alive. It was formed of the skin of a moderately sized pony; and being embellished with picturesque attachments in the shape of mane and tail was a really creditable object. But it was expensive to carry as it took up much space. Arnott and two of his men ran up to fetch this down as there was not time to make a new profile horse. When they got to Paddington he found that the [railway] authorities refused to carry the goods by weight on account of its bulk, and asked him something like £4 for the journey. He expressed his feelings freely, as men occasionally do under irritating circumstances, and said he would go somewhere else. The clerk in the office smiled and Arnott went away; he was a clever man who did not like to be beaten, and railways were his natural enemies. He thought the matter over. Having looked over the timetable and found that the cost of a horse-box to Bristol was only £1 13s., he went to the department in charge of such matters and ordered one, paying for it at once and arranging that it should go on the next fast train. By some manoeuvring he so managed that he and his men took Koveski's horse into the box and closed the doors.

When the train arrived at Bristol there had to be some shunting to and fro so as to place the horse-box in the siding arranged for such matters. The officials in charge threw open the door for the horse to walk out. But he would yield to no blandishment, nor even to the violence of chastisement usual at such times. A little time passed and the officials got anxious, for the siding was required for other purposes. The station at Bristol is not roomy and more than one line has to use it. The official in charge told him to take out his damned horse!

"Not me!" said he, for he was now seeing his way to "get back" at the railway company, "I've paid for the carriage of the horse and I want him delivered out of your premises. The rate I paid includes the services of the necessary officials."

The porters tried again, but the horse would not stir. Now it is a dangerous matter to go into a horse-box in case the horse should prove restive. One after another the porters declined, till at last one plucky lad volunteered to go in by the little window close to the horse's head. Those on the platform waited in apprehension, till he suddenly ran out from the box laughing and crying out:

"Why you blamed fools. He ain't a 'orse at all. He's a stuffed 'un!"

Bram Stoker

SIR SQUIRE BANCROFT (1841–1926)

169 *Actor and manager of the Prince of Wales's Theatre and the Theatre Royal, Haymarket. These passages are from Bancroft's autobiography, which he wrote jointly with his wife, the actress Marie Wilton.*

I hope my vanity will be pardoned for relating an incident I remember after acting with them [Mr and Mrs Charles Kean] in *Much Ado about Nothing*. On the following evening I was seated in the green-room, when Charles Kean entered dressed as Othello. He sat down, and after staring at me some time in a way which rather frightened me, beckoned to me to go near him. I advanced, fearing I had innocently distressed him on the stage. To my great surprise he said, 'Sir, I was at the wing last night waiting to go on, and heard you give Borachio's difficult speech in the last act. I can only say that if I were still the lessee of a London theatre, it would be your own fault if you were not a member of my company.' I stammered out some words of thanks for this unexpected compliment, which was paid to me before a full green-room; fortunately I was 'called' almost direcly for the stage; and so was able to beat a blushing retreat.

Kean, although at this time not quite fifty-two, had the appearance and manner of a much older man, and he was watched and guarded with what seemed unnecessary fuss by those around him. At rehearsal the green baize was laid down on the stage,* the gas lighted, the stage enclosed – precautions which were taken for no other person. His memory was growing treacherous, especially in long soliloquies, as, for instance, the fall of Wolsey; either Cathcart or Everett would then be always at the wings to prompt him, while Mrs Kean, ever the most devoted woman in the world, would hover round the scenes to stop the smallest noise. One night I witnessed a very comic incident, through her absolutely insisting on a member of the company, who was crossing the back of the stage on tip-toe, taking off his boots *because they creaked*, and continuing his journey to the stage-door in his stockinged feet.

170 *As the next two passages show, Bancroft was always prepared to challenge theatrical traditions.*

It may be curious to mention here the first morning performance we ever gave at the Prince of Wales's Theatre, which was on March 6th [1869], in the height of the run of *School*, when all the seats were booked every night long in advance. The experiment, however, was so novel, that it only attracted a moderate house in the daytime, and it was not for some years that *matinées* became popular.

*see reference to the green room, p. 27.

171 To take the events of that opening night [at the Haymarket, Saturday, January 31st; 1880] in proper sequence, I must begin with the Pit question, and the riot that occurred when the curtain rose. Anonymous reports had reached me that there would most likely be a disturbance. I was sanguine enough, however, to hope that the following advertisement issued beforehand, and the nature of the accommodation offered in place of the old pit, would have prevented anything of the kind. Those hopes were vain:

> 'As some disappointment may be felt at the abolition of the pit, Mr and Mrs. Bancroft deem it necessary to explain the alteration. With the present expenses of a first-class theatre, it is impossible to give up the floor of the house – its most remunerative portion – to low-priced seats, and the management, being unwilling to place any part of the audience in close and confined space under the balcony, the only alternative was to allot to the frequenters of the pit the tier usually devoted to the upper boxes, and now called the second circle. In carrying out the structural alterations of the theatre, Mr. and Mrs. Bancroft have, they hope, specially attended to the comfort of visitors to these seats by raising the ceiling, building a new stone staircase, a refreshment-room, and by removing all obstacles to a clear view of the stage.'

Naturally enough, I think it may be expected that I should here express some views on this then important subject, and tell what led me to the bold measure of daring to abolish the pit, more especially from the Haymarket Theatre, which had been long known to boast, and truly enough, the possession of the best and most comfortable pit ever to be found in a playhouse, from the reason that it did not go under the dress circle.

To begin, it is perhaps necessary to remind young play-goers that the pit in the old days occupied the entire floor of the theatre, extending to the orchestra, and as the charge for admission in the leading houses was three shillings and sixpence, the pit quite earned its title of being 'the backbone of the theatre'. The dress circle and private boxes were the resort of the better classes, the wealthy, or the fastidious. The modern stall was then unknown. Gradually this luxury was introduced. Row by row, very insidiously, the cushioned chairs encroached upon the narrow benches, which, year after year, were removed further and further from the stage, until at last, in many theatres, all that was left of the old-fashioned pit was a dark, low-ceilinged place hidden away under the dress circle, which, by contrast with its former proud state, seemed but a kind of cellar, or reminder of the black-hole of Calcutta.

That thousands of earnest play-goers would far rather sit there in heat and discomfort than go up aloft to better accommodation I don't doubt for a moment, nor do I for another moment deny that I should very likely find myself of the party under their circumstances; but that seems to me outside the question. Matters had entirely changed. The pit had long lost, in most West End theatres, the possibility of being the support it used to prove, owing to the managers of them having, row by row, robbed it of its power, and made the stalls instead their 'backbone'. This grew to be eminently the case with our management, which could not have endured without high-priced admission.

I don't think anything I might add to these remarks would advance the argument, I will return to the hooting and howling which greeted the raising of the curtain, mingled with noisy cries of 'Where's the pit? At the great disadvantage of being dressed for Sir Frederick Blount*, in which I wore a flaxen foppish wig and pink complexion, I walked upon the stage and faced the anger of the few who made the noise, which quite drowned the friendly greeting of the many. Utterly unprepared what to say, for I had disregarded the anonymous warnings, I believe I owed something to the manner in which I spoke the few broken sentences I was allowed, through the tumult, to utter, and to never showing during that *mauvais quart d'heure* (to be exact, more than twenty minutes) the least sign of temper. What I said was not of much moment, and very likely my attempts to speak were neither soothing nor judicious; but I am not of a 'knuckling-under' disposition, and, at least, I thought myself justified in claiming the respect of the audience. Unfortunately the diversion tended largely to disconcert the actors, and to add greatly to the nervousness due to the position of all concerned.

SARAH BERNHARDT (1845–1923)

172 *Probably the most versatile actress of her time, Sarah Bernhardt was as triumphant in London in 1879 in* Phèdre *as in New York a year later as Marguerite in* La Dame aux Camélias. *In later life she even played Hamlet. Numerous stories circulated about her eccentricities, many of which were well-founded. In this first passage Mrs Patrick Campbell who played Mélisande to Bernhardt's Pelléas in a production of the play that bears their names, describes some unscripted business.*

Her company indiscreetly told me that Madame Sarah had never been known to make fun or to laugh on the stage.

In a tobacconist's shop I saw a tobacco pouch made in the shape of a fish, and painted to represent one. I bought it, took it to the theatre, and tied it down to a bit of canvas at the bottom of the well at the Fountain.

At the performance, when Sarah came to the second act and stood by the *fontaine des aveugles*, she spied the fish and began improvising about *les poissons là*. . . . She stooped gracefully over the edge to take the fish

*Character in *Money*, by Lord Lytton (1840).

out; as it was tied, she nearly lost her balance. Without concern she went on calmly with her part. I laughed, spoiling my lovely little scene.

When the curtain fell Sarah did not allude to what had happened, neither did I. The next day when we lunched together she had a strange, preoccupied expression on her face. Later, at the matinée, when we came to the Cave scene, at the point where she tenderly takes my hand and helps me over the rocks, she took hold of my hand, hard – squash – she held a raw egg in hers.

I did not smile, but with calm dignity I went on with my part. I can see now the tears of laughter trickling down her cheeks, and her dear body shaking with merriment as I grew more and more dignified to the end of the scene.

Her company told me afterwards, almost with awe, that Madame must love me very, very much.

173 *Although feeling feverish one day Bernhardt disregarded her doctor's orders not to go on that evening in* L'Entrangère *at the Gaiety Theatre. He was furious but insisted that she at least took 'a prescription in case of a relapse'.*

The opium I had taken in my potion made my head rather heavy. I arrived on the stage in a semi-conscious state, yet delighted with the applause I received. I walked as though I were in a dream, and could scarcely distinguish my surroundings. The house itself I only saw through a luminous mist. My feet glided without effort over the carpet, and my voice sounded to me far away – very far away. I was in that delicious stupor that one experiences after chloroform, morphine, opium, or hasheesh.

The first act went off very well, but in the third act, just when I was to tell the Duchesse de Septmonts (Croizette) all the troubles that I, Mrs. Clarkson, had gone through during my life, just as I should have commenced my interminable story, I could not remember anything. Croizette murmured my first phrase for me, but I could only see her lips move without hearing a word. I then said, quite calmly:-

"The reason I sent for you here, madame, is because I wanted to tell you my reasons for acting as I have done, but I have thought it over and have decided not to tell you them today."

Sophie Croizette gazed at me with a terrified look in her eyes; she then rose and left the stage, her lips trembling and her eyes fixed upon me all the time.

"What's the matter?" everyone asked, when she sank almost breathless into an arm-chair.

"Sarah has gone mad!" she exclaimed. "I assure you she has gone stark mad. She has cut out the whole of her scene with me."

"But how?" everyone asked.

"She has cut out two hundred lines," said Croizette.

"But what for?" was the eager question.

"I don't know. She looks quite calm."

The whole of this conversation, which was repeated to me later on, took much less time than it does now to write it down. Coquelin had been told, and he now came on to the stage to finish the act. The curtain fell. I was stupefied and desperate afterwards on hearing all that people told me. I had not noticed that anything was wrong, and it seemed to me that I had played the whole of my part as usual, but I was really under the influence of opium. There was very little for me to say in the fifth act, and I went through that perfectly well. The following day the accounts in the papers sounded the praises of our company, but the piece itself was criticised. I was afraid at first that my involuntary omission of the important part in the third act was one of the causes of the severity of the Press. This was not so, however, as all the critics had read and re-read the piece. They discussed the play itself, and did not mention my slip of memory.

WILLIAM TERRISS (1847–97)

174 *Known as 'Breezy Bill', because of his numerous roles in muscular melodramas, Terriss was one of the most popular actors of his day. Ellen Terry said that when he had presents from the front, which happened every night, he gave them straight to the call boy or the gas man. All the sadder therefore that, at the age of 50, he should have been murdered at the stage-door of the Adelphi Theatre by a demented small-part actor with an imaginary grievance.*

Irving, who had a very warm corner in his heart for William Terriss, used to be immensely amused at the almost effortless way in which he could sweep a great audience before him, often without having taken the trouble to dive very deeply into the inner meaning of the text. On one occasion at rehearsal the great man, who was listening to him declaim magnificently, stopped the scene and mischievously asked, "Bill, my boy, what do those last two lines mean?" "What do you say, guv'nor?" said Terriss. "The last two lines – what do they mean, my boy?" "Oh! the last two lines – well – what about them?" "What do they mean?" came the enquiry again. "Oh! the lines," again replied Terriss, "you want to know what they do mean?" "Yes," said Irving, "what do they mean?" "Well, guv'nor, they mean, of course, they mean – " Here he paused. "Well, Bill, What *do* they mean?" "Oh, well," said the ever-undefeated Bill, "so help me goodness, guv'nor, I'm blowed if I know what they *do* mean." "No, I thought not," retorted Irving, joining in the shout of laughter which the very frank reply brought forth.

Seymour Hicks

ELLEN TERRY (1847–1928)

175 *'All brains and sympathy' said George Bernard Shaw of Ellen Terry who was Henry Irving's partner at the Lyceum for over twenty years. The first passage is a charming, poignant description of her visit to Irving during his last months.*

He was taken ill at Wolverhampton in the spring of 1905.

We had not acted together for more than two years then, and times were changed indeed.

I went down to Wolverhampton when the news of his illness reached London. I arrived late and went to an hotel. It was not a good hotel, nor could I find a very good florist when I got up early the next day and went out with the intention of buying Henry some flowers. I wanted some bright-coloured ones for him – he had always liked bright flowers – and this florist dealt chiefly in white flowers – *funeral* flowers.

At last I found some daffodils – my favourite flower. I bought a bunch, and the kind florist, whose heart was in the right place if his flowers were not, found me a nice simple glass to put it in. I knew the sort of vase that I should find at Henry's hotel.

I remembered, on my way to the doctor's – for I had decided to see the doctor first – that in 1892 when my dear mother died, and I did not act for a few nights, when I came back I found my room at the Lyceum filled with daffodils. "To make it look like sunshine," Henry said.

The doctor talked to me quite frankly.

"His heart is dangerously weak," he said.

"Have you told him?" I asked.

"I had to, because the heart being in that condition he must be careful."

"Did he understand *really?*"

"Oh, yes. He said he quite understood."

Yet a few minutes later when I saw Henry, and begged him to remember what the doctor had said about his heart, he exclaimed: "Fiddle! It's not my heart at all! It's my *breath!*" (Oh the ignorance of great men about themselves!)

"I also told him," the Wolverhampton doctor went on, "that he must not work so hard in future."

I said: "He will, though, – and he's stronger than any one."

Then I went round to the hotel.

I found him sitting up in bed, drinking his coffee.

He looked like some beautiful grey tree that I have seen in Savannah. His old dressing-gown hung about his frail yet majestic figure like some mysterious grey drapery.

We were both very much moved, and said little.

"I'm glad you've come. Two Queens have been kind to me this morning. Queen Alexandra telegraphed to say how sorry she was I was ill, and now you – "

He showed me the Queen's gracious message.

I told him he looked thin and ill, but *rested*.

"Rested! I should think so. I have plenty of time to rest. They tell me I shall be here eight weeks. Of course I sha'n't, but still – It was that rug in front of the door. I tripped over it. A commercial traveller picked me up – a kind fellow, but d–n him, he wouldn't leave me afterwards – wanted to talk to me all night."

I remembered his having said this, when I was told by his servant, Walter Collinson, that on the night of his death at Bradford, he stumbled over the rug when he walked into the hotel corridor.

We fell to talking about work. He said he hoped that I had a good manager . . . agreed very heartily with me about Frohman,* saying he was always so fair – more than fair.

"What a wonderful life you've had, haven't you?" I exclaimed, thinking of it all in a flash.

"Oh, yes," he said quietly . . . "a wonderful life – of work."

"And there's nothing better, after all, is there?"

"Nothing."

"What have you got out of it all. . . . You and I are 'getting on,' as they say. Do you ever think, as I do sometimes, what you have got out of life?"

"What have I got out of it?" said Henry, stroking his chin and smiling slightly. "Let me see. . . . Well, a good cigar, a good glass of wine – good friends." Here he kissed my hand with courtesy. Always he was so courteous; always his actions, like this little one of kissing my hand, were so beautifully timed. They came just before the spoken words, and gave them peculiar value.

"That's not a bad summing-up of it all," I said. "And the end. . . . How would you like that to come?"

"How would I like that to come?" He repeated my question lightly yet meditatively too. Then he was silent for some thirty seconds before he snapped his fingers – the action again before the words.

"Like that!"

I thought of the definition of inspiration – "A calculation rapidly made." Perhaps he had never thought of the manner of his death before. Now he had an inspiration as to how it would come.

We were silent a long time, I thinking how like some splendid Doge of Venice he looked, sitting up in bed, his beautiful mobile hand stroking his chin.

*Charles Frohman, see also p. 151.

176 *The Terry family was a large one. Ellen's sisters Kate, Marion and Florence were all fine actresses.*

All the Terrys had very bad memories. Marion, at the end of her life, used to go to play the big scene from *Lady Windermere's Fan*, with my aunt Mabel Terry-Lewis, her niece, at charity matinées, and I remember my mother trying to hear her go through her words at our house. She kept making endless mistakes, although she had known the part for many years. However, they all had a lot of skilful ways of covering their lapses of memory, as many old actors do. Irene Vanbrugh, in her last performance, had the same trouble, but she would shout or stamp her foot or look at the other actor, making it seem as if he was the one who had dried up. This was a much more common occurrence in my days as a youthful playgoer. The prompter was often a good deal in evidence, particularly on first nights, and the audience did not mind, they thought it was all part of the fun. When I saw Ellen Terry as the Nurse in Doris Keane's *Romeo and Juliet* in 1919 she could hardly remember a word, and Basil Sydney and Leon Quartermaine, who were playing Romeo and Mercutio respectively, whispered every line in her ear, and then she said the line herself and it sounded as if she had just thought of it. One would have thought it would have made her nervous, but she still had confidence in her charisma and in the audience, and managed to enchant them just the same.

John Gielgud

177 *The following was found on the fly-leaf of Ellen Terry's copy of* Romeo and Juliet. *She had played Juliet at the Lyceum Theatre in 1882.*

Get the words into your remembrance first of all. Then, (as you have to convey the meaning of the words to *some* who have ears, but don't hear, and eyes, but don't see) put the words into the simplest vernacular. Then exercise your judgment about their sound.

So many different ways of speaking words! Beware of sound and fury signifying nothing. Voice unaccompanied by imagination, dreadful. Pomposity, rotundity.

Imagination and intelligence absolutely necessary to realize and portray high and low imaginings. Voice, yes, but not mere voice production. You must have a sensitive ear, and a sensitive judgment of the effect on your audience. But all the time you must be trying to please *yourself.*

Get yourself into *tune.* Then you can let fly your imagination, and the words will seem to be supplied by yourself. Shakespeare supplied by oneself! Oh!

Realism? Yes, if we mean by that real feeling, real sympathy. But people seem to mean by it only the realism of low-down things.

To act, you must make the thing written your own. You must steal the words, steal the thought, and *convey* the stolen treasure to others with great art.

DAME MADGE KENDAL (1849–1935)

178 *With Sir John Hare, Madge Kendal had a long and successful partnership at the St James's Theatre. Pinero's play,* The Squire, *was produced here in 1881.*

"The Squire" was unquestionably one of the greatest triumphs of the Hare and Kendal management and created a phrase which was current for a long time in the newspapers that it "wafted the scent of the hay over the footlights," so perfect a picture was it of country life.

Its production created a sensation, for its plot was everywhere assumed to have been borrowed without admission from Thomas Hardy's *Far from the Madding Crowd*. Mr. Pinero, as he then was, stated emphatically that he had never read the novel so that the similarity of the stories was merely one of those coincidences which if not frequent are not unknown either in the theatre or in literature.

The result of this acrimonious discussion was that, one night, when the curtain went up, I noticed in a private box Mr. Hardy himself, Sir George Lewis, presumably his solicitor, and Mr. Comyns Carr who had come to see the play and discover how far the plot of "The Squire" agreed with the novel.

The trouble arose through Mr. Hare having mislaid the manuscript among the hundreds he had received. Mr. Comyns Carr lost his temper at the delay in receiving an answer and asked for the play.

Eventually, Mr. Hare wrote that he did not like it as "Mrs. Kendal did not like her part."

Alas! I had never even seen the manuscript.

Some considerable time later Mr. Hare did find the manuscript and he and Mr. Comyns Carr became good friends again.

In the second act of "The Squire" I wore an evening dress, the material for which I searched carefully to get, as it had a thread of gold which I wanted the fire to play upon in the great scene of the play in which I burned some love letters.

One day a lady, the wife of one of the members of the company, came to me and said she did not like the dress and she thought something more becoming ought to be got.

I did not agree with her and I continued to wear it.

One evening, her husband, who was playing in "The Squire," was taken suddenly ill and, as it was thought his illness was serious, a telegram was sent asking her to come at once.

She was at a dinner-party and came straight on. As she threw off her cloak, she revealed the fact that she was wearing a dress made of the same material and cut in the exact manner as the one I was wearing which she did not like!

Tableau!!!

The Comyns Carr version of "Far from the Madding Crowd" was produced later at the Old Globe Theatre with Mrs. Bernard Beere as the heroine and Mr. Charles Kelly as Gabriel Oak, but it had no great success.

179 At rehearsal she could be terrifying. She once asked a manager to bring a kitchen chair and to place it in the middle of the stage. The company was summoned to gather round while she knelt down and said: 'Oh Lord, we pray Thee out of Thy infinite mercy that Thou will cause some notion of the rudiments of acting to be vouch-safed to this company for Jesus Christ's sake, Amen.' She got up and dusted her knees. 'Well, now we'll see what *that* will do!' she snapped.

James Harding

J. W. COOKE (fl. 1850s)

180 The celebrated American tragedian, Mr. Cooke, was always fond of frolic on his benefit night, declaring he never took liberties with his friends at any other time.

It once happened during an engagement at Philadelphia that on such an occasion he was short of money and at a loss to know where to raise the wind for the accustomed breeze. In this dilemma he started up the town in a speculative mood, determined to inspirit himself in some way or other.

Having reached the corner of Callow Hill and Eighth Street, he perceived one of those enticing signs of three golden balls. He turned the corner and entered the fatal door, and addressed the man behind the counter thus:

> "My name is Cooke. This is my benefit night. The manager can't do without me. I am up for Richard III. I want something to eat. I have no money. Now I propose to pledge myself for ten dollars, and you may lay me upon one of your shelves."

The joke was a queer one. The pawnbroker paid the ten dollars, and Cooke was laid up. The theatre that night was crowded, and at seven o'clock the manager came forward to apologise, stating that with the permission of the audience, the performance would commence with a farce.

He had sent in different directions, but was unable to find Cooke in the city. He promised that the tragedian would be forthcoming in the course of half an hour.

As the manager retired, he was told that a boy wished to see him in the green-room. He found the boy, who presented a note written in cypher, which he at length translated thus:-

"MY DEAR JONES, – I am pawned for ten dollars; send and redeem me, or it will be impossible for Richard to be himself to-night.
"Yours, &c.,
"W. COOKE."

The manager started immediately after the fixed star, and found him nicely shelved with a plate of biscuits and cheese. In the button-hole of his coat was a piece of paper marked "No. 1,473; pawned for ten dollars."

The amount was paid, a cab called, and Mr. Cooke and the manager returned to the theatre, where the former had just time to dress and commence, "Now is the winter of our discontent." It is said that he never acted better or received more applause.

J. B. Howe

SIR HERBERT BEERBOHM TREE (1852–1917)

181 *Tree's fame rests on the years in which he managed Her Majesty's Theatre (where he founded an academy for stage training that later became the Royal Academy of Dramatic Art), on his 'character' parts such as Fagin in* Oliver Twist, *Svengali in* Trilby, *and on his own gift for repartee.*

Once upon a time, a then budding and now a fully-grown young star actress, was engaged by Manager Tree, who really did a great deal to advance her on her stage career. Soon, however, the young novice began to tell Tree that she and her parents (whom we all love and honour) insisted on her being billed in larger type than she was getting. Nay, more, the radiantly beautiful girl claimed that she was to be given the "and" – which is so coveted by professionals when their names are advertised. "I want," said she, "to be announced thus, 'Sir Herbert Tree *and* Miss (So and So).' " "Yes, my dear child," retorted the Chief, "but why 'and'? Why not 'but'?"

In my opinion, however, the best answer this epigrammatic actor-manager ever gave in this announcement connection was that which he administered to a very Cockney, not to say illiterate but certainly clever, low comedian whom he had thought of engaging. "But, look 'ere, guv'nor, yer know," remarked our low com. warningly, "I shall expect you to bill the 'and' before my naime!" "Alas! my dear friend," replied Tree, "how *can* I do so? You know it is 'ard to give the 'and where the Art can never be!"

H. Chance Newton

182 I feel that I ought, however, to tell this little story of an *au revoir* supper which Tree gave one Saturday midnight at the Garrick Club prior to his starting on tour at Manchester on the following Monday. There was quite a brilliant assembly of his brother actors and managers at this gorgeous midnight banquet – for being Tree's of course it was gorgeous – not to say Lucullus-like! He explained to his guests that he was staying at the Garrick that night – or morning – in order to catch the nine a.m. train from Euston to Manchester. Presently he asked to be excused while he summoned John, a wonderful waiter there, and asked him to be sure to call him in time for that train. Several times during the revels, which grew more and more revelsome, Tree called John again to remind him about the train. Each time the hilarious host grew more and more incoherent, but the diplomatic John kept assuring him that he had not forgotten the instructions and that all would be well!

In due course the host's guests departed, and Tree, taking from John a heavy candlestick, started up the Garrick Club's noble staircase *en route* for bed! When nearing the top, Tree and his candlestick fell to the bottom of the stairs! John, in alarm, bent over him to lend first aid. Tree, however, suddenly pulling himself together, murmured, "John! John! *I have returned to remind you that at nine o'clock* — !" Tableau!

H. Chance Newton

183 *Tree was so completely preoccupied with himself on stage that he was always surprised when anyone else spoke. George Bernard Shaw, one of whose hardest tasks as a producer was to induce his actors to speak as if they had never heard their cues before instead of betraying the fact that they knew all about it beforehand, writes of Tree's peculiarity.*

Tree always seemed to have heard the lines of the other performers for the first time, and even to be a little taken aback by them. Let me give an extreme instance of this. In *Pygmalion* the heroine, in a rage, throws the hero's slippers in his face. When we rehearsed this for the first time, I had taken care to have a very soft pair of velvet slippers provided; for I knew that Mrs. Patrick Campbell was very dexterous, very strong, and a dead shot. And sure enough, when we reached this passage, Tree got the slippers well and truly delivered with unerring aim bang in his face. The effect was appalling. He had totally forgotten that there was any such incident in the play; and it seemed to him that Mrs. Campbell, suddenly giving way to an impulse of diabolical wrath and hatred, had committed an unprovoked and brutal assault on him. The physical impact was nothing; but the wound to his feelings was terrible. He collapsed in tears on the nearest chair, and left me staring in amazement, whilst the entire personnel of the theatre crowded solicitously round him, explaining that the incident was part of the play, and even exhibiting the prompt-book to prove their words. But his *morale* was so shattered that it took quite a long time, and a good deal of rallying and coaxing from Mrs. Campbell, before he was in a condition to resume the rehearsal. The worst of it was that as it was quite evident that he would be just as surprised and wounded every time, Mrs. Campbell took care that the slippers should never hit him again, and the incident was consequently one of the least convincing in the performance. . . .

184 Dear old friend Tree soon developed a passion for being interviewed. Not only was he more interviewed than any actor-manager before or since, but also it fell to my lot to interview Tree for the *Referee* and other papers more than I ever interviewed anybody!

Herbert's habits at interview-time were peculiar. He was (to quote the old comic song) "Always all over the shop." As I entered by the stage-door he would grasp my arm and drag me, first into the Prompt Box. There he would cause me to begin questioning him! In a few moments he would find (as he ought to have known before) that we were in the way of the prompter, the curtain men, the scene shifters, and other rehearsers.

Next he would drag me down into the P.S. Stage-box, saying: "We shall be quieter there!" Then, in a jiffy, he would suddenly climb on to the stage to attend to some point in the play then being rehearsed. A few moments later he would beckon me to climb up to him and to stand there to ply him with questions under the Tee-piece!*

Then, finding – as was only to be expected – either that we two were interfering with the rehearsals, or that the rehearsals were interfering with us – the restless Tree would drag me up to his dressing-room! There we were soon interrupted by 'phones from the stage, by callers, and what not! So at last – when our meeting place was His Majesty's – Tree, luring me into a lift, next piloted me up into the Dome!

Once in the Dome – far, far up into the Haymarket sky – Tree generally forgot about the interview for a time and babbled of his books there, his pictures, and his articles of the kind that another humorist called "bigotry and virtue."

How we ever got any interview through puzzles me to this day! Usually I had to go away in despair and dazement and piece out a sort of scenario, embodying (as far as I could) Tree's broken-up views, remarks, jokes and criticisms of his critics!

H. Chance Newton

---

*A portable gas bracket used at rehearsals, placed down stage centre, which gave off a rather dim light through which the cast were supposed to read their lines and arrange their moves.

SIR JOHNSTON FORBES-ROBERTSON (1853–1937)

185 *A successful actor-manager, whose* Hamlet *at the Lyceum in 1897 was particularly admired for the beauty of his voice. All but the last of these entries come from his autobiography.*

Once when I was bemoaning to Clayton the trouble I had in wording with sufficient tact letters to authors whose plays I could not accept for production – "My dear fellow," said Clayton, "I solved the question only yesterday. I wrote to a man who had sent me an abominable play, and said, 'My dear Sir, I have read your play. Oh– my very dear Sir! Yours truly, John Clayton.' " I told this story on many occasions with great success. At last I told it to one who did not laugh. He was my secretary. It seemed to me hard, indeed, that one's own secretary should not laugh at one's funny stories. It appeared to me that he had mistaken his vocation, and I said in a tone of some irritation, "You don't seem to think that funny." Said he, "No, I don't. It was to me Mr. Clayton wrote that letter!"

186 But to return to the Lyceum. Loveday was always much concerned at Irving's lavish expenditure on the furnishing of the stage, who would discard at once any property or scene, no matter what it cost, if it did not quite satisfy him. I remember on one occasion I was sitting in Irving's dressing-room while he was making up, when Loveday came in with a very beautiful sceptre he had had made for *Richard III*. He drew it from its case and showed it to Irving with much pride. Irving handled it for a moment, and said sharply, "No good, too heavy." Poor Loveday appealed to me silently from behind Irving's chair, with a most eloquent look as who should say, "What is to be done with this man?" Upon this I seized the sceptre and waved it about, walking up and down saying, "Too heavy? Oh, no! It's got to be heavy. It is not a fairy's wand, it's an imposing sceptre. Please stand up and try it properly." Irving said meekly, 'Is it? Well, let's see." He got up and paced the room, trying it this way and that; then turning to Loveday said very humbly, "Thank you, Loveday. Yes, it's a nice sceptre. I'll use it." Loveday was all beams, and his look of gratitude to me I shall never forget.

187 *The Light that Failed*, in spite of its poignant story, proved a great success. The stage version of Kipling's novel was done by Miss Constance Fletcher, who kept most happily the flavour and the character of the book.

Aubrey Smith, Sydney Valentine, William Farren, and Leon Quarter-main, Miss Margaret Halstan, my wife, and Miss Nina Boucicault were in the cast; all gave of their best and played their parts to admiration.

A rough-haired terrier, a friend of Aubrey Smith's, had a very important part, "Binkie, by himself," as he very properly appeared with his brother actors in the bill of the play.

Every night he waited at the wings during the second act with his master, showing impatient interest as his cue came near; when the door was opened, he trotted in with the greatest regularity and, leaping on the table in the centre of Dick Heldar's studio, sat him down with his tongue out, smiling at the audience, and seldom failed of a reception. One night, however, he began to growl lowly, which was not set down in his part, and in spite of his master's saying, "Lie down, Binkie," the growls became louder, and ended in continuous barking, which after a few minutes subsided. There was a silence, and the dialogue proceeded, when suddenly the barking was renewed.

What had angered him was this. Two ladies and a man were making their way to seats in the middle of the stalls, and Binkie, very properly, entered a protest against his scene being disturbed. The people having, with great deliberation, seated themselves, the man of the party presently rose to take off his overcoat, which action caused the second outbreak on Binkie's part. The unhappy late comers were between two fires, the protests of the dog and the hearty laughter of the audience.

During the whole of Binkie's scene, I, as Dick Heldar, was lying on a sofa supposed to be asleep, so that it was only after the act was over that I learned from Smith, when he apologized for his dog giving tongue, what had happened in the audience. I told him that Binkie's behaviour in the matter entirely met with my approval and filled me with respect in that he would not suffer the interruption of his scene by late comers. Human actors may put up with this sort of thing, but dog actors never. That, I am persuaded, was Binkie's attitude of mind on the question.

188 Apropos of mishaps upon the stage, I recall one that happened to that greatly gifted woman, Miss Elizabeth Robins, during a performance of Miss Constance Fletcher's play of *Mrs. Lessingham*, at the Garrick. It was in a scene where I, as her husband, was trying to soothe her distressed condition. She had bought for the part a necklace of imitation diamonds and pearls, which she wore clasped firmly round her throat. Suddenly, to my consternation, the necklace broke, and the jewels, that I knew had cost her a considerable sum, began to drop on the carpet. While trying to comfort her, I managed to get most of the jewels into my joined hands. So far so good, but we were both in evening dress, and, my hands being full, I could not stow the things into my pockets without exposing the mishap to the audience, as we were standing in the middle of the stage. She at that moment gave a deep sigh which caused a momentary hiatus between her bodice and her chest. With what I consider a magnificent inspiration, I quickly poured the whole lot into that slight gap and got from her a stifled, gasping "Thank you," and we continued the scene.

189 *This charming recollection of Forbes-Robertson at the Garrick Club comes from the pen of the Canadian actor, Raymond Massey.*

Some of the most pleasant hours of my London years were spent at the Garrick. I always found it fascinating and on occasion enchanting. The building is a beautiful example of early Victorian architecture, exactly as it was when the club moved there in 1864. Since it was founded, practically every great actor of the English stage, the actor-managers who ran the theatre, the great dramatists who wrote the plays, have all been members of the Garrick, along with many of the leaders of arts and letters and the bar. There has always been a great feeling for the past, and a sense of history.

The English actors who visited Toronto during my boyhood days, like Forbes-Robertson, Martin Harvey, Cyril Maude, were great heroes to me. Just after I was elected to the club in 1928, Sir Johnston Forbes-Robertson came to see *The Constant Nymph* in which his daughter Jean and I were playing our first leading roles. The old gentleman came backstage after the show, one of the great moments of my life.

Soon after that, there was a supper in his honour at the Garrick and of course I went. Gerald du Maurier presided. It was an impressive affair. The dining-room was packed and there were many fine speeches, witty and affectionate. Finally Sir Johnston rose to make his remarks. I still think that even at eighty he had the most beautiful voice ever heard in the theatre, a voice with the quality of a violoncello. He spoke well without notes, describing many amusing or moving incidents in his life, and in his peroration referred to the lovely ladies with whom he had had the privilege of acting, mentioning four or five of them by name. "How those dear names crowd in upon me!" he said, citing Mary Anderson, Madame Modjeska, Kate Rourke, Mrs. Patrick Campbell, Genevieve Ward. "And last but, oh, not least," he concluded, "the lovely lady who has been my inspiration and my comrade in so many theatre ventures, my dear wife – eh – " But this name did not crowd in upon Sir Johnston. The tall, noble figure stood straighter than ever, surprise on his face. There was silence as we waited. Was this magical occasion to fizzle out with a missed cue? No. With perfect timing, from the other end of the long table came the gentle prompt from Gerald du Maurier: "Easy does it, Forbie – Gertrude Elliott!" Sir Johnston's surprise turned into a smile. All of us stood and cheered. I understood Sir Johnston's predicament. I have had trouble remembering names all my life.

DAVID BELASCO (1853–1931)

190 *During his career on Broadway he directed or produced over 300 plays and was accepted as the master of naturalism. This made him the prime target when a reaction against this form of theatrical realism set in. The well known critic, George Jean Nathan, claimed derisively that he had seen a signed photograph of Dante on Belasco's inlaid onyx commode. But during Belasco's heyday plays such as his Civil War drama* The Heart of Maryland *set him in the forefront of American dramatic art.*

Although Belasco was often sued for plagiarism, he was never convicted. He could prove that the Belasco stamp was unique. Once he contributed a series of learned articles about acting to *The Booklovers Magazine*. It turned out that they had originally appeared in England under the signature of George Henry Lewes, an eminent British critic. Belasco explained that his name on the article was a clerical mistake made by a subordinate who had since disappeared. Just a regrettable oversight in Belasco's opinion.

He measurably improved the standards of stage décor by his ingenious use of lighting and his meticulous attention to the details of scenery. He was the first manager to conceal footlights in the interest of reality. He was one of the few men in that time to understand the importance of direction. He rehearsed his companies remorselessly. He did not so much interpret as invent and mold performances. He tortured his actors. He stuck a pin in Frances Starr's beguiling behind to make her scream dramatically. In the heat of a rehearsal, he sometimes threw his watch on the floor and stamped on it. It was a dollar watch that he kept in stock for the purpose, but the gesture was sobering.

All the actors whom he took in charge were gratified. He expected to take charge of them in every part of their lives. When Mrs. Leslie Carter married for the second time without telling him, Belasco excommunicated her and never saw her again, although she kept on writing to him and hoping for a reconciliation. He was a tyrant and an artist manqué.

Brooks Atkinson

RICHARD MANSFIELD (1854–1907)

191 *Mansfield achieved widespread success and wealth from his dual role as Dr Jekyll and Mr Hyde (first performed in Boston in 1887) and he was also the first to introduce Shaw to American audiences with* Arms and the Man *(1894) and* The Devil's Disciple *(1897).*

His major productions were lavishly mounted and prepared with scrupulous attention to every detail. And each detail was supervised by the intense, high-strung star whose explosions, when things went wrong, were the terror of managers and fellow performers. Once the production was prepared, however, and once the actor was ready to perform, he lost himself in the role he was playing. An incident which occurred in 1894 during his production of *Scenes and Incidents from the Life of Napoleon Bonaparte* illustrates his power of absorption and concentration. Shortly before the curtain rose Mansfield had exploded in fury when a stage hand had accidentally dropped a broom against his dressing room door. But during the performance, when Mansfield was waiting in the wings to begin the crucial scene at Waterloo, a supernumerary stumbled over a stack of rifles and sent them clattering to the floor. The cast was petrified, expecting a titanic outburst. But Mansfield did not move or blink an eye. He appeared not even to have heard the noise – so absorbed was he in the thoughts and feelings of his imaginary situation.

Garff B. Wilson

SIR ARTHUR WING PINERO (1855–1934)

192 *Sir Seymour Hicks records this splendid* bon mot *by the author of such plays as* The Magistrate *and* Trelawny of the Wells.

Of me, the critics usually said: "He seemed to perspire more than usual on this occasion"; a notice of this kind drew from the then Mr. Arthur Pinero the remark, "Seymour, I'm not sure they are wrong. If I were you I shouldn't advertise 'Doors open at eight,' I should alter it to 'Pores open at nine' "

EDMUND TEARLE (1856–1913)

193 Edmund Tearle was married to Kate Clinton. They were both creatures of such size that beside them I should have looked like Jack in Beanstalk Land. Edmund as Hamlet, a mastodon in tights, was always good for an unscheduled laugh when he soliloquized, "O, that this too, too solid flesh would melt." Kate, squeezed into costume as Portia, equalled him as a provoker of laughter when she complained, "My little body is a-weary of this great world." But they would both pause for the inevitable laughs to cease, then reassert their control over their audiences.

Their voices matched their girth. One story tells how Edmund was appearing in a Lancashire town one night while Kate stayed up in a hotel opposite the theatre waiting for him to return. When he got back after his performance, she had some disturbing news. "You were not in good voice tonight, my dear," she said. "I kept the window open, but I couldn't hear a word from where I was sitting"

Cedric Hardwicke

MRS BERNARD BEERE (1856–1915)

194 *'A woman capable of such wit and aplomb', said Madge Kendal, 'should have this anecdote told to her credit.'*

I only met her once. This was at a large bazaar which was attended by everybody who was anybody, and at which I was asked to preside at the photograph stall. Mrs. Beere had just made a sensational success in "As in a Looking Glass," an adaptation of the novel of the same name, and her photograph was in every shop window, so that I knew her well by sight.

As I stood at my stall, this lady, beautifully dressed – she was a striking figure, for she was very tall – came slowly up to me and raising her lorgnette and staring at me fixedly said, in a supercilious tone, "Are you selling *your* photographs, Mrs. Kendal?"

"No," I replied, "but I have some excellent ones of Mrs. Bernard Beere."

"Show me some," she drawled.

I took up a few small photographs which were retailed in the shops at a shilling each.

"Very good," she said. "How much are they?"

"Five pounds each," I replied in my blandest tones. "I'll take this one," she rejoined. "How cheap!"

Several years afterwards, when the Garrick Theatre was being built by Sir W. S. Gilbert for Sir John Hare, a delay occurred because water was struck when they were digging for the foundations of the stage.*

Not anticipating such an accident Sir John Hare had engaged certain members of his company for the opening play on a given date. Among them was Mrs. Bernard Beere.

When it was decided that the opening of the theatre must be postponed, Sir John Hare informed Mrs. Beere.

"Water under the stage," she replied, "has nothing to do with me," and she claimed that her salary should begin on the appointed date.

Madge Kendal

GEORGE BERNARD SHAW (1856–1950)

195 *'A testy Irish terrier – spirited and spry.' This is how the distinguished actress Helen Hayes describes the great Anglo-Irish dramatist.*

Shaw found fault at rehearsal with the last-act explosion in Barry

---

*At the time, Gilbert said that he didn't know 'whether to continue with the building or sell the fishing rights.'

Jackson's production of *Heartbreak House* and demanded a bigger bang. The stage manager assured him that on opening night there would be a bang to remember and accordingly warned the cast to that effect. When the cue came up, Edith Evans spoke the line, then prudently covered her face with her hands. Nothing happened. The audience was halfway out of the theatre when a sudden, thunderous crash brought the ceiling down and sent two playgoers to the hospital. Shaw for once, seemed satisfied.

Cedric Hardwicke

196 *Arnold Daly was an actor who sprang into prominence in New York as the producer of Shaw's plays. He came to London in 1911 both to play Bluntschli in* Arms and the Man *and, he hoped, to secure the American rights to Shaw's subsequent plays. However, when Shaw saw him act he was appalled.*

My Dear Daly

It is no use our squabbling. I am within my rights; and defiance of them, however earnestly you may believe it to be justifiable, is not possible, because you cannot do it single handed, and no-one would join you in the enterprise. I quite understand that it is very hard on an artist to be unable to use the material for his art which he feels to be the right material, and sees lying ready to his hand if only it belonged to him. I have suffered a good deal in that way myself. I have had to look on at actors and actresses who could have made my plays successes for themselves and for me, wasting their time and money and reputations on stuff which they were injudicious enough to prefer to mine. But I could not help that. Their talent was at their own disposal; and they did not choose to place it at mine. Well, the same thing is happening to you. You want my stuff; and I choose to dispose of it otherwise. I may be wrong; but I must follow my own judgment. And just as I found other actors who did believe in me, so you must find other authors who believe in you – not that I disbelieve in you for *all* stage purposes, you understand. I mean that, in my opinion, you are not as good for my purposes as other actors who are at my disposal.

The fact that Arms and the Man has been a failure will not stop you in other directions, as it is not known to the public, and your notices have been very good. It would be waste of time for me to explain the failure to you: if you could see the play as I see it, the failure would not have occurred. As to what you say about drugging and so forth, let me say that I can give you a good character as to your physical training for the work. I have made no complaint of that, because I have none to make. On the contrary, I was struck with the way in which you got into trim and kept in it. You behaved badly in other ways. You neglected your own work and claimed for yourself the position of manager, producer and author, with the result that all that part of your business which required minute study and swift, brilliant work: that is, the whole part except the last half of the First Act (which you did very well) was hopelessly bad, and let the performance down, in spite of all the others could do, to a point at which the play was hardly recognizable by anyone who had seen it played before. But though I blame you strongly for not having been so good as you might have been if you had stuck to your work and minded your own business as the others were minding theirs, I do not think you could have saved the situation even if you had done your best. I will not tell you why: you would not believe me.

Whether you believe me or not, I will now tell you exactly how you stand at present. In your own theatre, with your own company under your own management, you are worth what you can make. In an engagement, you are worth in London £15 a week in a certain line of parts. As a juvenile leading man you are worth absolutely nothing at all: any management can lay his hand on half a dozen young ambitioners who can beat you at that for half the money. If you stayed in London for five years and worked hard and made yourself agreeable enough to be welcome as a member of a company, you would improve a good deal; but you are not built that way, and would not do it. Your best plan is to induce Whitney to back you for an American campaign in a new play or plays, and give you another chance on the strength of your London notices. But in selecting the plays, DO face your age and limitations frankly. You are all right for comic and character juveniles; but for staid sympathetic ones in realistic modern tailoring you are out of the question. Your day for Eugenes and Valentines and Apjohns is gone by: you must bow to the clock and the calendar as other men have to do. You are not, for stage purposes, an English gentleman. You are a bit of a genius, and a bit of a blackguard, and a bit of a spoilt child; and you are quite unable to shake any of these bits off on the stage. You have never been hammered by others into the hard-beaten professionalism that makes the capable and biddable actor; and you have been too fond of yourself to hammer yourself hard enough. You must try to get parts in which your qualities and your faults contribute equally to a likeable effect. In addition to your cleverness, you have a sort of Irish Emigrant pathos about you that will always secure you more indulgence than you deserve. With that stock in trade, there is a chance for you yet; and you have my friendliest wishes that you may have luck.

And so farewell, as far as professional relations are concerned. I have done my best for you; and you have done your worst for me; but I bear no malice, and quite recognize that you want to make my plays a success, and honestly believe you could if I would let you. Only I won't, for which you must forgive me as cordially as you can.

Yours sincerely
G. Bernard Shaw

197 *Having failed to make a pre-arranged visit to Shaw, Helen Hayes recalls her eventual meeting with him some years afterwards.*

I was, however, given a second chance with Bernard Shaw some years later, when we met at Lady Throckmorton's at Coughton Court, Warwickshire. The stately home was built for Lord Francis Throckmorton by Elizabeth I. He had been her ambassador to Mary Stuart. Since the Gunpowder Plot was hatched there, the ensuing explosion resulted in a cloud over the family. The Crown reduced the family title to a simple baronetcy.

The Dowager Lady Throckmorton, whose charming but drowsy son Sir Robert was dubbed The Sleepy Baronet by Charlie [Chaplin], had a pleasant exchange with the then 80–year-old playwright, who was not in the best of moods. For the first time in his life, he was about to have a tooth pulled and he was furious.

Shaw was a testy Irish terrier – spirited and spry – a grizzled, ancient puppy of a man with a complexion so beautiful that it was remarkable. Mary Anderson, herself an octogenarian, who, I believe, had been painted as Juliet by Rossetti, remarked about it with an envy all the ladies present shared.

"Now, Bernard," she teased, "I don't want to hear any canard about splashing your face with icewater and rubbing it off with the sleeve of your Norfolk jacket. You don't have a line or a wrinkle. What is the secret?"

"Comfortable boots and open bowels," he snapped, putting an end to her.

As for me, he had remembered the unfortunate incident that took place years before. Perhaps too well. We were all to suffer that day from his fear of dentistry, and consequently not to be spared his bite.

"You're appearing in Housman's *Victoria*, aren't you?" he asked amiably enough.

"Yes, Mr. Shaw," I replied. Laurence Housman had told me that G.B.S. was mad about his play.

"Silly little part, isn't it?" Shaw now observed, dispensing with the zenith of both the British Empire and my career in one fell swoop.

OSCAR WILDE (1854–1900)

198 *Brilliant dialogue and richly comic characterizations abound in Wilde's plays. The wit employed in his plays was surely honed in his own conversation.*

A Woman of No Importance first appeared at the Theatre Royal, Haymarket, on April 19th, 1893, and repeated the success of *Lady Windermere's Fan*. The critics had complained that in the earlier comedy the action of the play had been held up while the characters delivered themselves of epigrams. But 'English critics always confuse the action of a play with the incidents of a melodrama', said Wilde. 'I wrote the first act of *A Woman of No Importance* in answer to the critics who said that *Lady Windermere's Fan* lacked action. In the act in question there was absolutely no action at all. It was a perfect act.' The critics were duly irritated, and the audience were thoroughly exhilarated. They could have gone on listening for ever to the absent-minded 'Lady Hunstanton', who says of 'Lord Illingworth': 'I was in hopes he would have married Lady Kelso. But I believe he said her family was too large. Or was it her feet? I forget which.' And the interchanges between 'Lord Illingworth' and 'Mrs. Allonby' kept the house in a state of animation:

> *Lord Illingworth (not wishing to follow the rest of the party indoors):* Yes, let us stay here. The Book of Life begins with a man and a woman in a garden.
> *Mrs. Allonby:* It ends with Revelations.

Thunderous applause and cries of 'author' at the close of the play brought a large man, who was sitting in a box in full view of the audience, to his feet. In clear tones, which were heard in every part of the theatre, he announced: 'Ladies and Gentlemen: I regret to inform you that Mr. Oscar Wilde is not in the house.' As the speaker was Mr. Oscar Wilde, he was in a position to know. Much felicitation was in progress behind the scenes, and when Wilde joined the happy throng in Tree's dressing-room such words as 'marvellous', 'unique', 'wonderful' and 'great' were being bandied about. Author and actor congratulated each other. Then:

'I shall always regard you as the best critic of my plays', said Wilde fervently.

'But I have never criticised your plays,' said Tree reproachfully.

'That's why', said Wilde complacently.

Hesketh Pearson

199 *The Importance of Being Earnest* was originally in four acts. Alexander [the actor-manager Sir George Alexander] said that it should be in three. Wilde did not like to scrap any of his lines, which, after all, however easily conceived, had been indited with some effort. In telling me that Wilde had fought for nearly an hour to retain a scene, Alexander could only remember the end of their bout:

'Do you realise, Alec, what you are asking me to sacrifice?'

'You will be able to use it in another play.'

'It may not fit into another play.'

'What does that matter? You are clever enough to think of a hundred things just as good.'

'Of course I am . . . a thousand if need be . . . but that is not the
point. This scene that you feel is superfluous cost me terrible exhausting
labour and heart-rending nerve-racking strain. You may not believe me,
but I assure you on my honour that it must have taken fully five minutes
to write.'

Hesketh Pearson

SIR PHILIP BEN GREET (1857–1936)

200 *One of the great Victorian and Edwardian 'characters' of the theatre, Greet helped Lilian
Baylis to run the Old Vic Theatre when she took over its management in 1912.*

When he came to the Vic in 1914, Greet was already fifty-six, with thirty-
five years experience of many kinds of stages. Although an ardent
playgoer from boyhood, he had been forbidden to attend the Vic by an
otherwise broad-minded father; and he obeyed the veto (with, no doubt,
little temptation to break it) until the night that he approached Miss
Baylis. Trained in the old stock companies – he claimed that he had to
play nineteen roles in his first week as an actor – he became a touring
manager who at one time had twenty-five companies on the road,
playing small provincial dates. He worked with William Poel on
experiments in near-Elizabethan production,* and in presenting
Everyman; he ran a school of acting in Bedford Street; he was a pioneer
of professional open-air theatre, and (in 1886) inaugurated the Open Air
Theatre in Regents Park; for two years he had presented Shakespeare to
audiences of LCC schoolchildren at the invitation of the Board of
Education; and he had toured with a Shakespearian company throughout
America.

The spiritual qualifications of B.G. – as he was usually called – were,
for Miss Baylis, more impressive. Like her, he was a devoted Anglican.
He was a pillar of the Actors' Church Union, and of the Church and
Stage Guild. B.G. viewed Shakespeare as a moral oracle who helps us
all to achieve 'serenity of mind' and 'the way of gentleness and mercy'
and whose works must therefore be brought to the widest possible
audience. In Dame Sybil's [Thorndike] words, Shakespeare was 'the
nearest approach to Almighty God that B.G. knew'. (In the nursing
home where he died, many years later, he asked the doctor to change his
nurse, because the one in attendance didn't know a line of the Bard.) But
if he revered Shakespeare, it was not as someone supernatural and remote.
As Margaret Webster put it, 'Shakespeare, to him, was bread, breathing

---

*Poel (1852–1934) was a curious figure, totally involved with his efforts to stage Shakespeare
in a proper 'Elizabethan manner of presentation', believing that the nearer a production is to
the text, the more theatrically effective the result.

and a cup of tea'. He believed in simplicity – and that suited Lilian Baylis's budget very well.

B.G. was tall and sturdy, with a shock of white hair, deep blue eyes, and a cherubic face, which frequently went scarlet with violent rages. He got angry when he couldn't remember his lines, which happened frequently; he would stuff them up his sleeves, or into his hat, or pin them behind a property tree, but he would still drop sections of speeches, and rhubarb his way through the gap. He got angry when he saw (or imagined) that a property had been moved. In the middle of a speech he would say, quite audibly to the audience. '*That* bloody thing should be *there*' – transferring it to the place in which he expected to see it – or 'I'll bloody *kill* him (meaning the ASM) when I get off. As I was saying . . .' He was a belligerent, explosive man; and it was not long before he was at war with Lilian. They had terrible rows, forgave each other and then did battle royal again. Both were shrewd enough to realize that they couldn't do without each other, at that time. His value to her is plain. He knew about Shakespeare – as much as, if not more than, anybody in the theatre. He knew about actors: he had trained scores of them, and he brought a number to the Vic. He knew about management and production on the cheap, having to survive one disaster after another and come up smiling – or fighting. He knew about opera – enough, at least, to help in productions. He knew about audiences. As he never demanded – indeed, never encouraged – novel readings or original business, and as most of the actors were used to working together, the plays could be staged in rapid succession with little rehearsal – a necessity at the Vic. And he did it all free – for the first year, at least. Later he took 'expenses'.

Richard Findlater

SIR CHARLES HAWTREY (1858–1923)

201 *The leading comedian of his day, Hawtrey created a style that was widely imitated. He became manager of Her Majesty's Theatre in 1885 and of the Comedy in 1887.*

He was always just in – or just out of – some awful money muddle, and either worried to death or else in the greatest good humour.

He seemed to spend half his life rushing about to get money to stave off creditors, and there is a characteristic true story of how he once dealt with a writ-server. He received the man in his most fascinating Hawtrey manner, accepted the writ gracefully, and insisted on giving the bewildered visitor one of his best cigars.

"Are you doing anything this evening?" he asked presently. "Have you seen my play?"

The man replied, no, he hadn't seen Hawtrey's play.

"Then, my dear fellow, you must – I insist," he exclaimed. "I will get you two seats."

He disappeared into the adjoining office, calling to his secretary, and then returned with an envelope.

"There you are, my dear chap, two for to-night," he said.

The man, overcome by Hawtrey's charm, stammered all the grateful thanks he could think of, and took his departure. What he said when, later, he opened the envelope and found the writ inside it, I do not know!

Gladys Cooper

SIR FRANK BENSON (1858–1939)

202 *With great energy, Benson threw himself into the task of performing Shakespeare all over England. He had, said James Agate, 'presence, profile, voice and vitality'.*

Benson wanted *Macbeth* to be a major revival. Before Janet Achurch appeared he had produced the play with Winifred Beadnell, who left the cast shortly afterwards (to return to it next year), as Lady Macbeth. He confessed that, thus early, he knew everything about the play except his words. Even when familiar with these, he was unsure of himself, allowing his voice to saw the air and his attitudes to stiffen into what [W.S.] Gilbert, in another context, called both angular and flat. Fresh to the part which he played, to the horror of traditionalists, bare-legged, and with an intricate production to consider, he kept the company hard at it. When they had been rehearsing for nearly seven hours without meals, and Macbeth had reached the cry, 'They have tied me to the stake!' William Mollison exclaimed, 'I wish to God they would tie me to one!' Benson, returning to the rude fact that the company had not eaten for hours, dismissed rehearsal.

J.C. Trewin

203 Sport in the country makes me think, too, of Sir Frank Benson. I suppose no actor who ever lived has been such an all-round athlete as this old 'Varsity Blue. It is said of him, that if he were debating which of two actors to engage for a certain part, the slightly inferior artist, if he was a fine cricketer, would most certainly have obtained the coveted honour of employment under the Bensonian banner.

I have heard, though I cannot vouch for the story, that Sir Frank's contracts with his artists were always worded: "To play the Ghost in 'Hamlet' and keep wicket," or "To play Laertes and field cover-point"; and it was said that no Polonius need apply unless he happened to be a first-class wicket-keeper.

Seymour Hicks

CHARLES FROHMAN (1860–1915)

04 *When the* Lusitania *was torpedoed in 1915 she claimed among her victims Charles Frohman, the fifty-five year old impresario. As a manager he started out by organising touring companies.*

The Northern Pacific Railroad had just been opened to the coast, and Charles followed the new route. A series of tragic, dramatic, and comic experiences began. The tour was through the heart of the old cow country. One night, when the train was stalled by the wrecking of a bridge near Miles City, Montana, a group of cowboys started to "shoot up" the train. Frohman, with ready resource, singled out the leader and said:

"We've got a theatrical company here and we will give you a performance."

He got Rowland Buckstone to stand out on the prairie and recite "The Smuggler's Life", "The Execution," and "The Sanguinary Pirate" by the light of a big bonfire which was built while the show was going on. This tickled the cowboys and brought salvos of shots and shouts of laughter.

At Miles City occurred what might have been a serious episode. When the company reached the hotel at about eleven in the morning Charles Wheatleigh, the "first old man," asked the hotel-keeper what time breakfast was served. When he replied "Eight-thirty o'clock." Wheatleigh pounded the desk and said:

"That is for farmers. When do artists eat?"

The clerk was a typical Westerner, and thought this was an insult. He made a lunge for Wheatleigh, when Frohman stepped in and settled the difficulty in his usual suave and smiling way.

Now began a return journey from Portland that was even more precarious than the trip out. Baggage had to be sacrificed; there was scarcely any scenery. One "back drop" showing the interior of a cathedral was used for every kind of scene, from a gambling-house to a ball-room. To the financial hardship of the homeward trip was added real physical trial. Frohman showed in towns wherever there was the least prospect of any kind of a house. The company therefore played in skating-rinks, school-houses, even barns. In some places the members of the company had to take the oil-lamps that served as footlights back in the make-shift dressing-rooms while they dressed.

At Bozeman, Montana, occurred an incident which showed both the humour and the precariousness of the situation. Frohman assembled the company in the waiting-room of the station and, stepping up to the ticket-office, laid down one hundred and thirty dollars in cash.

"Where do you want to go?" asked the agent.

Shoving the money at him, Frohman said, "How far will this take us?"

The agent looked out of the window, counted up the company, and said, "To Billings."

Turning to the company, Frohman said, with a smile, "Ladies and gentlemen, we play Billings next."

Just then he received a telegram from Alf Hayman, who was on ahead of the company:

> What town shall I bill?

Frohman wired back:

> Bill Billings.

Hayman again wired:

> Have no printing and can get no credit. What shall I do?

Frohman's resource came into stead, for he telegraphed:

> Notify theaters that we are a high-class company from Wallack's Theater in New York and use no ordinary printing. We employ only newspapers and dodgers.

At Bismarck, North Dakota, the company gave "Moths". In this play the spurned hero, a singer, has a line which reads, "There are many marquises, but very few *tenors*."

Money had been so scarce for months that this remark was the last straw, so the company burst into laughter, and the performance was nearly broken up. Frohman, who stood in the back of the house, enjoyed it as much as the rest.

Through all these hardships Frohman remained serene and smiling. His unfailing optimism tided over the dark days. The end came at Winona, Minnesota. The company had sacrificed everything it could possibly sacrifice. Frohman borrowed a considerable sum from the railroad agent to go to Chicago, where he obtained six hundred dollars from Frank Sanger. With this he paid the friendly agent and brought the company back to New York.

Even the last lap of this disastrous journey was not without its humor. The men were all assembled in the smoking-car on the way from Albany to New York. Frohman for once sat silent. When somebody asked him why he looked so glum, he said, "I'm thinking of what I have got to face to-morrow."

Up spoke Wheatleigh, whose marital troubles were well known. He slapped Frohman on the back and said:

"Charley, your troubles are slight. Think of me. I've got to face my wife to-morrow."

It was characteristic of Frohman's high sense of integrity that he gave his personal note to each member of the company for back salary in full, and before five years passed had discharged every debt.

Isaac F. Marcosson and Daniel Frohman

205 Peter Pan, *by J. M. Barrie, was probably Frohman's most celebrated London production.*

The very beginning of "Peter Pan", so far as the stage presentation was concerned, was full of romantic interest. Barrie had agreed to write a play for Frohman, and met him at dinner one night at the Garrick Club in London. Barrie seemed nervous and ill at ease.

"What's the matter?" said Charles.

"Simply this," said Barrie. "You know I have an agreement to deliver you the manuscript of a play?"

"Yes," said Frohman.

"Well, I have it, all right," said Barrie, "but I am sure it will not be a commercial success. But it is a dream-child of mine, and I am so anxious to see it on the stage that I have written another play which I will be glad to give you and which will compensate you for any loss on the one I am so eager to see produced."

"Don't bother about that," said Frohman. "I will produce both plays."

Now the extraordinary thing about this episode is that the play about whose success Barrie was so doubtful was "Peter Pan," which made several fortunes. The manuscript he offered Frohman to indemnify him from loss was "Alice-Sit-By-The-Fire," which lasted only a season. Such is the estimate that the author often puts on his own work!

When Frohman first read "Peter Pan" he was so entranced that he could not resist telling all his friends about it. He would stop them in the street and act out the scenes. Yet it required the most stupendous courage and confidence to put on a play that, from the manuscript, sounded like a combination of circus and extravaganza; a play in which children flew in and out of rooms, crocodiles swallowed alarm-clocks, a man exchanged places with his dog in its kennel, and various other seemingly absurd and ridiculous things happened.

But Charles believed in Barrie. He had gone to an extraordinary expense to produce "Peter Pan" in England. He duplicated it in the United States.

No one will be surprised to know that in connection with "Peter Pan" is one of the most sweetly gracious acts in Frohman's life. The original of *Peter* was sick in bed at his home when the play was produced in London. The little lad was heartsick because he could not see it. When Frohman came to London Barrie told him about it.

"If the boy can't come to the play, we will take the play to the boy," he said.

Frohman sent his company out to the boy's home with as many "props" as could be jammed into the sick-room. While the delighted and excited child sat propped up in bed the wonders of the fairy play were unfolded before him. It is probably the only instance where a play was done before a child in his home.

Isaac F. Marcosson and Daniel Frohman

SIR C. AUBREY SMITH (1863–1948)

206 *Smith forsook the British stage and became the uncrowned king of the English colony in Hollywood.*

It was not customary in Cardiff to play a mid-week matinée, but we did, and our little company of seven outnumbered the paid admissions by the margin of one! Aubrey Smith claimed we had set a record. Henry Miller countered that he had been with a touring company which had topped the paid audience by two to one. "What was the play?" demanded Aubrey testily. "*Henry IV, Part II*," was the answer. I remember the old cricketer's reply, "Good God, sir, that play has a cast of thirty – two to one means an audience of fifteen. Ours is the victory – by a margin of nine, sir, nine!"

Aubrey Smith was then in his late fifties, handsome, rugged, a monolith of probity, wildly miscast as a philandering husband. In spite of his excellent performance, those who saw the play knew for certain that the virtue of Miss Carson as the other woman was never in jeopardy. Aubrey, a great cricketer, had captained the English Eleven on two tours. He was an ardent golfer too, and in the wings while waiting for his entrances he would practise short approaches with his stick and a ball of paper. On one occasion during a performance he chipped his paper ball through a window of the setting onto the stage. He was terribly cut up about it. I whispered that nobody would notice. He was one of those people who cannot whisper and replied in a resonant tone, "I know, but I shanked my shot!" It was always his custom to clear his vocal cords before an entrance. Sometimes the audience would be puzzled to hear offstage a distant voice booming "Hip bath! Hip bath! Hip bath!"

Raymond Massey

LADY TREE, née Helen Maud Holt (1863–1937)

207 She was a very talented woman and before she went on the stage had taught mathematics, Greek and Latin at Queen's College. It was then that she fell madly in love with Herbert Beerbohm Tree [see p.ooo] and her ambition, when they were married, was that they should act together.

She rather thought in those days that being on the stage was something of a game. She soon discovered, however, that work at the theatre began at 10.30 a.m. and ended at 11.30 p.m.

On one occasion she was called on to play at short notice a part which had been acted by Lady Monckton, who was a much older woman.

In the company was Mr. Harry Kemble, who said to her, "If you will come to me, I will tell you everything about the part and give you all the wrinkles."

"Wrinkles!" replied Mrs. Tree, bridling. "Don't talk to me about wrinkles. Go away to the other side of the stage and stop there. Wrinkles, indeed."

In those days Lady Tree did not know that "wrinkles" is the term we apply to the little bits of stage business which give finish to a part and not the indelible marks which come on our forehead, whether we like it or not.

Madge Kendal

FRED TERRY (1863–1933)

208 *A member of the famous Terry family, Fred was a handsome romantic actor, often remembered for his part as Sir Percy Blakeney in* The Scarlet Pimpernel.

He once mounted a production of *Romeo and Juliet* for his daughter Phyllis. He had intended to act Mercutio, but became ill during rehearsals and finally directed the play without appearing in it himself. A shy young actor, engaged to play the part of Paris, was given an elaborate Carpaccio costume to wear – parti-coloured tights and an Italianate wig falling to his shoulders. Some of the older members of the company, with whom he shared a dressing-room, mischievously drew attention to the inadequacy of his make-up, and finally persuaded him to add mascara to his eyelashes, rouge to his lips, and a dangling pearl to his right ear. Deeply self-conscious in all this finery, the young man slunk timidly on to the stage at the dress parade and bashfully announced himself. Fred, who was asleep in the darkness of the stalls, woke suddenly, rammed his glasses on to his nose, and, roaring with laughter, shouted out, 'My God, it's a tart I once slept with in Bury St. Edmunds!'

John Gielgud

MINNIE MADDERN FISKE (1865–1932)

209 *When she married, Minnie Maddern Fiske retired from acting. But her absence was only short-lived and her return saw her as one of the leading champions of Ibsen on the New York stage. The intensity of her acting was much admired, though her delivery did not always find universal favour, as Franklin Pierce Adams indicated in his oft-quoted lines:*

> Some words she runs togetherso;
>   Some others are distinctly stated
> Somecometoofast and s o m e t o o s l o w
>   And some are syncopated,
> And yet no voice – I am sincere –
> Exists that I prefer to hear.

One of Mrs. Fiske's most successful scenes in *Salvation Nell* was a scene lasting ten minutes during which she sat on the floor, almost motionless, holding her drunken lover's head in her lap without uttering a word. Even though hurried activity was going on around her, she riveted the attention of the audience on her own silent agony. After watching this scene in performance, the distinguished actress–singer, Mary Garden, is said to have exclaimed, "Ah, to be able to do *nothing* like that!" George Arliss, a fellow actor, said: "Her great moments come in flashes – in silences, in exclamations, or in brief utterances." She certainly threw herself (and occasionally others) into the rehearsal of her great roles.

On one occasion, in preparing the role of Hedda Gabler, she locked her cousin, Emily Stevens, out in the cold while she recreated a scene between Hedda and Lovborg, and later, when Emily expressed astonishment over the fact that the scene was not in the play – having been imaginatively conjured up by Mrs. Fiske – the older actress answered: "Ibsen shows us only the last hours. To portray them I must know everything that has gone before. . . . I must know all that Hedda ever was. When I do, the role will play itself."

Garff B. Wilson

MRS PATRICK CAMPBELL (1865–1940)

210 *Tremendous brio, enormous confidence, considerable talent – all were characteristic of Mrs Patrick Campbell's performances. Her voice, says Emlyn Williams, was 'throaty and over-articulated'. She was nearly fifty when she created Eliza Doolittle in Shaw's Pygmalion in 1914. Off stage, with her fellow actors, she could often be difficult, to say the least.*

One foolish anecdote of this time has clung to me: – Mr. Alexander in this play by Mr. Jones had to look into my face and tell me I was beautiful and that he adored me, or some such words, and one night he said it with such a look in his eyes, as though he would willingly have wrung my neck, that I burst out laughing. When the curtain fell, his stage manager came with pompous dignity to the door of my dressing-room and said, "Mr. Alexander's compliments and will you please not laugh at him on the stage?" I replied, "My compliments to Mr. Alexander, and please tell him I never laugh at him until I get home." I was a most horrible leading lady, surely!

211 One of the members of Irving's staff was very proud of his distant relationship to "Mrs. Pat," and never lost an opportunity of dragging into his conversation some reference to "my cousin, Mrs. Patrick Campbell." On the first night of *Hamlet*, Mrs. Pat had scarcely mastered her reading of the part of 'Ophelia,' and some unfavourable comment was heard on the performance. A friend of mine was met by him in the foyer after the Mad scene, and gaily he enquired: "Well, and how has my cousin, Mrs. Patrick Campbell, got on?" Said my hyper-critical friend, "Humph, I'm afraid – I'm *afraid* your cousin . . . !" "Oh, I'm sorry for that," said the distant relative, and after a moment's pause, added: "She's only my *second* cousin you know."

John Martin-Harvey

212 *She could certainly be a wilful spirit, as John Gielgud relates in the next couple of passages.*

Everyone referred to her as Mrs Pat, but I always hated the familiarity and took care always to address her by her full name until the day when she rewarded me by asking me to call her Stella. I had been introduced to her, in the early Twenties, at a luncheon party in Brighton in a private suite at the Metropole Hotel given by a Lord who loved the stage. She was playing Hedda Gabler at a theatre on one of the piers and someone told her that the performance was a *tour de force*. 'I suppose that is why I am always forced to tour,' she replied mournfully.

Her company dreaded her, except for the few worshippers who dared to stand up to her when she was in a bad mood. She loved rich and titled people and would allow them to give her presents and entertain her, but she was very proud with younger folk and generous both in advice and criticism. She could be wonderful company, though I think she was often cruel to men who fell in love with her – even Forbes-Robertson and Shaw – and sometimes even more unkind to her women friends, letting them fetch and carry for her for a time and then making fun of them or casting them aside. But somehow I was never afraid of her, though the only time I acted with her, as Oswald in *Ghosts* in 1929, she played some alarming tricks and made a fool of me at one performance. The dress-rehearsal had gone off without mishap, and Mrs Campbell was word perfect and sailing through her scenes. At the first performance, however, she seemed less at ease, though still charming to me at the fall of the curtain, when she graciously thanked me for having helped her through. I beamed with delight and thought I had passed my test. At the second performance I was sitting at a table smoking. No ash tray had been provided, and I looked helplessly round when the cue came for me to put out my cigar. Not daring to leave my chair, for fear of complicating the moves that had been arranged by the director, I stubbed it out on the chenille tablecloth and dropped the butt under the table and then, a few moments later, stupidly put my hands on the table before lifting them to cover my face. Mrs Campbell, turning upstage, shook with laughter for the rest of the scene, and pouted, 'Oh, you're such an amateur!' as the curtain fell. During the second interval my aunt, Mabel Terry-Lewis, never famous for her tact, burst into my dressing-room. 'Tell her we can't hear a word she says,' she announced, 'the Charing Cross Road is being drilled outside!' This counsel I naturally preferred to ignore, though it hardly tended to improve my already shaken confidence. But worse was yet to come. At the end of the play Mrs Alving stands aghast, staring at her son as he mutters, 'Mother, give me the sun. The sun! The sun!' In her hand she still holds the box of pills which she does not dare to give him. Mrs Campbell had evidently decided suddenly that she must make the most of this important final moment. With a wild cry, she flung the pillbox into the footlights and threw herself across my knees with her entire weight. 'Oswald. Oswald!' she moaned. The armchair (borrowed by Mrs Campbell herself from a friend, because, as she said, 'the back is high enough to hide my chins') cracked ominously as she lay prone across my lap, and as I clutched the arms in desperation for fear they might disintegrate, she whispered fiercely, 'Keep down for the call. This play is worse than having a confinement.' Yet she had been of the greatest help during rehearsals and I always thought she could, if she had chosen, have been a fine director herself.

213 When the first rehearsal of *Strange Orchestra* began, 'Mrs. Pat' pretended that she did not understand the play. 'Who are all these extraordinary characters?' she demanded. 'Where do they live? Does Gladys Cooper know them?' She invariably arrived late every morning, and we would hear her talking loudly all the way from the stage-door to the stage. She said to David Hutcheson, whom we got for a certain part after tremendous trouble: 'Oh, how-do-you-do. I hope you'll stay. We have had four already!' She kept on reminding us, 'I am leaving in a fortnight; you must get someone else to play this part.' Every afternoon she went off to sit with her beloved Pekinese, which had been locked up in quarantine on her return with it from America. Her distress about her pet was quite genuine, and a real obsession with her. In the end she left us, as she had threatened to do, and I was in despair. She had rehearsed the part magnificently, and I felt sure that if she would only open in it that the play's success was certain. And how wise she was about all the other parts! Here, just as in *Ghosts*, she was extremely well informed about every detail of the play, though she pretended to be quite indifferent to everything that was going on. One day she was sitting at the side of the

stage. I thought she was asleep. I was rehearsing one of Hugh Williams's scenes, and asked him to cut a certain line. Suddenly the famous voice boomed out: 'You know his whole character is in that line; I shouldn't cut it if I were you'. Of course she was perfectly right.

214 *Emlyn Williams describes his first meeting with Mrs Campbell, at John Gielgud's home.*

One night I arrived later and the one caller still there was spread on the sofa: a stout old lady in a rag-bag of a black evening dress ornamented with what looked like jet. Her hair, an improbable black, was done in old-fashioned loops above a face to which, earlier in the evening, make-up had been applied, hastily and liberally. She looked like a grand theatrical landlady on a night out, who had herself once trod the boards.

'Stella dear, this is Emlyn Williams – Mrs Patrick Campbell.'

'Oh, he won't recognize the name of an old has-been . . .'

She would anyway have been identified by a voice imitated in a hundred anecdotes: throaty and over-articulated, sounding anxious to please until you realize that the humble pie was flavoured with arsenic.

It was my first and last meeting with a sacred monster who so perfectly lived up to herself that next day I wrote it down. I waited for the darts, and they came.

John said, 'Emlyn has a great success at the St James's, with Edith [Evans] and Cedric.' I wondered if the mention of the foremost contemporary actress was the happiest of strokes.

'*Do* tell me more, but you look a *child*, did you write it all by yourself?'

She cannot have known how lethal that dart was. John looked nervous. 'He's adapted it from the French.'

The black eyes fixed on me with horror and there was a weightlift of beringed fingers. 'Oh, you poor dear, a *translation?*' She made it sound like a dirty book. 'Translations remind me of those short-sighted spinsters slaving over their abominable copies in the Louvre. John, dear, do you remember our *Ghosts*, the programme should have read "*Mangled* from the Norwegian by William What-was-his-name . . ." Bowmen? Arrowsmith? *Archer*, that was it . . .'

She turned to me again, 'Now I've got a *spiffing* idea, why not write a play out of your *very own head*, for a penniless old harridan who can still act? Goodbye dear John, such lovely costumes, and goodbye you naughty *cribber*, goodbye . . .'

WILLIAM BUTLER YEATS (1865–1939)

215 *Irish poet and dramatist who, in 1923, was awarded the Nobel Prize for Literature. With Lady Gregory, he founded the Abbey Theatre in Dublin.*

Where can we go from here? It seems to me that this is the end of the road for what is falsely labelled 'realism.' The theatre never was and never can be 'real.' Its rule of life is not 'let us *be*,' but 'let's *pretend*.' The actor portraying a murderer cannot drum up a 'real' impulse or his performance would clap him in the electric chair. The stage lovers can only pretend their romantic ardour, or the play would be padlocked.

I am reminded that at the Abbey Theatre in Dublin one day, W. B. Yeats, the poet and playwright, was looking for realism in creating the lighting effects for a glorious sunset. Hour after hour, until evening came, he had the electricians try every conceivable combination of colours and rheostats. At last, he saw exactly the effect he wanted. "That's it!" he cried. "Hold it, hold it!"

"We can't hold it, sir," came a stage hand's apologetic voice. "The bloody theatre's on fire."

Cedric Hardwicke

DAME MARIE TEMPEST (1866–1942)

216 *The leading comedienne of the early twentieth century. Rex Harrison describes her technique in handling an audience during Robert Morley's play,* Short Story.

We opened out of town, in Glasgow, and then came to London. It fascinated me to see Dame Marie, on opening nights, shaking with nerves to such an extent that, during the tea party which seemed always to feature in her plays, her tea cup had to be glued to the saucer.

I had a short scene with Dame Marie, after which we left the stage together through the inevitable french windows of that period. Almost before we were out of sight of the audience, Dame Marie started to clap her hands loudly; whereupon the audience, thinking that the noise came from some enthusiast in their midst, took up the clapping. I looked sidelong at Dame Marie, thinking it was a joke, but not at all – she was quite serious, and it happened at every performance.

Her curtain calls, too, were masterfully handled. After the routine cast calls, she appeared by herself, and then most graciously brought on Sybil Thorndike from one side and Matthews from the other. By that time the applause was dying down, but still the curtain went up, and a maid planted in the wings would catapult on to the stage Dame Marie's little white Sealyham dog. The audience adored it. Dame Marie made a great pantomime of shooing the dog away, and wondering how he could have followed her on to the stage, and then finally would take the trembling, unwilling creature into her arms and hug it, and get two more curtain calls all to herself.

217 Off stage he [James Agate] found her a perpetual delight. There had been a fire at her pretty little St John's Wood house, and he arrived in the morning to commiserate. She, wearing pyjamas, was rampaging through the mess brandishing a coal hammer and about to demolish a grand piano. It would look better for insurance purposes. He protested that it wouldn't seem at all like fire damage. She reversed the hammer and bounced the spike along shelves of rather shabby calf-bound books. Again he protested. 'The hose-pipe, dear,' she reproved him in her patrician voice, 'the hose-pipe!'

James Harding

SIR SEYMOUR HICKS (1871–1949)

218 *Hicks was a fine comedian who had learnt his craft from the great J. L. Toole. He appeared in London's first-ever revue,* Under the Clock, *in 1894. He built the Aldwych and Globe Theatres in London. These extracts come from his autobiography,* Me and My Missus.

1887 was just at the end of what is known in the theatrical profession as the lesser palmy days. It was at this time that every piece perpetrated by any kind of author was tried out at a matinée. I often prompted four new productions a week. This gave amateur playwrights an opportunity of paying to see their absolute rubbish performed by professional actors, while distinguished amateurs often had the impertinence to appear in any classic parts supported by a first-class London company, many of whom were obliged through lack of means to subject themselves to this, the greatest possible indignity.

As may be supposed, most of these performances were thrown on anyhow, and so many amusing things occurred at them that if ever members of my profession happened to be dull or in doubt as to how to spend a happy afternoon, it became the fashion for them to go and have a good laugh at some anæmic Richard the Third, or enjoy some atrocious nonsense labelled a "New and Original play in four Acts." One of these poor souls played Hamlet, with a cast of many of the best actors in London, his only qualification for the part being that he was the son of rich parents, his father having made his money in a flourishing carrier's business. The matinée must have cost £500 in salaries alone. The laughter commenced on Hamlet's entrance, and continued merrily throughout the afternoon, a mighty roar arising when the King (was it by accident or design?) misquoted his lines to the Queen, and instead of saying, "Full thirty journeys hath the sun and moon," etc., substituted for them, "Full thirty times has *Pickford's van* gone round." A week later the melancholy matinée-giver left England for the Cape of Good Hope.

219 Of course there were occasionally good matinée productions, but they were few and far between. One, I remember, was of an historical drama that went smoothly enough until almost the very end of the last act, when there came one of the biggest unintentional laughs I have ever heard in a theatre.

The scene was a dungeon, and in it, chained to the wall, was a Royalist hero on the eve of execution. The heroine entered to bid him farewell, and a scene was enacted between the pair in which the withers of the audience were wrung watching as they did the parting of a devoted man and woman. The main object of the heroine's arrival in addition to saying her last good-bye, was that she brought for her lover's use a small phial of poison with which he would cheat the hangman on the morrow and spare himself the indignity of a public execution. In the nervousness of a first performance, however, the lady who played the heart-broken girl forgot this part of the plot entirely, and left without handing over the all-important means of escape. The actor realized her mistake when it was too late. She had gone; in vain he called for her return, but she came not. In vain he walked to the prompt corner, but, as is usual when a prompter is really wanted, he was not there. The situation was a hopeless one, and he stood in the centre of the stage, beginning his last farewell to the world without the faintest notion of how he was to get out of it. No sword, no gun, no poison, no anything. The actors and actresses in the audience were quick to see his dilemma, and waited with sympathetic eagerness to see what he would do. The inspiration of genius came to him, and with tragic intensity he declared:

"And so to-night I die. Yes. Never, oh never shall it be said that the last of the De Courceys fell by the hand of the paid executioner; no, never! never!" And suddenly, with a convulsive twitch of the head and the raising of his arm, he fell prone and cried, "Thank God! I have broken my neck!"

220 Many years ago at the Richmond Theatre, a remark from the pit amused the house enormously. An actor who was playing the part of the Cardinal in "Under the Red Robe" was by no means good. The audience were fidgety throughout the evening, being thoroughly conscious that they were witnessing a most inferior performance on the gentleman's part. At the end of the last act all the characters in the play attacked the Cardinal, and he, finding himself alone and without power, turned on his tormentors crying, "Am I then only a howling pelican in the wilderness?" A man in the pit rose, saying, "Oh! is that it? I've been wondering what the hell you were all the evening."

EDWARD GORDON CRAIG (1872–1966)

221 *Craig and his sister Edith were the children of Ellen Terry. Before becoming an innovative designer and director Craig had been an actor with Henry Irving's company at the Lyceum Theatre.*

We were sitting round the Green Room (E. T. [Ellen Terry] not there) while Irving read us his version of this play. It began at twelve o'clock, I see, and ended at two-fifteen. I and Ben Webster were seated side by side on some sort of a seat or bench which looked out through the window, across Burleigh Street, to the public house opposite. And as we settled into our places to listen to Irving reading, the vision of the public house came upon us. It made no immediate effect, but there it was.

Then Irving's voice began to inform us of the words of this play which, it occurred to me (looking at the public house), I could quite easily read to myself later on, without his taking all this trouble to read it to us. I began to puff and blow a little – gently. The words entered into my ears now and then, in a sort of corkscrew way which somehow irritated me – my eyes still on the public house. Those chaps in there, drinking beer. . . . I began to move restlessly. Irving's voice went on and on. Ben Webster gave me a poke in the ribs with his elbow. What did he do that for? Men drinking beer . . . On goes the voice, on goes the beer. Something began to stir in me which I believe is called 'the devil.' But the result was not devilish, it was merely idiotic. I began to titter. Can one be drunk by thinking of beer and so lose control over some organ or other? My speech was all right, but I hadn't to use that. Looking was all right – I could see. I think it was the hearing that was troublesome. Irving's voice went on and on, and at last I was almost overcome by a desire to roar with laughter. The scene 'Public House' – the voice 'Irving doing the play' – these not of a piece. I bottled up the laughter with thoughts of the beer; but it became worse, and I let out a squeak with a pop. Irving, you know, was a saint: otherwise he would have risen up and told me to leave the room. I didn't laugh, but by this time I was gasping. Ben Webster gave me a kick on the leg, which didn't mend matters. I wanted to kick him back, but that would have meant catastrophe. Then I frowned. I frowned hard and in doing so, lowered my head and began to breathe heavily through my nose. My lips were sealed – no more squeaks. But I did not hear another word. All Irving's beautiful speech was lost on me, and the reading came to an end and I think I must have given him a glance out of the corner of my eye. And then he went out of the room, nobly – and I had no further desire to laugh – suicide was the thought then.

222 *Kenneth Tynan, the critic, dined with Craig and recorded their conversation in his book* Curtains.

Far from being pent up in the past, Craig keeps in touch with every new development in theatre, cinema, and even television. He was soon urging me to see the new French underwater documentary, *Le Monde du Silence:* "It's like nothing you've ever dreamed of. Or, rather, it's like *everything* you've ever dreamed of." He showed a keen interest in "this fellow Orson Well-ess." of whose films he had heard much. "I'll tell you a thing about Well-ess," he said. "A Paris paper published an interview with him, in which he said that one day he was standing in the American Express in Paris when the door *flew* open to reveal a cloaked figure in a funny hat. *Me!* He threw himself to the ground in veneration. I gathered him up and took him to my studio and spent six months teaching him the art of the theatre." Craig was now shaking with glee. "Magnificent, isn't it? *Because I've never met the fellow in my life!*" He nudged me and we rocked.

223 I once knew an actor-manager who would look eight times at his gold watch in the course of a two minutes' stroll down my street. His first look would be casual, his second rather interested, his third pensive, his fourth as though slightly surprised. At his fifth look he would mutter "Tut-tut" with his tongue and teeth, at his sixth he would quicken his pace, at his seventh he would stop suddenly, exclaiming "By Jove, half-past ten," and at his eighth he would shake his head.

Once I caught him at the eighth look. "What is the time?" I asked him. "Don't know, my dear fellow," and out came the watch for the ninth time. "Whew!!" he whistled, "half-past ten, I *shall* have to hurry," and on he rushed as though something were really doing at last. But nothing was doing; it was not half-past ten; all was acting.

The fact is, he owed me five pounds and his company another thirty.

Edward Gordon Craig

GEORGE CRAM ('JIG') COOK 1873–1924

224 *Fired by a vision of a new society 'Jig' Cook founded, in 1915, the Provincetown Players, the most influential of the groups in America's Little Theatre movement. Turning their backs on bourgeois materialism and the conventional realism of the theatre at that time, they set out to establish a new order of dramatic art which would concentrate on 'the relation of the modern writer's social feeling to his art'. Cook and his wife Susan Glaspell left the company in 1922, but not before they had discovered and established probably their most famous member, the playwright Eugene O'Neill.*

Still another problem was the law. As a small, unlicenced theatre, the

Provincetown was not allowed to sell tickets at the box office. Anyone interested in the burgeoning group had to subscribe, receiving seats by mail for all performances. As such a group, the Provincetown changed plays every two weeks and gave three performances a week, one on Sunday. Jig was eventually arrested and ordered by a judge to justify the Provincetown Players and their Sabbath performances. He rose magnificently to the occasion. Already conspicuous because of his leonine mop of blue-white hair, he jumped to his feet and told the judge: "We are doing it for fun. Of course, profound fun. The fun of death, for instance – the profound amusement of imagined death, followed swiftly enough, Your Honour, by the real moment." To this rather surprising explanation, the judge responded even more surprisingly. He whipped out his wallet and on the spot took a season subscription. The arresting policeman watched this in bafflement. "What shall I do if they play again on Sunday?" he asked the judge. "Oh, do something else," the judge snapped.

Allen Churchill

SIR GERALD DU MAURIER (1873–1934)

225 *Du Maurier – the first, and many people say the finest, exponent of the naturalistic style of acting – excelled in playing such parts as Bulldog Drummond and the master-cracksman Raffles. He was not one to take the profession too seriously.*

Nobody on the stage was ever safe when Gerald was present: he would go to the most appalling lengths, and take infinite time and trouble with his experiments. Nothing pleased him more than a successful joke, and, back in his dressing-room, he would rock with laughter until the tears ran down his cheeks, while he told the story of one of his latest shock discoveries. He would invent strange contraptions with string, and place them under the tablecloth, then press some sort of bulb and the plates and cups and saucers would jump about in undignified fashion before their respective owners, who were trying to look as if they were really eating eggs and bacon; there were rolls filled with cotton wool, bananas made of soap, and apples that squeaked a protest when moved; there were cushions that uttered significant and unmistakable sounds when sat upon, collapsible knives and forks that crumpled in the hand, tumblers that melted at the first drop of liquid.

He even once went to the trouble of staging that well-known Chinese torture of the drip of water . . . and made scientific arrangements for a drop to fall periodically from above on to the forehead of a wretched and innocent performer, who was tied by his part to sit in a certain chair and conduct a very serious conversation for many minutes on end.

Daphne du Maurier

LILIAN BAYLIS (1874–1937)

226 *During her management of the Old Vic Theatre Lilian Baylis presented every one of Shakespeare's plays between 1914 and 1923. She was also well known for what Russell Thorndike here describes as her 'oddities'.*

I once saw her receiving Queen Mary, and heard her address Her Majesty as "dear" in a perfectly natural conversation.

This was on the occasion of the Vic's Centenary Matinée [1918].

It was to be a long programme, strengthened with many West End Stars. Sybil and I had been asked to arrange a number of scenes played by different people, showing the history of the old theatre. The first scene was between the Duke of Wellington and Grimaldi. It was due to ring up at two sharp, and at five to, a reception committee waited to receive the Queen at the Stage door, which led to the Royal Box.

Our Royal Family are noted for their punctuality, but on this occasion, the King was inspecting the Union Jack Club. The King's arrival there caused a congestion of traffic on the Bridge and in Waterloo Road, and the Queen's arrival at the Vic was therefore held up.

The minutes ticked on. Knowing that it would be a very long performance, Miss Baylis began to fear that her Early-doorites [i.e. the early arrivals] would be inconvenienced for the evening's opera. This she would not tolerate, and said that we must really start the show, and ring down directly the Queen arrived. It was pointed out that this would not be at all in order.

But "I won't keep my Opera Patrons waiting," was another slogan of Miss Baylis. At ten past two, while Henry Vibart as Wellington and myself as Grimaldi were waiting on the stage, to our horror the curtain suddenly rose without warning. Miss Baylis had taken it upon herself to push the curtain bell, as she called out quite loudly: "Queen or no Queen, we really must make a start."

In confusion we began our dialogue, and then half-way through the episode, Miss Baylis cried out from the wings: "Ring down, She's here."

She rushed on to the stage, and said: "Come on, Mr. Vibart, you're dressed as a soldier, and she'll like that. Come on, Sybil, and Russell, bring your red-hot poker and hold it like a gun, so that she'll see you've been a soldier."

We were pushed down the steps into the crowd of receptionists, just as Her Majesty and Princess Mary were being received by Mrs. Randall Davidson.

Miss Baylis treated the Queen as just one of her Vic patrons. "I'm glad you've turned up at last, dear," she said, "and I know it's not your fault being late, as I hear that your Dear Husband going to the Union Jack Club has held up the road. But we've got a long programme to get through, and had made a start, so let's get on with things. Here's John

Booth, who has written a history of the Vic, price ninepence, post free tenpence. But we've had a special copy made for you, in a cover made near Stratford-on-Avon, where Shakespeare's wife lived. What's the name of the village?" Someone prompted her, Shottery.

Miss Baylis then asked the Queen not to look at it till later, and pointed to the steps leading to the Royal Box. The Queen, with a smile of appreciation, began to mount the steps, when Miss Baylis dashed at the Curtain leading to the stalls and called out towards the Orchestra well: "Go on, Corrie. She's here. Play the King."

The various people who were privileged to visit the Royal Box recounted the extraordinary things which Miss Baylis said. She pointed out the large picture of Emma Cons,* and told Her Majesty that she had hung it there on purpose, as she thought it would be interesting to the Queen.

"We have always had a photograph of the dear King in this Box, but I've hung him over there on the prompt side for to-day. You can see it in the box opposite."

She went on to say how very fond her patrons were of the dear King and how the Vic Theatre throughout the War had not only had "His song" (meaning the National Anthem) played by the Orchestra right through, but had insisted on the audience singing it too. She ended her conversation about the King by feeling sure that the Queen was very happy in her Family.

Certainly the oddities of Miss Baylis added to her personal attraction. People just loved her, because she was herself.

227 *The director Tyrone Guthrie describes his first interview with Lilian Baylis at the Old Vic.*

I remember arriving at the stage door; I remember the doorkeeper; the stone steps up into a corridor and a woman cooking a whiting for Miss Baylis's lunch on a little gas ring behind a festoon of faded pink cotton, which was supposed to conceal the fact that the cooking area was in a public corridor.** The office was densely crowded: here a 'Hamlet' chair, there a rickety sofa, a pretty little marquetry chair – forlorn stray from some Edwardian drawing-room. As I wait, the sapphire plush

---

*Emma Cons, a social worker, bought the Old Vic after it had closed in 1880. She re-opened it as 'The Royal Victoria Hall and Coffee Tavern', offering a 'purified entertainment and no intoxicating drinks', but the Old Vic it would always be called, and in 1898 Emma Cons' niece, Lilian Baylis, joined her as manager.

**'She was mortal enough,' says Russell Thorndike, 'to require a little food during the day besides her cups of tea. Towards the end of a long matinée the salubrious fumes of sausage, bacon or kippers would float over the footlights and fill the stalls accompanied by the sound of fizzling and spitting.'

cover of a side table is violently agitated and two dogs rush snarling out
– Scamp and Sue. They were quite nasty little dogs, spoiled and bad-
tempered. Miss Baylis, someone once said, came to dogs too late in life.
She loved them not wisely but too well. Beneath that table Scamp and
Sue had a home from home – basket, water, bones and so on. The top
of the table was covered with portfolios, sketches for sets and dresses.

But the room was dominated by The Desk; a large affair in oak with
a roll top. It was densely covered with papers; on the top were knick-
knacks. Presents from Margate, Lucerne, the Trossachs, a bowl of
Benares brass full of rusty paper clips and shrivelled rubber bands; a
bunch of flowers, a tray of dirty tea things and three telephones. Tacked
to the roll top was a postcard reproduction of Dürer's *Praying Hands*. All
this I remember perfectly – and hearing Miss Baylis in the corridor,
asking the person with the whiting what the dogs were getting for lunch.
Of her entrance into the office, what she looked like, or said, I have no
recollection whatever. Nothing was concluded at that interview. I
gathered later that she had not liked me very much, and when eventually
she did engage me it was with no feeling of pleasure or confidence. She
did not, I'm afraid, regard me as one of those God-sent shining ones,
those saviours upon whom she liked to believe her life and that of the
Old Vic depended. There was a vacancy; I was willing to fill it. The
salary being what it was, I guess the queue of applicants did not stretch
far.

228 *Miss Baylis puts John Gielgud in his place.*

I had an amusing encounter with Lilian Baylis about this time. The Vic
was about to open again for a new season, and Lilian sent me one of her
characteristic letters (neatly typed, with most of the typing crossed out
and her own writing crowded in on top of it) asking me to come down
to see her and discuss some of her plans. Delighted and flattered at being
considered so important, I stepped into my car and drove to the Vic. I
marched in to Lilian's office in my best West End style, with a new hat
and yellow gloves held negligently in my hand. Lilian greeted me
warmly, and we talked enthusiastically together for half an hour. As I
got up to go I said grandly, 'I should simply love to come down some
time and act and produce again at the Vic for you if you'd let me, but of
course I'm awfully busy for the next month or two.' Lilian, looking
steadily at my rapidly receding hair, said briskly, 'Oh no, dear, you play
all the young parts you can while you're still able to!' I left the Vic in a
distinctly chastened frame of mind, determined that I would never again
attempt to impress so shrewd a judge of character as Lilian Baylis.

229 *As Sybil Thorndike discovered, Miss Baylis wouldn't let a little thing like a war interfere with her productions.*

We were playing "Richard II," and I was not on till half-way through the show, so was arriving a little late. As I got out of the train in Waterloo Tube Station I met crowds pouring down the stairs with the Air Raid look on their faces, and in their talk too. Lilian was more to be reckoned with, however, than any raid, so up I fought my way to the street. I was stopped by a bobby, who said: "You can't go outside here, my dear, raid's on."

"I can't help the raid," I cried, clinging to his brass buttons, "the curtain's up at the Old Vic, and I shan't be on for my entrance."

"Old Vic, is it," he said. "Oh, I know Miss Baylis; yes, you're right," and a lull coming in the bomb sounds, he gave me a push into Waterloo Road with a: "Now run for your life, and if you're killed, don't blame me – blame Her!" I got to the pit door – first door I reached – and found Lilian in a fume and fret. "Why on earth weren't you in before this?"

"A raid," I said, "everybody underground at Waterloo – everything impossible."

"Raid," she snorted. "What's a raid when my curtain's up!"

The Heavens may fall – peradventure the darkness may cover us – the Philistines be upon us, but the Curtain must go up and the play must go on!

Sybil Thorndike

230 *The next two anecdotes come from Sybil Thorndike's brother, Russell, who was also appearing at the Old Vic.*

There was a very old man in the company who had gained his position by reason of the scarcity of men owing to the War, so old was he that he used to say to the ancient chorus ladies of the Opera, "Good luck, girls." He had the right to this hilarity. He was a very old Vic-ite, too, which first stabilised his position. He also claimed the privilege of old age by thinking and talking a good deal about his state of health. He put the best of his failing strength into such parts as he was called upon to play. As often as not his exertions brought him to the dressing-warren (I will not say room) in a state of nervous or temperamental breakdown. He had the greatest sympathy with me, because when I joined the company I was perhaps a sicker man than he. In fact Miss Baylis realised that I was not really fit enough to play such parts as I was cast for, but she, on the Doctor's advice, let me keep in the dressing-room a bottle of brandy which I was allowed to quaff at my own discretion. One night I noticed towards the end of a scene, in which this old gentleman had played an important part, that he was seriously distressed and faint. I gave him a drink of brandy, and told him to help himself whenever he felt he needed it.

A week or so later we had all run out of spirit gum, and as it was cheaper to buy it in large quantities one of the men voluteered to call in on Thomas the chemist in St. Martin's Lane, who sold the best spirit gum on the market. My brandy bottle being then empty, he took it with him to fill up with gum, for, like everything else, there was a scarcity of bottles. That night was a clean-shaven play, "Julius Caesar," so the bottle remained in my cupboard. I came off from the quarrel scene to find the gentleman gasping in the dressing-room. He had come into the room while I was on the stage to have a nip of the brandy. Unfortunately he took a good gulp of strong gum, so that his tongue and uvula were literally cleaving to the roof of his mouth. Someone meaning to be helpful suggested that when mending a puncture of a tyre, one sprinkled powder to take away the stickiness of the gum, and so he peppered talcum into the unfortunate old gentleman's open mouth. Hearing that it was extremely unlikely that the old gentleman would be able to play his small part in the battle scene, Miss Baylis came out of her office in a panic. She entered the room and saw the old man sitting on the floor and choking. She caught sight of the brandy bottle and jumped to the conclusion that he was drunk. "I won't have alcohol in the dressing-room," she declared hotly. "You must keep it locked up in the office."

"But, Miss Baylis," I said, "he's ill – he's not drunk."

She looked quickly at the sufferer and said: "Put out your tongue." He couldn't, but she saw the whiteness of the Talcum powder and said: "Quite right, he's ill, poor fellow. I've never seen a whiter tongue in my life." And she was very angry when we all began to laugh.

231 Miss Baylis was very exercised in her mind about a proposed production of *Henry V* which Ben Greet had told her would draw all the First World War soldiers in London. The only thing she knew about the play was The Prayer. At our first meeting, she asked me if I would kneel. Thinking she was about to ask me to play Henry, I told her that at present I could neither kneel nor walk, but that I hoped to get better soon. She then knelt down by her roll-top desk, with one hand resting upon the base of the telephone. The prayer which followed was exactly like a business talk over the telephone. The 'Dear God' she addressed seemed to be on the other end of the line. She told Him who she was and what she was praying for, and hoped that in the presence of the soldier home from the front (me), He would listen. She asked Him if it was right to do *Henry V*? It was a long cast and would need more actors. And that meant spending more money. The last sentence of the prayer was that God

should send her some good actors – and, as an afterthought – she added the word 'cheap.'

SIR LEWIS CASSON (1875–1969)

232 *Sybil Thorndike, who tells this story, played Volumnia in the Old Vic production of* Coriolanus *in 1938 (with Laurence Olivier in the title role), which was directed by her husband Lewis Casson.*

Tragedy you have to drag out of yourself, and it hurts so frightfully that many actors dodge it. But Larry's Coriolanus was magnificent. He and Lewis worked all-out on it. I remember them having a breathing competition during the rehearsals. Lewis said, "You've got to do this speech all in one breath', and Larry said, 'I bet you couldn't', but Lewis did. Larry has a longer breath than anybody I know. He could do the Matins exhortation 'Dearly Beloved Brethren' twice through in one breath. Lewis could do it in one and a half, and my father in one. All of which is pretty good. As children we used to listen fascinated in church to see if Father could get through the collect in one go.

JAMES AGATE (1877–1947)

233 *Early drama reviews for the* Manchester Guardian *led to work in London and the post of drama critic for the* Sunday Times *from 1923 until his death. Quixotic and intemperate as he frequently was, he was a generous and valiant supporter of merit and talent when he found it.*

In one of the rashest acts he ever committed, he and a collaborator dramatised *Blessed Are The Rich* and, worse still, persuaded Manchester friends to contribute several thousand pounds towards its staging. The first night took place at the Vaudeville Theatre in 1928 with a cast headed by the engaging Mary Clare. The curtain fell on a very indifferent comedy and there was a certain amount of encouraging applause – enough, in fact, to tempt the incautious author out front. The applause was a trap. As soon as Agate appeared before the curtain a hurricane of boos, whistles and loud calls of 'Rubbish!' poured about his bewildered head. Never had he been so taken aback, and never in his life had he been so humiliated. For once the master of repartee was stunned into silence before this onslaught. An eye-witness reports that the affair had been organised with care and precision, starting with the deceptively warm clapping and ending in the sudden torrent of invective from all parts of the house. *Blessed Are The Rich* limped on for thirteen performances, although at the last night both pit and gallery were full of people attracted by the notoriety of the event and, it is clear, by a feeling of *schadenfreude*.

The actors, authors, playwrights and other enemies who had suffered in
the past from Agate's barbs congratulated themselves on having obtained
a satisfying vengeance.

James Harding

234 In 1928 the Stage Society put on a matinée of a new play entitled *Journey's
End* by an unknown writer called R. C. Sherriff. Agate, expecting an
afternoon of intellectual flummery, was persuaded to accompany Bishop.
At five o'clock he emerged full of enthusiasm. In the foyer they met
three of London's leading theatre managers and stormed at them to put
on the play in a commercial house. No, came the reply, it was too good
for the general public. That evening Agate was due to broadcast one of
the fortnightly theatre talks which the BBC had recently commissioned
from him. He telephoned Alan Dent [his secretary], ordered him to tear
up the manuscript he was typing, and replace it with an ecstatic notice
of 'a marvellous play'. This it was not, being simply a fine and very
sincere example of craftsmanship. But, as he later observed, in a world
where everyone talks at the top of his voice any way, you need to shout
loudly about something worthwhile. A fortnight later, on hearing that
a manager had actually bought the play for production, he exploded
another bombshell with ironic advice to cancel *Journey's End* because the
public was utterly unworthy of such a play. The trick worked, abusive
letters from outraged listeners flowed in, and theatregoers were stung
into buying seats. 'Nobody can boost a bad play,' Agate said afterwards,
'and this play was good enough to run when once it had got a start. And
in the theatre the start is ninety-nine hundredths of the battle. Without
the thousands of wireless listeners who bombarded the box-office before
the Press got busy, this play must have failed.' Whenever, and this was
often, people accused him of over-statement, he would quote the
episode of *Journey's End* as proving the uses of deliberate and cunning
exaggeration.

James Harding

CHARLES DORAN (1877–1964)

235 Charles Doran's Shakespearean Company was not exactly famous, but
at any rate it was better known than the St. Nicholas Players. It was then
appearing at the Devonshire Park Theatre in Eastbourne, and one
afternoon in June 1921, [Ralph] Richardson cycled over from Brighton
to try and get a rise in his profession. He interviewed Doran after a
matinée of *The Merchant of Venice*, and was told to recite something. He
began, "Friends, Romans, countrymen." "Stop", said Doran. "Am I

no good?" cried Richardson, showing his first sign of disquietude. "It isn't that. You're standing on my trousers. You're engaged." "Wait a minute," said Richardson, who at that time prided himself on his financial acumen . . . "I am not, as you might suppose, a rich man. I shall want £2 a week." Now, Doran, possibly recalling that the Actors' Association minimum was three, said, "I will give you £3, but you must hand me ten shillings back." So both of them made a profit.

Harold Hobson

JULIAN WYLIE (1878–1934)

236 *A theatre manager who became the Pantomime King of his day.*

I saw no signs of the temperamental storms and rages for which he was said to be famous among pantomime artists. Leslie Henson once told me of a rehearsal of *Dick Whittington*, in which he had appeared under Julian's direction. There was an unusually complicated change of set to be negotiated, from a 'Desert' scene to 'A Staircase in the Palace'. In the first there was a trap-door which had to be closed before the curtain went up on the second, in which a lady was discovered singing on the stairs. After a verse or two she was supposed to descend in stately fashion. But this she dared not do, fearing that the trap might still be open.

'For heaven's sake, come *forward*', Wylie yelled each time.

But the lady demurred, and the change had to be rehearsed all over again. At last Wylie could bear it no longer. He bounded on to the stage with a roar, and immediately vanished into the still open trap. There was a murmur of consternation. Then Julian's head suddenly popped up through the hole in the stage. 'I heard you laughing', he announced, though actually everyone had been too much alarmed to see the joke.

John Gielgud

ERNEST THESIGER (1879–1961)

237 The cast also included Ernest Thesiger, a great character who constantly referred to his great friend "Dear Queen Mary", with whom he used to do crochet work. He was very old by the end of his career and enjoyed telling the story of someone who stared hard at him in the tube and eventually said, "Excuse me, but weren't you Ernest Thesiger?"*

Derek Salberg

---

*Ernest told me this story, but claimed that he replied, 'Madam, I *was*.'

FREDERICK LONSDALE (1881–1954)

238 *An enormously successful playwright, whose greatest triumphs were behind him when Kenneth More first encountered him.*

As I came to know Lonsdale better, I liked him a lot. He appeared even grander than Noël Coward, but I sensed he had not been born to wealth, and indeed his background was humble.

Like me, he had spent his childhood in Jersey, and money was generally short. One Friday afternoon, when he was a boy, his parents were so hard up that his mother told him they had no meat at all for the weekend. Freddie decided to remedy this in the only way he could – by nipping out to the local butcher's shop and pinching a leg of lamb when the butcher's back was turned.

Years later, in the 1930s, at the height of his fame, when he owned a yacht and two Bentleys, Freddie went back to that shop, because the theft had played on his nonconformist conscience. The butcher was alone behind the counter, cutting up a carcass.

'Good morning,' Lonsdale began. 'Do you know who I am?'

The butcher looked at him blankly.

'No,' he admitted. 'Who are you?'

'I happen to be Mr. Frederick Lonsdale. You may have heard of me? I write plays.'

'Oh, yes?'

'Yes. As a matter of fact I have two plays running in London now, at this very moment.'

'Really?' said the butcher, quite unimpressed. 'So what do you want here, Mr. Frederick Lonsdale? Some meat?'

'Actually, no,' Freddie went on. 'You won't remember, of course, but twenty-five years ago a small boy came into your shop one Friday afternoon and stole a leg of lamb. Well, I was that boy, I have come to pay for that meat and to apologise.'

'Ahhh!' shouted the butcher. He picked up his cleaver and swung it above his head. 'So *you're* the little bugger? I've waited all these years for this!'

And he chased him out of the shop and down the street.

DAME SYBIL THORNDIKE (1882–1976)

239 *'Lively, passionate, argumentative', says John Gielgud of Sybil Thorndike. Her long association with the Old Vic under Lilian Baylis began in 1914. Earlier, in a letter to her father, she recounts an incident while on tour with Ben Greet's company in America.*

Then we went to the Spanish Mission – the monks are too adorable and showed us all over the monastery – all the allowable parts that is – some parts females aren't allowed in – and what do you think? – Ben Greet has given them 2 boxes for a performance of *Everyman* – the Superior let them come because B.G. said it was a religious service and not a play proper at all.

. . . The monks all came to the show last night with their nice bare feet and their sweet simple faces. We had the shock of our lives when Death came on – we thought they'd be awfully impressed, instead of which they all burst right out laughing – just like I do – at the wrong time. We were absolutely flabbergasted, till some one told us that in the mediaeval times Death was often the comedy character, just as the Devil was, and that no true Catholic could treat them seriously – so here were these darling old monks being truly mediaeval – never having changed in feeling since those long-back times. It gave me a great cheer and a lump in my throat. You see they used to play this very play, Father, in the Churches in the Middle Ages, one almost felt these old dears were reincarnated from them.

240 Miss Tempest (who two years later was to become the next actress after Sybil to get the honour of Dame) and she did not often see eye to eye, largely because Miss Tempest used to knit ostentatiously downstage during Dame Sybil's big scene. Finally, and in some desperation, Sybil began playing cards equally ostentatiously during Miss Tempest's big scene, and next night in the wings there was a hissed confrontation: 'Clever little actress, aren't you, dear?' said Miss Tempest. 'No,' replied Sybil sweetly, 'but clever enough to act with you, dear.'

Sheridan Morley

241 "I was much in awe," Ralph Richardson recalls. "Dame Sybil was the first great star I had played with. Five minutes before the curtain went up I wondered if I dared pay court and wish her well. I went to the door of her dressing-room, but I was afraid to knock in case she was communing with herself before that big part. Then I heard a buzz of talk inside, and tapped. 'Come in, Ralph dear,' Sybil said. 'Won't you have a bun? There isn't really time for introductions.' She was feeding half-a-dozen schoolgirls with buns a few moments before the performance.

Elizabeth Sprigge

242 *Dame Sybil opened in April 1951 in* Waters of the Moon *with Edith Evans at the Haymarket Theatre. The play ran for a couple of years.*

All things considered, they got on remarkably well together though later in the run Frith Banbury had on Dame Edith's [Edith Evans] advice to reprimand Dame Sybil for overacting at one matinée: 'Yes,' replied Sybil, 'I was rather naughty on Saturday afternoon, but I had two grandchildren in front and I was determined that they should know exactly what the play was about. Consequently much underlining. . . . However I've pulled myself together now and if you come again I think you'll find all is in order.'

This was the only occasion on which Dame Edith and Dame Sybil ever did a prolonged run together, and while Dame Edith cascaded from a great height ('like Royalty opening a bazaar', said Tynan) Dame Sybil contented herself by playing Schumann on the stage and, when the grandchildren weren't in front, capturing the few good scenes she did have almost by stealth . . . .

. . . Twenty years later I asked Dame Edith what she remembered of it all: 'Sybil I always envied for having so many relatives. She had the dressing room above mine, and all I ever seemed to hear was the tramp of children's feet.' Legend has it that when the play had been running successfully for a year, the Tennent management announced to Edith that she'd be getting a whole new wardrobe from Balmain. 'Good,' said Edith, 'but you'd better do something for Sybil too, what about a new cardigan?'

Sheridan Morley

243   How fitting it was that her very last public appearance should have been at the Old Vic on its farewell night. At the end of the performance, she was wheeled down the aisle in her chair, to smile and wave for the last time to the people sitting in the theatre she had always loved so well. Lively, passionate, argumentative, always travelling, acting, learning a new language or a new poem, a magnificent wife and mother, she was surely one of the rarest women of our time. 'Oh, Lewis,' she cried once, 'if only we could be the first actors to play on the moon.'

John Gielgud

JOHN BARRYMORE (1882–1942)

244   *John Barrymore, a fine actor to begin with, in serious and comic roles, squandered his talent in later life in second-rate plays and films. 'He had a wild soul, and no one could discipline him', said a colleague. Willie Collier said that he liked Barrymore too much ever to fire him for his misbehaviour, tardiness or eccentricity. Nevertheless, Collier's patience must often have been stretched to breaking point by Barrymore's unnerving performances. In fact, on the opening night of the London run of* The Dictator, *Collier had not one but two recalcitrant actors to handle on stage.*

The Dictator proved so popular in America that in 1905 Mr. Frohman suggested that Collier take the company to England. Marie Tempest, another Frohman star, was at this time appearing most successfully at the Comedy Theatre, a London playhouse controlled by Frohman. It was the producer's novel intention that Collier and Miss Tempest make a trans-Atlantic interchange, each artist to appear for a four weeks' season at the other's stand. Instead of four weeks, Miss Tempest played for a year in New York, and Collier for more than a year in London.

On the opening night in London, and with much at stake for Collier, two of his actors put him in a fine predicament. Jack, of course, was the worse offender.

At the rise of the curtain on *The Dictator*, Collier, as Travers, is found in desperate need of a new name to cover his identity as a fugitive from the law. Ordinarily, in the play, one of his actors, in the role of Bowie, comes on-scene to sell his name to Travers for twenty-five thousand dollars. But tonight the actor appeared with alcoholic hauteur, and when Collier asked, "By the way, what is your name, the one I am to purchase?" he refused point-blank to tell it. Nor could Collier, as Travers, squeeze the name "Bowie" out of his suddenly obstinate actor. He wheedled him, but the actor refused any information. In fact he made an exit, leaving the first-nighters in ignorance of his identity. Finally Collier improvised, saying, "Of course I know his name. Knew it right along. Happened to meet his wife. She told me it was 'Bowie.' "

Hardly had Collier hauled himself out of this pit than Jack arrived on-stage to make matters worse, far worse.

The first entrance of the wireless operator was important for a proper understanding of the play. the business provided that Jack give Collier a wireless despatch written on two long sheets of paper. Collier would read the report aloud, thus advising the audience of the why, when, and wherefore of the action.

Jack appeared on cue, but had in his hand only a small fragment torn from a menu card, a triangle about the size of a Cape of Good Hope postage stamp. He offered this tiny absurdity to the astounded Collier with the usual dialogue, "Here, Chief, is the despatch."

Collier, his eye upon the scrap of paper, improvised, "But where is the real despatch? The longer one?'

Jack also improvised. "Here it is, sir. Or have your eyes gone back on you again?"

"Go to the wireless room,' said the desperate Collier, "and bring the *first* despatch. There are two sheets of it. Remember? That's the one I want to read. Not this piece of confetti."

"But this *is* the first despatch," Jack insisted. "I took it down myself, word for word. Put on your bifocals."

Collier knew that the long, plot-point speech he was supposed to deliver hardly could be accepted by a London audience as being read from the menu-fragment.

"Look," he said, then added under his breath, "if you don't go for the prop, I'll break your leg!" Then, so that the audience might hear, "Someone is trying to double-cross us. Go back and look again. I'm sure you will find the genuine message."

"But I *know* this is the one, sir," Jack insisted. "It was sent by a well-known female impersonator."

"Then have her, or him, send us another."

"But," Jack said, "he, or she, can't. He, or it, just died." He wiped away a tear, and sniffled, "Are you going to the funeral?"

"No," said Collier. "How can I?"

"Why not, sir?"

"Because," said Collier, "I haven't got a black dress!" He barked, "Now go for the other message." He added under his breath, "It's a terrible thing to be stranded in London. Catch on?"

Jack went off-stage, leaving Collier to ad lib once again for almost half a minute. Then Barrymore re-appeared to present Collier with exactly the same triangular bit of paper!

"Sir, I have had this authenticated," and he held up the little scrap. "It was not written by the late female impersonator, but by the very clever fellow who engraves the Lord's Prayer on the heads of pins."

There was no other course for Collier than to take the miserable paper, hurriedly edit down his regular speech, and hope for the best. But Willie barely had reached the close of his abridged reading when the actor who hitherto had refused to give the name "Bowie," entered unexpectedly to shout: "I've decided to tell you my name. It's John P. Murphy!"

Gene Fowler

245 *An extraordinary outcome to a typical outburst of Barrymore's temper.*

Some weeks afterward, and in another city, he lost his temper entirely. It was at the end of the first act. At this point in the play Peter picked up the Duchess of Towers' bouquet. After looking at it tenderly for a long moment, he pressed the flowers to his lips. Then he murmured, "*L'amour.*" It was one of the most touching scenes in the play. It sent the ladies into near-swoons.

On this particular evening some girl in the gallery, hysterical with delight, giggled. Jack called out: "Damn it! If you think you can play this better than I can, come on down and do it."

He hurled the bouquet into the audience. It struck a woman in the face. The curtain fell. Barrymore stomped off-stage to his dressing-room to lock himself inside it.

Sounds of outrage came from the audience. Miss [Constance] Collier was dismayed to hear high-pitched voices filtering through the curtain. The actors stood in their places on the stage as if paralyzed. Then the manager of the theatre, purple and blowing, charged round from the pass-door.

"I'll bring a damage suit against you!" he shouted at Miss Collier. "Barrymore has ruined the reputation of my theatre. I'll not allow you to fulfil your engagement for the remainder of the week. My God! Nobody is safe with this man. I'll have him barred from every . . . "

He paused to regain his wind. The actress took this opportunity to beg the manager to allow the curtain to rise for the second act. He said no. The audience would throw things.

"They're sitting out there now, desperate and waiting," he said. "Peek out at 'em. You'll see. They're like a sheriff's posse."

Miss Collier did peer out to observe the audience waiting as if to exercise some terrible judgment. She finally persuaded the manager to allow the curtain to rise. He recommended that Miss Collier make a speech of apology and offer to return all box-office moneys to the patrons. She declined to do this.

"All right then," the manager warned, "but if you're killed, don't say I didn't tell you."

There had been half an hour's delay. Jack refused to come out of his dressing-room. No threats could move him. Finally Miss Collier informed him that he really had injured an inoffensive woman in the audience, and that the victim's eye had been bandaged.

"In that case," Barrymore said, "ring up the curtain."

The curtain rose for the second act. It seemed remarkable that so few persons had left the theatre or asked for their money back. There was the type of quietness that obtains before a prison riot. The slight plop of a moth against a spotlight slide sounded like a howitzer shell in the challenging silence.

Jack's entrance did not occur until halfway through the second act. Ordinarily, before this appearance of Peter, there were moments of laughter or hand-clapping. Tonight there was no laughter, no applause. Silence.

The cast was terrified. The suspense led Miss Collier to issue whispered instructions of an "abandon ship" nature. She admonished the crew to lower the curtain the moment the audience began to tear Jack apart.

The moment arrived, and Jack arrived with the moment. He entered with profound self-assurance. He was casual. He might have been on his way to a church, so poised was he. And now the presence that mysteriously was his on any stage, and always would be strangely his, spread its electric influence over the whole house.

He received the wildest sort of applause. Cheers even, and the waving of women's kerchiefs.

It is said that the manager of the theatre sank to his knees, either to pray or to keep from collapsing on his face. No one was sued. The play could have gone on for weeks to capacity business in that city.

Gene Fowler

246 *One of Barrymore's biggest successes was his 1925* Hamlet *in London.*

One thing that enchanted Jack with the *Hamlet* play was the physical leeway it permitted the actor. "You can play it standing, sitting, lying down, or, if you insist, kneeling. You can have a hangover. You can be cold-sober. You can be hungry, overfed, or have just fought with your wife. It makes no difference as regards your stance or your mood. There are, within the precincts of this great role, a thousand Hamlets, any one of which will keep in step with your whim of the evening. Why, one night in London, after I had been overserved with Scotch at the home of – never mind her name – I got halfway through my 'To Be' soliloquy when it became expedient to heave-ho, and quickly. I sidled off to the nearest folds of the stage draperies and played storm-at-sea. I then resumed the soliloquy. After the performance one of the fine gentlemen who had sponsored me for membership in the Garrick Club confided: 'I say, Barrymore, that was the most daring and perhaps the most effective innovation ever offered. I refer to your deliberate pausing in the midst of the soliloquy to retire, almost, from the scene. May I congratulate you upon such imaginative business? You seemed quite distraught. But it was effective!' To which I replied: 'Yes, I felt slightly overcome myself.' "

Gene Fowler

247 There was always a feeling of good humour and good fellowship on tap. I was explaining one day to the girls who carry on the body of Ophelia in the burial scene that, owing to the extraordinary and suggestive lighting of Robert E. Jones, they would not be recognized as having appeared in earlier scenes. I cautioned them that they should remember that in this scene they were virgins. One of them said to me: "My dear Mr. Barrymore, we are not character actresses, we are extra ladies." This is the spirit in which the whole production was done.

John Barrymore

GEORGE JEAN NATHAN (1882–1958)

248 *One of New York's severest theatre critics. Though he lambasted what he saw as the crassness of Broadway he was a loyal supporter of playwrights such as Eugene O'Neill.*

I thought again of how I had served as a witness for Eugene O'Neill in the suit brought against him for alleged plagiarism in the case of his drama, *Strange Interlude*. In the course of examination by the attorney for the plaintiff, one Cohalan, I testified that O'Neill some years before he wrote the play had outlined to me its theme, plot, and general treatment. "Where did this take place?" Cohalan asked me. I replied that O'Neill was living at the time in the old Lafayette Hotel in University Place, that he had started the outline there, and had expanded on it during the walk to an oyster house on Sixth Avenue in the neighborhood of Sixteenth Street, where we had a dinner engagement with a mutual friend.

"There was a bar in that restaurant, wasn't there?" observed the interrogator. I answered that there was. "And you and O'Neill, with your friend, did some drinking there?" he continued. I allowed that he was correct in his surmise. "What did you drink?" he questioned. "Three Old-Fashioned cocktails apiece," I apprised him. "What else?" he asked. "Nothing else at the bar," I replied, "but at dinner we engaged two bottles of Orvieto and rounded off with a couple of Rémy Martin brandies each." "Did you then return once again to the bar?" he pursued. I said, yes, we had. "And what did you drink?" he went on. "Three Old Oscar Pepper highballs apiece," I volunteered. A look of triumph crossed Cohalan's features. "And still," he shouted in my face, "after all those drinks, enough to make any man drunk, you say that your memory was so good that you remember exactly the conversation you allege O'Neill had with you on a walk immediately previous!"

"If," I replied, "I can recall exactly the number and character of the drinks, which you assert were enough to intoxicate anyone, why should I not be able to recall exactly a conversation before I had so much as even one?"

BALIOL HOLLOWAY (1883–1967)

249 *The finest Falstaff, Othello and Richard III of his time. His long experience in the theatre left him with an enviable sense of stagecraft.*

I went off to consult my old friend Baliol Holloway, by then aged eighty-four, who had spent the whole of his theatrical career in the classical repertoire. In his minute flat in Thayer Street, 'Ba' gave me a two-hour lesson in the art of the aside:

An aside must be directed to a given seat in the theatre – a different seat for each aside, some in the stalls, some in the circle. Never to the same seat twice – the rest of the audience will think you have a friend sitting there. If you are facing to the right immediately before the aside, then direct it to the left of the theatre, and vice versa. Your head must crack round in one clean movement, look straight at the occupant of the seat, deliver the line and crack your head back to exactly where it was before. The voice you use must be different from the one you are using in the play. If loud, then soft; if soft, then loud; if high, then low; if low, then high; if fast, then slow; if slow, then fast. During an aside, no other characters must move at all – the time you take does not exist for them.

'Ba' and I practised what he preached, using a scene from – I think – *Still Waters Run Deep* in which two characters speak in asides for twenty or more lines, until he was satisfied that I could do it. It worked and it was a proud moment when 'Ba' later saw a performance and congratulated me.

Donald Sinden

250 Soon after the turn of the century Ba read in a theatrical newspaper that a leading man was required for a stock company in Northampton. In answer to his letter an appointment was made for the following Saturday. Ba put on his best suit, caught the train to Northampton, asked his way to the theatre and presented himself outside the manager's office. 'Come in,' a voice bellowed. Standing behind a desk was a portly man with his jacket off, braces supporting his trousers and a bowler hat on his head.

'My name is Holloway sir – Baliol Holloway.'

'Yes, well I'm glad you've come, 'olloway – I want you to start Monday.' He then opened a drawer, took out six scripts and threw them one by one on the desk: 'There you are; Monday night, Tuesday night. Wednesday matinee same as Monday. Wednesday night. Thursday night. Friday night. Saturday matinee same as Thursday. Saturday night. Six wonderful parts 'olloway. Monday night's the best one – forty-two rounds [rounds of applause] in it. And you've got the best line in the play: I'll give it to you. "I may be only a trooper, Kendrick, but I would rather be a trooper – ten times rather – than an ensign with an 'eart as black as Villiers." Brings the house down, 'olloway. Good luck.'

Considerably shaken, Ba found himself some digs and started to swot up his six leading parts over the weekend. On Monday night he opened and at the end of the performance the manager appeared in his dressing room. 'Not bad 'olloway, not bad. Thirty-six out of the forty-two. But 'olloway, "'eart as black as Villiers" – what 'appened to it?'

'I don't know, sir,' said Ba. 'I shouted it as loudly as I could.'

'SHOUTED IT!? It's yer right arm. YOU DROPPED IT! . . . Look, I'll give it to you again: "I may be only a trooper, Kendrick, but I would rather be a trooper – *ten times rather* – [the manager here raised his arm ominously and pointed] than an ensign with an 'eart as black as Villiers." Hold it; keep yer arm up there till they do applaud.'

Donald Sinden

LAURETTE TAYLOR (1884–1946)

251 *This notorious first night – unsurpassed for its rowdiness, surely, since the 1809 Old Prices Riots at Covent Garden (see p. 61) – ended in the stoppage of the play and the dismissal of the audience halfway through the performance. Laurette Taylor, making a return visit to London, was, in Katharine Hepburn's view, the most gifted actress she ever saw.*

Miss Laurette Taylor was making her reappearance in London after several years' absence in a new play by her husband, Mr. J. Hartley Manners, entitled "One Night in Rome." The piece was presented by Mr. Charles B. Cochran.*

The origin of the disgraceful scene, during which stink bombs were thrown from the gallery, has not to this day been publicly explained.

The trouble began on the rise of the curtain. Hardly a word had been spoken on the stage when a voice in the gallery exclaimed, "Raise the curtain. We can't see the stage."

The audience then observed that the act-drop had not ascended more than one-third of the proscenium height. If it had been raised any higher the "flies" would probably have been exposed to view above the ceiling of the scene – a low-built interior representing a palmist's room, a striking apartment with purple hangings and the mystic appurtenances of a professional clairvoyante – the character played by Miss Taylor.

"What a charming room!" said one of the characters as he entered.

"We can't see it; raise the curtain!" replied the gallery.

A little later another character remarked of the palmist, "She makes it difficult for people to see her," an observation which provoked a roar of laughter in the gallery.

"Give the play a chance!" said someone.

"Give us a chance of seeing it!" retorted the gallery.

A third unfortunate remark by one of the characters (played by Mr. Arthur Wontner), "What a horrible room!" was received by the malcontents with exclamations of delight.

Then the gallery apparently resigned itself to the situation, the play was allowed to proceed in quiet for about half an hour, until the end of the act.

On the fall of the act-drop, all the principals acknowledged enthusiastic

*see footnote, p. 213.

calls. When Miss Taylor's turn arrived, at the end of the procession of players, she was greeted with an ovation.

"I'm awfully sorry about this," she said, pointing to the curtain. "In the next act we will have it higher. The scenery was made in America – where we do things so small. We didn't know we were coming into a theatre so high."

(The Garrick Theatre, it should be mentioned, has three tiers – dress circle, upper circle, and gallery.)

Miss Taylor retired amid the plaudits of the whole house.

Directly the curtain rose on the second act, about nine o'clock, the storm broke out again, more violently than before. It raged incessantly until 9.30.

"Shut up and go back to America!" shouted the gallery. A performer, Mr. Barry Baxter, began to play the violin. The strains of the instrument were drowned in cat-calls and coppers were thrown on the stage.

At this juncture there was a good deal of sneezing and coughing in the auditorium. I was among the afflicted members of the audience. I had to bury my face in my handkerchief for fully ten minutes. Both stink bombs and "electric snuff" were thrown from the gallery.

The uproar had now become so great that the performance could not be continued. Miss Taylor, greatly agitated, entered and advanced to the footlights.

"If all you people who cannot see will come downstairs," she said, "you shall have seats in the orchestra stalls tomorrow night."

Mr. Cochran then appeared. Taking Miss Taylor by the hand, he began to speak.

Miss Taylor interrupted him.

Addressing the audience, she said, brokenly, "It isn't like England for you to do this."

Mr. Cochran went on.

"I have brought Miss Taylor, this great artist, so beloved, three thousand miles to appear here to-night," he said. "I will not allow her to appear amid this scene of disorder. I have decided, therefore, to ring the curtain down and to dismiss this audience to-night."

The announcement was received with some commotion, and a few moments after the curtain had fallen it was rung up again, and Mr. Cochran reappeared.

"Why not let every one upstairs go?" shouted a man in the stalls. The suggestion was cheered by stalls, pit, and circle, which showed their antipathy to the gallery in loud expressions of disgust.

"It's not us," shouted a galleryite. "It's an organised gang at the back."

"I'm not blaming anybody," said Mr. Cochran. "I am only saying that I will not allow Miss Taylor to continue after the strain she has undergone. There will be another first night of this play. The scenery will be altered to allow of the line of sight from the gallery.

"I am told now that the gallery can see. Whether that is so or not, Miss Taylor is not going to continue this performance to-night."

The curtain was rung down again for the last time. A voice called "Three cheers for Miss Taylor!" They were given very heartily. The band played the National Anthem.

The gallery and the upper circle were immediately cleared, but the people in the circle, pit, and stalls remained in the auditorium for about twenty minutes, discussing the affair with considerable agitation.

Meanwhile the vestibule was besieged by excited pittites and galleryites, giving their views of Miss Laurette Taylor, and expressing the opinion that the riot was "a put-up job."

A number of stink bombs and other missiles were found in the auditorium.

Archibald Haddon

SIR GODFREY TEARLE (1884–1953)

252 Hidden away in Godfrey's entry in *Who's Who in the Theatre* is the most delightful sequence. Between 1904 and 1906 he toured in his own company playing Hamlet, Othello, Shylock, Brutus, Romeo and Sir Peter Teazle. Years later at His Majesty's Theatre he is playing Marcellus in *Hamlet*, Ludovico in *Othello*, Lorenzo in *The Merchant*, Octavius in *Julius Caesar* and Trip in *The School for Scandal*. Big fish in little ponds to little fish in big ponds.

He told me that in *Antony and Cleopatra* in 1946 at the Piccadilly Theatre, the young actor playing his servant Eros was suddenly taken ill and an unprepared replacement was pushed on at the last moment to assist in removing Antony's armour. Godfrey spoke: 'Unarm, Eros; the long day's task is done. Off, pluck off.' The young replacement looked aghast. 'I'm so sorry,' he said and retired from the scene.

Donald Sinden

RUSSELL THORNDIKE (1885–1972)

253 *Just as Lilian Baylis insisted that the play must go on during a First World War air raid (see p. 169), so Russell Thorndike also shakes his thespian fist at the Germans.*

That season we did "King Lear" for the first time – Sybil in the seventh heaven because, through the scarcity of good men, she was cast for the Fool. She did lots of men's parts afterwards, including Prince Hal in

"Henry IV", but the best of her efforts in that direction was undoubtedly the Fool. I never hope to see it better played. During the first night there was a bad air raid. We carried on the performance while the gunfire grew louder. It was interspersed with those dull reverberations that told of dropping bombs. The guns were kicking up pandemonium as I, attempting the part of Lear for the first time in my life, and a Dardanelles back throbbing merrily, reached the great moment of:

> "Blow, winds, and crack your cheeks! rage, blow,
> You cataracts and hurricanoes, spout,
> Till you have drench'd our steeples, drown'd the cocks!
> You sulphurous and thought-executing fires,
> Vaunt-couriers to oak-cleaving thunderbolts,
> Singe my white head! And thou, all-shaking thunder,
> Strike flat the thick rotundity o' the world!
> Crack Nature's moulds, all germens spill at once
> That make ingrateful man!"

I had just reached the passage, "And thou, all-shaking thunder, strike flat the thick rotundity o' the world," when there was the most appalling explosion and the Old Vic shook. I was so angry at these uncalled property-men so overdoing the storm that I strode down-stage, with Sybil at my heels, and shaking my fist at the roof of the auditorium, shouted, "Crack Nature's moulds, all GERMANS spill at once!" The audience at the Old Vic are intelligent, quick to seize the slightest point, and their applause swept through the theatre, and drowned the sound of the guns, so delighted were they with the aptness of the misquotation and so in sympathy with the sentiment. The applause had barely died when the Fool capped Lear's remark with "Here's a night that pities neither wise man nor fool!" Once more the house rocked with delight. I am afraid the Germans would have thought us a strange people if they could have seen us at that moment. They would have realized that we did not take our pleasures sadly – but gladly. Certainly, that night the raid gave an added zest to our performance. Not until the play was over did we discover how near the Germans had been to us in the Old Vic. It was the night that Waterloo Station was bombed.

ROBERT ATKINS (1886–1972)

254 *Actor and director, Atkins served his apprenticeship with Beerbohm Tree and Frank Benson. For many years he was associated with the Old Vic and the Open Air Theatre, Regent's Park, believing strongly in presenting plays as close to the Elizabethan model as possible.*

And then there was Robert Atkins. What actor has not tried to imitate his voice – the essence is there but never that idiosyncratic timbre wherein all his bass vowel sounds came through a cavern and down his nose. He it was, at the Open Air Theatre at Regent's Park where the stage is of grass surrounded by real trees and bushes, who stopped a rehearsal and, advancing on an inept young actor, delivered himself of a resounding Johnsonian phrase: 'Scenery by God. The words by the greatest poet the world has ever known. A director – not bad, and then . . . YOU come on.'

I would love to have been present when he and the actor Ralph Truman were walking beside the docks in Bristol as they espied a four-masted schooner. 'Look at her,' mused Atkins. 'That beautiful barque has sailed the seven seas bringing us tea from Ceylon, jewels from India, silks from China, spices from Samarkand and there she lies about to depart at our behest.' He called to a deck-hand: 'Sailor! Whither sailest thou?' Hardly bothering to turn, the deck-hand replied, 'F — off.'

He was incredibly perceptive over theatrical matters. He could immediately put his finger on a fault. He attended the first night of Peter O'Toole's *Hamlet*. The settings by Sean Kenny, directed by Sir Laurence Olivier at the Old Vic Theatre, the first home of England's National Theatre Company. Expectation was in the air. The house lights lowered. In the stygian gloom of the battlements Francisco and Bernardo began the play . . .

'Have *you* had quiet guard?'
'Not a mouse stirring.'

Atkins turned to his companion and his hollow boom, ventured, 'That's a *very interesting* intonation – I don't think I'm going to like this.' Theatrically he was right. You cannot be so particular in the first ten or fifteen lines of a play.

Again when John Neville was playing Hamlet at the Old Vic during the Fifties, Atkins was asked later what he thought of him. 'Well, with a little more sex and a little less sanctity he'd make a very passable Laertes.'

At Stratford-upon-Avon it was always the custom for the leading actor to read the lesson in Holy Trinity Church on the Sunday nearest Shakespeare's birthday. In 1945 Atkins was not asked. Extremely annoyed, he cornered Canon Prentice in the High Street. 'Can you adduce any cogent reason why *I* should not reading the f — ing lesson?' The Canon humbly tried to explain that someone else had been booked earlier, etc. 'Well,' grumbled Atkins. 'You can stuff yer church and you can stuff yer steeple! – except of course the bells which I understand are the most melodious in Warwickshire.'

Donald Sinden

255 *The writer and actor Robert Speaight is given a piece of Atkins's mind.*

I recall a rehearsal of *Othello* at which I slipped up over a trifling piece of business. Atkins advanced with menacing tread from the auditorium on to the stage and, after his characteristic gestatory pause, delivered himself of the following tirade:

'It's all this bloody education. Forget your Latin, forget your Greek, forget all the French and German that you've ever learnt . . . for God's sake, be *primitive*.'

256 Everyone who has ever worked for Atkins has endless stories of his remarks, my own favourite being one of Michael Bentine's, dating from the time when that genius was a struggling juvenile and cast as Demetrius opposite the statuesque Helen Cherry. "Put in some lifts, my boy" advised Robert, and Michael experienced his first uncomfortably high heels. Tottering uncertainly on to the stage he was greeted by a roar from the auditorium. "You're supposed to come from Verona, my boy. Not bloody Pisa."

Kitty Black

JIMMY ALLEN (fl. 1890)

257 Poor Jimmy Allen deserves a niche in the Chronicle of the Lyceum. He was an old Indian Mutiny N.C.O. How he drifted on to the stage I never heard, but he was, all through my time under Irving, his prompter. It was Allen's pride to make out elaborate prompt-books of all the Lyceum plays. He was a very faithful servant. He used to take the rehearsals of supers, minor people, and under-studies. His only difficulty was in selecting the correct moments to introduce or to eliminate the aspirate . . . There was a scene in *Louis XI* in which certain Burgundian Lords (local) were required to breathe defiance at the old and crafty monarch. "Look 'ere, boys, you swagger on, see? Stare at the old King, as much as to say 'Oo are *you?* With a look of 'ate, see?" "Please, Sir," objected a certain waggish super, "there are only seven of us."

"Now then, you ladies," he shouted, as he was rehearsing the witches in the Brocken scene in *Faust*, "don't let me see any grinnin' faces, you're not on 'Ampstead 'Eath, remember, you're in 'Ell."

By dint of rigid economy exercised over a wilderness of years, he scraped together enough upon which to retire. He had taken for a wife a woman much younger than himself who entirely consumed his hard-gained substance. There was nothing before him but the workhouse. One night he came down to the theatre when I was playing *The Only*

Way, handed over to me his precious, careful prompt-books, went home and shot himself.

John Martin-Harvey

EUGENE O'NEILL (1888–1953)

258 *O'Neill won four Pulitzer Prizes for his plays and was awarded the 1936 Nobel Prize for Literature. His one-act play* Bound East for Cardiff *(1916) consolidated the Provincetown Players (see p. 164). After the departure of Jig Cook, O'Neill became one of the 'Triumvirate' that steered the group, until he too left in 1926, three years before the Provincetown closed for good.* All God's Chillun Got Wings *was first produced by the Provincetown Players in 1924.*

Though the Triumvirate [O'Neill, Kenneth Macgowan and Robert Edmond Jones] appeared to be heading up a far more formal Provincetown than the one under Jig Cook, it was still capable of arousing violent controversy – as a truly Bohemian theatre should. This happened first with *All God's Chillun Got Wings*, which dealt with the ever-touchy subject of marriage between a Negro and a white girl. At one point onstage, the girl kisses her husband's hand and this, together with the idea of miscegenation, produced a storm in the press. Even before the play opened a photograph of Mary Blair, who played the wife, was syndicated under the heading: WHITE ACTRESS KISSES NEGRO'S HAND. The Provincetown subscribed to a bureau which up to now had duly delivered small monthly batches of newspaper clippings. Now the clippings began to arrive in bales. Later, it was figured that the cost of the clippings on *All God's Chillun* exceeded the cost of scenery for the play.

All God's Chillun appeared to contain such potentialities of ugliness that the Triumvirate decided on a preliminary stratagem. In the lead they had cast an actor named Paul Robeson who, after graduating from Rutgers, had combined the study of law with an interest in amateur theatricals. His massive physique and resounding voice had been noted by Augustin Duncan, the actor brother of Isadora, who had brought him to the attention of the Triumvirate. Robeson was promptly given the lead in *All God's Chillun*, but it was decided to revive the *Emperor Jones* first, with Robeson in the lead. This was "an attempt to focus the attention of the public on an actor instead of a controversy." As expected, Robeson scored a triumph as Brutus Jones. One reviewer, commenting on his superb vocal equipment, asked "One wonders if he had ever tried to sing?"

But even with Robeson established as a personality, the controversy over *All God's Chillun* boiled on. Poison pen letters flooded the theatre; the lives of O'Neill's children were threatened; and one man promised to place a bomb in the cellar of the O'Neill home if the play were allowed to open. The sensitive O'Neill then stepped forward to issue this statement to the press:

> Prejudice born of an entire ignorance of the subject is the last word in injustice and absurdity. The Provincetown Playhouse has ignored all criticism not founded on a knowledge of the play and will continue to ignore it. . . .
>
> All we ask is a square deal. A play is written to be expressed through the theatre, and only on its merits in a theatre can a final judgment be passed on it with justice. We demand this hearing.

Such tempered words failed to stop the fray. The District Attorney of New York City was Southern-born Joab A. Banton. He was anxious to prevent the play from opening, but no legal means for this were at his disposal. The best he could do was stop the appearance of child actors used in the first scene. On the opening night stage manager Harold McGee read the children's lines and continued to do so through the run of the play. A cordon of police protected the front of the theatre as the first-nighters entered, thus adding an air of unprecedented excitement to a MacDougal Street opening. Nothing untoward happened, nor did any disturbance take place for a full week. Then a large man rose in the midst of a performance to deliver himself of a series of ear-splitting yells. Plunging up the aisle, he tumbled into the arms of a frightened usher. "Where the hell am I?" he demanded, his breath giving off the pungent fumes of bottled-in-bond.

Allen Churchill

DAME EDITH EVANS (1888–1976)

259 *The greatest actress of the first two-thirds of the twentieth century. Her phrasing of 'A handbag?' in* The Importance of Being Earnest *has passed into legend. Older playgoers drool about her Millimant and her Rosalind. Peter Ustinov describes a production of* The Rivals *in which they both appeared. In the orchestra were members of the Berlin Philharmonic, under their leader, Lance-Corporal Professor Doktor Strietzel, as well as members of the Vienna Philharmonic, led by Private Professor Doktor Stiasny.*

The play, performed in garrison theatres in very flimsy yet evocative sets, assuring a rapid continuity of action, opened in Salisbury, and was an instant success. One distinguished admiral was even compelled to admit to Edith Evans, 'By Jove, I'm embarrassed to say that this is the first play by Shakespeare I've seen since Richard of Bordeaux!'

One drawback to these garrison theatres was that there was no method of concealing the orchestra. Its members sat on the same level as the audience. It was merely the actors who were elevated. I noticed on the first night that the orchestra made use of a miniature chessboard in order to while away the time during the histrionics, and often musicians crept forward like troops in a dugout to make some snide move. As far as I could understand it was a permanent championship, Berlin versus Vienna.

I hoped and prayed that Edith Evans wouldn't notice what was going on, but on the fourth night, during a brilliant tirade, she stopped dead. One eye had alighted on the tiny chessboard just as an Austrian viola player had spotted a crack in the enemy defence, and was creeping forward on all fours to deliver the *coup de grâce*.

She faltered, fumbled, and then, with superb dramatic instinct, she looked at me and said, in a tone of pained surprise, 'What did you say?'

Determined not to be placed on the defensive, I invented a little Sheridan: 'Madam, though the humours of Bath be but a diversion to our contumely, I will not presume on your generosity to the extent of belittling those very qualities which, while they do us but scant justice before the evil tongues of the town, nevertheless becalm the odious, and bring success to fools.'

Neither I nor the audience knew what on earth I was talking about, but I said it, or something like it, with immense conviction, with the result that our exit was rewarded by a burst of spontaneous applause.

Poor Edith was livid, and kept referring to the chess playing as a 'Gilbertian situation'. After the show, I accosted Professor Strietzel. To soften the blow somewhat (for after all, he *was* a lance-corporal, and I had seen how hostile he had become towards poor Private Stiasny) I told him he had never played better than on that night.

His face lit up.

'You are a *real* musician,' he counter-flattered, 'tonight, for ze *först* time, ze Boccherini was good, alzo I still have trouble mit ze Mozart und ze Dittersdorf.'

'Yes,' I replied reasonably, 'but even there, I noticed a distinct improvement.'

'Even there, even there!' he agreed.

'There's only one thing . . . one criticism.'

'Ach!' His face darkened once again in anticipation of some searing words of truth.

'The game of chess,' I said.

He bridled like a frisky horse. 'Are you serious?' he asked quietly.

'I'm afraid so. There has to be an end to it. It is frightfully distracting for the actors. We can see your every move down there, and – '

'It distracts you?' he enquired, all innocence and soft surprise.

'Yes,' I said.

'No!' he roared. 'You are too fine an artist to be distracted. It's zis voman!'

'Now come on!' I snapped, simulating crossness. 'She's a most distinguished actress and a wonderful person – '

'It's not as zough it vas a big chessboard,' he shouted, and then his voice became dramatically diminutive. 'It vas a little chessboard.' His two index-fingers reduced its imaginary size to about one inch square.

'The smaller the chessboard the greater the distance you have to travel to make a move, and the greater the distraction for us,' I declared.

He knew a checkmate when he saw it, and retired from the scene of battle.

The next night, Edith found it hard to concentrate, which was unlike her, being a creature of a ferocious inner discipline, and usually impervious to external influence. As soon as I hobbled on the stage in the guise of my gouty paterfamilias, I saw what was happening.

The orchestra, deprived of its chessboard, had now arranged the lights from its music-stands so that its members were lit from beneath, and they now followed Edith's every move in this ghostly light, looking for all the world like war-criminals following the arguments of their advocate with misgiving and resignation.

Once again, at the end of the performance, I was compelled to accost Professor Strietzel.

'Tonight,' I said sternly, 'it was not so good.'

He was in surly temper.

'Once again,' he grumbled, 'you give proof of your musicianship. Stiasny is like a mule so stubborn. The Boccherini vas one Funeral March, not one minuet. A disgrace. The Mozart vas a little better, and the Dittersdorf superb. The rest – '

'I have a criticism.'

'Please.' He smiled like a head-waiter confronted with a fly in the mayonnaise.

'Why do you follow Edith Evans with your eyes in a manner calculated to disturb any performer, any artist?'

What was left of his smile faded, and he became controlledly rational.

'First, it vas the chessboard. Correct me if I am wrong. Chess ve shouldn't play . . .'

'That is correct.'

'So ve leave the chessboard at home. Vot else can ve do? Ve follow the play. Ve look at the voman.'

Suddenly the constriction of his voice and the coolness of his presentation of the facts deserted him. He shouted volcanically: 'You think it gives us *pleasure* to vatch zis voman? Ve, who have seen Paula Wessely at her height!'

I tried to top him in bluster, but he lowered his voice to a kind of lugubrious mutter, at the same time looking into the distance to lend a cosmic significance to his words.

'You know, ven ve left Germany, mit concentration-camps and persecution, ve thought ve would come to a land vere ve could breathe – '

Here he gave an ingenious impression of a plant opening its petals to the sun, but he quickly shrivelled. 'But no,' he said brokenly, 'it's all ze same . . . persecution . . . prison bars . . .'

I was outraged. I told him angrily that I saw no connection between myself and a Gauleiter.

'Not you, dear friend – '

Nor did I think that any more ludicrous comparison could be made than one equating a dear, human, and profoundly religious creature like Edith Evans with Heinrich Himmler.

He nodded in a way which suggested that everyone is entitled to his own opinion, no one more so than he who has suffered a deprivation of liberty to play chess in an orchestra pit.

The next night Edith was brilliant. The only trouble was the almost entire absence of laughs. I made my entrance, and, inspired by the zest and brio of Edith Evans, I acted as well as I knew how, in complete and utter silence. It was acutely depressing. Not even the presence of three generals in the front row could justify the extraordinary dullness of the audience.

When I had a free moment, I rushed to the back of the auditorium in order to unravel the mystery. I did not have far to seek. The musicians had now reversed their positions, and sat facing the audience, their heads just visible above the rail of the orchestra pit. Lit from beneath, like mournful skittles waiting for the usual knocks of fate, they dampened the spirits of the onlookers.

Edith was very upset by the deterioration in the audience's quality, and left the stage with the unspoken conviction that she was face to face with *force-majeure*. I found no words to express my horror at such diabolical ingenuity. I just shook a negative head at Professor Strietzel, who smiled imperceptibly and shrugged a fatalistic shoulder.

The rest of the run was most successful, and for the record, I must add that the chess-games on the miniature board were resumed, and Edith never seemed to notice them any more. By the last performance, the Austrians were leading the Germans by twenty-four matches to twenty-one, with nineteen matches drawn.

260 *Derek Salberg, for many years manager of the Alexandra Theatre, Birmingham, recalls one memorable opening night.*

The most notable event in 1956 was the British premiere of "The Chalk Garden" with an all star cast including Edith Evans, Peggy Ashcroft and Felix Aylmer, produced by John Gielgud. The first night was the most glittering I can remember at the Alex, with an audience which included Laurence Olivier, 'Binkie' Beaumont, under whose management it was presented, Robert Helpman and many other notables. Our rather elderly stage doorkeeper who, after the performance, was simultaneously trying to control autograph hunters, deal with requests for taxis, give advice on restaurants and attend to his normal duties, answered a telephone call. By now distraught, and afraid to leave his stage door unattended, he shouted up the stairs, "Is there an Edith Evans in the theatre? If so, she's wanted on the 'phone!"

261 *The following three anecdotes appear in Bryan Forbes's biography of Dame Edith.*

Edith left little to chance. I particularly like the story of the young actor who once went up to her before the red light flashed for transmission time on a BBC drama broadcast. 'Good luck, Dame Edith,' he said. 'With some of us,' Edith replied, 'it isn't *luck.*'

262 During the run of *Coriolanus* she was involved in a car crash; she was thrown out of the front passenger seat and broke her wrist, cracked some ribs and was very badly bruised. She was out of the company for three weeks as a result, returning before she had completely recovered with her arm in plaster. It so happened that on the matinée of the day she resumed her role the young Albert Finney, understudying Sir Laurence, was called upon to deputise for him.* They had a rehearsal for Finney on the morning of the matinée. 'The set had a lot of steps in it,' Finney recalled. 'We all had to do a lot of going up and down, I remember, and there were a couple of occasions with Dame Edith where, as her son, I had to hold her and guide her and go up the stairs with her. When we broke at the end of the rehearsal, I said 'Dame Edith, is there anything I'm not doing right, anything that worries you or throws you?' She said, 'Just be careful when you hold me because my ribs are a little bruised. So don't hold me, because it'll make me want to wince. I'll become aware that I'm bruised. Just put your arm within an inch or so, so that I'll know it's there if I need it, but don't grip me.' I said, 'Okay, yes, but is there anything, any move I'm making that's not the way Larry does it, that's sort of, you know, wrong?' 'Albert,' she said, 'move where you like, dear. I'll get my face in somewhere.'

263 Edith's views on full frontal nudity when that fad hit the West End hardly coincided with those of the perpetrator of *Oh, Calcutta!*. 'I can't think what they're all after, what they're *at*, what they're trying to find out.

---

*Albert Finney's own account of his understudying in this production is on p. 283.

What does it mean? One woman's just like another. I see myself every
morning in the bath and it doesn't interest me to stay any longer than I
have to. Even when I was young and considered to have quite a good
figure . . . I'm not interested. I can't be bothered with it, really. Mystery,
that's what the theatre's all about and there's no mystery in a lot of goose-
pimples.'*

DAME GLADYS COOPER (1888–1971)

264 *Gladys Cooper was popular on both sides of the Atlantic, in such plays in J.M. Barrie's*
Peter Pan *in London just after the First World War and Enid Bagnold's* The Chalk
Garden *in New York nearly 40 years later. These passages come from her autobiography.*

At Drury Lane I got to know a delicious type of old-time actor, who,
according to his own story, had in the 'sixties (or perhaps it was the
'fifties, I forget) created "a furore" in nearly all the best parts Shakespeare
wrote. If you believed him he had been, in his time, about the most
marvellous Hamlet, Iago, Julius Cæsar, Jew in *The Merchant*, and so on,
ever to walk the stage.

He was a great talker, and one night, recounting some of his alleged
triumphs, he was proceeding, "From the moment I make my appearance
on the stage I always forget everything but my part. I leave my own
personality behind me – I am Hamlet, Romeo, Othello, Anthony, as the
case may be, the theatre disappears, the audience vanishes – I am . . . "
when one of his irritated listeners interrupted:

"Yes, I have noticed that," remarked the interrupter.

"You have noticed what?" demanded the old actor.

"That your audience vanishes," was the unkind but deserved reply.

265 An actor I knew was playing a very tragic part in a drama, and in one
scene he is discovered sitting at a table in a country inn. He has ordered
some food and the maid brings in a plate and sets before him what is
supposed to be a mutton chop. The actor usually turns from the table as
she approaches, to say his lines. One night they could not find the
"property" chop, so a small brown gingerbread biscuit was put upon
the plate. The maid placed it before the unfortunate actor, who was so
petrified at what he beheld before him that, instead of declaiming to the
air the line "Oh, God, how long will it last?" (meaning his agony of
mind) he addressed the words to the biscuit. A roar of laughter went up

---

*Sybil Thorndike's reaction was similar. 'My dear, I am a mother, a grandmother, and a great-
grandmother. There is *nothing* I haven't seen.'

from the whole audience and a ribald voice from the gallery shouted "Cheer up, guv'nor! It's treasury night to-morrow – you'll 'ang out."

266   It may be heretic of me, but I am inclined to hold and maintain that *Peter Pan* is really more of a play for grown-ups than for children. Hook is a terrifying character. When children are asked "Do you believe in fairies?" they are egged on to call out "Yes" by the elders. When I played in the piece we did as big business in the evenings with adult audiences as in the afternoons with children.

It is fatal to introduce children to the back of the stage after you have asked them to believe in *Peter Pan*. One afternoon a small boy was brought to my dressing-room. He looked at me suspiciously for some moments and then he said: "Well, now fly." There absolutely does not seem to be any adequate answer to that sort of demand.

GEORGE S. KAUFMAN (1889–1961)

267   *George S. Kaufman, a celebrated member of the Algonquin Hotel's famous Round Table, was also a playwright and director. In 1936 his play* You Can't Take It With You, *written in collaboration with Moss Hart, won the Pulitzer Prize. He also wrote scripts for the Marx Brothers. He was a director of tact but tenacity.*

Directing a great actress of that day, Jane Cowl, in the play *First Lady*, Kaufman allowed her to rehearse with hat, gloves, all the necessary hand props in the play. During one scene, she had a very long speech, after which she put on her hat, gloves, picked up her purse, took some props from the table, put them into the purse, and then made a grand exit.

"Miss Cowl," Kaufman asked, "wouldn't it be better if instead of saying that speech and *then* doing all that, you did all the stage business while you were delivering the speech?"

"Oh, but that's impossible," Miss Cowl snapped.

"Why is it impossible?" Kaufman asked softly.

"It just can't be done!" the actress called out.

"Why not?" he persisted, lowering his voice as she raised hers.

"Do you want me to begin," she demanded, "and say . . . " and she started the speech, put on her hat, her gloves, picked up her purse, crossed to the table, snatched up the props, opened the purse, threw the props into it, snapped it shut, and walked off, her cheeks blazing with indignation.

When she came onto the stage again, Kaufman just looked at her and murmured, "My mistake."

During the run of the play Miss Cowl was the recipient of a Kaufman telegram. After an absence of several weeks, he returned one night and found that Jane Cowl, a playwright herself, had added scores of new lines for her own role. Off shot the telegram: DEAR MISS COWL. YOUR PERFORMANCE IS BETTER THAN EVER. DELIGHTED I CANNOT SAY AS MUCH FOR YOUR LINES.

It wasn't difficult to make an enemy of Kaufman. All one had to do was talk during the performance of a play, especially if he was part of the audience. Many a time he would turn around in his seat or lean forward and tap the shoulder of a between-the-lines talker.

The best record of such an action was when a group came into the theatre after the curtain had gone up. Ignoring the play, they continued to press their previous conversation in loud whispers. Kaufman burned.

"I wish you people would speak up," he snapped. "These actors are making so much noise, I can hardly hear what you're saying."*

When *he* didn't care for a play, things were different. At an opening that bored him beyond endurance, he tapped the shoulder of the woman seated in front of him. "Madame," he whispered, "would you mind putting on your hat?"

During the intermission of another production he disliked, he heard Peggy Pulitzer coughing. "Peg," he flipped, "save that cough for the play."

Howard Teichmann

SIR CHARLES CHAPLIN (1889–1977)

268 *One of Chaplin's earliest stage engagements, before moving to America, was in* The Painful Predicament of Sherlock Holmes, *with William Gillette (see p. 223) in the title rôle.*

Holmes was an immediate success. During the engagement Queen Alexandra saw the play; sitting with her in the Royal Box were the King of Greece and Prince Christian. The Prince was evidently explaining the play to the King for, during the most tense and silent moment, when Holmes and I were alone on the stage, a booming voice with an accent resounded through the theatre: 'Don't tell me! Don't tell me!'

*For a parallel, a century or more earlier, see p. 61.

269 *John Gielgud recalls his first meeting with Chaplin.*

Many years later, in 1952, at a cocktail party in Hollywood, I was introduced to Charlie Chaplin. He took me aside and began to talk to me about his boyhood in London when he used to see Tree's productions from the gallery at His Majesty's. For some reason we talked about Duse.* Chaplin described an occasion on which he saw her act. He began to imitate the actor who had appeared that night with Duse. He whipped out a chair and sat astride it and began to jabber bogus Italian. In a brilliant mime, he showed how the actor was enthralling the audience with a long speech when suddenly the curtains behind began to move and a little old lady came out very quietly and glided across the stage and put her hands towards the fire. Duse. And at this point the poor actor who had seemed so remarkable a moment before was completely blotted out.

DAME AGATHA CHRISTIE (1890–1976)

270 The Mousetrap *has entered theatrical history as the world's longest-running play. Derek Salberg recalls the original pre-London tour to Birmingham.*

On Monday, 17th November, came the now legendary "The Mousetrap" with Richard Attenborough and Sheila Sim, about which, on leaving the theatre, one old-age pensioner was heard to say to another, "Well, this won't run. . . ." Neither did it receive good notices here or at its opening in Nottingham the previous week. At the lunch to celebrate the 25th year of "The Mousetrap", Richard Attenborough recalled that after its initial poor reception, the producer, cast, and Agatha Christie all held a conference. There was much gloom and to dispel it Agatha Christie, then halfway up the stairs on her way to bed, leaned over the bannister and said, "Don't worry children. I'm sure we will get a nice little run out of it."

One who thought it might succeed (but was not wildly enthusiastic about it) was my cousin Victor Saville, once one of England's top film producers with such films as "Goodbye, Mr Chips" and "South Riding", with Ralph Richardson and Ann Todd, to his credit, and who made Jessie Matthews the darling of the British film public. He bought a half share of the film rights for £5,000; there was, however, a proviso in the contract, namely that the film could not be made until the play had terminated its London run. Victor is now eighty-one!**

---

*Eleanora Duse (1858–1924). Her acting was all the more impressive for seeming to be so simple. A legendary theatrical figure wherever she appeared, in England or America, audiences were spell-bound at her ability 'not so much to act as to live'.

** . . . and Victor is now dead!

ROBERTSON HARE (1891–1979)

271 *Delightful English character actor known to all as Bunny. In the first passage John Mills describes the production of* Aren't Men Beasts *in which he appeared with Hare and Alfred Drayton in 1936.*

On two occasions, however, things happened that strained control to breaking point. During one scene with the three of us on stage Bunny Hare had to say, 'Indubitably' (a word he made famous), and then in excitement jump up in the air. On one momentous occasion at a matinée, after I can only suppose a large helping of baked beans for lunch, 'Indubitably' Bunny jumped as usual into the air and a foot from the stage produced one of the loudest and most spectacular farts it has ever been my pleasure to hear. There was no question this time of it being an 'in' joke – the audience heard it. There was no need to go through the agony of suppressing the laughter; the house went up in smoke and we went up with it.

The next happening, however, was much more difficult to cope with. At one point Alfred had to shout at the top of his considerable voice, 'Shut up.' During one performance we were all in a line facing front, obeying Leslie's instructions and barking it into the abyss. As Alfie shouted the words the top plate of his false teeth flew out of his mouth making a bee-line for the stalls. With a miraculously quick reaction he shot out his right hand and caught them in mid-flight. The whole thing was so fast that the audience didn't see it, but unfortunately Bunny and I did. The rest of the scene was torture for us, Alfie turned up-stage and returned his high-flying choppers to their rightful home, while we struggled with the agony of suppressing the laughter that threatened to overwhelm us. Somehow we managed to get through it. But Alfie himself was livid. We were in disgrace. The audience didn't pay to see that sort of behaviour. It was two days before he forgave us.

272 Tall, handsome, with a splendid profile topped by dark wavy hair, Leslie Faber was quite the opposite of a young actor by the name of Robertson (Bunny) Hare who was very short. Bunny hero-worshipped the magnificent Faber who was everything that Bunny was not or ever could be. An incongruous friendship sprang up between them. One day as they entered The Volunteer, a public house in Baker Street, a youngish, ill-kempt man with pale face and hollow cheeks, and wearing a crumpled raincoat was leaning on the bar; his eyes suddenly glazed and uttering a strangulated cry he collapsed to the ground. In complete control of the situation, Faber said, 'Stand back' and, demanding a glass of water from the barmaid, he filled his mouth and 'squirted' it into the man's face. With a shudder the man revived, and Faber, taking his lapels in one hand, lifted him to his feet. With the other hand Faber extracted his wallet, peeled off a pound note and gave it to the unsteady man saying, 'There you are – if you have any sense you'll eat with it. If you haven't you'll drink with it. Get out into the fresh air!'

Bunny stood gaping with admiration at his hero – the aplomb, the wisdom, the sheer strength of this man. He never forgot it.

On holiday in Budleigh Salterton many years later, Bunny had just reached the bottom of a zig-zag staircase that led from the top of the cliffs to the beach below, when his wife said that she would like a box of chocolates. 'Very well, my dear – I'll get you some', and he started back up the steps. Halfway up a panting Bunny arrived at a small landing, to find an ill-kempt man with a pale face and hollow cheeks wearing a crumpled raincoat, leaning on the balustrade. As he passed, the man uttered a strangulated cry and with glazed eyes collapsed to the ground . . . Bunny's experience of his youth leaped to his mind – this would be his moment of triumph. He had to stop three passers-by before one agreed to search for water. Eventually some arrived and Bunny echoed Faber's command: 'Stand back.' Taking a mouthful of water, he 'squirted' it in the man's face. But even using two hands he failed to lift him without assistance. He fumbled for his wallet, remembering the pound note and the advice that went with it, but the man had already revived – shaking the water from his face, he glowered at Bunny and his eyes widened. 'You dirty rotten bastard,' he said and chased poor Bunny up the steps.

Donald Sinden

ALFRED LUNT (1892–1977) and LYNN FONTANNE (1887–1983)

273 *The 'fabulous Lunts', as they became known, were fine comedians as well as serious actors. They played on both sides of the Atlantic with equal style and success: S.N. Behrman's version of Giraudoux's* Amphitryon 38 *was a particular triumph in New York in 1937.*

During the early rehearsals for *Amphitryon 38*, Alfred arrived at the theatre in a great tizzy, the stage manager recalls, and called the company together for a talk. "Ladies and gentlemen, it is impossible for me to play this role, so we can not go on with this play. Please consider the production cancelled. Speak to the company manager and pick up your cheques. I can't go on. I can't find the green umbrella." He turned and left the theatre.

Lynn sat quietly down near the footlights and watched the perturbed actors who stood transfixed with dismay. Then she spoke, "Don't worry, we'll go on, and he will find it."

The rehearsal began and half an hour later, completely re-inspired by his respite, Alfred returned and raised his arm, announcing, "Don't worry. I've found it. We'll start again at the beginning of the act."

The exact origin of the green umbrella, meaning the inspiration for a role, seems shrouded in mystery. Noël Coward told Raymond Mander and Joe Mitchenson in June 1957 that the term dates from rehearsals for the repertory tour in 1927 which included *Pygmalion*, when Lynn suggested that he should use a green umbrella as Higgins, as he was depressed over his interpretation of the part. George Greenberg, many times their stage manager, was sure his first knowledge came at the time of the above incident in connection with *Amphitryon* 38. All members or former members of the Lunts' companies know the umbrella well.*

George Freedley

274 After the run of *The Pirate*, they decided to go to London to act in Sherwood's re-written *There Shall Be No Night*. there was a strong reason for Lynn's decision. Though she had raised considerable sums of money for the American Theatre Wing of the British War Relief Society with her broadcast readings and recording of *The White Cliffs of Dover*, she felt that she must be on the spot as a born Englishwoman and Alfred naturally wanted to go with her. Since Russia at this time was England's ally against the Nazis, a play in which she was exposed as an aggressor nation would not be fitting, so Sherwood transposed the situation in the play to the German invasion of Greece and it opened that way at the Aldwych Theatre in London on 15 December 1943.

One night during the London run of *There Shall Be No Night* a bomb fell right next to the theatre and, as was customary, the fire curtain was lowered. Alfred called out, "Take it up, we're going on." The audience applauded. Lynn had been offstage awaiting her entrance when the blast came. When she entered, Alfred's line was, "Are you all right, darling?" It was too apropos for Lynn, so she paraphrased until she could collect her senses and give the proper lines.

Terence Morgan, playing their son, was standing near the stage door and had disappeared. He had been blown out of the theatre; somewhat shaken, brushing the dust off his uniform, he reappeared on cue, smoothing his hair as he entered. This was wartime playing, indeed.

George Freedley

---

*Lynn told me that Alfred had been very worried during rehearsals of a certain play until one night he suddenly sat up in bed, shook the sleeping Lynn, and exclaimed, 'I'll carry a green umbrella!' From that moment he was quite happy. The phrase is now quite common in the theatre.

275 The Lunts specialized in 'daring' love scenes and physical intimacies that would be considered tame today. For example, during a scene in which Alfred stretched out on a sofa and Lynn took off his shoes, he stroked her face with his feet – in socks of course, but still a caress that might not have been quite so acceptable night after night from just any leading man to the puritanical American public. Once when the curtain fell on the scene, an old lady in the audience remarked with relief to her elderly friend, 'How nice to know they're married.'

Lilli Palmer

NORMAN BEL GEDDES (1893–1958)

276 *One of America's most influential and inspired theatre designers, Norman Bel Geddes first attracted attention in 1916 with a play he wrote and designed about the Blackfeet Indians. Exuberant sets for the Chicago Opera initiated plans for a lavish staging of Dante's* Divine Comedy, *a production that never saw the light of day but still established itself as a landmark in the theatre of what might have been, with its myriad lighting changes and 523 costume and mask designs. In New York he was a virtuoso designer for the Metropolitan Opera. Among his innovations was the move away from what he saw as the restrictions of the proscenium arch towards the greater freedom of the arena stage.*

To design the scenery, he [Max Reinhardt] hired another superman, Norman Bel Geddes, who despised anything less than ten feet tall. Putting their imaginations together, Reinhardt and Geddes reversed the usual practice of producing: they adapted the Manhattan Opera House to fit the show. Since the orchestra pit was not deep enough to contain part of the spectacle, they deepened it by drilling into bedrock under the theater. Before they got down as far as they wanted to, a spring of water spouted twenty-one feet into the orchestra: they had punched into a flowing underground creek. It was some time before the creek could be capped and the water diverted out of the orchestra pit. This was the most serious of the obstacles, but it was not the only one. There were ten postponements before the play could open, and the costs rose to $540,000. Everything was on a colossal scale. The cast included forty-three principal actors and singers. The scenery represented not only the earth where Moses morosely trudged across sand dunes, but also a modern synagogue on the lower level, with heaven above where a choir of angels burst into song in the blue empyrean.

When the production opened on January 7, 1937, the four acts ran until three o'clock the next morning, and exhausted the audience. But the critics left at midnight after seeing the first two acts, and most of the notices were rhapsodic. Beginning on the second night, the last two acts were furtively discarded, and *The Eternal Road* was a hit. There was not an empty seat during the 153 performances. But after the play opened the producers discovered that the operating expenses were greater than the revenue from capacity audiences and the production lost $5000 a week.

Brooks Atkinson

KATHARINE CORNELL (1893–1974)

277 *In the years following the Second World War Katharine Cornell contended with Helen Hayes for the title of 'First Lady' of Broadway. She worked hard to achieve her success and never tired of trying to perfect her technique.*

By breathing, you can raise the tension and excitement in you so that you can come in on top of a scene, where you've got to come in high. The old actors used to call it "shaking the ladder". They used to have the old string ladders, rope ladders, that came down from the flies. And the old actors, for the big, big scenes, you know – the tremendous scenes – they'd go and take this ladder and shake it. And they'd shake it so hard. And I can do it in a minute; you can do it in a minute. You can get your circulation up in one second. Then you get so you don't have to shake that ladder, you can do it by breathing. And often I do it with my breathing. That's nothing I've learned from anybody outside. And I've often done it with my hands on my knees. And I did it when I came in in *The Green Hat* at the end, where – no, I didn't do it, Leslie Howard did it – when after I killed myself . . . I showed Leslie how to put his hands on his knees, and he'd come in like that. Because your whole flow of blood is very high. It's just a mechanical thing, to get your circulation up. I don't have to live through anything in a cellar; I don't have to see somebody dead down there. I can do it myself, mechanically, and with the help of my imagination.

DAME CICELY COURTNEIDGE (1893–1980)

278 *Harold French appeared with Cicely Courtneidge in the* Little Revue, *directed by her husband Jack Hulbert, and describes one memorable scene from it.*

The undertaker sketch opened with me alone on the stage, my back to the audience, polishing some sherry glasses. A second later, Cis made her entrance with a tray of rock-cakes, speaking in a 'refained' voice: 'I do hope as how the Whaite's aren't going to be lait.'

I had then to turn, see her for the first time, look at her admiringly and greet her with the line, 'You look a treat, Martha old girl, you reely do.'

On that first dress rehearsal, I polished my glasses, Cis made her entrance, said her first line. I turned, and that was as far as we got. The sight of Cis, in an obviously dyed red wig, hideous mauve dress, high-heeled bronze shoes, teetering across the stage with her rock-cakes was too much for me. I started to say my line, but couldn't get it out. I started to giggle. At that moment I saw Cis take in my sleazy frock-coat, my balding wig, my moustache. Then our eyes met, a deep gurgle rumbled in her throat. We tried, we tried desperately to behave, but it was no use, hysterical laughter took over.

'When you've quite finished behaving like children . . .' Jack's voice from the stalls, 'perhaps we can get on with the sketch.'

'I'm sorry, Jack', I blurted.

'Yes, I'm sorry, Jack', came from Cis, 'do you mind if we start again?'

'Please do.' The tone was icily polite.

Cis went off, and I started to polish my sherry glasses with one thought in my mind. Whatever happens, I must not catch Cis's eye. She teetered on, saying her line. I turned, looked somewhere in the direction of the dress circle, and said, 'You look a treat, Martha old girl, you reely do.' The fact that I hadn't looked, even vaguely, in her direction, was too much for Cis. The gurgle started again. Somehow or another we got through the lines leading to the entrance of Mai and Tommy. Cis had then to offer the rock-cakes to her guests. Suppressed laughter had made her hand unsteady, the rock-cakes left the plate and bounced about the stage. It was too much. All four of us collapsed, irretrievably, helplessly.

A roar came from the stalls. 'You're supposed to make *me* laugh, not yourselves. Get off-stage, the lot of you, we'll get on with the next number.'

I have to confess that never once did Cis or I go through that sketch without one or other of us 'drying up'. It was unprofessional, unforgivable, but there it was. There is nothing an audience dislikes more – and quite rightly – than actors enjoying their own private joke. Yet, curiously enough, the audience who came time and time again to the *Little Revue* not only forgave us, but anticipating our 'break-up', encouraged us, and heartily joined in. It is the only time in my long career I have ever known this to happen.

SIR CEDRIC HARDWICKE (1893–1964)

279 *Hardwicke – Bernard Shaw's favourite actor – was at his best in good character parts, with a fund of stories in his repertoire. These passages come from his autobiography, A Victorian in Orbit.*

It may have been the manager of this same company [at the Alhambra] who encountered an earnest student of the drama with a problem on his mind. The student, clearly a forerunner of the Method and its insistence on motivations wanted to know, "Did Hamlet have an affair with

Ophelia?" The manager did not have to rack his brains to answer that. "In my company, always," he replied.

Another scholar who thought perhaps too long and too hard about the same play was an old vaudevillian whom I knew very well in later years. He had saved all his money to fulfil his life's ambition of playing Hamlet. At his invitation, I went to see the production, and was startled to find that Hamlet's first appearance opened on the soliloquy "To be or not to be . . . " In his dressing room after the performance I asked him why he had shuffled the tragedy in this way.

"Well," said the old stager, pulling off his tights to change and go home, "in that speech, Hamlet mentions 'that bourne from which no traveller returns.' Now if you think about it, how could he say that *after* he's seen the bloody Ghost?"

The touring Shakespeareans always played *Richard III* on Saturday nights, after they had been handed their pay on Saturday afternoons so that they could settle up with their landladies before they moved on to the next town. One Saturday, the actor playing the Duke of Gloucester devoted his money to a more gratifying cause than paying for his lodgings. He made his entrance in *Richard* swaying like a ship at sea. The rowdies in the audience took only one look at him before they started yelling, "Get off; you're drunk!"

Gloucester steadied himself and straightened out his assumed hump back. At full height and in a voice that reached the gallery, he intoned, "What? Drunk? Me? Just wait 'til you see Buckingham."

280 I spent my evenings walking, and my daylight hours working at the Academy . . . Part of our training was in elocution, and I was glad to discover that I had not the problems in pronunciation encountered by one genteel young woman, who sorely harassed Tree. He pulled her up short one morning, during her reading of *Antony and Cleopatra*. "You may have a 'skay' in Kensington," he observed ironically, "but please understand that in Egypt it is only a 'sky.' "

My modest means saved me from another hazard, too, which a rich young American student stumbled over repeatedly in another early example of a typical Method problem – having to relate a playwright's line to your own experience. The line she balked at was, "I lunch at the Berkeley and dine at the Savoy." She attempted it time and again, but the words would not come right.

"For the love of Heaven, what's wrong with you today?" our instructor cried in despair.

"I'm sorry," she said, "but the line doesn't make sense to me. I always lunch at the Savoy and dine at the Berkeley."

281 On my way back from Italy, I was captured in London by Olivier, to play King Edward IV in his film production of *Richard III;* this performance in the theatre had been dazzling. With Sir John Gielgud, and Sir Ralph Richardson also in the cast, it was a veritable Birmingham Rep reunion, and I reminded them about the old actor seeing a playbill on which, as in this project of ours, four knights were featured. "Imagine that," exclaimed a friend of his, "four knights in one cast."

"That's what I give the play," said the old actor, not in the least impressed.

BEATRICE LILLIE (LADY PEEL) (1894–   )

282 *A splendid comedienne, known to all as 'Bea', and renowned for her wit, she is on the receiving end here.*

You'll *never* guess what happened next. Well, almost next, after an up and a down or three. I became a sort of paid, professional transvestite. I learned how to knot a bow tie, wear a top hat, wrestle with dress studs, swing a cane. I could toy with a cigarette like Gerald du Maurier and ogle a girl like Gilbert the Filbert, the King of the Knuts.

I was known, in fact, as the best-dressed man in London, and thereby hangs a tail that we'll get to in a minute. But beneath the starched shirt front there beat a heart emerald green in its innocence. I scarcely knew anything about *anything*, let alone the ways of the theaytah. After all, I was a *concert* artiste.

I was appearing in *A to Z* with Jack Buchanan, a tall, debonair Scot, who was making his London debut. He'd never had a singing or a dancing lesson, but with his smoky-grey eyes and dark brown wavy hair, with a look of wearing evening clothes as though he'd been poured into them, he went on to become a world-wide idol of the stage and cinema.

Backstage, I was still classified as a girl even if I hardly ever got into a skirt. We girls had dressing rooms on one side of the theatre – the Prince of Wales's – while the men were accommodated on the other.

Jack used to kid me about my being a girl hero, decked out in tails or flannel slacks (tennis anyone?) or whatever costume was called for. 'Tell me, Beattie,' he said one day, 'how do you dress, left or right?'

I hadn't a clue to what he was talking about, not the glimmer of an idea about the meaning of the twinkle in his eyes. I still thought *flies* were something you swatted.

'Come on, Beattie. Don't be shy. On which side do you *dress?*'
Suddenly, the light dawned, or so I thought.
'Oh, yes,' I answered. 'In Number Five. Stage left.'
Jack roared with laughter; thought I was brilliant.

ANEW MCMASTER (1894–1962)

283 *The last of the great Irish actor-managers, McMaster founded a company in 1925 to present Shakespeare on tour, not just in Irish provinces but as far afield as Australia. Harold Pinter here recalls early days on tour with this colourful, impressive figure.*

Joe Norton, the business manager, came in one day and said: 'Mac, all the cinemas in Limerick are on strike. What shall I do?' 'Book Limerick!' Mac said. 'At once. We'll open on Monday.' There was no theatre in the town. We opened on the Monday in a two-thousand seater cinema, with *Othello*. There was no stage and no wingspace. It was St Patrick's night. The curtain was supposed to rise at nine o'clock. But the house wasn't full until eleven-thirty, so the play didn't begin until then. It was well past two in the morning before the curtain came down. Everyone of the two thousand people in the audience was drunk. Apart from that, they weren't accustomed to Shakespeare. For the first half of the play, up to 'I am your own for ever', we could not hear ourselves speak, could not hear the cues. The cast was alarmed. We expected the audience on stage at any moment. We kept our hands on our swords. I was playing Iago at the time. I came offstage with Mac at the interval and we gasped. 'Don't worry,' Mac said, 'don't worry.' After the interval he began to move. When we walked onto the stage for the 'Naked in bed, Iago, and not mean harm' scene (his great body hunched, his voice low with grit), they silenced. He tore into the fit. He made the play his and the place was his. By the time he had reached 'It is the very error of the moon; She comes more near the earth than she was won't, And makes men mad,' (the word 'mad' suddenly cauterized, ugly, shocking) the audience was quite still. And sober. I congratulated Mac. 'Not bad, was it? Not bad. Godfrey Tearle never did the fit, you know.'

284 In the trial scene in *The Merchant of Venice* one night I (as Bassanio) said to him instead of 'For thy three thousand ducats here is six,' quite involuntarily, 'For thy three thousand *buckets* here is six'. He replied quietly and with emphasis: 'If every *bucket* in six thousand *buckets* were in six parts, and every part a *bucket* I would not draw them – I would have my bond.' I could not continue. The other members of the court scene and I turned upstage. Some walked into the wings. But Mac stood, remorseless, grave, like an eagle, waiting for my reply.

RAYMOND MASSEY (1896–1983)

285 *Although best known for his roles in American films Raymond Massey acted a great deal in England between the wars.*

Like all actors, I had been called on for numerous charity shows. Charity leaned heavily on the theatre for support between the wars, but this would be my first time in one of the big so-called "command" perform-ances. King George [the Fifth] was not fond of the theatre. He paid his annual visit to his Actors Pension Fund Performance, grimly determined to do his duty in the best tradition of the senior service in which he had served with distinction. Queen Mary, on the other hand, was stage-struck in her regal way, genuinely enchanted by the theatre.

Command performances were at that time revivals of full-length plays produced for one occasion only and inevitably under-rehearsed. Gerald du Maurier did dozens of them both as actor and director. It must have been agony for him, the most meticulous of actors, to take part in such untidy operations. They were forced on him. Usually, the shows squeaked by without incident and were forgotten. But not this peform-ance of *Bulldog Drummond*.*

Rehearsals had gone well. There were four of the original cast in the matinée production including Gilbert Hare, Alfred Drayton and Ronald Squire. Hare had retired from the theatre after the play had ended its long run and for five years he had been engaged in biochemical research at Cambridge. He now returned to the theatre to play his part of a wicked biochemist, Dr. Lakington, in the command matinée. He seemed very nervous.

We were to play at the Adelphi, a huge theatre in the Strand. As the young American millionaire kidnapped by the bad guys, I made my first entrance in the second act supposedly drugged to the extent of semi-consciousness and with my arms pinioned, led by the arch-villain, Dr. Lakington. I got myself trussed up by props and, a good five minutes before the cue, took my place by a scene door which opened onto the stage.

In the darkness I was relieved to see Mr. Hare – his luxuriant wig identified him – standing near the door. I thought to myself, What a professional! All ready for our entrance! As our cue came closer, I whispered, "Here I am, Mr. Hare." The figure turned and to my horror it wasn't Gilbert Hare, but a stagehand waiting to hand some props to him.

I rushed to the prompt corner and told the stage manager. The stage wait was the time it took to bring Hare from his dressing-room on the second floor. I suppose it was only two or three minutes, but in stage time it seemed eternity.

Edith Evans and Alfred Drayton were on stage. They had been warned of a delay. Back at the door I heard our cue. I was helpless. I felt like a traitor. I could do nothing without Hare. Through a peephole I watched

---

*In a version by A.E.W. Mason, who accompanied the King on this particular occasion.

Edith Evans keep things going in one of the most astonishing improvisations I have ever seen. She was playing a fake Russian countess, and she started off with a stream of Russian double-talk which so bewildered Drayton that he panicked and left the stage. Alone, she proceeded to toy most seductively with a long cigarette holder while softly humming snatches of "The Volga Boat Song." The audience apparently was in her hand. All, that is, but the Royal Patron of the Pension Fund. Just as the breathless and shattered Gilbert Hare was about to make his belated entrance, the Monarch's quarterdeck tones were clearly heard – "Mason, is this one of your damned, dramatic pauses?"

GERTRUDE LAWRENCE (1898–1952)

286 *Bryan Forbes recalls a performance of* September Tide *by Daphne du Maurier.*

I had an arrangement with Michael Gough whereby I partly shared the services of his dresser, an engaging and eccentric character named Herbert. Herbert's principal responsibility came during the second act when Micky had to dive from the balcony of the house into the harbour to rescue the drifting boat. He dived, of course, into a pile of mattresses strategically placed off-stage and out of sight of the audience. He then had to plunge into a bath of lukewarm water to simulate the real thing for his reappearance. Herbert had to be standing by to assist.

During one matinée when the Aldwych was packed with middle-aged matrons all balancing tea trays on their knees, one of the cleats securing Michael Relph's weighty set suddenly gave way. Ossie dashed in search of stage-hands to repair the damage before the set caved in. Now it so happened that this incident took place a few minutes before Micky was due to make his celebrated plunge into the harbour. Herbert was waiting in the wings and before he disappeared Ossie handed him a support rope and told him to hang on to it until help arrived.

Meanwhile on-stage Gertie and Micky continued with the scene, unaware of the drama being enacted in the wings. Micky leapt from the balcony and groped his way in the semi-darkness to the bath of water.

During his absence Gertie went to a cupboard in the supposedly totally deserted house and took some towels out in readiness for Micky's drenched return. It was a vital plot point and carefully established in the dialogue that she and her son-in-law were isolated and alone – the storm was raging and there was nobody for miles around.

Unbeknown to Gertie, Herbert was standing holding the rope on the other side of the cupboard door. It was a hot afternoon and he was curiously dressed in pin-stripe trousers, collarless shirt and white tennis shoes. I should also add that he had a small Hitler moustache. The total effect was startling.

Gertie opened the cupboard door as she had done for the last two hundred performances and revealed Herbert. She was too dumbfounded to close the door again, and for a few seconds she and Herbert stood transfixed like characters in a Disney cartoon. Herbert, being of the old school of theatrical dressers, was also a stickler for etiquette. He couldn't help himself. He gave a little bow and said, 'Good afternoon, Miss Lawrence.'

Up to this point the audience had been mystified but not unduly alarmed by this sudden plot twist. After all, since they hadn't seen the play before, it was conceivable that Miss du Maurier had intended that her central character be suddenly confronted with Hitler in tennis shoes inside a cupboard.

But when Herbert paid his respects to Miss Lawrence the game was up. Gertie managed to close the door and then started to collapse. She turned away up-stage in a futile attempt to conceal her mounting hysteria and, of course, minus towels, bumped straight into the wet and unsuspecting Micky. He had clambered back over the balcony and was greeted with a howl of laughter from the audience and a leading lady staggering around as though inexplicably drunk.

In such circumstances an actor's first instinct is to check his flies, which Micky did. Finding that everything was intact, he began his dialogue as per cue, but received no answering cue for by now Gertie – one of the world's great gigglers – was on the floor. Micky assumed that she had gone temporarily insane and carried on, giving her dialogue as well as his own and attempting to retrieve the situation. Needing a towel, he went back to the cupboard. Renewed hysteria, this time in anticipation, from the audience. Micky opened the cupboard door. The cupboard was bare. And so the second act staggered to its conclusion, Micky having to wait until curtain-fall for an explanation.

CHARLES LAUGHTON (1899–1962)

287 *Born in England, an excellent character actor and a great success on the London stage in the 1930s, Laughton showed his attachment to the American film world by becoming an American citizen in 1940.*

The last night of the Old Vic season was memorable. The theatre was crowded to its utmost limit: the audience was in festive mood. Charles Laughton made the first speech, to hoarse calls from the gallery of "Good old Nero!" – he had played that part in a recently shown film [*The Sign of the Cross*]. Then they called for Elsa Lanchester, who was in the audience. She had made a success in all her parts, and was a great favourite.

"Bring her up!" shouted some one in the gallery.

"Many people have tried to do that, my friend, but they have not succeeded," swiftly answered Elsa's husband.

Janet Dunbar

288 Charles went on tour in *On the Spot* when the London run finished. He was away for a few weeks and visited all the 'key' cities with the play. For the whole of the London run Charles had given the impression to audiences that he really played the organ in *On the Spot* – his rendering of Gounod's *Ave Maria* in particular was supposed to be an excellent interpretation. But one night in Manchester something went wrong. He was walking towards the instrument and it began to play before he got there . . . his off-stage accomplice had mistimed his cue and started too soon. The audience yelled with laughter and it was some time before Charles could pick up the broken threads of the play again and keep them quiet. At the end of the show Charles made a speech. He said: 'Ladies and Gentlemen of Manchester, you are the only people in the world who know that I cannot play the organ. Will you please keep my secret?'

Elsa Lanchester

SIR NOËL COWARD (1899–1973)

289 *Coward's achievements spread over many fields – as actor, playwright, director, singer, composer and lyricist. In Singapore, John Mills was playing Raleigh in R.C. Sheriff's First World War drama,* Journey's End, *when the leading actor, playing Stanhope, fell ill. On holiday at the time, Coward stepped willingly into the part.*

Stanhope is a long and complicated part, full of army jargon and technicalities. I shall never know how he did it, but Noël was word-perfect in three days. He must have had a photographic memory. Apart from the actual lines, he had all the complicated moves and business to remember. As we were playing different shows every evening, he only had time for one run-through with the cast on the afternoon before we opened. I simply couldn't believe how calm and collected he appeared: not only was he word-perfect – I don't remember a single fluff – but he actually had the confidence to alter one or two moves that had already been set in the play.

In the last scene Raleigh dies on the bed in the dug-out. Stanhope leans over him and then walks to the dug-out steps. There is a loud rattle of machine-gun fire. Star shells illuminate the parapet above, as Stanhope walks slowly up the steps to face the barrage. At the dress rehearsal Noël, after he had played the scene, said: 'I've got an idea, Johnnie. If you think it'll work, would you like to try it out tonight?' This was one of his most endearing characteristics. He would frequently ask people in very lowly positions what they thought. It wasn't condescension. He genuinely wanted their reaction. 'Yes, of course, sir. I'm sure the scene could be improved.' I was still very much in awe of him, and had quite a problem preventing myself from jumping up and standing to attention every time he addressed me.

'Right. But before we go any further, although I find it enchanting and flattering to be addressed as sir, we are two actors working together in a play, and having watched you perform on several occasions from the front, I am delighted to have the opportunity of being on the stage with you, and I'm sure unless I pull out all the right stops at the right moment, I shall, at the drop of a tin hat, be acted right off it. And so, Johnnie dear, I think it calls for Christian names from now on.'

I stared at him. 'Well, I, I shall never forget what you've said, sir, but somehow it just doesn't seem right. After all, you are, well, I mean, well . . . you're the Master.'

That title stuck. He was known as and called the Master by many people and friends who loved him throughout his career, and one of my claims to fame must be that I was the originator.

The Master then suggested the following alteration to the direction of the scene. After Raleigh's death, he said he thought it would be more effective if, when Stanhope reached the dug-out steps, he put on his tin hat, then instead of making his exit walked down the stage once more, leaned over Raleigh, looked at him for a moment, and then walked slowly back upstage, and without pausing, continued up the dug-out steps into oblivion. I naturally said I thought it was terrific, it would obviously make the final curtain.

We had always done excellent business with *Journey's End*, but on this unique occasion the House Full boards were outside the theatre when we arrived for a run-through that afternoon. The atmosphere in the theatre that evening was electric, and also cool – in fact, arctic. Air-conditioning had been installed since our previous visit and the system must have been slightly beyond the engineer in charge because our audience in white dinner jackets and backless evening dresses were practically frozen stiff by the end of the first act. We, on the other hand, for the first time, were comfortable in our heavyweight uniforms.

The first act went well. The adrenalin was running and Noël's first-night nerves worked for him and gave his performance all the edge and inner tensions that were an integral part of Captain Stanhope's character. The second act really took off. Noël was giving a magnificent perform-ance. He'd sparked off vibrations like a dynamo, raising the cast to a standard I'm sure we had never attained before. My death scene finally arrived, and after the first few lines of dialogue with Captain Stanhope young Lieutenant Raleigh emitted a heartbreaking (I hoped) cry and died in the Captain's arms.

I lay there on the bed in the dug-out with my eyes closed, holding my breath so that my diaphragm wouldn't pump up and down. I sensed Stanhope rise to his feet, then heard him walk up-stage; there was a pause, the rat-tat-tat of machine guns, the footsteps returned, and I knew that, as rehearsed, he was standing at the bed giving Raleigh a last poignant look before his final exit. I was still holding my breath and had nearly reached bursting-point when suddenly I let out a piercing scream, sat bolt upright and stared at the gallant Captain, who was bare-headed – from quite a considerable height his tin hat had fallen on to the most treasured and delicate part of my anatomy.

Having come back to life in this startling fashion the gallant young lieutenant emitted another rather *sotto voce* second death-cry and collapsed again on the bed. I lay there, waiting for the laugh that I felt must come and ruin everything, but to my relief not a sound came from the audience. They were obviously so caught up with the emotion that was being generated, so held by the play, that nothing, with perhaps the exception of the theatre collapsing on their heads, would have broken the spell.

The curtain fell. The show was a riot, as it thoroughly deserved to be.

290 The tour of *Private Lives* was, as Noël said, swathed in luxury, with first-class trains and hotels provided by Cochran.* Adrianne Allen remembers their first train-journey to Edinburgh and the four of them having their first meal of the tour together, slightly shocked by Larry's behaviour at the end of it, throwing bits of bread at Noël and then anything stickier he could lay his hands on until the two of them turned the fight into a Mack Sennett custard-pie comedy. Noël adored Larry, there is no other word for it, and Larry adored Noël. He, Larry, was then the worst giggler on stage that Noël had ever encountered, or ever did. The slightest thing would set him off; he had already been sacked from a production for giggling, and was very nearly expelled from Birmingham Rep for the same reason. Noël thought this a very serious matter and solemnly warned Larry of his intention to *try* to make him break up at every performance until he was cured. Noël could himself be as wicked as he liked on stage and keep a straight face; judging by the merriment with which he used to recount the tale, he evidently enjoyed administering the cure. He invented a dog called Roger, unseen but who was always on stage with them when he and Larry had a scene together. Roger belonged to Noël but was madly attracted by Larry, especially to his private parts both before and behind, to which he invisibly did unmentionable things in full sight of the audience. 'Down, Roger,' Noël

*C.B. Cochran (1872–1951) was a splendid showman, a producer who presented several of Coward's plays, notably *Bitter Sweet* and *Cavalcade,* with elaborate scenery and costumes.

would whisper, or, 'Not in front of the vicar!' until in the end, as though this time the dog really had gone much too far, a shocked 'ROGER!' was quite enough. The day did eventually come when Larry could not only stand up to this without a flicker, but beat Noël at his own game. He had a line which ran, 'A friend of mine has a house on the edge of Cap Ferrat'; Noël quickly ad-libbed, 'On the *edge*? 'Yes,' Larry said firmly, 'on the *very* edge,' and looked Noël straight in the eye. His cure was complete. What is more he got a big laugh; and the line was slightly changed and incorporated into the play.

Cole Lesley

291 In 1964 we decided to put *Hay Fever* into the repertoire of the National Theatre and to ask Coward to direct it. Nobody alive knew more about sophisticated comedy, and I remembered Coward's remark to Rex Harrison: 'If you weren't the finest light-comedy actor in the world next to me, you'd be good for only one thing – selling cars in Great Portland Street.' Coward himself was astonished by the invitation. Soon after it was issued, I was walking along a Mayfair street when a Rolls pulled up at the kerb. The electric window zoomed down and Coward peered out. 'Bless you,' he said, 'for admitting that I'm a classic. I thought you were going to do nothing but Brecht, Brecht, Brecht.' When he arrived to start rehearsals with a company led by Edith Evans and Maggie Smith, he made a little speech that began, 'I'm thrilled and flattered and frankly a little flabbergasted that the National Theatre should have had the curious perceptiveness to choose a very early play of mine and to give it a cast that could play the Albanian telephone directory.'

The rehearsals yielded a classic *mot*. Dame Edith persisted in upsetting Coward's rhythm by saying 'On a very clear day you can see Marlow,' instead of 'On a clear day you can see Marlow.' After weeks of patience Coward interrupted. 'Edith,' he said, 'the line is "On a clear day you can see Marlow" On a *very* clear day you can see Marlowe *and* Beaumont *and* Fletcher.' The production was a huge success, and spawned a still-continuing vogue of Coward revivals.

Kenneth Tynan

292 *Kenneth More meets 'the Master' for the first time.*

In April, at the Fortune Theatre, luck – that independent and elusive spirit which uplifts or casts down all human enterprises – played its part in our affairs. After months of cold, April was unexpectedly warm. But people recovering from the miserable weather did not flock into London theatres; they wanted to enjoy the sunshine. As a result, we never played to more than £375 takings in any week. Although we were highly praised, we were still unknown. The play lacked the draw of big names. But unknown to me, our performances had attracted the attention of the biggest name in the theatre – Noël Coward.

One evening I was making myself up when the call boy came into my dressing room.

'Mr. Coward on the telephone for you,' he announced brusquely.

'Mr. Who?'

'Said his name was Coward.'

'Coward? You don't mean Noël Coward?'

'Yes. That's him.'

I followed him out to the stage-door keeper's telephone and picked it up.

'Kenneth More here.'

The Master spoke in his clipped, precise way.

'Is that you Kenny, dear boy?'

Good heavens, I thought. It is Noël Coward. And speaking to *me*.

'Yes, sir. Here, sir.'

'Good. Well, I would like you to come and see me in my dressing room after the show tonight. I think I've got something that will interest you.'

Somehow, I survived that evening's performance, then I hurriedly wiped off my make-up, caught a taxi to the Haymarket where he was starring in his own play, *Present Laughter*, with Moira Lister, and timidly knocked on the door of the star dressing room.

Noël Coward was standing in front of his mirror, wearing the blue and white silk polka dot dressing gown he wore so often that it almost became like a trademark.

'Come in, dear boy. Come in and sit down.'

We shook hands. I sat carefully on the edge of the nearest chair. Noël smoothed back his hair and turned sideways, still looking at himself in the mirror.

'Aren't I beautiful?' he asked. 'Absolutely beautiful?'

I was too nervous to know whether he was serious or just pulling my leg, so I replied very earnestly: 'Yes, sir. Of course, you are *very* beautiful.'

A plate of thinly cut smoked salmon sandwiches and a Thermos of tea stood on a table. As we ate and drank, Noël explained that he had written a new play, *Peace in our Time*, which dealt with what might have happened had the Germans won the war and occupied Britain. He had seen me in *Power Without Glory*, and now he offered me the part of the leader of the British Resistance Movement.

I was astonished and delighted. And to think that only days before I had felt sorry for myself because I believed no one had noticed my performance! Such are the switchbacks of fortune in the theatre.

Coward gave me a copy of the script, and invited me to his flat in Chelsea for dinner in a few days time. I accepted with alacrity. We were alone and as before he was wearing his polka dot dressing gown. We had a delightful meal. There were two grand pianos in the room, and, after dinner, Noël sat down at one of them and played, 'I'll see you again', and some of the other lovely melodies he had composed. The atmosphere was very intimate. Subdued lights, a fire burning low, and the tinkling piano in the background.

I sat by the fire feeling rather apprehensive as to how the evening might end. Noël Coward finished playing, and stood up and walked slowly towards me. I lost my nerve and jumped up as he approached.

'Oh, Mr. Coward, sir!' I cried, fearful of what might be about to happen. 'I could *never* have an affair with you, because – because – *you remind me of my father!*'

Noël paused. He looked as enigmatic as a Chinese mandarin. Had I offended him beyond all apology? Then he smiled. 'Hello, son,' he said in his clipped way and roared with laughter!

The air was instantly cleared between us, for I think he appreciated my honesty. Thereafter, until his death, we remained the best of friends. And although he would frequently call me 'son' in front of friends no one ever knew the reason why. In every way he was a most wonderful man.

MILDRED DUNNOCK (1900 –   )

293 *One of the most respected supporting actresses of the American theatre, Mildred Dunnock made her debut in 1932 in* Life Begins. *Arthur Miller here describes how she won the part of Linda Loman, the prelude to one of her best remembered performances.*

It is here that the still unsolved mystery begins, the mystery of what makes a stage performer. There are persons who, in an office, seem exciting candidates for a role, but as soon as they step onto a stage the observers out front – if they are experienced – know that the blessing was not given them. For myself, I know it when, regardless of how well the actor is reading, my eyes begin to wander up to the brick wall back of the stage. Conversely, there are many who make little impression in an office, but once on the stage it is impossible to take one's attention from them. It is a question neither of technique nor of ability, I think, but some quality of surprise inherent in the person.

For instance, when we were searching for a woman to play Linda, the mother in *Death of a Salesman*, a lady came in whom we all knew but could never imagine in the part. We needed a woman who looked as though she had lived in a house dress all her life, even somewhat coarse and certainly less than brilliant. Mildred Dunnock insisted she was that woman, but she was frail, delicate, not long ago a teacher in a girl's college, and a cultivated citizen who probably would not be out of place in a cabinet post. We told her this, in effect, and she understood, and left.

And the next day the line of women formed again in the wings, and suddenly there was Milly again. Now she had padded herself from neck to hem line to look a bit bigger, and for a moment none of us recognized her, and she read again. As soon as she spoke we started to laugh at her ruse; but we saw, too, that she *was* a little more worn now, and seemed less well-maintained, and while she was not quite ordinary, she reminded you of women who were. But we all agreed, when she was finished reading, that she was not right, and she left.

Next day she was there again in another group, and the next and the next, and each day she agreed with us that she was wrong; and to make a long story short when it came time to make the final selection it had to be Milly, and she turned out to be magnificent. But in this case we had known her work; there was no doubt that she was an excellent actress.

The number of talented applicants who are turned down because they are unknown is very large. Such is the crap-shooting chanciness of the business, its chaos, and part of its charm.

CHARLES GOLDNER (1900–55)

294 *Kitty Black describes Goldner in Lillian Hellman's play* Watch on the Rhine.

Charles Goldner, as the villain, ran a sweepstake on the box office figures every night – most of the cast, being stars, were on a percentage and entitled to be given the figure. He always won for he made his first entrance from the french windows centre stage, came down to kiss Athene's hand and then straightened up, his bulging eyes sweeping the house from stalls to gallery, and counting any empty seats that might be visible in inconspicuous corners.

The only other time I saw that trick performed was during a production of *Two Gentlemen of Verona* when the dog that Michael Aldridge had bought from the Dog's Home in Bristol, and who had behaved perfectly during rehearsals, was so startled at seeing the auditorium full of people on his first entrance that he walked down to the footlights, stared straight out in front, surveyed the theatre from floor to ceiling as if counting the house and got the biggest round of the evening.

SIR TYRONE GUTHRIE (1900–71)

295 *Guthrie's skills lay in producing and directing, in England, America and Canada (where he established the Shakespeare Festival at Stratford, Ontario). He began, however, as* *an actor. After a successful performance in a student production of* Henry IV *at Oxford, Guthrie was offered the part of Captain Shotover in Shaw's* Heartbreak House *in a new repertory company founded by James Fagan.*

Came the first day of rehearsals.

We assembled in a parish hall in London. It was in the basement of one of those tall, damp, dilapidated houses, unlovely and unloved, behind Victoria Station. It was exciting to meet the company. Miss Dorothy Green, a very handsome, auburn lady with a purring voice, had been leading lady at Stratford; her Cleopatra had made quite a stir. Miss Florence Buckton had been at the Old Vic. The gentlemen were no less eminent. Mr. Earle Grey had played leading parts in Shakespeare. Mr. Peter Cresswell had once played in the West End.

The three of us from Oxford felt very young, very small beer. I was the youngest of the three, the youngest person present . . . no, there was a girl younger than I, a tall, dark girl with beautiful grey eyes, who had just left the Royal Academy. Her name was Flora Robson [see p. 000].

Soon Mr. Fagan arrived with Mr. Reginald Denham, who was to produce some of the plays. Goodness! Mr. Denham was quite young, hardly any older than I was, really very, *very* young to be a producer. Somehow this seemed a vaguely hopeful sign in an afternoon which was otherwise depressing and ominous.

Now Mr. Shaw appeared and was going to read his play to us. I should like to be able to describe this reading and to give some impression of George Bernard Shaw at this time. It was 1923 and he was finishing *Saint Joan*, which would be produced the following year. Alas, the essentials of the scene have entirely faded from my memory. I cannot remember what Shaw wore nor where he sat. I think we were ranged in a sort of oblong formation round a table with a broken table-tennis net (very 'parish hall'). I remember that I was in a wicker chair and, when the reading started, became self-conscious because my chair creaked whenever I took a breath.

Shaw is always said to have read his own plays wonderfully. I cannot remember. I was charmed by the modest gravity of his demeanour, when he arrived and received our deferential greetings. Then I recall being a little surprised when, during the reading, he would go into fits of laughter at his own jokes.

The next morning we were to start rehearsal. I was there first, word-perfect, humbly but smugly conscious of being one of the youngest members of the company yet playing the longest part – the wonder-boy. The rehearsal began. The wonder-boy, who had been free all summer and knew the words inside out, strode about, now whispering, now shouting, throwing his arms about in the way which had been so effective in Glendower, making long, thrilling pauses. Miss Green, bless her, was in glasses with her handsome nose pressed to the very small print. Mr. Grey was hardly attempting to act at all, just reading, just mumbling really. I hoped he would eventually do better than that.

When we broke for lunch, Mr. Fagan beckoned me to follow him out of the room. We paced a dingy basement passage – three dustbins and a door marked 'Mr. Fothergill – strictly private'.

He took my arm. It had all been a great mistake, he said; he was to blame, not I. He had never realized *quite* how inexperienced I was, not only technically, but in every way.

'After all, you *are* rather young for your age – twenty-one, is it?'

Twenty-three, I had to confess, aware of development abnormally, ridiculously retarded. He was a good psychologist. He did not attempt to gild the pill with flattery. The interest of the whole company, the whole venture, must come before my private interest. I must give up the part. I might leave, if I liked, right then, not come back after lunch; or I might stay on at the same wages, assist the stage manager and make myself as useful as I could.

I could feel that he liked me, that he still felt I had some talent – for something. I could sense and respond to something humorous and merry in the way that he was handling the situation. I suddenly saw that the little episode was not in the least tragic, and not even very absurd. When I said I'd like to stay, he said 'Good, I'm glad'. And I believe he meant it.

When we resumed after lunch, Mr. Grey read Shotover. I was on the book – theatrical parlance for prompting. No one caught eyes; no one looked at me with contemptuous pity; best of all, no one was obtrusively kind. The next day Mr. Grey invited me out to lunch and we talked of this, that and the other, but never alluded to you-know-what. The episode was closed. I had found my level, and not too painfully. The satisfactory thing was that I had had the chance to leave, to get out, to turn back, and had instinctively, finally rejected it. My foot was on the ladder, albeit upon the very lowest rung. He that is down, I reflected cosily, need fear no fall.

296 *Guthrie was part of Lilian Baylis's company when it was invited to take its production of Hamlet to Elsinore to inaugurate an annual festival performance in the Castle of Kronborg.*

Elsinore was no picnic. The performances were arranged by the Danish Tourist Board and were to take place in the courtyard of Kronborg, a seventeenth-century castle on the sound which divided Denmark from Sweden. This was the first venture of the kind and the Tourist Board, understandably enough, was hardly conversant with the peculiar problems of theatrical management.

We had sent over plans of the stage set and a list of requirements for rehearsals, dressing-rooms and so on. We were assured that all would be in perfect order and that, for good measure, we should have the full co-operation as 'extras' of a hundred of the Corps of Officer Cadets who were quartered in the castle.

We arrived a week before the performance. The cadets were perfect – a hundred blond and intelligent young men ready to do or die in the service of art. A stage set had been built to the design of a Danish artist, who was considerably huffed when we insisted that the use of his set would involve rearranging the entire production, and that the whole thing must be rebuilt in precise conformity with our plans. More serious was the fact that the authorities in control of the castle had never been informed that we needed to rehearse.

The castle was open to visitors all day and the authorities were not prepared to close it. Accordingly we rehearsed all night. Even this arrangement was rather upsetting to the authorities, who were convinced that theatre was in some way synonymous with fire; reluctantly they permitted us to rehearse from midnight until six in the morning, but insisted on our employing a large posse of elderly firemen in steel helmets with axes in their belts. Since the courtyard is built of stone, with walls at least a foot thick, and since the weather was exceedingly wet, the precaution seemed excessive, but the firemen did us no harm and seemed, dear old things, to enjoy the play.

I had never before done a production out-of-doors, and was amazed to find how much less quickly we all got tired in the fresh air. The stuffy, frowsty atmosphere of most theatres and rehearsal rooms makes work much more physically exacting; after six or seven hours everyone is tired, has a headache, needs a break. In these rehearsals, although it was pretty cold in the small hours and we were often soaked through and through, we would find ourselves full of energy at the end of the long night; the great problem was not how to keep awake, but how in the freshness of a May morning to commit what seemed the sacrilege of going to bed and trying to sleep.

Like a good commander she [Miss Baylis] shared the hardships of her troops. Night after night she sat through the rehearsals, dispensing from a window sandwiches and lemonade. We used to break for twenty minutes at about three in the morning: the company and the cadets and the orchestra – military musicians resplendent in skin-tight, sky-blue uniforms with silver lace. One night the rain was more persistent and more violent than ever before. Miss Baylis was not at her usual window, but in a sort of porter's lodge, and word got round that she had laid in a keg of rum. Came the break and with it an ugly rush towards the porter's lodge. At the head of the hunt was the colonel who commanded the band.

'Not you!' screamed Miss Baylis in the raucous tones which English-women reserve for foreigners who, naturally, are stone deaf, 'Not you!' and we heard a resounding whack on a sky-blue behind. 'You're just band. This stuff's for *my* people.'

The opening was to be an important occasion – the Tourist Board had left no stone unturned. Royalty was to be present; a special train was chartered to convey the royal party and the diplomatic corps from Copenhagen. The press was there in force. And that night it rained as never before.

The performance was at eight; at seven-thirty the rain was coming down in bellropes. Miss Baylis, Larry Olivier and I held a council of war. It was out of all question to abandon the performance, indeed the special train had already steamed out of Copenhagen. To play in the open air was going to be nothing but an endurance test for all hands. We would give the performance in the ballroom of the hotel. There was no stage; but we would play in the middle of the hall with the audience seated all around as in a circus. The phrase hadn't yet been invented, but this would be theatre in the round.

Larry conducted a lightning rehearsal with the company, improvising exits and entrances, and rearranging business; George Chamberlain and I, assisted by the critics of *Dagbladet*, the *Daily Telegraph* and *Paris-Soir*, arranged eight hundred and seventy basket chairs in circles round the ballroom. Miss Baylis put on her academic robes and kept things going with royalty and ambassadors till we were ready.

The audience thought it a gallant effort and were with us from the start; actors always thrive on emergency and the company did marvels. But *Hamlet* is a very long play. After two hours of improvisation the actors became exhausted and a little flustered. The finale was a shambles, but not quite in the way the author intended. Still it had been quite a good evening; royalty looked pleased, ambassadors clapped white-gloved hands and the press next morning acclaimed a 'sporting gesture' and a *Hamlet* of more than ordinary vitality.

The performance would have worked better if we had been permitted to use all the entrances to the hotel ballroom. But one – the most effective one, a double door at the head of a short flight of steps – was strictly forbidden. The head porter, six foot six, in frock coat and brass buttons, was obdurate. 'This door cannot, it must not, it will not open.' Ours not to reason why; besides, there was no time for argument. The reason emerged next morning. I asked the man, who seemed a reasonable and friendly person, why he had been so firm. 'I will show you,' he said, and tiptoed down a veranda towards the double door. In the architrave was the nest of a pair of blue-tits; the little hen, nervous but gallant, fluttered about our heads. 'If this door had been used, she would have deserted her eggs; you wouldn't have wanted that.'

ANTON WALBROOK (1900–67)

297 *The play is Lillian Hellman's* Watch On the Rhine. *Spoliansky is the child actress Irmgard Spoliansky.*

The closing scene was so unbearably poignant that the stage managers maintained nobody had ever actually *seen* the printed page. Anton was in floods of tears himself and little Spoliansky became agitated.

"Tell me, Mr Walbrook," she asked. "Are you going to cry like this every night?"

"Certainly not," snapped Anton. "In rehearsal *I* cry, in performance it is the bastards in front who cry."*

Kitty Black

HELEN HAYES (1900–)

298 *Of the several actresses to be accorded the title of First Lady of the American Stage surely none has been held in greater affection than Helen Hayes. It was in 1955 that she 'became' a theatre.*

There are probably no more than a dozen actresses in the whole history of world theatre who have had playhouses named after them; of those, only one has to my knowledge managed to outlive her own building, and she is Helen Hayes. When a couple of years ago, property-hungry Broadway developers tore down the New York theatre named in her honour, a number of actors led by Jason Robards and Colleen Dewhurst took to the streets in protest, and some even got arrested trying to halt the bulldozers. Miss Hayes viewed the inexorable march of time rather more tranquilly:

"People kept calling to commiserate with me but I thought, well, I've outlasted all that brick and stone and steel. My theatre may have gone but I'm still here, and I rather liked the feeling. But then they took another theatre just next door to Sardi's and named that after me instead, only now we have a little problem there too. The show that happens to be playing there at the moment is Harvey Fierstein's *Torch Song Trilogy*, about homosexuality, and on the neon sign they don't have room to explain about it just being the theatre that bears my name, so the neon lights read HELEN HAYES TORCH SONG TRILOGY. The other day two old ladies were standing outside and one of them said 'Well, dear, I really hadn't intended to pay 30 dollars just to see a lot of homosexuality, but if Helen Hayes is doing it then it must be all right'. So at least I'm still good for something at the box-office."

From *The Times*

---

*And cry they did. One afternoon John Gielgud came to the matinée. Soon he was awash, his handkerchief clapped to his face, tears rolling into the sodden linen.

299 Mr. Gillette* once told me a story of a small boy who was a mathematical genius – a true prodigy, who awed everyone but his parents. They were petrified of him. His life was so totally involved with equations that his parents feared monomania. In an effort to help them, Mr. Gillette suggested that they take the child to the theatre in order to divert him and stimulate his imagination. With this end in mind, he presented them with tickets to Maude Adams's *Peter Pan*.

The anxious mother and father now sat in the theatre watching their son with gratitude and relief. He was obviously and utterly engrossed.

When intermission came, they happily asked how he liked the play.

"Do you know?" the boy answered. "There were 71,832 words in that act."

LEE STRASBERG (1901–82)

300 *Lee Strasberg must accept responsibility for Method acting, the style that characterized his work with the Group Theatre, of which he was a co-founder with Harold Clurman and Cheryl Crawford in 1931. They created outstanding productions including Paul Green's* The House of Connelly *(their first, in 1931) and Clifford Odets's first play* Awake and Sing! *These extracts from Clurman's book about the Group Theatre,* The Fervent Years, *point to Strasberg's distant and doctrinaire personality.*

One Sunday afternoon the members of the company were invited to a near-by country home. On their return to rehearsal that evening, Lee waited till they were all seated, paused ominously, and asked: "Do you feel tired?" Most of the company answered that they didn't. Lee paid no attention to the answers, but said with frozen control: "There will be no rehearsal tonight. You had such a good time today that you are in no condition to rehearse." The company was a little stunned and marched out meekly, because Lee's face at such moments became a relentless mask.

On the surface this was simply Lee's way of making a point the actor would not soon forget. The actor couldn't come to rehearsal casually: he had to be physically and mentally prepared. From the viewpoint of theatrical discipline this was altogether correct. Apparently some of the actors had had a few more highballs than their sober director deemed judicious, and he wanted to teach them that alcoholic conviviality was not the proper preparation for rehearsal. Yet there was something so tense and bitter in his manner that I couldn't help thinking that some scratch had been inflicted on his ego during the course of the afternoon. Whether this was so or not, one or two asked me later to explain Lee's harshness. They were hurt, and I tried to soften the effect Lee had made

*William Gillette, who played Sherlock Holmes in the original dramatization of the Arthur Conan Doyle stories.

by pointing out the lesson he had wished to draw from the episode. Lee heard that I had spoken to these people and had perhaps mollified them. "You will please not speak to my actors," he flashed.

301 The two particular aspects of the system emphasized during the first summer were the aspects most sensational to people new to its use. One was improvisation. This required the actors to do extemporaneous scenes based on situations emotionally analogous to those in the play, but not actually part of the play's text. A further step in improvisation was the acting of the play's scenes in the actor's own ad lib speech. The purpose of improvisation was to make the actor face each of the play's situations spontaneously – that is, without the support of the play's actual lines, which often serve merely to disguise from himself his own lack of relation to the basic matter of the play.

The second, and most striking, feature of the system, as we knew it then, was what Strasberg called an "exercise" – short for "an exercise in affective memory." "Affective memory" may be defined as the "memory of emotion," which, historically speaking, is the root discovery that led Stanislavsky to the elaboration of his system. In this "exercise" the actor was asked to recall the details of an event from his own past. The recollection of these details would stir the actors with some of the feeling involved in the original experience, thus producing "mood." These "exercises" were used to set the mechanism of the actor's emotion rolling, so to speak. When the actor was in the grip of this mood – although that is not what we called it, nor was it the purpose of the exercise to capture it directly – the actor was better prepared to do the scene calling for the particular mood that the exercise had evoked.

It is necessary to say at once that, besides the hilarious tales that were later recounted concerning these "exercises" – it was reported, for instance, that our actors prayed before going on the stage – they can and did provoke much serious theatrical discussion. But whatever its validity or error, the fact is that this procedure was used by us for the first four years of our work, and it unquestionably produced results – of all kinds.

The first effect on the actors was that of a miracle. The system (incorrectly identified by some actors as the use of the exercises) represented for most of them the open-sesame of the actor's art. Here at last was a key to that elusive ingredient of the stage, true emotion. And Strasberg was a fanatic on the subject of true emotion. Everything was secondary to it. He sought it with the patience of an inquisitor, he was outraged by trick substitutes, and when he had succeeded in stimulating it, he husbanded it, fed it, and protected it. Here was something new to most of the actors, something basic, something almost holy. It was revelation in the theatre; and Strasberg was its prophet.

302 Our first program read: "The Group Theatre (under the Auspices of the Theatre Guild) presents —" The official announcement that preceded the opening merely said: "This theatre is an organization of actors and directors formed with the ultimate aim of creating a permanent acting company to maintain regular New York seasons."

The opening took place the evening of September 23, 1931, at the Martin Beck Theatre on West Forty-fifth Street, New York City. It was the only Group Theatre opening I ever watched from beginning to end. Most of the others I never attended at all.

Cheryl Crawford, Lee Strasberg, and I stood in the rear of the auditorium, a little worried and let down because the actors that night were not up to their usual pitch. Their nervousness in this instance tended to lower their vitality. I could not tell how the play was going; the audience was subdued. When the final curtain descended, I felt the actors had proved themselves fine-spirited people whose accomplishment I would forever cherish beyond the mere value of their talent or success. Tears came to my eyes, and I began to shout "Bravo" before I was sure that anyone would join me in applause. The applause and cheering were general. Not till four years later would there be anything in opening night receptions to equal this.

The company, Paul Green, some friends or Group Associates, as they became officially known, made for an actor's apartment somewhere on West Forty-seventh Street. We had come to celebrate our achievement. This was the only opening-night party free of the tension that came later when we began to appreciate the power of the press in relation to the New York theatre.

At two a.m. word from Cheryl Crawford came over the phone that some reviews had already appeared, and that they were unqualified raves. A loud cheer broke out among us. Clifford Odets and I taxied over to Times Square to buy the morning papers. We read such praise as we hardly dared imagine. We rushed back to the expectant company, and Lee Strasberg read the reviews aloud.

Here is what some of them said: "Paul Green has his match in these young players. They are not only earnest and skillful, but inspired. They play like a band of musicians . . . Their group performance is too beautifully imagined and modulated to concentrate on personal achievements. There is not a gaudy, brittle or facile stroke in their acting. For once, a group performance is tremulous and pellucid, the expression of an ideal. Between Mr. Green's prose poem and the Group Theatre's performance, it is not too much to hope that something fine and true had been started in the American theatre." Another reviewer spoke in comparisons that we had not instigated: "They [the Group] must have convinced the fascinated audience that their way is the only way to prepare a play for all the play is worth . . . I cannot remember a more completely consecrated piece of ensemble work since the Moscow Art masters went home." Still another reviewer, after describing "the rafter-rocking cheers which are all but unknown at first nights nowadays," pointed out that "the truest reason for these cheers was not Mr. Green's play. Instead it was the simple fact that in this Group Theatre jaded Broadway seems finally to have found the young blood and new ideas for which many of us have been praying."

I tried to embrace Strasberg, but a certain rigidity in his posture made it difficult. His attitude bespoke an unwillingness to be moved by the superficial rewards of an enthusiastic press. I clapped him on the back. "Now," I said, "we shall be able to get everything," by which I meant the financial support to carry out our program.

MAURICE EVANS (1901–   )

303 *This English actor-manager was particularly successful in America. His* Richard II *ran for 170 consecutive performances in New York in 1937 and his* Hamlet, *the following year, was the first unabridged version to be seen there. The critic John Mason Brown took his nine-year-old son to a matinée of* Hamlet.

We lunched first. Not at home. At a restaurant. At Giovanni's, in feast-day style worthy of the event. While he sipped a preliminary coke downstairs and I an old-fashioned, I tried to explain what he would see. It took more explanation than I had thought it would. I noticed that his eyes brightened whenever the Ghost was mentioned. Or whenever, in my narration, a cadaver bit the dust.

"Why don't they use pistols?" he asked while I was outlining the duel scene with its multiple jobs for the court mortician. It was only when I had described the poisoned foil, the poisoned wine, and the fury of the duel that he appeared to forgive Shakespeare for not having anticipated the age of the machine.

When he demanded, "They won't really be dead, will they?" I knew he was interested. For him, make-believe and reality were still blissfully, terrifyingly one – at least up to an uncertain point.

Traffic held us up so that we were a minute or so late in getting to the theatre. Hence we missed the first scene on the parapet. But a friendly Negro doorman did his bit for Shakespeare that afternoon.

"Yessuh," the doorman said to him, "the Ghost is walkin' now. It's too dark to go in there. You gotta wait. But never you fear – he'll walk again."

While we were waiting for the first scene to be over, I assured him for the tenth time that the Ghost was not real, and tried to tell him how the illusion of his disappearance would be achieved.

The auditorium was dark when, with other stragglers, we pushed our way in. After we reached our seats, I could hardly persuade him to take off his coat and muffler. His eyes were glued on the stage. I was pleased to see how, even for the young, *Hamlet* sweeps forward on its own feet without having to rely on footnotes.

He listened to every word. He was never bored. He sat far back in his seat, relaxed only during the soliloquies. Whenever there was a threat of action, he pushed forward. Whenever the Ghost appeared, he stood up. Once, when an offstage cannon sounded in the darkness, he came close to turning a somersault into the lap of the woman who was sitting beyond him.

"Holy smokes, what's that?" he cried.

The intermission almost broke his heart. When I suggested that he go out with me while I had a cigarette, he was at first unwilling to leave. His was that nicest of nice fears. He was afraid they might start without waiting for the audience.

On the sidewalk we encountered the doorman for the second time. "Did you see the Ghost?" he beamed. "Well, you'll see him again. He ain't done walkin'."

On the way back to our seats came, "Is Mr. Maurice Evans married?"

"No," I replied, "I don't think so."

"Why doesn't he marry Ophelia?" he suggested. "She's a mighty pretty girl."

He was standing bolt upright during the whole of the play-within-the-play scene. The death of Polonius grieved him. "He's such a funny, nice old man; he made me laugh." But he started laughing again when Hamlet reached behind the curtains for Polonius's body, to say, "I'll lug the guts into the neighboring room."

He jumped as if dynamited at that moment when Laertes and his followers were storming the castle. And I almost had to hold him to prevent his crawling over the seat in front of him during the duel.

After Hamlet's body had been carried by the four captains up the stairs and the curtain had fallen, he stayed – taped to his seat – applauding. He applauded, and applauded, and applauded.

"How'd you like it?" I asked in the taxi, homewardbound.

"Gee, it was swell! I liked it better than *Oklahoma!*" Then a pause. "I like it a little better than Donald Duck." Another pause – a long, reflective one. " 'A little more than kin, and less than kind.' – Gee! That's pretty, isn't it?"

TALLULAH BANKHEAD (1902–68)

304 *Famous for her husky voice, quick wit and outrageous behaviour, Tallulah Bankhead
seldom found roles that did full justice to her potential. At fifteen she won a competition
in a film magazine that included a trip to New York as part of its prize. There she stayed
to begin a distinguished stage career.*

The holidays came and went, and still no word from New York that
producers were clamouring for my services. Suspicion started to chew
at me. Was I to be retired on the brink of a career? I started to toss on my
cot. Grandmother kept the cold water tap turned on. Then came an
incident that went far toward convincing me I was destiny's darling.

In late February *39 East* came to Washington for a week's engagement.
Written by Rachel Crothers, it was produced by Lee and J. J. Shubert in
association with Mary Kirkpatrick. Miss Kirkpatrick was from Alabama.
Her brother had been a classmate of Daddy's in college. The Bankheads
and the Kirkpatricks were friends of long standing.

Mary called up Grandmother: "I know how stage-struck Tallulah is.
Please bring her to the matinée tomorrow. I'm leaving two tickets for
you at the box office." Coming home in Grandmother's limousine after
the performance I started to wail like a banshee. "I can play that part as
well as she can," I keened. "If I'm not permitted to return to the stage
I'll kill myself."

The "she" whom I traduced was Constance Binney. My suicide threat
impressed no one but because a smouldering Tallulah is far from an ideal
companion, Daddy, my aunts, my grandparents, all agreed I should
return to the Algonquin, job or no job. Their lives would be more
peaceful. So, they hoped, would mine.

I idled through most of the summer. Through the kindness of Lyman
Brown I played for two weeks in summer stock in Somerville, Mass.,
another two weeks in Baltimore. Two years had almost elapsed since I
invaded Manhattan, and I had yet to speak a word on its stage. I dreaded
every visit of the postman . . .

One day the awesome Jobyna Howland, then playing in Rachel
Crothers' *The Little Journey*, tapped me in the lobby. "They're casting a
second company of *39 East*, and I've spoken to Miss Crothers. She's
agreed to hear you read for the Constance Binney part. There will be
fifteen other girls trying for the role, but I think you might get it. And
please, Tallulah, don't make up like a tart. Wear a simple little dress.
Look and act your age."

Jobyna briefed me thoroughly on how to behave: "Miss Crothers is
a very opinionated person who knows exactly what she wants. Should
she stop you after you've read only four or five lines, don't be disappointed. She may have made up her mind that quickly. Don't waste her
time pleading for a second chance if she thumbs you down."

The reading was on a cold, badly lit stage. I was paralysed with fright. i had never read or had sides in my hands before. Just before my ordeal I was upset when a fifteen-year-old girl read for one of the minor roles. She was accompanied by her father who in his fright started off with: "Miss Carruthers . . . " "*Crothers* is the name," the author replied in chilly fashion. I wanted to bawl in sympathy.

In those days I felt stark naked unless I had my hat and gloves on. Handed the part, I was unable to get my gloves off. The sides of the part were typed on flimsy paper. I had difficulty trying to turn the sheets with my gloves half on, half off. I had read only ten or twelve lines when Miss Crothers stopped me. Despite Jobyna's briefing, I felt I had failed. I was certain my fumbling, my quivering voice, had betrayed me. Without further ado I burst into tears. To my astonishment Miss Crothers spoke up: "That's very good indeed. Come to my house Friday evening and you can go over the role with the young man who will play opposite you." Believe it or not, I had started crying at the moment the lines indicated emotional upset.

DAME FLORA ROBSON (1902–84)

305 *Fortunately Tyrone Guthrie coaxed Flora Robson back to the stage after she had given up acting in her mid-20s.*

During the summer several members of the O.U.D.S. [Oxford University Dramatic Society] rented a theatre at Oxted, in Surrey, to put on a verse morality play which Christopher Scaife had written. This was a curtain-raiser, with one of Goldoni's comedies for the second play. Tyrone Guthrie was to direct both, and he wrote asking Flora to play the part of the woman in the morality, with Christopher Scaife and Robert Speaight in the other chief parts.

Flora was supposed to turn into a skeleton at one point, and hide her face in a curtain while a death-mask was slipped on; she was then to fall like a collapsed puppet. She had made herself a mask of papier-mâché, with a painted skull face, and was to lie dead for some ten minutes. At the dress rehearsal, after her death fall, she crept off the stage to watch the rest of the play. On the opening night a stage-hand pushed the mask on to her face, and as Flora fell in a heap to the ground she realized she had forgotten to make nose-holes to breathe through, in the mask. The next few seconds were agonizing. She was afraid to make the slightest move, as she was now supposed to be dead; but she had begun to heave for breath, and it took all her will-power to keep still. Her mind leapt forward to the moment when they would pick up her body at the curtain call and find a real corpse. Then she remembered that Tyrone Guthrie, who used darkness as a stage effect, had the lights dimmed right down for the re-entrance of Death in the play. Choosing the right moment, she quickly pushed up her mask in the dark, took a long gulp of air, and lay still as the lights went up again.

Janet Dunbar

306 *The Cherry Orchard* opened to an appreciative house [in 1933]. Athene Seyler was a lively Madame Ranevsky, and Charles Laughton gave the rich peasant, Lopahin, an earthy vigour. The notices were good, and Flora [playing Varya] had a mention in most of them. The week would have gone by smoothly if it had not been for a near-disaster at one performance.

Flora had sometimes tried to imagine what she would do if she fell flat on her face while making a stage entrance. One night it happened. Entering hurriedly to chase one of the characters, Epihodov – played by Marius Goring – Flora tripped over a rug and fell, her face smothered in the woolly pile. As quickly as possible she scrambled up and went on with her speech. The audience gave no reaction; Marius Goring remained solemn. When they were both safely off the stage they could give way to laughter, but it might have been tears of humiliation. James Whale, the producer, who was over on a vist from Hollywood, visited Flora later in her dressing-room, and when she asked why nobody had laughed at her tumble, he said, "But why? We all thought, How very Russian."

Janet Dunbar

307 *The play here was* Mary Read *by James Bridie and Claude Gurney, at His Majesty's Theatre in 1934.*

With a large cast and much violent movement, there were many incidents, especially during the clashes between the pirates. Flora sometimes came in for occasional incidental blows. Charles Farrell, a tough Canadian boxer who played one of the pirates, had to slap Robert Donat's face at one point. Donat always hit back, and there was an occasional loss of temper between them. They would turn to Flora, who was supposed to part them, and say she did not come between them quickly enough. At one rehearsal she ran in too soon, and received blows from both on her face, at which she lost her own temper.

"Look!" she said. "This is only a play, you know."

They were both upset and ashamed, kissed her apologetically, and all went well thereafter. The next night, at the final dress rehearsal, another incident happened which might have had serious consequences. There was an exciting scene in the last act of the play, where Mary Read's lover, about to be tortured as a suspected spy, begged her to kill him quickly;

as she kissed him good-bye she had to pull out her gun and shoot him through the heart. There was a flash of gunpowder from the touch-hole of the gun when she fired, which made it all very realistic. On this night Flora fired right into Robert Donat's bosom, and, to her horror, his shirt immediately began to belch smoke; as he fell dying she could see his fingers crushing out fire which flamed from the shirt. There was a tremendous noise on the stage: guns were booming, the orchestra rising in a crescendo, the pirates rushing about the deck, shouting as they prepared for battle. Flora was unable to get across the stage to Donat, who now lay still. When the curtain came down, however, he sat up with a blackened face and called out, "Flora has singed my navel!" After that she always fired the gun beyond him.

Janet Dunbar

SIR DONALD WOLFIT (1902–68)

308 *Donald Wolfit was a splendid actor-manager. He loved life, and he loved touring. The first three entries come from his autobiography,* First Interval.

The first play [in Wolfit's first season in rep] was *Julius Caesar* with Charles Doran as Brutus. I howled with the rest of the Roman mob to the full extent of my lungs, and hurriedly rushed to the dressing-room to equip myself as a Roman centurion, one of the three who had to carry the dead Brutus from the field of battle. My helmet was large but an old actor hissed: " Put your grease towel inside it"; I added an enormous brown crêpe-hair moustache which was totally out of period and none too secure on my shining cheeks. Thus accoutred, and looking more like a music-hall edition of a fireman than a Roman, I took up my position by the beech-tree whilst the noble Brutus expired. Then, as rehearsed, I stepped forward to hoist the defunct tragedian on my shoulders. Whilst lifting him up a far from Roman voice hissed at me: "For God's sake mind my toupée." I had not until that moment realized that our Brutus was not the possessor of a full head of hair, and in a flash I knew that the whole dignity of this final procession of seven majestic figures depended on me. So taking the by no means slim Brutus on my right shoulder I proceeded to pat the toupée gently with my right hand, whilst with my left I clutched firmly some yards of Roman tunic and a large portion of human flesh beneath it; and thus did I make my long first exit from the professional stage to slow and solemn music.

309 *The setting for this memorable performance was King William's School, Castletown, on the Isle of Man.*

In those days a well-known firm of theatrical publishers used to purvey

232 SIR DONALD WOLFIT

paper scenery. On strong lithograph paper was printed in large squares (about five feet) a woodland scene, an oak-chamber scene and a drawing-room scene. The proper method for mounting was to paste or glue the squares on to the canvas frames to the size required. The school had omitted to do this and had only tacked them on to the frames. It was, of course, the woodland scene that we used for *As You Like It*, reserving the oak-chamber scene for *Twelfth Night* in the evening.

After an excellent lunch in the masters' common-room we prepared ourselves for the play, crowded in the narrow space behind the wings. The play went smoothly, and the laughter from the crowded hall was continuous as the comedy unfolded. Many of the boys were seeing their first play. There was much doubling of small parts in the company and one actor had a very quick change from William, the country man, to Jaques de Boys, the second son of old Sir Rowland. He dashed off the stage, tore off his tunic and furry leggings, and as he dived to the wash-stand to clean his tanned face and body his tights fell about his knees. Suddenly we heard a veritable gale of laughter sweep the hall in the middle of what should have been a quiet scene. We gazed at one another in the wings in amazement as the laughter grew louder and louder. Nothing seemed wrong on the stage, but on turning to look in the corner we discovered that the unfortunate actor immersed in frantic ablutions had pushed against the paper scenery and split it asunder presenting a completely naked posterior (framed by the enchanting Forest of Arden) to the full view of three hundred schoolboys. "Know I am set naked upon your kingdom," wrote Hamlet to his uncle! We dragged the unfortunate man into the wings again and repaired the damage as best we could, but the performance never recovered from that incursion.

310 For two performances we moved to Versailles and played in a delightful theatre which one approached through the stables below. The little boxes were actually on the side of the apron-stage and packed with six men in each box. At the second performance I made a quite terrible mistake. I still blush when I remember it. Coming from scarred and bombed England it did indeed seem that the war would never end. Momentarily I forgot that here in Versailles we were playing to SHAEF, to the men whose sole aim was to conclude the war as soon as possible, and who had a pretty good idea as to when it might be concluded. In response to a storm of applause at the fall of the curtain I ventured to express our thanks for the way the performances had been received, thanked one and all for their generous hospitality and expressed the hope that we might be allowed to come again next year!

311 *Ronald Harwood (whose play* The Dresser *drew heavily upon his experiences with Wolfit) offers these glimpses of Wolfit on and off the stage.*

During a rehearsal of *Macbeth*, a young actor, Nicholas Baker, took his turn in a queue of processing 'Kings' waiting to take their crowns from a box of props. Each took his crown quickly, for there was no time to make a choice of sizes, and Nicholas's crown was so large that it rested across the bridge of his nose. Wolfit was gabbling, in a casual undertone, Macbeth's lines. Nicholas appeared before him on the line: "Thy crown doth sear mine eyeballs!", and his boyish grin at the ludicrousness of standing in a crown that was as good as resting on his own eyeballs was quickly effaced by Wolfit's furious cry of: "IT'S NOT FUNNY, BAKER!!!!"

312 One night at Belfast, as Othello lay on the floor dying, a young officer knelt over the floor to make sure he was well and truly dead. Othello whispered, "My boy, you must do something about your breath."

313 Wolfit's padding for Falstaff was a monstrous piece of old-fashioned engineering. Hot, heavy and Gothic, it caused the actor to sweat mercilessly. Its worst drawback was that it had to be removed entirely if the actor was to relieve himself during the performance. Falstaff, luckily, is off-stage for some length of time during the course of the play, and this provided Wolfit with the necessary opportunity. "Brilliant craftsman, Shakespeare. Knew the actor would want to pee and constructed the play accordingly. A master, a master!"

314 *The entry in Peter Hall's diary for 1 May, 1978 provides this nugget.*

Dinsdale Landen told today a wonderful story of his days as assistant stage manager at Worthing. He was a walk-on when Wolfit was there as guest star, playing Othello, but was not told what to do until the dress rehearsal, at which the great man said it would be a very good idea for Othello to have a page who followed him everywhere. He handed Dinsdale a loin cloth, told him to black-up, and said he'd got the part. Dinsdale did not know the play and just went wherever Wolfit went, the complete dutiful page, always in attendance. But at one point he found himself in a scene in which he felt rather ill at ease; he had an instinct about it. Suddenly he heard the great man's voice roaring, 'Not in Desdemona's bedroom, you cunt.'

SIR RALPH RICHARDSON (1902–83)

315 *Richardson, Gielgud, Olivier are the three great actor-knights of the modern era. Richardson was the most eccentric, spawning scores of stories about his 'oddities'. He was a splendid actor, equally at home in comedy or tragedy, and played a wide variety of roles, from Shakespeare (his Falstaff in 1945 was a triumph) to Pinter (whose* No Man's Land *in 1975 teamed him with John Gielgud).*

After an abortive period at the Brighton Art School, Richardson saw Frank Benson in *Hamlet*, and immediately decided to become an actor. In December, 1920, when he was seventeen – he was born at Cheltenham on December 19, 1902 – he took himself off to a certain Frank Growcott, who ran a little theatre – the St. Nicholas Players – in a disused bacon factory at the back of Brighton station. Growcott received him with the lack of enthusiasm that managers show to all young men who wish to become actors. "Don't be hasty", cried Richardson, determined to dazzle him with the force of his personality; "I am a man of means. I will give you money: a pound a week for ten weeks. After that, if you like me, *you* can give *me* a pound a week." A bargain was struck, and soon afterwards, in his own exuberant words to an interviewer in South Africa some years later, he "burst on the English stage as a bombshell . . . I was employed primarily to imitate the bursting of bombs dropped in an air-raid scene in a war play. I did it with a petrol tin at the end of the scrap. I had a sheet of cues, which I read by the light of a candle under the stage. One night the candle went out. Bombs fell everywhere regardless of cues or courtesy."

Harold Hobson

316 The recruits, Mouldy, Shadow, Wart, Feeble and Bullcalf, played by younger actors, keenly following Olivier's extra-terrestrial example [in *Henry IV, Pt.2*], would also adopt every kind of facial disfigurement to call attention to themselves – blackened teeth or fangs, huge whiskers, warts with bushy hairs. One night before they were about to go on Ralph stopped and, looking them over critically, pronounced, "You know, when I was a young actor, I had some very good advice given me by an old actor: 'If you're playing a character part,' this actor told me, 'just before you come down to the stage, take one last look in your dressing-room mirror and ask y'self, "Is it human?"'"

Garry O'Connor

317 *Two versions of the time that Richardson fell through the ceiling at the Oliviers' home at Notley.*

The men having left, the wives chatted over their coffee. Mrs Olivier

[Vivien Leigh] felt obscurely uneasy, but after five, ten, fifteen minutes had passed without incident, she was ready to scoff at her qualms. At this moment there was a prolonged splintering noise from above, followed by a colossal crash that made the whole house shake. The women dashed upstairs, where, in the main guest room, lovingly decorated under Mrs Olivier's personal supervision, they found Richardson on his back and covered in plaster, in a bed that had collapsed under his weight. Above it there was a gaping hole in the ceiling, through which he had evidently fallen.

Could one believe 13 stone of Ralph Richardson fell 8 or 9 feet, breaking 4–inch rafters as it crashed down? Tynan's report is reminiscent of an attempt made by Thomas Carlyle in 1853 to have a soundproof room constructed on his top floor: workmen fell through the ceiling into Mr and Mrs Carlyle's bedroom, one narrowly missing Mrs Carlyle's head. The tables and chairs all had their "legs in the air as if in convulsions".

A possibly more reliable account: The following Monday morning saw Richardson arriving at the New Theatre offices in Goodwin's Court off St Martin's Lane. "I've done it again," he told the secretaries, Vi Marriott and Kate Ashbury.

Then, before everyone's eyes, he began to act out the whole scene, using chairs and tables; how he and Olivier left the two ladies downstairs; how Olivier in the course of showing him the attic, "You must keep to the beams, dear chap, keep to the main beams." Of course he hadn't. But all of him hadn't gone through the ceiling by any means. Just his leg. Rather easier if it had, because he had great difficulty in getting his leg back. "Quick," said Olivier. "We won't tell her – we must tidy up." So they'd rushed downstairs to the bedroom, picked up what broken plaster they could, then stolen downstairs and unseen by their wives collected buckets and water, creeping back through the flower beds under the drawing-room window: then desperately tried to get the room straight again so Vivien shouldn't explode. All this Richardson enacted for the New Theatre staff by crawling about on hands and knees on the floor of the Goodwin's Court Office.

Garry O'Connor

318 The ill-fated *Macbeth* opened in June 1952. Richardson wore a red wig, having sent down his wig-maker into the stalls during one matinée of *The Tempest* to snip a lock of schoolgirl's hair he decided was just the right shade. . . .

"Has anyone seen a talent," Richardson remarked, waiting for notes in the Green Room the day the reviews appeared. "Not a very big one, but I seem to have mislaid it." One night after delivering the great dagger speech he came over to two members of the cast standing by the curtain and said: "I've lost the knack; if I was a member of the audience, I'd ask for my money back." At another time later in the season, during a performance of *Volpone*, he took aside another actor: "Give me five pounds." "What?" said the puzzled colleague. "Give me five pounds." The actor began to wonder if Richardson was still sane. Richardson: "If you don't give me five pounds I'll have it put about that you were in my *Macbeth*."

Garry O'Connor

319 In Sydney they opened the new National Theatre, and one night Richardson was going to the theatre in a taxi when the driver said to him, " How do you like it out there at this New Elizabethan?" (the name of the theatre). As Richardson recorded:

"I like it very much," I said, "it's a very nice theatre."

"You don't say?" said the driver.

"Oh yes," for some reason I went on, "very nice theatre to play in, very nice to speak in."

"You don't say," said the driver. I said no more.

"I drove two old ladies home from the Elizabethan last night, mister," the driver turned round to inform me, "and they were saying, in this cab, that they couldn't hear a word you said!"

Garry O'Connor

320 *Peter Hall writes in his diary about Richardson in rehearsal.*

A lovely day on *The Cherry Orchard*. I shall never forget Ralph walking through the last bit of Firs; not acting it but commentating on it to himself and to us. 'Now I come through the door in my slippers. Good heavens, there's nobody here. Good Lord, they've all gone. So I go off to the window and look out. Can't see anything. So I go over to the sofa feeling very tired now, sit down, drop my stick, too tired to take it up. So I lie back, want to put my legs up, but can't, I'm too tired. Then I die . . .'

321 *Coral Browne tells John Lahr, the biographer of Joe Orton, about Richardson's difficulties in learning Orton's lines.*

Sir Ralph, an august and lovably eccentric actor, was totally lost in the whirlwind of Orton's language. He had memorized the script, as was his custom, by writing it out on large music sheets which he put on a music stand. 'He learned it in rhythm and turned over each page as if it were a musical score,' Coral Browne explains. 'Sometimes it was difficult for him to learn because he had no idea of what the words meant. He couldn't get nymphomaniac right because I don't think he'd heard of one of those. He would refer to it as "nymphromaniac". When he had one of those long speeches with words like "transvestite" or "nymphomaniac", he was hopelessly at sea. He'd learned the rhythm of Orton but not all the words. And when he'd dry, he'd continue on saying "Di-da-di-da-di-da-di-da". Nobody in the audience seemed to take any notice.'

SIR JOHN GIELGUD (1904–   )

322 *Gielgud's roles in the 1930s at the Old Vic – principally in Shakespeare but also, triumphantly, in Gordon Daviot's* Richard of Bordeaux *at the New Theatre – emphatically confirmed his stature. Olivier describes him as 'always the poet, head upturned towards the stars'. He has a delicious sense of humour, but is also renowned for his gaffes. The first three entries are by the actor Emlyn Williams.*

Richard of Bordeaux being in its seventh month, its star was given two weeks' holiday, 'to make a break', took a suite in the Royal Crescent, Brighton, littered it with scripts, and asked me and Dick [Clowes] down for a couple of days.

He went for walks between us along the front, the ozone fertilizing his mind with ideas while his eyes spotted theatre faces with the excitement of a Gallery First-Nighter. 'I've got rather a good idea for *A Midsummer Night's Dream* – to do it nude, or as near as one could go – wouldn't it be superb?'

He made it sound just that, till he added, 'With everybody starkers we could just call it "Bottom",' and shrieked with nursery laughter . . .

One rainy afternoon he decided on a night out in London. By now I knew him well enough to guess that he would take us to a theatre, but not well enough to know which one.

After a fine early dinner at the Café Royal, Dick and I found ourselves sitting in the front of a stage box, with the holiday-maker lurking in the shadows. We were at the New Theatre, watching *Richard of Bordeaux*, 'I'm curious to see it from the front.'

As the theatre darkened Dick whispered to me, 'Would you call this "making a break"?'

Glen Byam Shaw was playing Richard as a rehearsal for his tour in the part, and playing well. At the end of one emotional scene between the king and his wife, I stole a look behind me: John G. was not just moved, he was weeping. I was in the company of a child playing with double mirrors.

When at the end we hurried through the pass-door, the stage-hands stacking scenery looked through the visitor without recognizing him. They had plainly never seen him in a suit.

Glen was staggered – 'Thank God I didn't know' – and delighted by praise generous and sincere. Then John took Dick and me out to supper as if after a first night he had enjoyed.

Dick said, 'John dear, I know the play moved you, but I did once see you lean forward and count the house through your tears.'

'Dickie Clowes, that's a wicked thing to say. Actually it wasn't at all bad, I was surprised . . .'

323   To jump ahead. Years later, a friend told me of an example of John's absorption in the theatre, which cropped up quite unexpectedly. The two of them, playing in the same film, were sitting on the set in their canvas chairs, whiling away one of the long waits; John was reading. The other, wrestling with his *Times* crossword, leant over, "Sorry, but is there a character in Shakespeare called the Earl of Westmoreland?"

"Yes," John answered, without looking up, "in *Henry IV Part Two*." Then, to break the bad news, he turned to my friend. "But it's a very poor part." And went back to his book.

in *The Ages of Gielgud*, Ronald Harwood (ed.)

324   Early in the Gielgud career, at the Ivy Restaurant, he was the luncheon guest of a prominent playwright of the time who was notoriously dull and garrulous company. Just as there came a pause for breath, a man passed the table. "Thank God he didn't stop," said John, "he's a bigger bore than Eddie Knoblock," and turned back to his host. Who was Eddie Knoblock . . .

. . . John was casting *The Laughing Woman*, a play about a brilliant young sculptor and his mistress. "Bronnie is insisting on Stephen Haggard for the part. He's splendid but *much* too well-bred. It calls for an actor who would convey somebody savage, uncouth – Emlyn, *you* should be playing it!"

in *op.cit*, Ronald Harwood (ed.)

325   *This anecdote refers to Gielgud's production of* Macbeth, *produced by Binkie Beaumont, for whom Kitty Black, the narrator, acted as a secretary.*

For a long time John couldn't make up his mind about the Lady, and finally announced that he would hold auditions in order to find a suitable new star. Among the letters was one application for the part of "Lady

McBeth" enclosing a photograph with the pathetic p.s. "I do take my glasses off often." Eventually he settled for Gwen Ffrangçon-Davies who had been his exquisite partner in the romantic smash-hit, *Richard of Bordeaux*, as well as in *Three Sisters* and *The Importance of being Earnest*.

From the first the disasters that seem to dog the Scottish play began to accumulate. First, William Walton disappeared. His agent had no idea where he was and as the music he had been commissioned to write had been conceived as an accompaniment to all the witches' scenes, which were to be spoken rhythmically against a recorded score, nobody could rehearse anything final until the composer had set down what had been agreed with the director. One day the office boy came into my room saying: "There's a bloke outside who says he's supposed to be composing the music for *Macbeth*."

"Mr Walton, Mr Walton," I cried, hurrying out to meet him, "where have you been? Where is the music?"

"I haven't written it yet," he replied.

"Not written it!" I gasped. "But we need it right away."

"It won't take long," he replied and proceeded to explain that composing the twenty-odd minutes of music required would barely take him a week, and he was as good as his word. He attended only one run-through of the play, made careful notes and when the score was delivered, every fanfare and musical bridge was correctly timed to the very last second. A piano version was made to enable the witches to rehearse their "Double double" bits and eventually the whole thing was recorded by HMV on acetate one-sided 78s with thirty minutes of the London Philharmonic Orchestra conducted by Ernest Irving. They over-ran the recording session by an incredible amount of overtime and poor John had to produce a personal cheque as nobody would leave the studio until every last penny had been paid. Came the day when there was a run-through of the play with the music, and in the empty theatre I felt like Ludwig of Bavaria listening to the final versions of *Tannhäuser* or *Lohengrin*.

John had put together a tremendously complicated effects score with wind howling at all the climaxes, bells ringing, doors being hammered on, etc. and the only way all this could be coordinated was for two operators – Mary and Viola – to manipulate the panatropes – gramo-phones with pick-up arms that could be spotted on to any given groove of the 78s – with the effects records on one machine and the Walton music on the other. John kept changing his mind and adding or subtracting effects with the result that finally there were one hundred and forty separate cues for effects, while the music was fed in to complement or underline the action. After the final matinée, John came to Viola and asked her to add another wind cue to the plot.

"But Mr Gielgud, there's only one more performance," wailed the harassed stage manager.

"Yes, I know, but I *would* like to hear it just once," said John, and who could resist him?

326 *Peter Ustinov saw Gielgud being interviewed on American television.*

I once saw him on a local late-night television interview in Saint Louis, Missouri. He was busy playing *The Ages of Man*, his one-man show, in half a ball-park, and now he was being interviewed by a long-winded intellectual.

'One final question,' the interviewer said. 'Sir . . . Sir Gielgud . . . did you . . . oh, you must have had . . . we all did . . . at the start of your very wonderful . . . very wonderful and very meaningful . . . let me put it this way . . . did you have someone . . . a man . . . or . . . or indeed, a woman . . . at whom you could now point a finger and say . . . Yes! . . . This person helped me when I . . .'

By now John understood what was being asked of him, and he prepared to answer, disguising his dislike of all that is pretentious by a perfect courtesy.

'Yes, I think there was somebody who taught me a great deal at my dramatic school, and I certainly am grateful to him for his kindness and consideration toward me. His name was Claude Rains.'

And then, as an afterthought, he added – 'I don't know what happened to him. I think he failed, and went to America.'

327 *The narrator is the playwright David Storey whose play* Home *was first produced with Gielgud and Richardson, and directed by Lindsay Anderson, in 1970.*

The beginning of rehearsals for *Home* was like watching two horses galloping along while, perched on a delicately fashioned carriage behind, a driver called out, 'Whoa! Stop!' finally turning to his fellow passenger and saying, wryly, 'Well, we'd better let them have a run . . .' If *The Contractor* [Storey's previous play] had seen the empirical method of directing at its most demanding, *Home* saw it at its most discreet:

'It isn't possible for an actor to sit on a stage without moving, Lindsay, for 25 minutes.'

'Is it 25 minutes?'

'It feels like 25.'

'Move, in that case, if you feel like it, John.'

Until a point had been reached:

'It's strange, but once sitting here, I don't feel I want to move again.'

'Don't, in that case.'

'I shan't.'

One critic observed:

'So perfect is the spell cast, indeed, that on the second night during one of the deeper silences, a mouse strolled on the stage, looked calmly round, and having satisfied its curiosity wandered off again . . . it would not surprise me that [he] too had been exhaustively rehearsed, his entrance and exit timed within the flick of a tail.'

CLIFFORD ODETS (1906–63)

328 *In spite of his later and disappointing work in Hollywood, Clifford Odets will be remembered as the Group Theatre's leading dramatist who brought the battle cry of the working classes to the stage in such plays as* Waiting for Lefty *(1935),* Awake and Sing! *(1935) and* Golden Boy *(1937).*

Sunday night, January 5, 1935, at the old Civic Repertory Theatre on Fourteenth Street, an event took place to be noted in the annals of the American theatre. The evening had opened with a mildly amusing one-act play by Paul Green. The audience, though attracted by the guest appearance of a good part of the Group company, had no idea of what was to follow.

The first scene of *Lefty* had not played two minutes when a shock of delighted recognition struck the audience like a tidal wave. Deep laughter, hot assent, a kind of joyous fever seemed to sweep the audience toward the stage. The actors no longer performed; they were being carried along as if by an exultancy of communication such as I had never witnessed in the theatre before. Audience and actors had become one. Line after line brought applause, whistles, bravos, and heartfelt shouts of kinship.

The taxi strike of February 1934 had been a minor incident in the labor crisis of this period. There were very few taxi-drivers in that first audience, I am sure; very few indeed who had ever been directly connected with such an event as the union meeting that provided the play its pivotal situation. When the audience at the end of the play responded to the militant question from the stage: "Well, what's the answer?" with a spontaneous roar of "Strike! Strike!" it was something more than a tribute to the play's effectiveness, more even than a testimony of the audience's hunger for constructive social action. It was the birth cry of the thirties. Our youth had found its voice. It was a call to join the good fight for a greater measure of life in a world free of economic fear, falsehood, and craven servitude to stupidity and greed. "Strike!" was *Lefty*'s lyric message, not alone for a few extra pennies of wages or for shorter hours of work, strike for greater dignity, strike for a bolder humanity, strike for the full stature of man.

The audience I say, was delirious. It stormed the stage, which I persuaded the stunned author to mount. People went from the theatre dazed and happy: a new awareness and confidence had entered their lives.

Harold Clurman

Lillian Hellman (1907–84)

329 *Lillian Hellman's abrasive independence was guaranteed to unsettle conservative values whether in the theatre or politics. This brought setbacks to her career during the McCarthy era, but plays such as* The Little Foxes *(1939) and* Watch on the Rhine *(1941) had established her as one of America's leading liberal writers.*

The Children's Hour was my first play. I don't remember very much about the writing or the casting, but I remember Lee Shubert, who owned the theatre, as he did many other theatres in New York, coming down the aisle to stare at me during a rehearsal day. I was sitting mid-theatre with my feet on the top of the chair in front of me. He came around to stand directly before me and said, "Take your dirty shoes off my chair."

I said, "My shoes aren't touching the chair, Mr. Shubert," but, after a pause, he pushed my right leg to the floor.

I said, "I don't like strange men fooling around with my right leg so don't do it again."

Mr. Shubert called out to Herman Shumlin, who was directing the play from the front row. They met in the aisle and I heard Herman say, "That girl, as you call her, is the author of the play," and went back to directing. About half an hour later, Mr. Shubert, who had been standing in the back watching the play for which he had put up the money, came down and sat behind me.

"This play," he said to the back of my head, "could land us all in jail." He had been watching the confession scene, the recognition of the love of one woman for another.

I said, "I am eating a frankfurter and I don't want to think about jail. Would you like a piece of it?"

"I forbid you to get mustard on my chairs," he said and I was never to see him again until the play had been running for about six months and then I heard him ask the doorman who I was.

Sir Laurence Olivier (Baron Olivier of Brighton)
(1907–)

330 *Olivier's theatrical achievements are far too numerous to be recounted here. 'An active actor', in his own words, he is at his best in parts demanding physical presence and using his own instinct and individuality. In 1970 he became the first actor to be made a life peer. Here he describes his entry onto the professional stage.*

We were in the Brighton Hippodrome on a Sunday evening in the autumn of 1925.

I passed through the stage door and the stage doorkeeper said sharply, 'Name, please? Oh yes, you're new, aren't you? Well now, I've been told to warn you: be careful the way you make your entrance. This is the old type set. The doors in the set are framed right out – the same width all the way round, top, both sides *and bottom*. That means across the bottom of the doorway there is a sill – ooh – four and a half to five inches high. It's quite difficult not to trip over this, see?' The stage doorkeeper turned away to his books again. Taking my small suitcase containing my ready-made dinner jacket, shirt, shoes, studs, etc., and a tin with a few sticks of Leichner greasepaint in it, a tin of Cremine, a towel and a piece of soap, I went up to the topmost floor to dressing-room No. 12; here were quite a few old actors, already at their make-up. After a while one said, 'Listen, laddie' (no, *honestly*) 'it's possible you may not have come across this,' and told me about the sill. I said it was kind of him but I did know about it. Dressed, made-up and ready (rather too much black under the eyes), I sat and waited for the first time for my call, praying that my name would be pronounced correctly. Eventually, the sharp knock and the boy's voice, 'Mister Oliver, please.' I sighed in disappointment and realized I was probably in for quite a battle with this problem. . . . The call-boy was on the lowest rung of the theatrical ladder, though advancement was quite possible; I imagine that Claude Rains must be the most spectacular example of one who started life as a call-boy. I followed the one who had called me 'Mr Oliver' down the back-stage stairs of the Brighton Hippodrome. On the way he said, 'Oh, you have to be careful, the entrance is a bit awkward.' 'I know, thanks,' I said. This was getting tedious.

Some of my generation may remember an ancient ghost of a habit that still haunted *les grandes dames* of our theatre in our early days. It was a device, we assumed, deliberately cultivated to lend dignity, grandeur, hauteur, not to say majesty to their image as leading ladies, which was accomplished by raising their beautiful skirts and seemingly sailing across the threshold on their entrance. It was born of forgotten years' early training in how to cope with *that sill* somehow, without looking undignified.

I stepped on to the stage, which as I had guessed was pretty sizeable. Several yards away the stage manager was beckoning me from the traditional left-hand prompt corner. (Stage-right prompt corners were unusual, except for odd places like the Birmingham Rep.) I came up to him and said, 'I know, you're going to tell me about that old sill, aren't you?' He waved me impatiently round the back of the set to the upstage right entrance at the end of the back wall of the set, which of course flapped about like a becalmed sail; I waited two or three yards up right of it for my cue from the stage. There was a friendly stagehand standing near me. My cue came and I started forward, the stagehand just touched me on the sleeve and pointed to the bottom of the door; it was my turn to wave someone impatiently away. I gave the canvas door a push and strode manfully through it.

Of course I did a shattering trip over the sill, sailed through the air, and before I knew what was happening to me I found my front teeth wedged firmly between a pink bulb and a blue one in the middle of the footlights. I was appearing before a very ample house, which means that an audience reaction of any kind makes a thunderously loud noise to one on the stage facing it. The particular reaction stunned me for a second or two by its volume. I scrambled to my feet dusting myself off, and stood a while blinking at the audience; then turned and blinked at Ruby Miller, who was pro enough not to have turned a hair. I looked back once pleadingly to the audience, but they were not to be robbed as easily as that of their biggest laugh for ages.

331 His Birmingham debut was in a new one-act comedy by Eden Phillpott, *Something to Talk About*, put on as a curtain-raiser. Olivier – Hitlerish in hair style and moustache – played a monocled aristocrat at a manor house party that is interrupted by the arrival of a burglar. 'Who are you?' the intruder asks. 'We are Conservatives,' was Olivier's haughty reply. But he didn't think this quite funny enough, and on the last night he changed it and said, 'We're Freemasons, froth-blowers and gugnuncs.' He thought that a marked improvement on the script and the audience reaction confirmed him in his opinion. But producer W. G. Fay did not share it. A matter of principle and discipline was at stake, and for once this small and gentle-natured Irishman displayed anger. Olivier has since acknowledged that he was 'a stupid little idiot' and that he might very easily have been fired but for Jackson* having mercy on him. . . . Recalling those early days at Birmingham, Sir Cedric Hardwicke remembered Olivier as being noisy and lacking in subtlety, 'but I knew instinctively that he'd be a great actor'. Eileen Beldon, who worked many times with him, also noted a certain lack of subtlety. Half a century later she still vividly recalled their dialogue as members of the company were parting at the end of a production. 'He said to me in a very grand manner, "Thank you for a wonderful performance, Miss Beldon. I *do* hope we'll be working together again." And I snapped back, "I *do* hope we don't." '

John Cottrell

*Sir Barry Jackson (1879–1961), founder of the Birmingham Repertory Theatre in 1913

332 *In Tyrone Guthrie's Old Vic production of Othello, with a perplexed Ralph Richardson in the title role, Olivier decided to give Iago a homosexual edge.*

There was, I am bound to say, a dichotomy of purpose between Ralph's Othello and my Iago. Tony Guthrie and I were swept away by Professor Jones's contention that Iago was subconsciously in love with Othello and had to destroy him. Unfortunately there was not the slightest chance of Ralph entertaining this idea. I was, however, determined upon my wicked intentions, in cahoots with Tony; we constantly watched for occasions when our diagnosis might be made apparent to the discriminating among an audience, though I must say I have never yet discovered any means of divulging something that is definitely *subconscious* to any audience, no matter how discerning they may be. In a reckless moment during rehearsals I threw my arms round Ralph and kissed him full on the lips. He coolly disengaged himself from my embrace, patted me gently on the back of the neck and, more in sorrow than in anger, murmured, 'There, there now; dear boy; *good* boy. . . .' Tony and I dropped all secret connivance after that.

I had one more trick up my sleeve; Ralph had to fall to the ground when Othello, frenzied by Iago's goadings, is helpless in the clutches of a paroxysm. I would fall beside him and simulate an orgasm – terri*fically* daring, wasn't it? But when the wonderful Athene Seyler came round after a matinée she said, 'I'm sure I have *no* idea what you were up to when you threw yourself on the ground beside Ralph.' So that was the end of that stroke of genius and out it came.

333 *The first night of Richard III at the New Theatre, 1944.*

. . . . One of his truly great, if not the greatest, performances began on the opening night of *Richard III* at the New Theatre in London in 1944, when he limped slowly downstage to begin the soliloquy:

> 'Now is the winter of our discontent
> Made glorious summer by this sun of York . . .'

Yet during rehearsals he had been full of self-doubts and for the first time in his career he had found it difficult to learn his lines. In his well-documented biography, *The Oliviers*, Felix Barker reports: 'On the night before the opening Olivier was up until 4 a.m. in a room at Claridge's going over and over his part while Vivien Leigh and an old friend Garson Kanin, the American producer, gave him the cues.'

Another old friend, John Mills, has a story which illustrates that Olivier's fears and forebodings had reached a neurotic pitch just before the curtain went up. When Mills was getting ready to go to the first night he received a phone call from Olivier asking him to come round to the dressing-room before the performance.

Mills arrived to find Olivier pacing up and down the dressing room in costume and fully made-up as Richard. He stared down the long, dagger-like, nose at Mills, fixed him with a piercing eye and opened the thin slit of a mouth to say: 'You are about to see the worst performance I've ever given. I haven't even been able to learn the bloody lines. I'll be terrible, terrible. I want you to know as one of my old friends. You can tell any of my other friends who're out there to expect the worst. If you're all warned in advance you won't be too disappointed.'

Mills, who had never seen him so deeply sunk in despondency tried to humour him, but it was useless. Now, full of foreboding himself, he went to the front of the house to await disaster. Then, as we know now, the curtain rose on a performance of such transcendent quality it will never be forgotten by those who were privileged to see it.

The pre-curtain moments of self-laceration were never again mentioned by Olivier to Mills. However there can be no doubt that the fears were very real and much in excess of the usual first-night nerves. They may have been related to an instinctive assumption of the tortured, sado-masochistic character of Richard. Whatever the cause it is interesting to speculate as to whether the heights of achievement he reached that night were in inverse ratio to the depths of self-doubt he touched before the performance.

His attitude was very different on another occasion involving John Mills. After a long spell in the film studios Mills was apprehensively preparing for a return to the stage in *Ross*, the Terence Rattigan play about T. E. Lawrence. Mills had been persuaded to do it by Olivier who had warned him of the dangers of staying off the stage for too long a period, and it was to Olivier that he turned for help, especially about the conquering of first-night nerves. Olivier told him, 'There's a trick I've used on occasions and I find it works. Try it. Go to the theatre early on the first night, and get made up well in advance of the curtain. Then walk on to the stage and imagine that the curtain is already up and that you are facing the audience. Look out at them and shout, "You are about to see the greatest fucking performance of your entire theatre-going lives. And I will be giving it. You lucky people."

'Tell them that once or twice. Then go back to your dressing room and relax, and you'll find that when the curtain does go up you'll have the necessary confidence.'

Logan Gourlay

334 *Olivier himself writing about the famous 1945 double-bill of* The Critic *and* Oedipus Rex.

The gift of playing in *The Critic*, following immediately upon *Oedipus*, worked like a dream for me. I could really sink myself deep into the Greek tragedy without reservation, secure in the anticipation of the joyous gaiety that was to follow it. I felt I was in for the greatest enjoyment ever allowed me in the work of acting (I was still under the thrall of having directed the film of *Henry V*). My pleasure was indulged for barely a month before a frightening accident occurred. I had worked out an elaborate routine for the finishing of Mr Puff. Anxiously concerned that all was not going as it should up in the flies, waving messages upwards he stepped unwisely across a bar that carried two sizeable cutout pieces at each end of it. Whereupon, up it came, and catching him in the crutch, took him up into the flies with it. Here I quickly changed over on to a swing-seat, which had a painted cloud on the front of it; down on this, supported by piano wires, at an easy pace sailed Mr Puff, but at a reasonable stepping off distance from the stage a huge explosion blew his cloud hastily up again into the flies. The company on the stage manfully supported these antics with actions of terrified anxiety: 'Where has he got to now?', gazing upwards following Puff's apparent cavortings in various directions at the same time. Meantime, my cloud was brailed off towards the stage right fly-rail, where I inched myself off from my swing-seat on to a rope, which I shinned down to dash downstage to climb a rope-ladder to seize hold of the right-hand half of the divided theatre curtain. In the meantime, my cloud came sailing down, to the general consternation of the company, minus any Mr Puff. The curtains descended finally towards each other with Mr Puff clutching on to the right festoon to be thrown in a somersault between it and the footlights. Needless to say, it was all great fun to do, for me that is; the rest of the company must have felt a bit stoogey.

Then came the occurrence which turned all the fun into terror. It wouldn't have done so for men of sterner stuff, but as must be clear by now, I am a moral and a physical coward. I had got through the routine up to being brailed off on my cloud towards the stage right fly-rail and, keeping my right hand around its piano wire, I inched off my cloud-seat, stretched out and grasped the rope to shin downwards and . . . ! The rope moved downwards under the pull from my left hand and – Oh! my Christ! – the thing had not been fastened to the fly grid up top. I continued pulling and screamed at the fly-men to *do* something. The rope slipped through its last few feet and snaked down to the stage floor thirty feet below. I thought desperately of jumping for it, but immediately underneath me was a five-foot groundrow of battleships in full sail, cut out of 3–ply, and I didn't fancy trying that out as a saddle. The fly-boys, only six feet away from me, began to panic: 'It's all right, guvnor, we'll find it. Which line is he on, Bert, for Chrissake? No, surely he's on thirty-eight, in't he? Hang on, guvnor, hang on, we'll find it in a tick.'

I think hanging on with a wire through one's hand and wondering how long before one has to drop is a nightmare common to most of us. After an eternity of the boys arguing and trying one line after another: 'Okay, guvnor, we got you. For Chrissake hold on,' and in full view of the audience, to whom it must have looked to be a singularly ineffectual joke, I was slowly lowered to the stage. Until then the prompt corner had been much too gripped by the situation to think of lowering the curtain.

335 *The actor Alan Webb relates this anecdote.*

Many years later I had a part in a celebrated production of *Titus Andronicus* with Larry in the name part. My part was small, but it involved a good deal of standing alone on the stage with Larry and occasionally speaking a line or two while he went through a storm of emotions. At one point he was kneeling half back to the audience and preparing to chop off his hand with an axe. I was transfixed, and I wondered what must be passing through his mind. I think it must have been during the first performance when, to my horror, just as the axe was about to fall, out of the corner of his mouth he said sharply: 'Get out of my light!' I was most upset and extremely mortified, and as consolation I said to myself: 'He cannot be really in his part if he's thinking about the lights.' I realized later that it was the highest kind of professional behaviour.

336 An actor who played with Laurence Olivier in his triumphant *Othello* told me of one performance that transcended all the others. His fellow actors were used to being thrilled by him on stage, but this night they huddled in the wings, uneasy, as if in the presence of real tragedy.

At the end of the play, after his last call – with the audience still cheering – Olivier made his way to his dressing room through two lines of fellow actors who were also applauding him. He ignored them all and slammed the door. When someone knocked and said, "What's the matter, Larry? It was *great!*" the cast heard his voice boom through the door.

"I know it was great, damn it, but I don't know how I did it so how can I be sure I can do it again?"

Helen Hayes

337 *This is Olivier's foreword to William Hobbs's book* Technique of the Stage Fight.

I have always felt very strongly that a stage fight offered the actor a unique opportunity of winning the audience, as great almost as any scene, speech or action. That Shakespeare put it high in his estimation of stage effects is proclaimed by the amount of times he trustingly leaves it to this element to provide him with his denouements, and this, as Mr Hobbs points out, for an audience commonly practised in the art and therefore shrewdly critical of the goings on.

There is a traditional paradox in reference to stage fights 'the safer the more dangerous'. Most accidents can be attributed to hesitancies and other symptoms of not wishing to hurt your opponent.

I have in my stage fighting life been more hurt than hurting, which would seem to absolve me in principle from this weakness, though in my mind's eye I see a couple of prone spectres of the past raising themselves upon a painful elbow aghast with speechless incredulity at my effrontery in making any such assertion.

I was first caused to muse upon these matters by an incident during *Romeo and Juliet* about Christmastime 1935. I had hurt Geoffrey Tonne quite badly in the Mercutio-Tybalt bout and the poor lad had to leave the cast for some weeks on account of his thumb *hanging by a thread*. The next evening I found myself squared up to the understudy – Harry Andrews no less. Each found something about his opponent that set his nostrils aquiver, if not his foot apawing and shrill neighing assailing the air. To each was flashed that instantaneous recognition of a kindred spirit. We both knew 'they' were going to get a good fight. From then on through the run no holds were barred and sparks flew like Japanese crackers and it was more up to the audience to defend itself as best it could rather than either of us.

We were using bucklers and hand-and-a-half hilted longish swords and hardly a performance went by that the tip of one of these did not go zinging out into the auditorium to be greeted by a female shriek, an outraged masculine snort of 'look here, I say', and a sobbing exit through one of the swing doors. How the management coped with it I shall never know.

Looking back over my career now, I see it as a long, a very long chapter of almost every imaginable kind of accident, which would seem to say that either I am a bad fighter or my rule of 'the safer the more dangerous' is a load of mallarkey.

Without pausing for reflection I can think of:

1 broken ankle
2 torn cartilages (1 perforce yielding to surgery)
2 broken calf muscles
3 ruptured Achilles tendons
Untold slashes including a full thrust razor-edged sword wound in the
    breast (thrilling)
Landing from considerable height, scrotum first, upon acrobat's knee
Hanging by hand to piano wire 40 feet up for some minutes (hours?) on
    account of unmoored rope

Hurled to the stage from 30 feet due to faultily moored rope ladder
Impalement upon jagged ply cut-outs
Broken foot bone by standing preoccupied in camera track
Broken face by horse galloping into camera while looking through finder
Near broken neck diving into net
Several shrewd throws from horses including one over beast's head into
    lake
One arrow shot between shinbones
Water on elbow
Water pretty well everywhere
Hands pretty well mis-shapen now through 'taking' falls
Quite a few pretended injuries while it was really gout
Near electrocution through scimitar entering studio dimmer while
    backing away from unwelcome interview
Etc., etc., etc.

Not to mention injuries inflicted upon my colleagues. (Memories of R. R. as Richmond, *sotto voce* but not unheard . . . 'Steady boy now', 'Easy fellow' or 'You've got two today boy . . .' 'Merely venture to submit'.)

Not to mention injuries inflicted upon my audiences.

I could go on a great deal.

Honourable scars? Well, I am not sure.

But why introduce, with a chapter of accidents and mistakes, a text book in which one is sure there are none?

DAME PEGGY ASHCROFT (1907–)

338 *Peggy Ashcroft, like Olivier, made an early mark at the Birmingham Repertory Theatre. From then on, she has hardly put a foot wrong in all the roles she has played, from Juliet in John Gielgud's production of* Romeo and Juliet *in 1935, to her Oscar-winning performance in the film of E. M. Forster's* A Passage to India. *The first passage concerns the dramatized version of Henry James's novel* Washington Square *which, under the title* The Heiress, *was directed by John Gielgud at the Haymarket Theatre in 1949, with Peggy Ashcroft in the leading role.*

One small but arresting piece of business was borrowed at the last moment from the novel. Catherine is sitting in her rocking chair, moving gently backwards and forwards. Her lover has not been heard of for years. Her aunt mentions casually that she has just seen him in New York; nothing is said, but instantly the rocking stops. Peggy Ashcroft remembered this one day at rehearsal, and Gielgud immediately sent out for a rocking chair. In the theatre the moment when it came to a standstill I recall as enormously exciting.

Eric Keown

339 *Here she leaps to the defence of a visiting actor from Nazi Germany.*

For Miles Malleson's adaptation of Gerard Hauptmann's *Before Sunset* the well-known German actor, Werner Krauss, had been brought over to play the old widower (who falls in love with a young girl, is baulked of marriage with her by his children, and dies of a stroke, holding her hand). For this highly theatrical part his lavishly powerful acting was ideally suited, and he had learned English with fair success in order to play it in London.

So far as was known he had no particular sympathy with Hitler, who in any case had only recently become a nuisance, but the first night offered too good an opportunity to be missed to a bunch of political exhibitionists caring nothing for the theatre and content to be ill-mannered at however undeserving a target. Their hooliganism had been shrewdly organised. In spite of a leavening of police, pandemonium broke out within a minute of the rise of the curtain: shouting, leaflets, stinkbombs and all the wretched paraphernalia of fanaticism in public. After three minutes of Hauptmann, the curtain was lowered. A man in the gallery demanded fair play, and a few seconds later, deathly pale, Peggy Ashcroft came out and waited for silence. Then she said: "There are about thirty British actors and actresses in this company, and all of us feel most deeply the honour which has been conferred upon us in acting with the distinguished artist who is a visitor in our midst. I appeal to you to give him and us a fair chance." Boos and catcalls were still mixed with the cheering aroused by this act of courage, but after further disturbances had spread as far as the dress circle peace was at length established, and the audience forgot its embarrassment in the excitements of the acting, of the poetic beauty of Peggy Ashcroft's performance and of the astonishing emotional voltage generated by Krauss (it is interesting that this pyrotechnical actor wore no make-up). At the end, a great ovation, and afterwards a kinder word than usual from Agate, who wrote of "Miss Ashcroft, who, conceiving the little schoolmistress as another Evelyn Hope, made her of spirit, fire and dew." Browning's words might indeed have been written for her.

Eric Keown

HUGH 'BINKIE' BEAUMONT (1908–73)

340 *Tyrone Guthrie sketches an early episode in the career of one of London's most famous impresarios.*

Only a few months before I met him he had been concerned with the management of a play by Clemence Dane. The producer was quite well known and experienced; the cast was led by Gertrude Lawrence, supported by three or four senior actors of the highest professional eminence. They opened in Bournemouth and the performance passed off without mishap. The leading players were invited to supper by Mr. Beaumont, champagne was quaffed and all was merry as a marriage bell.

Over coffee Mr. Beaumont, who was aged twenty-three – any of the others were the right age to be his parents – very quietly began to pull the performance apart. The production had seemed to him a little conventional (that is Binkie's way of saying outrageously dull); Miss Lawrence had seemed, here and there, just the least bit hesitant (that meant 'you'd better learn your words, dear, and learn them fast'), and so on down the line. The criticisms were of deadly accuracy and shrewdness, offered in a manner which not even the vainest or most sensitive actor could consider rude or even uppity.

It is not given to many managers after a not-too-disastrous first night to take five bulls by the horns, to say nothing of so glamorous and sacred a cow as Miss Lawrence, give them a good scolding and send them off to bed. Bear in mind that this particular manager was barely past his majority, utterly unknown and merely a paid hand of the firm which was presenting the play.

REX HARRISON (1908–)

341 *These two extracts are taken from his autobiography,* Rex.

I was cast as a native, Jimmy Kanaka, in a play by Eugene O'Neill called *Gold*. The thrill of getting that part is still with me: seeing my name on the call board inside the stage door, not as an understudy or a walk-on, but as being *in* the play with the other members of the company was, to me, like winning the Victoria Cross. The scene I had was with a lot of bearded, rough sailors on a desert island, and I was naked except for a loin cloth and a few shark's teeth around my neck. It took some hours to black up my body so that not a spot of white could be seen anywhere, even between my toes. At the centre of the stage was a palm tree, which I had to climb during the scene to sight a ship.

It was my big moment. My mother, father and sisters were out front on the opening night, and as it was the first British production of the O'Neill play, a lot of critics had come from London to see it. But the palm tree was my undoing. Nobody had thought to tell me that it had been fireproofed just before curtain time and was still wet. I went up black, and came down almost completely white. I sat cross-legged, trying to expose a piece of myself that was still black to the audience, but alas, without success. I was completely unnerved. Instead of making an exit like a noble savage I slunk off like a whipped cur, still trying to cover the white spots with my arms.

342 *A disaster just avoided during the New York run of the musical* My Fair Lady.

I was half-way through the song ['Accustomed to Her Face'] when a very heavy set which had been 'flown' – hoisted above the stage – fell immediately behind the frontcloth where I was performing. There was a thunderous crash, splinters and quite large pieces of wood came flying under the cloth, which had billowed out almost knocking me into the orchestra pit.

When I recovered from the shock, a matter of a few seconds, I found the stage littered and in total silence. The orchestra had stopped. Franz Ahlers had had such a fright that he obviously had forgotten to keep his arms whirling about. I had a moment of desperation, then, I suppose because I was hell-bent doing the number to a full house, recovered quicker than Ahlers (at whom I still didn't dare to look) and called loudly for a clarinet – mostly because it was about the only instrument in the orchestra I could think of – but I needed an introductory chord to get me back into action. There was a pause, then up came rather shakily from the pit the notes I needed and I finished the number to tumultuous applause.

When I came off I didn't know what I would find; it was a shambles, but incredibly nobody was hurt. We had been running nearly two years by then and apparently the ropes that supported this heavy set had frayed. It was a ghastly thought that had it fallen three or four minutes later we would have been taking our curtain calls and a great number of us would have been very badly injured if not killed.

SIR MICHAEL REDGRAVE (1908–85)

343 *A splendid actor – at his best I always thought when playing intellectuals such as Richard II, Hamlet or Crocker-Harris in* The Browning Version. *These extracts come from two of his books:* Mask or Face *and* In My Mind's Eye.

I last saw Mabel when I was an undergraduate. A letter arrived saying that she and her husband's company were playing at Saffron Walden, and would I care to come over from Cambridge to see a performance. I had not seen Mabel since the days when, with the help of her dressmaker, Mother had fitted her up with the costumes for *A Royal Divorce*, in which she played the Empress Josephine with her husband as Napoleon. But those were the palmy days.

The Woman Always Pays, said the poster outside the village hall. No mention was made of the author. Inside I found Mabel in the box office selling tickets. She greeted me with a cheerful smile and hurried backstage.

The play – seeming strangely familiar – was performed at a brisk pace. Henry Beckett, Mabel's second husband, was a fine actor who had played many seasons at Bridport.

'Did you like it?' asked Mabel.

'Yes, very much.'

'We had to change the title, of course. Good, don't you think? Good for the box office.'

'But what is the real title?' I asked.

'*Hindle Wakes*. Didn't you recognize it? Good little play, but of course we couldn't afford the royalties.'

344 *With the Old Vic company, he played the part of Rakitin in 1949. Valerie is the actress Valerie Taylor.*

It was in the course of a matinée performance of *A Month in the Country* at the St James's, half-way through our long run, and I was settling down to the first undisturbed duologue between the heroine and myself, looking up at Valerie with eyes brimful of affection and love, when I heard a lady in the stalls whisper to her companion, 'I like *her*.' I was noticeably quicker on my cues after that.

345 Very few members of an audience can possibly realise that the auditorium is in many ways a much better sounding board than the stage itself with its wings and borders and gaps which allow even the loudest and clearest voice partially to slide backstage. Much of what is muttered or whispered in an auditorium is not heard by the other members of the audience because for those in the audience who are sitting behind the mutterer the voice is projected away and for those who are sitting in front the shape of the human ear is directed away from it and attention is concentrated on the lighted stage. Funnily – and justly – enough, it is usually at moments when the actor is too pleased with himself that one hears some of these mutterings or whisperings. Again, I remember, when playing Macheath in *The Beggar's Opera* at the Haymarket Theatre, being disturbed to a point where I was for a few moments unable to continue. Macheath has, as you will remember, what we call a well built up entrance. For half an hour or so before he comes on the rest of the cast do little else but talk or sing about him and the director had devised for me a sensational entrance out of a cupboard on a landing, with pistols cocked, a jump over the banisters on to the counter of Peachum's shop and a further drop down on to the stage and straight into the duet 'Pretty Polly, say.' After the duet there is a short spoken scene, then one solo number by Macheath followed by the duet 'Over the hills and far away' and after another duet, 'Oh what pain it is to part,' an exit through a window, a rose and a kiss thrown to Polly. Curtain. The second act opens in a tavern where, after Macheath's gang have sung the opening chorus, Macheath enters, has a short scene with his highwaymen friends and settles down for the first solo that he had alone on the stage, his most charming number, 'If the heart of a man is depressed with cares.' Now it was true that in this production I, as Macheath, had on an overcoat for this second act, but otherwise my costume and make-up were the same. On this particular occasion the orchestra started the introduction to the song and I advanced with painted wine glass in my hand to sit astride a chair in order to sing it. I was careful, of course, to conceal the fact that I was husbanding my breath and, again perhaps I was feeling too pleased with myself, for I felt that I cut a fairly dashing figure. In the tiny pause between the end of the introduction and the beginning of the song I heard a voice whisper in tones worthy of Mrs. Pat Campbell: '*Who* is *this?*' On that particular occasion I lost my breath and a curious kind of snort came out. The conductor looked at me rather surprised and, after I had shaken my head at him like a dumb ox, he started the introduction again, and *The Beggar's Opera* continued.

346 An audience arrives at the theatre at Stratford-on-Avon with rather more than the common bond which links an audience together. Consciously or unconsciously – and without venturing into the shallow rapids of that dangerous term 'highbrow' – audiences drawn, as I say, from all over the world come to see Shakespeare's plays at Stratford-on-Avon with an extra sense of expecting something more (or rather, something else) than they can get at even the most exciting production in other theatres. Some of them come with a sense of dedication. Quite a few, I am sure, come with a feeling of penance. As a gentleman was heard to remark leaving that theatre one night after one or other of the 'tragedies': 'Every bloody play I come to now seems to last more than three hours.' Then, too, quite a number of people come, some of whom never come again, having perhaps some sense of expiation but not the least idea of what to expect. It sometimes astonishes me that the genius of Shakespeare and the combined skill of the director and actors should succeed in keeping such members of the audience quiet, let alone satisfying them. For really, a number of them have so little idea of what is in store for them that I can well believe the story which was told me by members of the Sadler's Wells Ballet Company who were performing at that theatre for a fortnight before Dame Peggy Ashcroft and I opened there in *The Merchant of Venice*. Two ladies were reading their programmes for the ballet *Coppelia*, and one said to the other: 'Oh dear! We've picked the wrong day. Peggy Ashcroft and Michael Redgrave aren't dancing.'

ELIA KAZAN (1909–   )

347 *Elia Kazan's position in American theatre is secure not only through his establishment of the Actors' Studio, but also through his superb staging of plays by Tennessee Williams and Arthur Miller. Other directors – in this case Joshua Logan – acknowledge his supremacy.*

Joshua Logan, of the cream of the directorial crop, was once accosted by a drunk during the intermission of one of his opening nights. The drunk was genial, effusive, flattering – and drunk.

"You," he shouted, pointing a wagging finger at Logan, "are the best damn director ever lived."

Logan blushed prettily and blurted out a modest, "Oh, come now."

"Oh, yes, you are," continued the drunk, "you're the best."

"I wouldn't say that," answered Logan in congenial protest.

"Oh, you wouldn't?" said his assailant, suddenly waxing bellicose, and he added challengingly, "You name me one director – one damn better director."

"Well," said Logan from his cul de sac, "how about Elia Kazan?"

The drunk glowered at him. Then the glower vanished and for a moment he thought, while Logan thought too of avenues of escape. Finally the drunk spoke.

"You're right," he said emphatically and made *his* escape first.

George Oppenheimer

MARGARET SULLAVAN (1911–60)

348 *'A true original,' says Josh Logan, about Margaret Sullavan. They first met long before she became a Hollywood star, in a very strange play at Falmouth, Massachusetts.*

We were building our new theatre at Old Silver Beach and rehearsing the opening production, a play called *The Devil in the Cheese*. She and Hank [Fonda] were the main characters. About four days before opening, Bretaigne Windust, who was directing the play – and always had a handkerchief tied around his forehead for some reason – said, 'No more rehearsals until the theatre's finished.' I said, 'We haven't learned our lines yet.' He said, 'We can't put on a play without a theatre. Go on, help work on it, we've got to get it finished.' So suddenly the whole company was nailing away, building scenery, installing seats: Fonda and I were way up on the grid for 72 hours putting in the counterweight system, Fonda face down most of that time, stretched out over the beams on his stomach, while I swung below him in a boatswain's gear with a mouthful of nails trying to thread the ropes through the sheaves; Windust was everywhere, still running around with a handkerchief around his head.

"It was a very complicated show, *The Devil in the Cheese*, one of the silliest and most difficult, and we had to have a lot of props. Just to give you an idea: the first act takes place in an old monastery on a Greek mountaintop and the only way to enter is to be hoisted up in a net from the earth below. Goldina Quigley, the part that Peggy played, is brought there by her mother and father on the pretext they are looking for Greek relics. The real reason is to get her away from Jimmy Chard, the boy she's fallen in love with (who eventually arrives by airplane and makes a spectacular crash landing), played by Henry Fonda. One of the monks gives Mr. Quigley an old amphora and a piece of cheese: 'Eat this cheese and know youth,' says the monk, so Mr. Quigley bites into the cheese, and suddenly there's a great green flash and out of the amphora leaps the Little God Min (some ancient Egyptian deity), who offers to take Mr. Quigley on a trip through his daughter's head. The second act takes place in Goldina's brain and consists of all her daydreams, enacted by Peggy and Hank: first they're on a sailboat, and while she washes dishes and drys them in a net strung out the cabin porthole, he catches a flying fish and pops it in the kettle for dinner; then they get wrecked on a desert island where they play the same scene, only this time he's found a turtle which she pops in the supposed dinner pot, and he brings her a monkey which they train – here there's a little time lapse and the monkey grows up into a gorilla – to take care of their baby. And so on.

"Well, you can imagine the props we had to round up. We never had any kind of dress rehearsal. Nobody had had any sleep for four days. The audience arrived for the opening; the curtain was six feet off the ground, so people could see us desperately trying to cover these white-pine steps that were supposed to be old rocks on the side of the Greek monastery. When we finally dropped the curtain, the audience applauded. I said, 'Windust, please go out and make a speech. Explain to them that we're not ready; maybe they ought to go home.' He said, 'No, no, I'll make a speech, but we're going to do this show come hell or high water. I've brought my full-dress suit and I will not make a speech without it.' He had to go downstairs; it took five or six minutes at least to put on a full-dress suit and white tie; when he walked out to make the speech, he still had that bloody handkerchief around his head. He made quite a speech, but the pounding of the nails was so loud the audience never heard what he said. There was such confusion, such hysteria; we were all in terror that this was going to be a failure, this, the beginning of all of our lives. Windust put on a monk's outfit over his full-dress suit (he had to be a monk along with me), we were ready to pull the curtain up, and he said, 'Wait a minute! We've got to get those lights out of the way. They'll cover everybody.' So the whole company came and pulled on the ropes but the ropes were twisted and the lights wouldn't budge. So Windy said, 'Put the lights on the floor.' Crash! When those lights hit, they made the biggest noise you ever heard. And the audience howled and applauded. The curtain went up.

"Unfortunately we'd never tested the apparatus for bringing up people from the cellar; Kent Smith, who played Mr. Quigley's butler, was supposed to be hauled up first, but the winches kept sticking and the basket that contained him started whirling at a dervish speed; it took ten minutes longer than we'd gauged to get poor Kent up high enough to be seen, so we all sang Greek chants until he finally appeared. And again the audience applauded. Now three people, the Quigley family, had to be brought up. A very old lady named Lily Jones was playing Goldina's mother; as the basket rose from the cellar below the stage, it whirled five times as fast as before, because it was so much heavier, and Lily Jones started screaming with the highest, most bloodcurdling scream that has ever been known, like a person being throttled to death. Finally the basket, still whirling, hove into view, two or three monks grabbed it, pulled it towards the stage for a landing, and out clumped the three Quigleys.

"This was Margaret Sullavan's début on the professional stage. And to my dying day, I will remember the first words out of her mouth. Just as though she were in the most successful play that had ever been written and she had the most wonderful lines to say, with the most aplomb I had ever seen, she said, 'Now don't get hysterical, Mother, we're here.' And I just thought, She must be the greatest actress who ever lived, because by rights she shouldn't be able to say anything at all. But she went right through the play, improvising with the same calm security, with everything around her going wrong, and that was just the beginning. It went wrong and went wrong ("Particularly the monkey," said Margaret Sullavan, "who, in the South Sea love scene between Hank and me, peed all over my very skimpy flowered bra." "She was absolutely magnificent," said Hank, "nothing fazed her"). Finally the curtain went down. I should say, from then on we lived happily ever after, because although it was a disastrous night, the people who were there formed a kind of club, the audience that had seen the opening night of *The Devil in the Cheese*.

SIR TERENCE RATTIGAN (1911–77)

349 *The anecdote refers to the opening night of Rattigan's first West End play,* French Without Tears *(1936), the rehearsals of which had gone particularly badly (although it then ran for over 1000 performances). Harold French was the director.*

Friday, 6 November, was a wet and gloomy day. Finding himself with nothing that he could usefully do and desperate to keep his mind off what was going to happen that evening, Rattigan went out and walked round London. Then he turned into a barber's shop and had his hair cut.

That evening, before the performance, he and his parents went out to dinner. They had a bottle of champagne in an attempt to celebrate, but it was a glum meal. Although they were too polite to say so, they all privately felt that it was going to be a disastrous evening. After the meal, Vera slipped the champagne cork into her purse as a souvenir. When they reached the theatre, their spirits sank still lower. It was still raining and there were two other first nights in London that evening: opera at Covent Garden and the première of a Marlene Dietrich film. The West End was choked with traffic and the audience was coming into the theatre soaked and bad tempered.

The curtain went up to reveal Trevor Howard, as the youngest of a group of students at a French crammer, eating his breakfast and trying to finish his French composition in time for a tutorial. He was joined immediately by another student, played by Guy Middleton, whose first lines consisted of ordering bacon and eggs in loud but appalling French. The sublime over-confidence with which he did it produced a peal of infectious laughter from Cicely Courtneidge, the musical-comedy star, who was sitting a few rows back in the stalls. That set the tone for the rest of the audience and, a few lines later, when Middleton translated, 'She has ideas above her station' as 'Elle a des idées au-dessus de sa gare', the audience gave a full-throated roar of delight. Only a page into the play and they were off to a good start.

The cast did not seem able to believe their ears. Still tense and nervous, they hurried on, without waiting for the laughs, or timing their lines so as to build them. Hovering at the back of his box, Harold French was uneasy. If the cast did not calm down and play the audience accurately they would lose their sympathy. The rush continued for fifteen or twenty minutes, until Roland Culver came on. A few seconds after his entrance, he played a line he knew should get a laugh; it came. Then with the self-assurance built of experience and his faith in the play, he waited. The laugh grew. There was applause. Only then, with perfect timing, did he complete the line. He had steadied the anxious cast and now they all started to play with that confidence and touch which is the greatest joy of an actor's craft. The evening developed into one of the most magical first nights of all time.

As the final curtain rattled down, there was a storm of applause and people rose in their seats calling 'Author, Author!' Harold French dived backstage looking for Rattigan, who had vanished from his place at the back of the Dress Circle. When he found him, in white tie and tails, he was green-faced and leaning for support against the back wall of the theatre. French virtually threw him on to the stage. The cheering grew louder. The success of the play was so unexpected that no one had arranged for the customary first night speeches. As Rattigan stepped forward to thank the audience the curtain unceremoniously came down on his head.

Michael Darlow and Gillian Hodson

350 Repeating that *The Deep Blue Sea* was the most striking new English play of the decade, Tynan looked hopefully towards Rattigan's future: 'There, to date, stands Rattigan, partially fulfilled, tall and softly smiling, crisp of speech and wise of eye. What next? Not, I am sure, a novel. He is scared of the freedom it implies; those infinite spaces of time and place terrify him; he prefers the limits of the stage, the specific actor and the deadline. He may now club us with a masterpiece. Or perhaps his so acute ear for dialogue will betray him with ditchwater fluency again . . .' But, Tynan concluded: 'One distinction will probably never be wrested from him: I support it with a completely unauthenticated story. It was told me by a friend who arrived at a Knightsbridge party and was ushered upstairs to doff hat and coat. Pausing on the cloakroom threshold and peering through the crack of the door, he saw someone talking to the mirror. Rattigan had stopped in the middle of combing his hair to muse, with a little groan, "If you're not very careful, Terry Rattigan, you won't be the prettiest playwright in London".'

Michael Darlow and Gillian Hodson

PETER BULL (1912–84)

351 *An English actor from whose autobiography these two extracts are taken. The play in the first piece is* The Lady's Not For Burning *by Christopher Fry.*

The play went very well on the first night, March 10th, 1948, but the notices were mixed. Some critics opined that the meaning was obscure and difficult to follow, but most of them had the good sense to realise that it was a new type of verse play. There was, however, no doubt about its popular appeal to the patrons of the arts or indeed the Arts, and we were packed for the short run. One's actor friends raved about it, and Miss Hermione Gingold came both Sundays. The dressing-rooms on the Sunday nights were thronged with stars, and it was quite droll one night, when the rafters had rung with praise and all the usual vociferous utterances of fellow actors saying "darlings, darlings, it was wonderful, marvellous, divine," when an old school friend of mine tapped at the door and said, "Thought I'd come and see you to tell you that I've had a most interesting evening and this is John Abercrombie who didn't like it at all," and a rather sad bespectacled gent was ushered into the room to face a lot of rather hysterical artistes.

352 *The original production of Samuel Beckett's* Waiting for Godot *took place at the Arts Theatre in London, then transferred to the Criterion because of its huge and unexpected success.*

In any case I kept a widow's cruse of brandy handy, not only for myself, but for those customers stalwart enough to stay the course.

It must be admitted that a lot of people didn't, and it was a remarkable thing to come on in the first act and feel a bungful house, only to return in the second to find a certain percentage of gaps in the theatre and the audience shrunk in size. Not that it was a great surprise, because those who had left did not attempt to cover up their movements. It was not just the banging of seats and slamming of exit doors, but quite often they would take the trouble to come right down to the footlights, glare at the actors and make their egress into outer space, snorting the while. Incidents were numerous and cries of "Rubbish", "It's a disgrace", "Take it off", "Disgusting", and I regret to say on one occasion "Balls", floated through the auditorium. There was one unforgettable night when, during the second act, the two tramps are alone on the stage cogitating about life as they were apt to do and one says: "I am happy," to which the other replies, "I am happy too," after which a gent in Row F shouted: "Well, I'm bloody well not."

At this point there was a certain amount of shushing, but the man would not be shushed and stood up and yelled at the audience: "And nor are you. You've been hoaxed like me."

A free fight ensued (well, fairly free; 15s. 6d. a head actually) and during a lull Hugh Burden observed quietly:

"I think it's Godot," which brought the house down and enabled our attendants to get rid of the angry middle-aged man.

But perhaps the drollest night was when I got my come-uppance. It had been reported to me by the stage manager that a party of eight had arrived rather late, and had made a good deal of noise sitting down in the front row. They were all in full evening dress with a fine display of jewels and/or carnations. By the time I'd been on for a bit I realised that they didn't seem best pleased by me or my performance. The muttering and whispering grew to a crescendo, until in a loud clear voice the dowager lady seated in the middle of the party said:

"I do wish the fat one would go."

I took a hurried look round at my fellow actors and decided that I had never seen a thinner bunch and guessed that she must be referring to me. I was a fraction shocked as, after a long and not terribly notable career in the service of the theatre, I have never actually been insulted DURING a performance. People have attacked me in the streets or in public transport, but never while I was actually doing it. I seethed inwardly with rage, but apart from glaring at the lady I was unable to make a come-back; luckily my beloved slave made handsome amends. As we were about to leave the stage, I shortened the rope which bound me to T. Bateson and he made as if to leap into the lady's lap, a threat which caused the entire party to leave hurriedly. Afterwards we were all filled with intense compassion and the milk of h.k., as it turned out that the party had arrived expecting to see a revue called *Intimacy at 8.30* which had vacated the Criterion Theatre a few weeks previously. Putting one and five together and realising the storm of criticism that would assail her at the end of the evening, the hostess had wisely decided to cut her losses.

SIR ALEC GUINNESS (1914–)

353 *One of the best anecdotes from his recent autobiography,* Blessings in Disguise, *a bestseller on both sides of the Atlantic.*

Martita Hunt was born in the Argentine in 1901, came to England as a young girl and was sent to school in Eastbourne, where she was horrified by the English climate and her first bite at an apple, which her father had cracked up to be the finest fruit in the world. She avoided apples for the rest of her life and escaped to France at any opportunity. Her early years as an actress were spent playing rather drab mackintoshed parts (except when she was at the Old Vic opposite John Gielgud) but there came a day when, after a holiday in Provence and Paris, she decided to alter her life-style. From flat shoes she took to high-heeled golden sandals, expensive sheer stockings – she had long, thin, elegant legs – and a generally French wardrobe. She also developed a taste for expensive food and the best wines. By the time I first met her, late in 1933, her habitat was a smart little flat in Knightsbridge; she was also to be seen frequently at Prunier's restaurant (not yet within reach of my pocket) in St James's Street. She had become a bird of rare plumage and was the first woman I had ever met who wore silk trousers and painted her toe-nails. Her work by now was mostly in the West End theatres, playing eccentric princesses, duchesses and other high-flying creatures, diversified with small parts in films. She said to me one day, in a tone of disgust, 'It's no use them trying to cast me as a woman of the people,' and yet one of her most memorable performances was as a Belgian peasant woman, hair scraped back, black-shawled and clogged, in the film of *Nurse Cavell*.

In 1933, working in a very minor capacity in an advertising agency for thirty shillings a week but determined to get into the theatre somehow, I applied for an audition at the Royal Academy of Dramatic Art, where I hoped to obtain the Leverhulme Scholarship. This, if achieved, would provide me with free training for two years and something like £5 a week. It was a shot in the dark from a blinkered and ignorant youth; so I paid my £1 audition fee and was given a list of short pieces to be learned from various plays; these included the Chorus from *Henry V*, speeches from *The Three Sisters* and *St Joan* and something of my own choice. The audition was to be held in January, in four months' time, and it dawned on me, as I held the list in my hand, that I hadn't a clue as to how to start work on it or, indeed, what would be required of me or how to comport myself at an audition. A wild idea struck me; perhaps John Gielgud would take me through my pieces or at any rate advise me. He lived then in a flat in St Martin's Lane and I found out his telephone number and had the nerve to call him. We were, of course, total strangers. He was kind on the telephone but in effect only said, 'You might try Martita Hunt. She'll love the money.' Because of my surname John must have assumed that I was one of the rich Guinnesses. And when I called Martita she undoubtedly thought the same, cooing and being formally respectful at the same time. When she saw me in her flat the following evening – a thin twenty-year-old in a well-worn suit I was gangling out of – she was visibly appalled and crestfallen. I had polished my shoes, cleaned my nails, brushed my dry, dark mouse-coloured hair and straightened my tie but the message was clear – no money.

Up and down the stairs to Martita's flat there plodded an assortment of ladies to minister to her; a French manicurist (and toe-nail painter), a French seamstress for mending gloves and hemlines, a French maid and a very English lady, known as Watty, with her higher-irrigation apparatus. All were called 'chérie'. The evening I arrived the door was opened by a dark-haired little soubrette. She explained that Mis' 'Unt was in her bath. The bathroom door was ajar and bubbling sounds, steam and exotic perfumes filled the air. 'Forgive me, dear Mr Guinness,' she cooed, 'I am in my bath. I think perhaps you are a little early.' (I was; I always am.) There was a sound as if she had submerged, followed by, 'Go into the sitting-room, there's a good fellow, and make us dry martinis.'

I was horrified and wished only to sink through the rich, deep pale-grey pile of the carpet. Being a very unsophisticated lad I wasn't even sure what a dry martini was composed of – gin and vermouth, I guessed, but I had no idea in what proportions, and why the heck it should be called dry. Stepping gingerly into the room, fearing to soil the carpet, I looked around with apprehension and a certain aesthetic pleasure. It was quite a small room but very elegant, with pale Regency-striped curtains, a sofa covered in a summery yellow silk, a handsome Louis Quinze desk, a Sickert painting above the over-mantel, bowls of exotic flowers, a huge gramophone and, horror of horrors, a glossy cabinet which had been converted for drinks. Staring at me, indeed, were bottles of vermouth, gin, sherry and whisky, beautiful crystal glasses and a jug with ice. The gin bottle in particular caught my attention; it was empty. 'Can't make cocktails without gin,' I thought and got as far away from the cabinet as possible. Bubbling in the bathroom ceased, water gurgled and then I heard Martita's voice call, 'Goodnight, chérie.' The front door closed. After a long dramatic pause Martita made her entrance.

She was tall, lean, and dressed in a blue-and-white striped silk blouse, royal-blue silk trousers, cut like a sailor's, with gilded sandals and scarlet toe-nails. She entered the room with a long arm extended, all smiles. It was a fine entrance for Act I. Then she saw me and the curtain almost fell; the glittering almond-shaped eyes darkened and dulled, the welcoming hand dropped to her side.

'You're not exactly an athlete,' she said.

'No, I'm sorry. It's an actor I want to be.'

'Where are the martinis?'

'There's no gin,' I said.

'I need a drink. Whisky.'

She sat down, and with a thin, trembling hand groped for a cigarette from an elaborate crystal box while I mentally struggled with the whisky. One inch? Two?

'There doesn't appear to be any soda,' I said, fumbling around.

'Neat!' she said. 'My God, I need it.'

She looked me up and down suspiciously.

'Your shoes are clean, I hope.'

I peered at the uppers, worn but polished.

'No,' she said, 'show me the soles.'

I turned up my feet, hopping and terrified they might reveal dog dirt. Clean enough. She seemed reassured. Not until later did I learn that Martita always put down druggets over her carpeting except when she was expecting important guests, fearing what lesser mortals might tread into her flat. In me she had been expecting an important visitor; seeing what she had got she was almost kicking herself. I gave her a tumbler half full of whisky and she told me to sit down, so I perched carefully on the edge of a Georgian chair. Later I would know that every time a guest departed, important or not, she, or chérie, would wipe where he had sat with some cleansing fluid.

After I had explained my ambition to try for the Leverhulme Scholarship she asked me to read something to her, so I unfolded the RADA audition syllabus and burst forth. 'O, for a Muse of Fire,' I wailed.

Martita buried her face in her hands, muttering 'Oh, my God!' while the smoke from her cigarette drifted through her hair.

'Think, when we speak of horses, that you see them . . .'

'I see nothing!' she said. 'Nothing! My dear boy, I see nothing.'

She got up suddenly and seizing me by the upper lip, tried to drag me across the room by it. It slipped from her fingers and lolled for a moment or two before returning to its proper position.

'Flab!' she said, contemptuously. 'No muscle. If you want to be an actor you must have muscle in your upper lip. Like mine!' She bared her teeth, wrinkling her nose rather unattractively. I had to admit there was plenty of muscle there and asked her if she would be prepared to take me through my audition pieces. She downed her whisky and stared at me.

'You are working in an office. What is your pay?'

'Thirty shillings a week.'

'Have you a private income?'

'About twenty-seven shillings a week but it won't last much longer.'

She exhaled a cloud of smoke, sighed a little, examined her finger-nails and then said, 'I will give you ten one-hour lessons at a pound a time. Once a week. We will start tomorrow. And now you must go; I am expecting someone important.'

She showed me the door. No 'chéri' for me as yet. I borrowed the ten pounds from an ex-schoolmaster and managed to repay him two years later.

354 She [Edith Evans] returned to Lilian's [Baylis] domain in October 1936. By then Harcourt Williams had been succeeded by Tyrone Guthrie. Guthrie was a man consumed, like Lilian, with a visionary idealism. After some protracted negotiations he obtained the terms and freedom he felt necessary in order to operate and quickly exerted his authority, denouncing the old policy of 'making do' and determined to abolish the general air of tattiness which Lilian scarcely seemed to be aware of. By the time Edith returned to her second home across the river he had transformed the image of the Vic with his own distinctive brand of radicalism, not always to everybody's liking, but at least ensuring that few could ignore it. Curiously, in spite of his overall plans for the reformation of the company, Guthrie greeted Edith with a somewhat conventional role: another Restoration overblown rose – Lady Fidget in Wycherley's *The Country Wife*. He had imported the American actress, Ruth Gordon, the wife of Garson Kanin, to play the role of Margery in partnership with Edith and when rehearsals started Alec Guinness was also in the cast. Guinness failed to impress Miss Gordon who brought to the Vic that particular brand of ruthlessness which so often characterises the Broadway scene. She halted rehearsals one day, came down to the footlights and shouted to Guthrie in the darkened stalls. 'Tony! this man is impossible. Can we have another actor?' Edith recalled the collective shock of the assembled cast. 'We'd never heard of such a thing, and of course we expected Guthrie to defend Alec as his choice. But he didn't. He fired him on the spot. Without a word. I still think it was a dreadful thing. Dreadful of Ruth and dreadful of Guthrie. There it was, it happened and poor Alec had to go.'

Bryan Forbes

KENNETH MORE (1914–82)

355 *Charles Denville was a born showman, going to bizarre lengths to publicize the melodramas he put on at the Grand Theatre, Byker, near Newcastle-upon-Tyne. Poor Kenneth More got caught up in one of Denville's madcap schemes in the late 1930s.*

Then came *Son of the Sheikh* which we had been busily rehearsing each morning. This involved a big scene around an oasis in the Sahara Desert. We were all tearing around with turbans on, and I was playing a Lancashire businessman who was on holiday there with his wife. Don't ask me why. Anyhow, he was very rich and very common. I had to talk Lancashire, to annoy the leading lady, my wife, who was very posh. To show I was rich, I had a big fat belly – a cushion stuffed under my shirt. Charlie Denville explained the background of the play to all of us.

'This is an eastern play, of course,' he said. 'Tons of atmosphere. It's an oasis, so we've got to have animals and sawdust. Animals for colour and effect.'

'What sort of animals have you in mind, Charlie?' I asked him.

'A camel, for one. The ship of the desert.'

'But where are you going to find a camel in Byker?'

'It's all been taken care of, dear boy. I've been to the local zoo, and they'll let me have one.'

'Do you know what to feed a camel on?'

'No, but it's going to eat anything I give it. We'll also have a few chickens and ducks.'

'But you don't have chickens and ducks in the middle of the Sahara.'

'*I* do,' Charlie replied with finality. 'Anything that moves and flys is good value. The whole stage is going to be covered in sawdust, and the scene will be set for the three nights, so the animals can stay on stage when the theatre's closed.'

Beryl protested, 'But, Charlie, the chickens and all those other animals will make an awful mess in the sawdust. The smell will be terrible.'

I felt especially unhappy about this because in one of my scenes I had to be knocked down by bandits.

'What about the chicken shit?' I asked Charlie. 'That's going to go all over me.'

Charlie Denville laid one hand gently on my shoulder.

'You're an actor,' he declared pontifically. 'That's all part of the fun. If you get a bit of chicken shit hanging out of your hair, they'll laugh.'

This play proved a terrible experience for us all. By the third night, the stage was covered with animal droppings. We had chickens, ducks, two goats and two donkeys, all contributing. The birds fluttered into the orchestra pit and had to be driven out by musicians wielding flutes and cornets like clubs. The whole theatre stank to high heaven.

Stagehands, who were playing the bandits, would trip me up and roll my face in the mess, having the time of their lives. And to cap it all, there was no room for the camel to get on the stage properly.

It was essential that he was seen, to prove that a camel was actually in the cast, and ideally the brute should have come loping across the desert with the hero on his back to rescue my wife and me from the villains. But so much other livestock was crowding the stage that there simply wasn't room for him.

So the camel came in, just as far as the base of his neck, with the rest of his body outside in the wings. This semi-entrance at least proved he existed. On this last night, with a fight going on around the stage oasis, the camel suddenly decided he had had enough and started to pee. The sight was as yet unseen, but the sound was unmistakable. Immediately, the audience forgot our fight and a wag shouted: 'Look at that camel! Eeeh! It's pissing, man!'

The man who had hired the camel was supposed to see that his charge performed this function before each performance, but he'd been in the pub and had somehow forgotten to do so.

Water just poured from the beast. It trickled out of the wings and on to the stage. At first, the leading lady tried to ignore this, but finally, realising that the audience knew what was happening, she called at the top of her voice: 'Put a bucket under it!'

One of the stagehands did so and now the water flooded like the Niagara Falls into the bucket, the metal base and sides magnifying the noise. At the same time, someone else had the idea that if he could give the camel a drink, it would stop peeing. So we had the curious sight of one person (an actor!) holding a bucket for the camel to drink from, and another holding a bucket at the other end to catch water coming out – and all the time we on stage were supposed to be playing heavy drama. The audience went wild.

ORSON WELLES (1915–85)

356 *Orson Welles was just twenty-three when he shook the theatre establishment. He became a leading light in the Federal Theatre Project, established under the Works Progress Administration (WPA) in 1935 to provide employment for theatre personnel made redundant by the Depression. With John Houseman he founded the Mercury Theatre in 1937. The stir he caused with his production of the 'Labor Opera',* The Cradle Will Rock *(described here by Brooks Atkinson), was followed a year later by his radio production of* The War of the Worlds *that brought widespread panic to an audience convinced that Martians were invading.*

In the spring [of 1938], Welles surpassed himself. He put the Federal Theater and Actors' Equity in their places by producing a play they had both excommunicated. It was Marc Blitzstein's *The Cradle Will Rock*, a militant, proletarian drama with music – part opera, perhaps, or oratorio – which Welles had been directing for several weeks. At Maxine Elliott's, it had a full suit of scenery and an orchestra which Lehman Engel conducted. The advance ticket sale numbered fourteen thousand. The final dress rehearsal was scheduled for June 15, 1937, before an audience. But two hours before the curtain was to go up, the Washington administration of the Federal Theater closed all Federal Theater performances pending reorganization of the entire project. No one doubted that the Federal Theater administration was, in Aesopian language, banning a partisan play that might embarrass the government.

Welles was as good a showman offstage as on. He and Houseman improvised a dramatic coup that humbled the bureaucrats. When the audience started to collect outside Maxine Elliott's Theater, the actors entertained them on the sidewalk by singing songs from the show. In the meantime, Houseman, working on the telephone, made an impromptu booking at the Venice Theater (originally Al Jolson's) at Seventh Avenue and 59th Street, paying $100 down. Actors and audience then proceeded uptown in buses and taxis – in a gratifying mutinous mood. Since the scenery had to be left at Maxine Elliott's, the stage at the Venice was bare; the props consisted of a borrowed piano, on which Blitzstein played the score, and a chair, where Welles sat as master of ceremonies. To circumvent the orders from Equity, the actors bought tickets and attended as members of the audience, sitting in the audience instead of on the stage. At 9:45, the performance began. Blitzstein sang some of the songs. Welles supplied the continuity. Actors popped up from various parts of the auditorium to sing or act their scenes, and orchestral instruments tooted and squealed wherever the players happened to be seated.

The performance was a rousing success* – partly because of the scandalous circumstances but, as later productions indicated, basically because of the astringent score, the biting lyrics and the graphic simplicity of the production. It ran ten nights at the Venice Theater at a $1.00 top. In December, it had three Sunday-night performances at the Mercury Theater with the actors in street dress seated in three rows of chairs onstage. Beginning the next January, it had a run of 108 performances at the Windsor Theater in 48th Street. It was again presented at the City Center on November 24, 1947, in a theater sponsored by the City of New York. A month later, it was put on at the Mansfield Theater on the night of the heaviest snowfall of the century, with a notable cast that included Alfred Drake, Will Geer, Vivian Vance, Dennis King, Jr., and Muriel Smith. *The Cradle Will Rock* is the classic proletarian musical

---

*'the cheering and applause lasted so long that the stagehands demanded an hour's overtime – which we gladly paid.' (John Houseman, *Entertainers and the Entertained*, 1986)

drama. Since a proletariat does not exist either on Broadway or in America, the play has never reached the masses. But it is cherished by music lovers and by playgoers who admire the theater arts.

357 *'Brilliantly theatrical' is how John Houseman categorizes the best of Welles's work. Brilliantly confusing might be a better term for Welles's London production of* Moby Dick, *described here by one of its cast, Kenneth Williams.*

Moby Dick was an open-stage production with no scenery, consequently the actors were seen as soon as they entered the pass door. Orson achieved his effects by lighting and stage grouping. In the chapel sequence, where he played Father Mapple, he stood holding a chair back for the pulpit with a multi-coloured spotlight casting the glow of a stained-glass window over the scene. It was economical and practical. When Orson spoke the lines, 'O Lord, I have striven to be thine', he was both vulnerable and moving. He used the stage area for the deck of the whaling ship *Pequod* and the auditorium was the sea. We lowered a rostrum as a symbolic boat into the front stalls when it came to the encounter with the whale. Orson was playing Captain Ahab and told me, 'You will be Fool to my Lear; kneel in the prow and I can tell my playing positions by standing above you for the harpoon throwing.' This was where he cried out, 'That whale – I'll have his blood!' It was all right rehearsing such a scene in an empty theatre, but on the night, with a packed house, it was a different matter. Sailors were clambering into the stalls trying to lower the boat into the central gangway while well-dressed spectators shrank in their seats from the proximity of burly perspiration. One lady's box of chocolates got squashed on her lap, and she protested loudly; and the spectators in the circle completely lost sight of the cast. They rose in their seats to extend their view, provoking cries of 'Sit down' from those seated behind. Orson, with his hand raised for the harpoon, was roaring 'Shut up' to the audience between his vengeful curses to the whale, and we eventually returned to the stage amidst considerable confusion.

In the interval I used to lie full-length on the dressing-room floor. The unaccustomed exercise had exhausted me and the continuity of the play was baffling because Orson frequently changed the scenes. One night I was playing the carpenter and during a long speech about carving Ahab a false leg made from ivory, Orson suddenly leant over my kneeling figure and muttered 'Get off'. I rose muttering a lame ad lib, 'God bless you, Captain', and backed away into the wings with the scene unfinished. As there was no set, we had been instructed that when we exited, we were to stand still at the side of the stage, and I was frozen in this position next to Joan Plowright who was playing Pip the cabin boy. 'What happened?' she whispered and out of the side of my mouth I replied, 'He told me to get off'. She looked heavenward: 'What about your speech?'

'It's cut', I whispered. At this point she realized it was her scene which followed the now absent carpenter episode. She rushed on saying her line, 'O Captain put they hand in mine, the black and white together . . .' with such incoherent haste that Orson was quite taken aback, but Joan rattled on with the speed of a gatling gun about white being black and black becoming white, till it sounded like a high-speed detergent commercial.

Afterwards I went to Orson's dressing room and asked why he had cut the dialogue so drastically. 'You bored me,' he said shortly, and if there's a snappy answer to that I haven't found it.

INGRID BERGMAN (1917–82)

358 *In November 1946 she forsook the screen for a New York run of* Joan of Lorraine.

I learned so much about an audience during that run. The public comes to the theatre not because they want to heckle and see things go wrong. They come because they hope it's going to be wonderful, and they're going to join in that one special occasion, that special night. The night things *did* go wrong, I was dressed in my armour, I was talking to my heavenly voices. I had to sit down on a narrow wooden bench with four small legs. Well, either I miscalculated or the bench wasn't in its proper place. Anyway, instead of sitting in the middle, I sat on the end. The bench tipped up, and bang, I sat down on my behind with a clash of armour. I sat there waiting for the laugh that was going to lift the roof off. But no. All I heard was one great breath of dismay . . . 'Oooohh' . . . a marvellous sound of pity. Then complete silence. I learned at that moment that the audience doesn't want anything to happen to you – they're sorry for you; they're on your side; they don't laugh at you; they weep for you. Yes, they laugh when it's funny – when you ask them to laugh – but when it's serious they hold their breath waiting for you to take hold again.

359 *Then nearly thirty years later she set off to tour America with* The Constant Wife. *The company manager, Griffith James, recounts an accident that befell her.*

We were playing in the Schubert Theatre in Century City and we'd been there two or three weeks. And one day, one of the actors told us about a French restaurant about a ten minutes' walk away. So after the Saturday matinee and before the evening performance we decided to pay it a visit. Ingrid stumbled, twisted her ankle on a stone and we had to half-carry her back.

'It was Saturday night and we couldn't find a doctor; when we finally did, he told us she'd broken a bone in her foot and began to put her leg in a plaster cast. I asked, "How is she going to go on stage with that great thing?" He said, "I'm the doctor. It's got to go on." I called the theatre manager and said, "She'll never be able to play tonight." He panicked. "But she must. We're sold out! We haven't got enough money in the box office to refund everybody. It's all gone to the bank!"

'So Ingrid said, "I'm going on!" I said, "How can you? We can't even get a wheelchair." She insisted: "I'm going on!" Then we got all the cast in and had a long discussion. Now, if so-and-so does this, and so-and-so does that, we can work out this scene and that scene. In the meantime, the manager went out and made the announcement. "Unfortunately Miss Bergman has broken a bone in her foot and it will be at least an hour before we can start the show. If anybody wants their money back they can have it."

'They all went into the bar, but not one soul left. And we were *an hour and a half late*. It took that long for the plaster cast to dry. Fortunately we had a butler in the play, so Ingrid sat in one of those swivel office chairs on casters and the butler pushed her on. She sat in the middle of the stage, swiveled around and spoke to each actor in turn. But of course this ruined their planned stage moves and they started bumping into each other. Ingrid had a whale of a time laughing at all the collisions. So the audience got a sort of play within a play and adored the whole thing.

'Then for the last act we managed to find a wheelchair, and we put her in that. The finale was just the two of them, the husband and Ingrid on the stage, with Ingrid saying, "I have to leave now," and going off. And I was saying to myself, "Now just stay there like a good girl and we'll bring the curtain down." But not likely. She spun the chair around, headed for the door, missed the door completely, nearly knocked the whole set down – all the books fell of the shelves – and the audience roared. They'd never had such a good time. Then the actors came on and she propelled herself back, and they roared and cheered some more. It was quite remarkable. We moved across the United States pushing Ingrid in her wheelchair. And she played it like that for five weeks.

'We found a bone specialist – the man who fixed up the bones of the New York Yankee baseball team – and he chiseled off the plaster cast and bandaged her. Then eventually a doctor said, "I think you'll be able to walk now,' but by now Ingrid so loved being pushed around and playing it in a wheelchair – it was a new theatrical experience for her – that she said, "Oh now, I think I should play it the way I am." And it was the second week in Washington before she decided she'd play it on her two feet again.

'Of course it was public knowledge now that she had played in a wheelchair and so, though the show went all right, it was really not as big a success as when she was in her chair. So she took her curtain call in the wheelchair and that brought the house down. Because that is what they'd come to see – Ingrid Bergman in a wheelchair. But she really is a very game girl. I couldn't think of any star I've ever worked with who would have gone on in such a situation.'

DIRK BOGARDE (1921–)

360 *Film actor and author who began his career in the theatre. The play he is describing is* Cornelius *by J. B. Priestley.*

If Ann Wilton taught me two of the most important lessons in the Theatre, devotion and dedication, Max Adrian, who was also in the play, taught me quite another. But not less essential or timely. Humility. Overimpressed with my modest notices in the Daily Press, and well aware that the audiences not only liked me but thought I was funny, I started, within a very few performances to attempt to take over the play from the Principals. I mugged about, invented bits of, I thought, irresistible business, extended my laughs and behaved as if I was a one-man show at the Palladium. One matinée, unable to bear my behaviour any longer, Max, who played a humbled, timid little clerk, took up a great leather ledger and brought it crashing down on my totally unsuspecting head with an infuriated cry of "Never do that again, I say!" Bewildered with the suddenness of the blow, the stars literally reeling about my head, I slammed into a wall and slid, winded and stunned, to the stage amidst the largest roar of delighted laughter I had ever heard in a theatre in my life. At my own expense. A salutary and necessary lesson for which I was ever grateful.

SIR BRIAN RIX (1924–)

361 *In England, Brian Rix and 'Whitehall' Farce are synonymous, and comic happenings seem to gather round farceurs like flies round a honey-pot.*

The *Ilkley Gazette* reported:

> "The new Ilkley Repertory Company were given a magnificent send-off on Monday evening when they opened to a capacity audience in the King's Hall with *Nothing But The Truth* by James Montgomery. There was an unfortunate incident at the start, when the cord of one of the stage curtains broke. The players were apparently unconcerned, however, and carried on to the end of the first act with half the stage hidden from view. From this point the play continued without a hitch."

Oh yes? Little did the *Ilkley Gazette* know. Colin Collins descended from the flies with his hired tails torn and filthy. The hire firm refused to take them back, so any profit we might have made in Easter Week went up the spout. However, I'm a careful man. Some might say a mean man. I kept those tails for ten years and Leo Franklyn eventually wore them for 1,200 performances in the first act of *Simple Spymen*. It's an ill wind . . .

Strangely enough, there was an incident with the front of the house curtains, known as "the tabs" when we were doing *Simple Spymen*. Maybe those tails were haunted. The fly-man lowered in the tabs at the end of Act I. Unfortunately, he'd left his brake off and the tabs continued to be lowered in, till we were staring at the audience over the tops of them. The fly-man realised his mistake, panicked, and heaved the tabs upwards till they shot above the proscenium arch, revealing the spot bars, the grid, the fly floor, the works. They also revealed a demented fly-man tugging frantically at a couple of thick ropes. The audience was in ecstasies – believing it to be all part of the play. The fly-man took a deep breath and the curtain was lowered in, a few inches too far. It is a well-known fact that a few inches can often cause trouble – and here was no exception. In the interval, the set was changed and a very heavy pianola placed down right. On this occasion it was placed on those unwanted inches of curtain – anchoring them firmly to the stage.

The interval being over – up went the curtain for Act II. At least *most* of it went up – leaving a torn section clinging to the feet of the pianola – looking for all the world like a giant cobweb. Leo Franklyn and I made our entrance.

"My God," said Leo, "that must be a bloody big spider. Get the scissors." I obediently trotted off stage – collected a pair of scissors – ran on – stood on Leo's back and cut the offending remnants down. The audience fell about – the fly-man had hysterics and fled from the theatre, never to be seen again.

362 That was a pretty dull year [1962] because we were so *successful!* Ridiculous, isn't it? Every night I pointed the car in the general direction of the Mall and every night when the curtain went up there would be yet another full house with maybe twenty or thirty standing. The cast grew as complacent as I did so that practical jokes to "corpse" your fellow actors – always a fatal sign – became the order of the day. I remember one elaborate joke I perpetrated night after night on Terry [Scott]. In the play I had just taken some peculiar drug and went off barking like a dog and Terry, as a furious father, would yell, "Look at him – just look at him. 'Alf way up that lamppost." This would be greeted by the necessary audience laughter, and all the cast left on stage would turn round to follow Terry's gaze – so it was a suitable time to get them all going. The antics I got up to were unforgivable and

unrepeatable in retrospect. All except the one on Terry's last night. As
he yelled his line about the lamppost, and as they all looked off left
through the windows, there *was* a lamppost, there *was* a dog and it *was*
lifting its leg. I had dressed my understudy Gerry Dawson, in a dog-
skin, had a lamppost built and a phallic tube and soda siphon completed
the necessary effect. The whole joke cost me about £5, but it cost a lot
more in actual fact for the cast were quite incapable of another word and
it was some time before we won the audience back. Oh dear – I blush
with shame when I think about it.

SIDNEY POITIER (1924–)

363 *Best known for his screen performances, Poitier began his acting career with the American
Negro Theater. His description of playing* A Raisin in the Sun *is a revealing glimpse
of a Method actor at work.*

I received the script almost a year before we went into production, right?
And I read it, naturally, many, many, many times and I knew, generally,
after ten or twenty readings, what the circumstances of the play were. I
knew what the individual characters were like, generally. I understood
my character kind of generally. Now I needed time to make my
understanding of my character specific. In so doing I must understand
all of the contributing elements that go to making up this character. First
I must understand what are the driving forces in the man. In order to
understand that, you must find out what are his political, social,
economic, religious milieus, and how they contribute to the personality
idiosyncrasies or whatever. And in so examining, I find that this, first,
is a Negro man thirty-six years old, living in Chicago on the South Side
– which of itself is quite significant in the building of a character, because
only a particular kind of Negro lives on the South Side in this particular
kind of circumstances, see? So that narrows the field already. And then
we take: Why is this man living here? Is he here by choice? What is his
relation to his community? What is his relation to his religion, if he has
one? What is his relation to his economic disposition? Is it one in which
he finds enough elasticity to function and maintain his manhood or is it
a constant badge or remembrance of his inadequacies – you follow? –
and all these things can be found in the script, or at least if they're not
there they can be made compatible with what is in the script at one point
or another. So that – after months of actually making specific this man
in his milieu – then I come to the final conclusion of what are his wants.
And when I find what are his general wants, I find what is his most
specific want or wants. And they aren't many – so with his most specific
want, I now have the man in total. I know what his reaction would be
to everything done and said in the play – see? I know what and how he

feels about his neighborhood, so that any question or reference to it strikes a certain chord in a man. Now with this kind of information, I then proceed to familiarize myself with the pros and cons of his life and his wants. I try to experience them, so by the time I'm ready to perform, I don't go in a corner – at least I don't have to go in a corner and concentrate and conjure up some mysterious magic. I walk on the stage and it happens. And I don't work Method because it's too late now to work Method. If you're not ready, forget it. You walk on the stage and you perform, because what begins to happen out there is that you find that you have taken on the milieu of the character, and you then begin to seek out and fulfill the very wants that are burning inside *you* now, which are his wants. Once you're on the stage you have no time, because the stage is to experience – you follow? – the stage is to experience . . . Once the curtain goes up and there is an audience out there, you, the artist, your responsibility is to experience, and only through your experiencing are you able really to transmit – you follow? There are many kinds of actors. There are actors who can get on a stage, but they can never quite enthrall, nor can they ever quite involve or hypnotize, but they can give a workmanlike job. Well, if they're not gifted, they don't enthrall and they don't involve, because they themselves are not able to involve on the level required by the artist.

MARLON BRANDO (1924–)

364 *In the same year that the German director Erwin Piscator expelled Brando from his dramatic workshop, the twenty-year-old actor made his Broadway debut in* I Remember Mama. *As Tennessee Williams describes here, it was Elia Kazan who spotted the talent of this brooding, passionate actor, recommending him for a part in* A Streetcar Named Desire.

For some reason the electricity and the plumbing went kaput simultaneously. Evenings were candle lit and for calls of nature the inhabitants of the cabin had to go out into the bushes.

Well, just about this time I got a wire from Kazan, informing me that he was dispatching a young actor to the Cape who he thought was gifted, and he wanted him to read the part of Stanley for me. We waited two or three days, but the young actor, named Marlon Brando, didn't show. I had stopped expecting him when he arrived one evening with a young girl, the kind you would call a chick nowadays.

He asked why the lights weren't on and we told him the electricity had failed. He immediately fixed that for us – I think he merely inserted a penny in the light fuse.

Then he discovered our predicament with the plumbing and he fixed that too.

He was just about the best-looking young man I've ever seen, with one or two exceptions; but I have never played around with actors, it's a point of morality with me and anyhow Brando was not the type to get a part that way.

When he had gotten the Rancho into shape by repairing the lights and plumbing, he sat down in a corner and started to read the part of Stanley. I was cuing him. After less than ten minutes, Margo Jones jumped up and let out a "Texas Tornado" shout.

"Get Kazan on the phone right away! This is the greatest reading I've ever heard – in or outside of Texas!"

Brando maybe smiled a little but didn't show any particular elation, such as the elation we all felt.

The part of Kowalski was the first important part he has ever performed on the stage, all the rest have been on the screen. I think this is a pity, because Brando had a charisma on the stage that corresponded to the charisma of Laurette Taylor in its luminous power.

That night we had dinner at home and we read poetry. I mean I read some poetry. Then we retired for the night. There was no bed for Brando so he curled up in a blanket in the center of the floor.

Brando was always shy with me for some reason. The following morning he wanted me to walk up the beach with him, and so we did – in silence. And then we walked back – in silence . . .

PETER BROOK (1925–)

365 *Some of Brook's productions have been controversial, but when his existentialist* King Lear *was taken to Europe it was received with rapture.**

Wherever they went in Europe, they were applauded. 'We must change our lives,' Iván Boldizsár, editor of the *New Hungarian Quarterly*, said in Budapest, a city famed for its Shakespearian scholarship and possessing in Miklós Gábor one of the majestic actors of his time. In Belgrade President Tito came to talk to the cast. On the last Rumanian night riots developed in the streets of Bucharest; students trying to break into the theatre, and every part of the house, except the President's box, packed to its distant crevices. Critics in Moscow praised a performance in depth, the emergence of 'psychological and philosophical realities'; at the opening Sviatoslav Richter, the Russian pianist, led twenty minutes' applause from the front row. I like especially a brief news story published

---

*Charles Marowitz, the assistant director, tells of an untoward incident during the original dress rehearsal in London. As Paul Scofield, in the title role, embarked on a long speech a photographer began taking shots. Scofield suddenly turned downstage, hurled his cloak at the man, growled 'Get that thing away from here', and continued his speech as Lear. It happened so quickly, and was so electrifying, that one observer remarked, 'I felt like saying, keep it in!'

in a Czech paper after the first performance in the great green and gold Smetanova Divadlo in Prague:

> Six minutes before *King Lear* was due to start, a man hailed a taxi far away in Strasnice. 'Can we get there in time?' The driver willingly gave it a try. One minute before the time the taxi stopped in front of the theatre. Neither the driver nor the passenger had small money. A banknote changed hands. 'I shall bring you the small change after the performance.' And he did. The name of the taxi-driver is Comrade Buldro, from the Trojická Street Garages. A truly exemplary service.
>
> J. C. Trewin

366 *John Kane, who played both Puck and Philostrate in Brook's production of* A Midsummer Night's Dream *at Stratford-upon-Avon in 1970, related this anecdote to the author and critic J.C. Trewin. Brook had decided to invite children to the rehearsals as he thought their response might be instructive.*

Most of the children at the *Dream* rehearsal, though they enjoyed the experience, really could not understand what was going on half the time. Still, Kane relates a conversation with one little girl at the end of the performance:

He: Did you enjoy the play?
She: Oh yes, very much.
He: Did you understand what was happening?
She: Oh yes.
He: How did you like the fairies?
She: Very much.
He: Would you have liked them better if they had worn wings and things?
She: Oh no. I liked them best when they were wearing their ordinary clothes. Wings and things don't matter.
He: Have you been to the theatre before?
She: Oh yes. Lots of times.
He: Does your daddy work in the theatre?
She: Yes.
He: What does he do?
She: He's a director.
He: What's his name?
She: Peter Brook.

RICHARD BURTON (1925–1984)

367 *No one disputes that Burton was on his day a brilliant actor, but he dissipated his talent. In this first piece Bryan Forbes reminisces about the time when Burton was appearing in Christopher Fry's,* The Lady's Not for Burning.

I envied Burton. He had so many qualities that I lacked and was totally without inhibitions. He was then appearing in *The Lady's Not for Burning* and constantly in hot water with the management. His various escapades were eagerly awaited and exhaustively discussed in Taylor's and Warwick Gardens: they encompassed some beguiling sexual conquests from amongst the flower of Shaftesbury Avenue as well as some bizarre practical jokes. Esme Percy, that eccentric actor who had enjoyed a distinguished career despite the fact that he had lost an eye, was one of the cast in *The Lady's Not for Burning*. In some Celtic mood of boredom Burton purchased a collection of glass eyes which, aided and abetted by Richard Leech, he secreted all over the stage. At the following performance the rest of the cast, Mr Percy included, were horrified by the surfeit of glass eyes that confronted them at every turn. Somebody proposed a toast and found an eye staring at them in magnified liquid fashion at the bottom of the glass. People trod on glass eyes, slipped on glass eyes, opened purses and were confronted with an abundance of glass eyes. Whether or not Burton exaggerated the effect in the hilarious retelling, I cannot say; I only know that I hugely and callously enjoyed the joke at the time.

368   Wales is the well-guarded reserve of its natural and principal species, the amateur. Someone suggested that Burton be invited to lead a National Welsh Theatre. A distinguished leader of the principality asked what were Burton's qualifications. It was explained that he had played Henry V at Stratford and a Hamlet at the Old Vic applauded by Churchill. The reply, which evoked no surprise, was, 'Yes, I see that. But what has he done in Wales?'

John Osborne

369   During that entire Broadway run there was only one disconcerting moment for Burton; on the night of 6 May a man from the balcony began booing loudly during one of the soliloquies. Others cheered to drown the one hostile voice, but the demonstrator would not be silenced. When players appeared individually for curtain calls, he reserved one solitary boo for Burton. At the next call, Richard asked for the curtain to be kept up. Then he approached the footlights and told the audience: 'We have been playing this production in public for over eighty performances. Some have liked it, some have not. But I can assure you – we have never been booed.' The fans cheered. The mysterious man in the balcony booed as loudly as ever.

Elizabeth had a touch of influenza that night and remained in their Regency suite. When Richard arrived home she was in bed enjoying a television movie in which she was seeing Peter Sellers for the first time.

'I was booed tonight,' he growled.

'Really?' said Liz, her violet eyes still glued to the gogglebox.

'Oh, turn that bloody thing off,' said Richard, sulkily seeking an audience.

'Shush! I can't hear.'

'Don't you understand,' he went on. 'I was actually booed. On the stage.'

'Yes, dear,' said Liz. 'Never mind.'

Richard stalked out of the room and changed into his pyjamas. When he returned and found he was still eclipsed by television, he stormed across the room and kicked the set over with a bare foot. It crashed against a wall and one of the knobs fell to the floor. He kicked it again. This time his foot struck the bared metal screw, and as the screw cut deep between his first two toes he let out an almighty yell of anguish. Blood gushed from the wound. Four-letter expletives sliced the air. Elizabeth, remembering his tendency towards haemophilia, automatically fetched the bandage and iodine, but at the same time she dissolved into fits of laughter and that literally made Richard hopping mad. Next day he went on stage with a pronounced limp and grumbled: 'Some critics have said I play Hamlet like Richard the Third anyway. So what the hell is the difference?'

Fergus Cashin

370 Though Burton says he could never be dedicated to the theatre in the way Olivier and Gielgud and Scofield are, he does genuinely enjoy acting. His handicap is his extremely low boredom boiling-point. 'I did many of those Shakespearean roles as a kind of duty,' he explained. 'I enjoyed them sometimes, but I found the stage a bit of drudgery for the most part; the terrifying thing of playing the same part eight times a week for, say a year, is enervating.' As a consequence of his restless disposition, he lacks a certain discipline as a stage actor, and during the course of a long run he can become somewhat unorthodox and cavalier. During his New York Hamlet, for example, when he knew that German adoption officials were visiting the theatre, he began his 'To be or not to be' soliloquy in German. And brother Graham recalls the night he went to see Camelot. 'There was the heaviest snowfall I have ever seen, and towards the end of the performance many people were slipping out to grab the first taxis. Richard came to the front of the stage and called out, "Hey, book a cab for me, too will you?" '

Fergus Cashin

BRYAN FORBES (1926–)

371 *Director, actor and writer. Here is a passage from his autobiography describing the effects of some pretty realistic make-up. Norman is the actor Norman Bird; Yvonne Le Dain ran a theatre in Rugby.*

The season ended in disaster for Norman and me. We exhausted ourselves in a series of unsuitable roles, gave, as they say, our all and somehow eked out and survived on our meagre salaries. Then came the moment when we were rehearsing yet another new play, never before performed, called *Charlotte Corday*. This was a dramatic episode of the French Revolution written by Helen Jerome and Yvonne cast herself in the name part. I was given the minor role of an aged jailer which I played as Charles Laughton in *Mutiny on the Bounty* down to the last lisping intonation. Norman got the flamboyant part of Marat, and of course the action included his murder in the hip bath at the hands of Charlotte Corday.

We took our work very seriously and it was tacitly understood that we would keep a watching brief on each other's major performances and feel free to proffer advice without fear or favour.

Since I only appeared briefly in the closing moments of the play I was able to sit out front during the dress-rehearsal and evaluate Norman's big scene. I thought he played it well enough but I was critical of the staging.

'The real problem is,' I said when we were once again in our shared dressing-room, 'that Marat took endless baths in order to relieve himself from a foul skin disease. Now, from the front, you look completely healthy, and when Yvonne stabs you with the knife nothing happens, there's no blood. I mean, it stands to reason that if anybody stuck a bread-knife into you with that force there'd be a great gush of blood, a fountain.'

Norman was only too anxious to agree with me and in the short time available to us between the dress-rehearsal and the first performance we devised ways and means of correcting the glaring faults.

I first concocted and then applied to Norman's body a mixture of cornflakes and glue to simulate Marat's foul scabs. Warming to my task, I then coloured them with sticks of carmine and brown until he resembled a leper in the last stages of deterioration.

Next I gave all my attention to the problem of the missing gush of blood. I unearthed an old motor car horn bulb in the prop room, filled this with liquid paraffin and tomato ketchup and then taped it under Norman's upstage arm with a roll of sticky plaster. I then carefully rehearsed him and was fairly confident by the time that Overture and Beginners was called that dramatic justice would be seen to be done. So engrossed were we that it never occurred to us that we should inform our leading lady and employer of these added pieces of finesse.

When the curtain went up on the second act Norman was revealed in his hip bath covered in suppurating scabs. With the added incentive of an audience to play to, he picked at them with ghoulish pleasure, causing a wave of horror to sweep through the Temple Speech Room. Then Yvonne made her appearance as Charlotte Corday and the scene progressed to the point where she plunged with the assassin's knife. I watched with a scientist's detachment from the wings. As Yvonne struck with the knife Norman timed his movement to perfection, bringing pressure to bear upon the bulb with his upstage arm, just as I had instructed. Yvonne was saturated with a great gush of imitation blood: it burst from Norman's imaginary wound with a force and authenticity that startled even me. Two people in the front row of the stalls leapt screaming to their feet and poor Yvonne must have thought she was going mad. She was drenched in our viscous mixture and quite unable to continue with her dialogue. Other members of the cast, rushing on stage, were equally dumbfounded. Norman, meantime, had died. He slumped half out of the hip-bath, a naked, blotchy corpse, diseased and bloodied. Yvonne, being a trouper, eventually recovered, and the play staggered to the curtain fall.

During the interval she committed verbal assassination on us both and we were given our notices on the spot. I don't think we were too dismayed, because we still had the rest of the week to go and were delighted with the startling success of our innovations. We took comfort in despising Miss le Dain for failing to recognize true dramatic genius.

DOROTHY TUTIN (1931–   )

372 *From a television interview with Derek Hart.*

DH: I remember seeing you in a play by John Whiting called *The Devils*, in which you played a prioress possessed by the evil spirit of the prelate, Grandier. There was a scene where the witch-hunting priest tries to extract the evidence from you and you actually became possessed. Now, that is a situation which must be wildly outside your own experience. When you're doing something of that kind, is it a particularly difficult thing for you to do?

DT: That part was impossible really, impossible. It was a marvellous play, absolutely marvellous. But when I read it I said to Peter Hall who was producing it, 'The play is so wonderful – it would be too awful if I played it and couldn't do it at all; I must audition for it.' I had done another play of John Whiting's before and he said it would be all right and I wasn't to be nervous about it and just do it. The awful thing was whenever we came at rehearsals to the possession scene, I kept on saying,

'Well do you mind if I don't do that today? You know, I'll do it tomorrow, can we skip that bit?' I was terrified of doing it, I was balking it. Then one of the nuns came up to me and said, 'Dotty, aren't you going to do that scene, because until you do it, we can't get started either?' I was appalled to think that I had been stopping them from acting. And so that day at rehearsal, when we came to the possession scene, instead of saying, 'Sorry I can't, I'll do it later,' I did it and we started off. I didn't know what would happen, I just made my mind a blank and tried to imagine possession. The extraordinary thing was that the other nuns picked it up and in fact we had the experience that happened in the actual play, in that nunnery, a sort of catching hysteria. We all got it; we never did it again like that. The problem about hysteria of that kind is that you can't portray it in any manner that is acceptable. The audience can imagine it for themselves far better than you could ever show it. In fact it was best when it wasn't seen, when it was either talked about or when you only saw a little bit of it.

MAGGIE SMITH (1931–   )

373 *In 1957 she was in a revue called* Share My Lettuce *with Kenneth Williams. He recalls the adroitness of her off-stage asides.*

Share My Lettuce became very fashionable. On the night of the 7th of September Terence Rattigan came backstage and was very complimentary. That seemed to set the seal of approval on us as firmly as the Royal Warrant and two weeks later we transferred to the Comedy Theatre in the West End.

The dressing-room windows overlooked an open space across which I could talk to Maggie, and I remember one night she called out, 'What's in this bottle of stuff you've given me for my eyes?'

'It's a balm to soothe the pupils,' I told her. 'Some sort of alkaline solution. Why?'

'W-e-ll,' she called back, elongating the vowel disapprovingly, 'I just spilled a drop of it on the window sill and it's gone clean through the paint.' I can recall my involuntary alarm and the subsequent laughter as if it were yesterday.

Share My Lettuce flourished through the rest of the year, at Christmas there was talk of yet another transfer, and on the 29th of January 1958, with Maggie remarking 'This must be the longest tour in town', we had our third London opening at the Garrick Theatre.

It was here that I misbehaved in more ways than one and incurred Maggie's wrath. There was a sketch in the show where four men stood selling newspapers; one, two and three cried, 'Star,' 'News,' and

'Standard' respectively and I called out 'Figaro'; then we shouted the virtues of our papers, each of us attempting to drown the others till Maggie appeared. Dressed in a slinky black mackintosh, she walked sexily across the stage and as she passed the vendors one by one, they fell silent. When she was almost at the proscenium arch, the first man asked, 'Paper, lady?' and she exited saying, 'No thank you, dearie, I won't be needing any paper.' It always got a big laugh and there was an immediate stage black-out.

One night I didn't stay mute when she passed me, I sang 'Figaro' basso profundo and then continued with 'When you're a barber . . . Figaro, Figaro,' etc. Of course Maggie couldn't say her line and after a momentary hesitation, she simply walked off stage, the electrics didn't get their cue, the blackout was late, and my choral efforts, while raising an initial titter, ruined the end of the scene.

During the interval an irate Maggie came into my dressing room demanding an explanation. I was sitting at the make-up bench doing my face and she perched herself on it between me and the wash basin, flicking cigarette ash into the bowl while she talked.

'Why did you put in all that operatic stuff?'

'I thought it was a funny idea.'

'It ruined my tag line.'

'I had this urge to do something new.'

'You need to rehearse something new.'

'I know, but I just couldn't wait.'

Maggie suddenly leant over the sink and asked, 'Have you been peeing in here?'

I started a stammering denial, reddened and faltered.

'Hmm,' she said. 'I suppose you couldn't wait for that either?' Then we both started laughing, and a potential row over a foolish ad lib had an entirely happy ending.

ALBERT FINNEY (1936–)

374 *From an interview with Clive Goodwin.*

Q. At Stratford you had the dream of every understudy come true. Laurence Olivier injured his leg and you took over the part of Coriolanus.*

A. Yes, that was smashing. I don't know what was wrong with my work at Stratford. I mean it was more wrong then than it's ever been before or since, and I was aware of it being wrong. It was one of those

*See also p. 194.

times when you feel that everything you do – you know that kind of tunnel – and there's nothing you can do to get out of it. The more you try to get out of it, the more you're in it. My work was awful, just vile. Every time I went on the stage I felt, get off, get off, what are you doing? But when I went on for Sir Laurence in *Coriolanus*, all the difficulties I seemed to be going through left me. Because, first of all, the audience kind of expect you to come on in flannels with a book. Sir Laurence isn't playing – big groan. His part will be played by Al – Albert Finney. And then I came on, and I had the costume on, and so they immediately think I'm talented because I've actually got into the clothes. I've put the body make-up on and then I start and they can't see the book. And I actually got through it without drying, so they think I'm very good. If you're an understudy and you go on, the card you've actually got in your hand is that they think you might not be able to get through at all, and if you can get through with any degree of professionalism, they think you're very good. And I kind of felt, get in there. But it's terrible to hear that announcement – you know, you're in your dressing-room putting on the make-up – Sir Laurence won't be playing tonight; terrible groan throughout the auditorium. That's nice.

But I felt a kind of freedom doing *Coriolanus* because I had no responsibility; I was his understudy, it didn't matter what happened. It didn't matter if I dried; they'd expect it. If I fainted, well it's a lot of pressure on the lad, you know. So I didn't worry. All the clouds which were around the rest of my performances, all the rubbish, the tunnel I felt in with my work, all the difficulties blew out of the window. I just went on and did it. I felt very free. I don't think it was a good Coriolanus. When you hear Sir Laurence's tones ringing in your ears for the number of times he'd done the performances, it's very difficult for you not to be similar, because you're working on his blueprint. I learnt from that how a great actor can take the peaks and the valleys of a performance, the ups and downs of a character as written, and push them even further apart. He makes the climaxes higher and the depths of it lower than you feel is possible in the text. It was marvellous to go through it during a performance, kind of putting on his clothes and feeling well they don't touch me here at all, you know. Just feel your own way – how big you are on the graph, as it were. Then you see he went right up there. I don't just mean vocally, but emotionally and everything, and he went right down there. That was a very interesting realisation. But I was glad when he was back actually. The theatre management gave me a steak between the matinée and evening show; I did it six times and it was always with a matinée and an evening show. So I quite enjoyed it.

SIMON GRAY (1936–   )

375 *The English playwright describes some of his experiences on Broadway.*

There was a party at Sardi's to celebrate the opening of my first play on Broadway. The producer, whose only venture into the theatre this was to be, sat sobbing at the end of a long table in an upstairs room that had emptied with the arrival of the *New York Times* review (epoch of Clive Barnes).

GRAY. Oh, come on now, no need to cry now. Only a play! (*Little pause.*) Old chap?
PRODUCER. Only a play? When I invested all my wife's money in it? And I haven't told her yet?

Early the following morning, my wife and I stole with our luggage through the hotel lobby, to avoid the manager who had given us cheap rates, a high standard of service and mysteriously obsequious smiles because, as we'd also learnt at the Sardi's party, he too had invested money in us.

Back in New York some months later, with a new piece. Standing in a bar next to the theatre during the interval of the second preview, my third large whisky smouldering in my mitt. A friendly figure hovers beside me, orders himself a drink.

FRIENDLY (*after a pause, turns*). Saw the same guy's last. That was crap too.
GRAY (*shakes his head gloomily*). State of Broadway.
FRIENDLY. Somebody ought to give him the bum's rush. Got enough crap of our own. Don't need his.
GRAY. Yeah.

A smooth theatrical production, though, interrupted only by life itself. Our youngest actor mugged twice in his dressing-room during the first week of performance. One of the understudies raped in a car-park during rehearsals. Our leading lady held at knife-point for two hours behind the theatre. Flying home after a week of previews, I phoned from the airport.

STAGE-MANAGER. Hello.
GRAY. Hello, Simon here.
STAGE-MANAGER. Oh, hi, Simon, what can I do for you?
GRAY. Just wondering how it went this evening.
STAGE-MANAGER. The first act went pretty well, I thought.
GRAY. Good. (*Pause.*) And the second act?
STAGE-MANAGER. There wasn't a second act.
GRAY. Oh. (*Pause.*) Any particular reason?

STAGE-MANAGER. The company went to see *Hello Dolly*.
GRAY. Instead of doing the second act, you mean?
STAGE-MANAGER. Right.
GRAY. Oh. (*After a pause.*) Any particular reason?
STAGE-MANAGER. Somebody reported a bomb in the theatre.
GRAY. Oh. (*Attempts lightness.*) Which?
STAGE-MANAGER (*laughs politely*). Ours.

On my third visit to Broadway, all went well apart from the discovery of the wardrobe mistress's body in the wardrobe an hour before curtain up on the first night. Natural causes, however, which in New York, opening doors on to inexplicable mysteries, are more alarming than the run-of-the-mill foul-play.

VICTOR HENRY (1943–85)

376 *An excellent actor who, following an accident, died tragically young. The narrator is Jack Shepherd.*

The Royal Court Actors' Studio was still operating at this time. Junior members of the company, such as myself, were encouraged to attend. There were classes in basic skills, movement, method acting, clowning, comic masks, full masks, and so on. Bill Gaskill used to take improvisation classes in which he would set out to explore the world of the epic narrative. These sessions were often very baffling . . . 'An old woman comes down to the river,' he said once. 'I want someone to act the narrative contained in that sentence.'

Everyone cringed. After a long silence an actor was picked out. A man.

'You want me to act out the sentence, "An old woman comes down to the river",' the actor repeated.

'Yes,' said Bill after another long silence.

The actor then tied a pullover round his head, hunched his shoulders, and started walking, as he hoped, towards the river.

'Start again,' said Bill, almost immediately. 'What you are showing me is . . . "The old woman comes down to the river." I want an old woman. Can you show me an old woman? Without using a headscarf, and without hunching your shoulders?'

The actor looked scared. 'I don't know,' he said.

'Try it again,' said Bill.

And so it went on.

I don't remember Victor Henry attending any of Bill's classes. He had theories of his own at this time. I remember him telling me that if you played a scene with your head on one side you could make middle-aged women cry. It had never occurred to me to want to do that but I showed interest, arguing that it seemed unlikely.

'Just watch me,' he replied. So I watched him one night, as Sparky in *Serjeant Musgrave's Dance*, playing a love scene with his right ear resting absurdly on his shoulder. I looked around the auditorium and, sure enough, middle-aged women were crying all over the place.

From Richard Findlater, ed., *At the Royal Court*

MARIA AITKEN (1945–)

377 *Her first speaking part in the theatre was in a provincial production of* Tom Jones, *starring an anonymous television personality.*

I also took my assistant stage-management duties extremely seriously, and in those few minutes before curtain up, although my heart was full of my village wench role, my head was methodically checking the prop table. Six drinking-cups, wooden platters, shot-gun, stuffed partridge . . . It was a litany I knew by heart; nevertheless I went through the motions of checking each object off on a list. The partridge was my particular concern, because it was the hub of the director's favourite joke. Tom Jones fired his twelve-bore stage right, and the partridge plopped out of the wings stage left. 'Don't argue, boyo – it's a classic,' said the director, and I was so bewildered by his sense of humour that I failed to get neurotic about his apparent sexual confusion.

My cue came, and I fled the sanctuary of the prop table for the wide unknown of the stage. I had evolved a sort of Loamshire sound for my comic village maiden, uneasily aware that regional accents were not my forte. My false hairpiece tumbled over my shoulders; my eyelashes were still tangentially attached; I had heaved and padded my unabundant bosom into a respectable cleavage, and every visible extremity was painted rustic nut-brown. They laughed. I only had eight lines and they laughed at five of them. I had the incredible disadvantages of an Oxford degree, a posh voice and the physique of an overbred setter, but the audience had believed in my common sexy wench enough to laugh at her.

'Quite the comedienne, boyo,' said the director in the interval. Rashly confident, I essayed some crack about his gender mix-ups, and was rewarded with the laugh accorded to my status as comic.

Act Two began, and I cavorted at the back of the stage with two other ASMs, busily representing a mob of three thousand. Tom Jones raised his gun. He fired. Nothing happened. Where was the partridge? Being a resourceful chap, the Star raised his gun again. 'Bang,' he said loudly. Suddenly I realized that I had hallucinated that bird on the prop table, that I had never set it there in the first place, absorbed in my own petty role, and that it was now up to me to Save the Play. Quick as a flash, I fell writhing to the ground, reasoning that as long as *something* died that Tom Jones wasn't aiming at, the director's favourite joke would remain intact. Unfortunately, a more practically minded member of our cavorting mob had simultaneously nipped off stage and thrown the partridge on. I never thought much of the original joke, but I can tell you with authority that when *two* things die that Tom Jones isn't aiming at, there is no joke at all. The entire episode was greeted with a bewildered silence.

I wept off my eyelashes as I swept the stage after curtain down, waiting for retribution. It arrived. 'Theatre is discipline, boyo. You can act your socks off, but it's no good if you're not reliable. Go back to your undergraduate amateurs where you can't spoil any more of my gags. You're fired.'

'But I bought three pairs of eyelashes for the run,' I sobbed, unable to believe that my career had ended the night it began. I trailed upstairs to pack up the barely used sticks of greasepaint, and wandered snuffling out of the stage-door. The Star was outside, engulfed in provincial pubescents waving autograph books. He took one look at my swollen face and led me to the nearest pub, heedless of the weeny-boppers' protestations. He extracted the story through my hiccups and gasps and towed me through a maze of carparks and alleys to another pub. I shied like a nervous horse when I saw the director propping up the bar, but the Star propelled me inexorably forward.

'Hallo,' he said pleasantly. 'I thought we'd find you here. I've brought Miss Initiative along for a drink.'

'She's fired,' said the director.

'No, I don't think so,' said the Star politely. 'I wouldn't feel the same about appearing here without her.'

I was dumbstruck. I'd never even spoken to him until that evening. By the time I re-focussed on what was happening, the Star and the director had their arms round each other's necks.

Later, much later, as they say in the women's magazines, I attempted to thank the Star.

'You've said thank you in the nicest possible way,' he said, putting on his clothes. 'Now I have to go home to my wife.'

My heart was broken, but I got my job back. I've never been able to look at a partridge since.

SOURCES

(Full titles are used for initial references,
thereafter short titles are given.)

1. *Gentleman's Magazine* (new series) vol. xxxiv, p. 234
2. Theophilus Cibber, *The Lives of the Poets of Great Britain and Northern Ireland to the time of Dean Swift* (1753), pp. 130–1.
3. Anon, *Dramatic Table Talk* (sometimes ascribed to Richard Ryan) (1825), ii. pp. 156–7.
4. *Diary of John Manningham 1602–03*, ed. J. Bruce (1868), p. 39.
5. Joseph Spence, *Observations, Anecdotes, and Characters of Books and Men*, ed. James M. Osborn (1966), i. 185.
6. Sir Henry Wotton, *Reliquiae Wottonianae* (4th edition 1685), pp. 425–6.
7. *Aubrey's Brief Lives*, ed. Oliver Lawson Dick (3rd edition 1971), pp. 177–8.
8. *Notes of Ben Jonson's Conversations with William Drummond of Hawthornden*, ed. David Laing (1842), p. 20.
9. *Diary of Samuel Pepys*, ed. John Warrington (1953), iii, p. 87–8
10. *An Apology For The Life of Colley Cibber*, ed. B. R. S. Fone (1968), p. 78.
11. Joseph Spence, *Anecdotes*, i. 319
12. Samuel Pepys, *Diary*, iii, p. 55
13. Ibid., iii, p. 137
14. Ibid., iii, p. 226.
15. Joseph Spence, *Anecdotes*, i. 322–3
16. Dr John Doran, *Their Majesties' Servants: Annals of the English Stage from Betterton to Kean*, ed. and rev. R. W. Lowe (3 vols 1888), i. 123
17. R. Wewitzer, *Dramatic Remains*, quoted in W. Clark Russell, *Representative Actors* (1888), p. 21.
18. Colley Cibber, *Life*, p. 71.
19. *The Guardian*, no. 82, 15 June, 1713 (collected edition 1797), i. 489–92.
20. John Dennis, *The Critical Works*, ed. E. Hooker (1943), ii. 405–6.
21. Ibid., ii. 409–10
22. Samuel Pepys, *Diary*, iii, pp. 74–5
23. John Doran, *Servants*, i. 262–3
24. Thomas Campbell, *Life of Mrs Siddons* (1834), ii. 87–88.
25. Thomas Davies, *Dramatic Miscellanies* (1785), iii. 444–5
26. Ibid., iii. 470–1
27. Colley Cibber, *Life*, pp. 113–5
28. Clark Russell, *Representative Actors*, p. 165 (note).
29. Thomas Davies, *Dramatic Miscellanies*, iii. 326–8;

30. Ibid., i. 180–1
31. Thomas Davies, *Memoirs of David Garrick*, ed. Stephen Jones (2 vols 1808), i. 370–1
32. Thomas Davies, *Dramatic Miscellanies*, iii. 88–90
33. Ibid., i. 8–9
34. Ibid., i. 183–4
35. *Macready's Reminiscences*, ed. Sir F. Pollock (1876), p. 22
36. John O'Keefe, *Recollections of the Life of John O'Keefe* (1826), i. 285–6
37. Ibid., ii. 316–7
38. *Macready's Reminiscences*, p. 22
39. Thomas Davies, *Dramatic Miscellanies*, iii. 498 (note)
40. Thomas Davies, *Garrick*, ii. 33
41. *Blackwood's Magazine* (1834), quoted in Clark Russell, *Representative Actors*, pp. 53–4.
42. W. R. Chetwood, *A General History of the Stage* (1749), pp. 224–6
43. *Johnsonian Miscellanies*, ed. George Birkbeck Hill (2 vols 1897), i. 386–7
44. *Johnsonian Miscellanies*, ii. 332–3
45. Ibid., ii. 318–9
46. Ibid., ii. 192
47. Thomas Campbell, *Siddons*, i. 38
48. Thomas Davies, *Garrick*, i. 42
49. Ibid., i. 376–7
50. Ibid., i. 55–7
51. Ibid., ii. 286–8
52. Ibid., i. 61–2
53. Ibid., ii. 5–6
54. *Table Talk of Samuel Rogers*, ed. Morchard Bishop (1952), p. 4
55. James Boaden, *Memoirs of Mrs Siddons* (1827), i. 23–5
56. Letter from David Garrick to the Duchess of Portland, presented to the Garrick Club in 1935 by Raymond Massey
57. Tate Wilkinson, *Memoirs of His Own Life* (1791), i. 153
58. Richard Cumberland, *Memoirs* (1806), pp. 250–1.
59. *Cornhill Magazine* (1867), quoted in Clark Russell, *Representative Actors*, p. 147
60. John O'Keefe, *Life*, i. 158–9.
61. J. H. Leigh Hunt, *Readings For Railways* (1849), pp. 104–5.
62. Richard Cumberland, *Memoirs*, pp. 269–70
63. W. R. Chetwood, *History*, pp. 42–4
64. George Anne Bellamy, *An Apology for the Life of George Anne Bellamy* (1785), i. 129–35
65. *Cornhill Magazine* (1863), quoted in Clark Russell, *Representative Actors*, p. 167
66. Tate Wilkinson, *Memoirs*, iii. 164–5
67. Clark Russell, *Representative Actors*, p. 191 (note)
68. William Hazlitt, *The Round Table: Northcote's Conversations, Characteristics, and Miscellania*, ed. W. Carew Hazlitt (1903), pp. 364–5
69. *Lichtenberg's Visits to England as Described in His Letters and Diaries*, trans. Margaret L. Mare and W. H. Quarrell (1938), pp. 28–9
70. Dr Doran, *Table Traits*, quoted in Clark Russell, *Representative Actors*, pp. 178–9.

71. Percy Fitzgerald, *Life of David Garrick* rev. edition 1899), pp. 169–70.
72. Tate Wilkinson, *Memoirs*, ii. 114–5
73. Ibid., iii. 83–4
74. James Boaden, *Life of John Philip Kemble* (1825), i. 193
75. John O'Keefe, *Life*, ii. 51–2
76. Ibid., i. 366–9
77. Thomas Campbell, *Siddons*, i. 88–9
78. Thomas Moore, *Memoirs of R. B. Sheridan* (1826), ii. 368
79. Thomas Campbell, *Siddons*, ii. 190–1
80. Ibid., i. 246–8
81. Ibid., i. 259–60
82. Ibid., ii. 143 (note)
83. Ibid., ii. 281–2
84. Ibid., ii. 336–7
85. Ibid., ii. 392–3
86. *Life of Mathews*, quoted in Clark Russell, *Representative Actors*, p. 226
87. William Dunlap (ed.), *Memoirs of George Frederick Cooke, Esq.* (1813), pp. 170–3
88. Ibid., pp. 187–8.
89. James Boaden, *Kemble*, i. 25–6
90. W. T. Parke, *Musical Memoirs* (1830), i. 71–2
91. *Wright's Caricature History*, quoted in Clark Russell, *Representative Actors*, p. 247
92. Donaldson, *Recollections of an Actor*, quoted in Clark Russell, *Representative Actors*, p. 251
93. Clark Russell, *Representative Actors*, pp. 257–8
94. Oral Sumner Coad, *William Dunlap* (1917), pp. 49–50.
95. Ibid., pp. 76–7.
96. William Dunlap, *History of the American Theatre* (1833), vol. 2, pp. 296–302.
97. George Raymond, *The Life and Enterprises of R. W. Elliston* (1857), pp. 224–5
98. Ibid., pp. 402–3.
99. Lester Wallack, *Memories of Fifty Years* (1889), pp. 80–1.
100. Ibid., pp. 87–8
101. J. R. Planché, *Recollections and Reflections* (1901), p. 252
102. From a contemporary paper, quoted in Clark Russell, *Representative Actors*, pp. 313–4
103. Mrs John Drew, *Autobiographical Sketch* (1900), pp. 54
104. *Recollections of an Actor*, quoted in Clark Russell, *Representative Actors*, p. 333
105. Richard Findlater, *Grimaldi King of Clowns* (1955), pp. 121–2
106. Ibid., pp. 181–2
107. John O'Keefe, *Life*, ii. 102–4
108. William Oxberry, *Dramatic Biography* (1825)
109. *Macready's Reminiscences*, pp. 12–13
110. F. A. Kemble, *Record of a Girlhood* (1878), ii. 179
111. *Macready's Reminiscences*, pp. 18–19
112. William Hazlitt, *A View of the English Stage*, ed. W. Spencer Jackson (1906), pp. 185–6

113. Alfred H. Miles (ed.), *The New Anecdote Book* (1900).
114. Thomas Colley Grattan, *Beaten Paths* (1862), ii. pp. 198–200
115. John W. Francis, *Old New York*, pp. 234–6
116. Edmund Stirling, *Old Drury Lane* (1881), ii. 145–7
117. Sir John Martin-Harvey, *Autobiography* (1933), p. 381
118. H. N. Hillebrand, *Edmund Kean* (1933), p. 199
119. Bram Stoker, *Personal Reminiscences of Henry Irving* (1906), i. 276
120. *Macready's Reminiscences*, pp. 29–30
121. Ibid., p. 215.
122. *The Journals of Macready (1832–51)*, ed. J. C. Trewin (1967), p. 35
123. Ibid., p. 38
124. Ibid., p. 58
125. Sir Seymour Hicks, *Me and My Missus* (1939), p. 106
126. Lester Wallack, *Memories of Fifty Years* (1889), p. 166
127. Dame Madge Kendal, *Madge Kendal* (1933), p. 100
128. *Macready's Reminiscences,* pp. 270–1
129. James Rees, *Life of Edwin Forrest* (1874), pp. 322–5
130. From a pamphlet published by H. M. Ramsey in 1849.
131. Rees, *Life of Forrest*, pp. 198–9
132. Mrs John Drew, *Autobiographical Sketch*, p. 22
133. Bram Stoker, *Henry Irving*, i. 166–8
134. Letter from Walter Lacy to W. Clark Russell and included by him in *Representative Actors*, p. 397
135. Sir Squire and Lady Bancroft, *The Bancrofts*, pp. 58–9
136. Dame Madge Kendal, *Madge Kendal*, pp. 211–2
137. Eric Barnes, *Anna Cora* (1954), p. 229
138. Lester Wallack, *Memories of Fifty Years*, pp. 80–1
139. Ibid., pp. 141–4
140. Ibid., pp. 48–50
141. Ibid., pp. 175–7
142. Dion Boucicault, *The Art of Acting*, printed for the Dramatic Museum of Columbia University *Papers on Acting*, Fifth Series, No. 1 (1926)
143. Helen Hayes, *On Reflection* (1974), p. 93
144. H. Chance Newton, *Cues and Curtain Calls* (1927), p. 223
145. J. C. Trewin, *Benson and the Bensonians* (1960), p. 43
146. J. B. Howe, *A Cosmopolitan Actor* (1888), pp. 34–7
147. Joseph Jefferson, *Autobiography* (1890), pp. 159–60
148. Ibid., pp. 215–6
149. Ibid., pp. 239–41
150. Ibid., pp. 318–9
151. Garff B. Wilson, *A History of American Acting* (1966), pp. 118–20
152. Stanley Kimmel, *The Mad Booths of Maryland* (1940), pp. 68–9
153. Garff B. Wilson, *A History of American Acting*, p. 77
154. Sir Squire and Lady Bancroft, *The Bancrofts*, pp. 85–6
155. Sir Seymour Hicks, *Me and My Missus*, pp. 144–5
156. Sir Cedric Hardwicke, *A Victorian in Orbit* (1961), p. 16
157. Joseph Francis Daly, *The Life of Augustin Daly* (1917), pp. 74–6
158. Ibid., p. 388
159. Edward Gordon Craig, *Henry Irving* (1930), pp. 54–6

160. Donald Sinden, *Laughter in the Second Act* (1985), pp. 156–7
161. H. Chance Newton, *Cues and Curtain Calls*, pp. 25–6
162. Ellen Terry, *The Story of My Life* (1908), pp. 182–3
163. Bram Stoker, *Henry Irving*, i. 170–2
164. Sir John Martin-Harvey, *Autobiography*, pp. 177–8 (note)
165. Ibid., p. 40
166. Sir Seymour Hicks, *Me and My Missus*, pp. 91–2
167. Bram Stoker, *Henry Irving*, i. 302–3
168. Ibid., i. 63–5
169. Sir Squire and Lady Bancroft, *On and Off The Stage*, p. 70
170. Ibid., p. 132
171. Ibid., pp. 296–7
172. Mrs Patrick Campbell, *My Life and Some Letters* (1922), p. 141
173. *The Memoirs of Sarah Bernhardt*, ed. Sandy Lesberg (1977), pp. 86–8.
174. Sir Seymour Hicks, *Me and My Missus*, p. 135
175. Ellen Terry, *Life*, pp. 335–7
176. Sir John Gielgud, *An Actor and His Time* (1979), pp. 24–5
177. From *Four Lectures on Shakespeare*, ed. Christopher St John (1932),
     pp. 14–5
178. Dame Madge Kendal, *Madge Kendal*, pp. 144–5
179. James Harding, *James Agate* (1986), p. 36
180. J. B. Howe, *A Cosmopolitan Actor* (1888), pp. 95–6
181. H. Chance Newton, *Cues and Curtain Calls*, pp. 142–3
182. Ibid., pp. 141–2
183. In Hesketh Pearson, *Bernard Shaw* (1942), pp. 296–7
184. H. Chance Newton, *Cues and Curtain Calls*, p. 118
185. Sir Johnston Forbes-Robertson, *A Player Under Three Reigns*, p. 112
186. Ibid., pp. 152–3
187. Ibid., 223–4
188. Ibi., p. 231
189. Raymond Massey, *A Hundred Different Lives* (1979), pp. 70–1
190. Brooks Atkinson, *Broadway* (1970), p. 46
191. Garff B. Wilson, *A History of American Acting*, p. 211
192. Sir Seymour Hicks, *Me and My Missus*, p. 50
193. Sir Cedric Hardwicke, *A Victorian in Orbit*, p. 38
194. Dame Madge Kendal, *Madge Kendal*, pp. 145–6
195. Sir Cedric Hardwicke, *A Victorian in Orbit*, p. 260
196. G. B. Shaw, *Collected Letters 1911–25*, ed. Dan Laurence (1985),
     pp. 41–3
197. Helen Hayes, *On Reflection*, pp. 134–5
198. Hesketh Pearson, *The Life of Oscar Wilde* (1946), pp. 236–7
199. Ibid., p. 254
200. Richard Findlater, *Lilian Baylis* (1975), pp. 120–1
201. Gladys Cooper, *Gladys Cooper* (1931), p. 58
202. J. C. Trewin, *Benson and the Bensonians*, p. 42–3
203. Sir Seymour Hicks, *Me and My Missus*, p. 114
204. Isaac F. Marcosson and Daniel Frohman, *Charles Frohman: Manager
     and Man* (1916), pp. 91–8
205. Ibid., pp. 243–4 and p. 257
206. Raymond Massey, *A Hundred Different Lives*, p. 30

207. Dame Madge Kendal, *Madge Kendal*, p. 271
208. John Gielgud, *Distinguished Company* (1972), pp. 18–19
209. Garff B. Wilson, *History of American Acting*, pp. 230–1 and 234
210. Mrs Patrick Campbell, *Life and Letters*, p. 96
211. Sir John Martin-Harvey, *Autobiography*, p. 196 (note)
212. Sir John Gielgud, *An Actor and His Time*, p. 32–4
213. Sir John Gielgud, *Early Stages* (1939), pp. 216–7
214. Emlyn Williams, *Emlyn* (1973), pp. 299–300
215. Sir Cedric Hardwicke, *A Victorian in Orbit*, p. 241
216. Rex Harrison, *Rex* (1974), pp. 43–4
217. James Harding, *James Agate*, p. 154
218. Sir Seymour Hicks, *Me and My Missus*, pp. 24–5
219. Ibid., pp. 26–7
220. Ibid., p. 28
221. Edward Gordon Craig, *Index to the Story of My Days* (1957), pp. 113–4
222. Kenneth Tynan, *Curtains* (1961), pp. 142–3
223. Edward Gordon Craig, *Books and Theatres* (1925), pp. 73–4
224. Allen Churchill, *The Improper Bohemians* (1961), p. 207
225. Daphne du Maurier, *Gerald: A Portrait* (1934), pp. 252–3
226. Russell and Sybil Thorndike, *Lilian Baylis* (1938), pp. 182–6
227. Sir Tyrone Guthrie, *A Life in the Theatre* (1960), pp. 76–7
228. Sir John Gielgud, *Early Stages*, pp. 255–6
229. Russell and Sybil Thorndike, *Lilian Baylis*, pp. 58–9
230. Ibid., pp. 136–8
231. Ibid.
232. Elizabeth Sprigge, *Sybil Thorndike Casson* (1971), pp. 226
233. James Harding, *James Agate*, pp. 80–1
234. Ibid., pp. 86–7
235. Sir Harold Hobson, *Ralph Richardson* (1958), pp. 16–17
236. Sir John Gielgud, *Early Stages*, pp. 193–4
237. Derek Salberg, *My Love Affair with A Theatre* (1978), pp. 108–9
238. Kenneth More, *More or Less* (1978), p. 139
239. Russell Thorndike, *Sybil Thorndike* (1921), pp. 166–7
240. Sheridan Morley, *Sybil Thorndike: A Life In The Theatre* (1977) p. 104
241. Elizabeth Sprigge, *Thorndike*, pp. 196–7
242. Sheridan Morley, *Sybil Thorndike*, p. 126
243. Sir John Gielgud, *An Actor And His Time*, p. 55
244. Gene Fowler, *Good Night, Sweet Prince* (1944), pp. 117–19
245. Ibid., pp. 169–71
246. Ibid., p. 210
247. John Barrymore, *Confessions of an Actor* (1926), p. 112
248. George Jean Nathan, *The Theatre Book of the Year 1950–51*
249. Donald Sinden, *A Touch of the Memoirs* (1982), p. 70
250. Donald Sinden, *Laughter in the Second Act*, pp. 167–8
251. Archibald Haddon, *Green-Room Gossip* (1922), pp. 115–8
252. Donald Sinden, *Memoirs* (1982), p. 159
253. Russell Thorndike, *Sybil Thorndike*, pp. 256–7
254. Donald Sinden, *Memoirs*, pp. 80–2

255. Robert Speaight, *The Property Basket* (1970), p. 94
256. Kitty Black, *Upper Circle* (1984), p. 79
257. Sir John Martin-Harvey, *Autobiography*, p. 96 (note)
258. Allen Churchill, *Improper Bohemians*, pp. 236–7
259. Peter Ustinov, *Dear Me* (1977), pp. 142–5
260. Derek Salberg, *My Love Affair With A Theatre,* p. 109
261. Bryan Forbes, *Ned's Girl* (1977), p. 149
262. Ibid., pp. 243–4
263. Ibid., pp. 201–2
264. Gladys Cooper, *Gladys Cooper*, pp. 71–2
265. Ibid., p. 92
266. Ibid., p. 188
267. Howard Teichmann, *Georges S. Kaufman, an intimate portrait* (1973), pp. 134–5 and 286–7
268. Charles Chaplin, *My Early Days* (1964), pp. 91–2
269. Sir John Gielgud, *An Actor and His Time*, p. 40
270. Derek Salberg, *My Love Affair With A Theatre*, p. 106
271. John Mills, *Up In The Clouds, Gentlemen Please* (1980) p.133
272. Donald Sinden, *Memoirs*, pp. 157–8
273. George Freedley, *The Lunts* (1958), pp. 71–2
274. Ibid., pp. 76–7
275. Lilli Palmer, *Change Lobsters and Dance* (1976), p. 230
276. Brooks Atkinson, *Broadway* (1970), pp. 342–3
277. Lewis Funke and John E. Booth, *Actors Talk about Acting* (1961), p. 176
278. Harold French, *I Thought I Never Could* (1973), pp. 77–8
279. Sir Cedric Hardwicke, *A Victorian in Orbit*, pp. 31–2
280. Ibid., p. 45
281. Ibid., p. 236
282. Beatrice Lillie, *Every Other Inch A Lady* (1973), pp. 54–5
283. Harold Pinter, *Mac* (1968), pp. 9–10
284. Ibid., pp. 13–14
285. Raymond Massey, *A Hundred Different Lives*, pp. 67–8
286. Bryan Forbes, *Notes For A Life* (1974), pp. 182–3
287. Janet Dunbar, *Flora Robson* (1960), p. 175
288. Elsa Lanchester, *Charles Laughton and I* (1938), p. 77
289. Sir John Mills, *Up In The Clouds*, pp. 80–1
290. Cole Lesley, *The Life of Noël Coward* (1976), pp. 137–8
291. Kenneth Tynan, *The Sound of Two Hands Clapping* (1975), pp. 61–2
292. Kenneth More, *More or Less*, pp. 121–2
293. *The Theatrical Essays of Arthur Miller* ed. R. A. Martin (1978) pp. 46–7
294. Kitty Black, *Upper Circle*, p. 66
295. Sir Tyrone Guthrie, *A Life In The Theatre*, p. 22
296. Ibid., pp. 168–171
297. Kitty Black, *Upper Circle*, pp. 65–6
298. Interview with Sheridan Morley, *The Times*, 19 December, 1984
299. Helen Hayes, *On Reflection.*
300. Harold Clurman, *The Fervent Years* (1957), pp. 40–1
301. Ibid., pp. 48–9

302. Ibid., pp. 54–5
303. John Mason Brown, *Morning Faces* (1950), pp. 25–8
304. Tallulah Bankhead, *Tallulah* (1952), pp. 63–4
305. Janet Dunbar, *Flora Robson*, pp. 65–6
306. Ibid., pp. 162–3
307. Ibid., pp. 183–4
308. Sir Donald Wolfit, *First Interval* (1954), pp. 76–7
309. Ibid., pp. 92–3
310. Ibid., pp. 223–4
311. Ronald Harwood, *Sir Donald Wolfit C.B.E.: His Life and Work in the Unfashionable Theatre* (1971), p. 24
312. Ibid., p. 24
313. Ibid., p. 24
314. *Peter Hall's Diaries,* ed. John Goodwin (1983), p. 349
315. Sir Harold Hobson, *Ralph Richardson* (1958), p. 15
316. Garry O'Connor, *Ralph Richardson* (1983), pp. 164–5
317. Ibid., pp. 172–3
318. Ibid., pp. 222–3
319. Ibid., pp. 230–1
320. Peter Hall, *Diaries*, p. 325
321. John Lahr, *Prick Up Your Ears* (1978), p. 331
322. Emlyn Williams, *Emlyn*, pp. 297–8
323. *The Ages of Gielgud*, ed. Ronald Harwood (1984), p. 33
324. Ibid., p. 44
325. Kitty Black, *Upper Circle*, pp. 74–5
326. Peter Ustinov, *Dear Me*, p. 157
327. *At The Royal Court*, ed. Richard Findlater (1981), pp. 113–4
328. Harold Clurman, *Fervent Years*, pp. 138–9
329. Lillian Hellman, *Three* (1979), pp. 455–6
330. Sir Laurence Olivier, *Confessions of an Actor* (1982), pp. 28–30
331. John Cottrell, *Laurence Olivier* (1977 edition), pp. 51–2
332. Sir Laurence Olivier, *Confessions*, p. 82
333. *Olivier*, ed. Logan Gourlay, (1973), pp. 10–11
334. Sir Laurence Olivier, *Confessions*, pp. 117–8
335. Logan Gourlay, *Olivier*, p. 45
336. Helen Hayes, *On Reflection*, p. 127
337. From William Hobbs, *Technique of the Stage Fight* (1967), p. 6
338. Eric Keown, *Peggy Ashcroft* (1955), p. 46
339. Ibid., p. 77
340. Sir Tyrone Guthrie, *A Life in the Theatre*, p. 144
341. Rex Harrison, *Rex*, pp. 22–3
342. Ibid., p. 23
343. Sir Michael Redgrave, *In My Mind's Eye* (1983), pp. 287–8
344. Ibid., pp. 200–1
345. Sir Michael Redgrave, *Mask or Face* (1959), pp. 111–2
346. Ibid., pp. 103–4
347. George Oppenheimer (ed.), *The Passionate Playgoer* (1958), p. 319
348. From Brooke Hayward, *Haywire* (1977), pp. 185–7
349. Michael Darlow and Gillian Hodson, *Terence Rattigan: The Man and His Work* (1979), pp. 81–2

350. Ibid., p. 204
351. Peter Bull, *I Know The Face, But* . . . (1959), pp. 97–8
352. Ibid., pp. 174–6
353. Alec Guinness, *Blessings in Disguise* (1985), pp. 51–4
354. Bryan Forbes, *Ned's Girl*, p. 177
355. Kenneth More, *More or Less*, pp. 73–4
356. Brooks Atkinson, *Broadway*, pp. 306–7
357. Kenneth Williams, *Just Williams* (1985), pp. 62–3
358. Ingrid Bergman, *My Story* (1980), p. 172
359. Ibid., pp. 486–8
360. Dirk Bogarde, *A Postillion Struck By Lightning* (1977), p. 226
361. Brian Rix, *My Farce From My Elbow* (1975), pp. 61–2
362. Ibid., pp. 190–1
363. Lewis Funke and John E. Booth, *Actors Talk About Acting*, p. 176
364. Tennessee Williams, *Memoirs* (1976), pp. 131–2
365. J. C. Trewin, *Peter Brook* (1971), p. 131
366. Ibid., p. 182
367. Bryan Forbes, *Notes For A Life*, p. 203
368. John Osborne, *A Better Class of Person* (1981), p. 238
369. Fergus Cashin, *Richard Burton* (1971), pp. 275–6
370. Ibid., p. 371
371. Bryan Forbes, *Notes For A Life*, pp. 87–9
372. From *Acting in the Sixties*, ed. Hal Burton (1970), p. 245
373. Kenneth Williams, *Just Williams*, pp. 75–7
374. *Acting in the Sixties* ed. Hal Burton, p. 200
375. Ronald Harwood, *A Night At The Theatre* (1984), pp. 39–40
376. Richard Findlater, *At The Royal Court*, p. 107
377. Ronald Harwood, *A Night At The Theatre*, pp. 12–14

ACKNOWLEDGEMENTS

The editor and publishers would like to thank the following for permission
to reproduce passages from the sources indicated.

Albert Finney, Maggie Smith and Dorothy Tutin: from *Acting in the Sixties*,
ed. Hal Burton (BBC Publications, 1970).

Random House Inc.: Lewis Funke and J. E. Booth, *Actors Talk about Acting*,
copyright © 1961 by Lewis Funke and John E. Booth.

Methuen & Co. Ltd.: James Harding, *Agate* (1986)

Century Hutchinson Ltd.: Eric Keown, *Peggy Ashcroft* (1955) (Rockliff
Publishing Corporation).

Secker & Warburg Ltd.: Oliver Lawson Dick (ed.) *Aubrey's Brief Lives*
(1969)

Laurence Pollinger Ltd.: Tallulah Bankhead, *Tallulah* (Victor Gollancz
Ltd., 1952)

Rosenfeld, Meyer & Susman: Gene Fowler, *Good Night Sweet Prince* (the
life and times of John Barrymore). Copyright 1943 & 1944 by Gene
Fowler. Renewed 1970 & 1971 by A. Fowler, G. Fowler Jr, J. F.
Morrison and W. Fowler. Reprinted by permission of the heirs of
Gene Fowler.

Penguin Books Ltd and A. P. Watt Ltd: Richard Findlater, *Lilian Baylis:
The Lady of the Old Vic* (1975)

Associated Book Publishers (UK) Ltd: Russell and Sybil Thorndike, *Lilian
Baylis* (Chapman & Hall, 1938)

Grafton Books Ltd: Max Beerbohm, *Around Theatres* (Rupert Hart-Davis
Ltd; Greenwood Press, 1969)

Century Hutchinson Ltd: J. C. Trewin, *Benson and the Bensonians* (Barrie &
Rockliff, 1960)

Michael Joseph Ltd and ICM: Ingrid Bergman, *My Story* (1980)

Associated Book Publishers (UK) Ltd and Curtis Brown: Kitty Black,
Upper Circle (Methuen London, 1984)

Chatto & Windus Ltd, The Hogarth Press and Holt, Rinehart & Winston:
Dirk Bogarde, *A Postillion Struck by Lightning* (1977)

Columbia University Press: Dion Boucicault, *The Art of Acting* (Dramatic
Museum of Columbia University *Papers on Acting*, Fifth Series,
Number 1, 1926)

Macdonald & Co. Ltd: J. C. Trewin, *Peter Brook* (1971)

The Estate of John Mason Brown: John Mason Brown, *Morning Faces*
(McGraw-Hill Book Co., 1950).

William Heinemann Ltd: Peter Bull, *I Know the Face, but . . .* (1959)

Weidenfeld & Nicolson Ltd: Fergus Cashin, *Richard Burton* (Arthur Barker
Ltd; Star 1984)

Macmillan Publishing Company: Allen Churchill, *The Improper Bohemians*
(Cassell & Co. Ltd.) Copyright © Allen Churchill 1961.

Alfred A. Knopf, Inc.: Harold Clurman, *The Fervent Years: the story of the Group Theatre and the Thirties.* Copyright 1945 and renewed 1973 by Harold Clurman. Copyright © 1957 by Harold Clurman.

The Cole Lesley Estate and Alfred A. Knopf, Inc.: Cole Lesley, *The Life of Noël Coward: Remembered Laughter* (Jonathan Cape and Alfred A. Knopf, Inc., 1976)

The Johns Hopkins University Press: John Dennis, *The Critical Works*, ed. E. Hooker (1943)

Bryan Forbes Ltd: *Ned's Girl: the authorised biography of Dame Edith Evans* (Hamish Hamilton Ltd, 1977)

Collins Publishers and A. D. Peters & Co: Bryan Forbes, *Notes for a Life* (1974)

The Garrick Club: Letter from David Garrick to the Duchess of Portland.

Sidgwick & Jackson Ltd and Clarkson N. Potter Inc.: John Gielgud, *An Actor and His Time*, copyright © 1979, 1980 John Gielgud, John Miller and John Powell.

Hodder & Stoughton Ltd : Ronald Harwood (ed.), *The Ages of Gielgud* (1984)

Heinemann Educational Books Ltd: John Gielgud, *Distinguished Company* (1972)

Macmillan London and Basingstoke: Sir John Gielgud, *Early Stages* (1939)

Macmillan London and Basingstoke: Joyce Grenfell, *In Pleasant Places* (1979)

A. P. Watt Ltd: Richard Findlater, *Grimaldi King of Clowns* (Macgibbon & Kee, 1955)

Hamish Hamilton Ltd and Alfred A. Knopf, Inc: Alec Guinness, *Blessings in Disguise.* Copyright © Alec Guinness 1985.

Hamish Hamilton Ltd and Wharton Productions: Sir Tyrone Guthrie, *A Life in the Theatre* (1960)

Hamish Hamilton Ltd: John Goodwin (ed.), *Peter Hall's Diaries* (1983)

Associated Book Publishers (UK) Ltd: Sir Cedric Hardwicke, *A Victorian in Orbit* (Methuen & Co. and Doubleday, 1961).

John Farquharson Ltd: Rex Harrison, *Rex* (Macmillan, 1976)

Associated Book Publishers (UK) Ltd: Ronald Harwood (ed.), *A Night at the Theatre* (Methuen London, 1983)

W. H. Allen & Co., plc: Helen Hayes, *On Reflection* (1974).

The Times: Interview with Helen Hayes by Sheridan Morley published on 19 December, 1984.

Alfred A. Knopf, Inc. and Deborah Rogers Ltd: Brooke Hayward, *Haywire.* Copyright © 1977 by Brooke Hayward.

The Estate of Lillian Hellmann: Lillian Hellman, *Three* (Macmillan Publishing Company, 1979)

Cassell Ltd: Sir Seymour Hicks, *Me and My Missus* (1939)

Columbia University Press: H. N. Hillebrand, *Edmund Kean* (1933)

Angus & Robertson Publishers and & Howard Teichmann: Howard Teichmann, *George S. Kaufman an Intimate Portrait* (1973)

Oxford University Press: *Lichtenberg's Visits to England as Described in His Letters and Diaries*, trans. Margaret L. Mare and W. H. Quarrell (The Clarendon Press, 1938)

W. H. Allen & Co., plc,: Beatrice Lillie, *Every Other Inch a Lady* (1973)

Longman Group Ltd: J. C. Trewin (ed.), *The Journals of Macready (1832–51)*.

Julie Haydon, Mrs George Jean Nathan: *The Theatre Book of the Year 1950–51*.

Macdonald & Co. Ltd: Sir John Martin-Harvey, *Autobiography* (Sampson, Low Marston, 1933)

Robson Books Ltd: Raymond Massey, *A Hundred Different Lives* (1979)

Curtis Brown and Doubleday: Daphne du Maurier, *Gerald: A Portrait* (Victor Gollancz, 1934)

Viking Penguin, Inc: Arthur Miller, 'The American Theater', in *The Theater Essays of Arthur Miller*. Edited with an introduction by Robert A. Martin. Copyright 1954 by Arthur Miller. Copyright renewed © 1982 Arthur Miller.

Weidenfeld & Nicolson Ltd: John Mills, *Up in the Clouds, Gentlemen Please* (1980)

Hodder & Stoughton Ltd, and Aitken and Stone Ltd: Kenneth More, *More or Less* (1978)

Weidenfeld & Nicolson Ltd: John Mortimer, *Clinging to the Wreckage* (1982)

A. M. Heath & Co Ltd: Eric Barnes, *Anna Cora* [Mowatt] (Secker & Warburg, 1954)

The Bodley Head Ltd: H. Chance Newton, *Cues and Curtain Calls* (1927)

Weidenfeld & Nicolson Ltd: Laurence Olivier, *Confessions of an Actor* (1982)

William Hobbs and Baron Olivier of Brighton: *Techniques of the Stage Fight* (Studio Vista and Macmillan New York, 1967)

Penguin Books Ltd and Curtis Brown: John Lahr, *Prick Up Your Ears The Biography of Joe Orton* (Allen Lane, 1978)

David Higham Associates Ltd, Faber & Faber Ltd and E. P. Dutton: John Osborne, *A Better Class of Person*, copyright 1981.

Methuen London Ltd and Judy Daish Associates: Harold Pinter, *Mac*, © 1968, first published by Emanuel Wax for Pendragon Press, 1968.

Quartet Books Ltd and Merrimack Publishers Circle: Michael Darlow and Gillian Hodson, *Terence Rattigan: The Man and His Work* (1979)

Lady Redgrave: *Mask or Face* (Heinemann Educational Books, 1959)

Weidenfeld & Nicolson Ltd: Sir Michael Redgrave, *In My Mind's Eye* (1983)

Hodder & Stoughton Ltd and Deborah Rogers Ltd: Garry O'Connor, *Ralph Richardson* (1982)

Secker & Warburg Ltd: Brian Rix, *My Farce from My Elbow* (1975)

Harrap Ltd and Janet Dunbar: Janet Dunbar, *Flora Robson* (1960)

Cortney Publications and Derek Salberg: Derek Salberg, *My Love Affair with a Theatre* (1978)

David Higham Associates Ltd; Hesketh Pearson, *Bernard Shaw* (Collins, 1942)

The Society of Authors on behalf of the Bernard Shaw Estate: *The Collected Letters of G. B. Shaw, 1911–25*, ed. by Dan Laurence (The Bodley Head, 1985)

Jack Shepherd and David Storey: Richard Findlater (ed.) *At the Royal Court* (Amber Lane Press Ltd, 1981)

Hodder & Stoughton Ltd and Richard Scott Simon Ltd: Donald Sinden, *A Touch of the Memoirs* (1982) and *Laughter in the Second Act* (1985)

David Higham Associates Ltd: Robert Speaight, *The Property Basket* (Collins, 1970)

Oxford University Press: Joseph Spence, *Observations, Anecdotes and Characters of Books and Men* (ed. James M. Osborn, 1966).

Curtis Brown: Sheridan Morley, *Sybil Thorndike* (1977)

The Estate of Elizabeth Sprigge: Elizabeth Sprigge, *Sybil Thorndike Casson* (Victor Gollancz, 1971)

Jonathan Cape Ltd and Holt, Rinehart & Winston: Kenneth Tynan, *The Sound of Two Hands Clapping* (1975)

The Estate of Kenneth Tynan: Kenneth Tynan, *Curtains* (Longman, 1961)

William Heinemann Ltd and Little, Brown Inc: Peter Ustinov, *Dear Me* (1977)

A. P. Watt Ltd: Hesketh Pearson, *The Life of Oscar Wilde* (Penguin, 1985)

The Bodley Head Ltd: Emlyn Williams, *Emlyn* (1973)

J. M. Dent & Sons Ltd: Kenneth Williams, *Just Williams* (1985)

The Estate of Tennessee Williams: Tennessee Williams, *Memoirs* (W. H. Allen & Co) © 1976 The Estate of Tennessee Williams.

University of Indiana Press: Garff B. Wilson, *A History of American Acting* (1966)

The Society for Theatre Research: *Drury Lane Journal: Selections from James Winston's Diaries 1819–1827*, eds. Alfred L. Nelson and Gilbert B. Cross

Syndication International (1986) Ltd: Sir Donald Wolfit, *First Interval* (Odhams Press).

Aitken & Stone; Ronald Harwood, *Sir Donald Wolfit CBE His Life and Work in the Unfashionable Theatre* (Secker & Warburg, 1971)

The editor and publishers have attempted to locate the owners of copyright of all the anecdotes included in this book, but not always with success. Acknowledgement is therefore necessary to the following, or their heirs, from whom we would be glad to hear:

Brooks Atkinson: *Broadway* (1970); Fergus Cashin: *Richard Burton* (Arthur Barker Ltd, 1971); John Cottrell: *Laurence Olivier* (Hodder & Stoughton Ltd); George Freedley: *The Lunts* (Macmillan); Harold French: *I Never Thought I Could* (Secker & Warburg, 1973); Logan Gourlay (ed.): *Olivier* (Macmillan); Harold Hobson: *Ralph Richardson* (Rockliff, 1958); The Hulton Press: E. G. Craig, *Index to the Story of My Days* (1957); Stanley Kimmel: *The Mad Booths of Maryland*; Sandy Lesberg, (ed.): *Memoirs of Sarah Bernhardt* (Pebbler Press, 1977); George Oppenheimer: *The Passionate Playgoer* (The Viking Press, 1958).

Index of Entries

(the figures refer to page numbers)